William Wye Smith

William Wye Smith

RECOLLECTIONS OF A NINETEENTH CENTURY SCOTTISH CANADIAN

edited by Scott A. McLean & Michael E. Vance

NATURAL HERITAGE BOOKS
A MEMBER OF THE DUNDURN GROUP
TORONTO

Library and Archives Canada Cataloguing in Publication

Smith, William Wye, 1827-1917.
    William Wye Smith : recollections of a nineteenth century Scottish Canadian / edited with annotations by Scott A. McLean and Michael E. Vance.

Includes bibliographical references and index.
ISBN 978-1-55002-804-1

    1. Smith, William Wye, 1827-1917. 2. Frontier and pioneer life-- Ontario. 3. Poets, Canadian (English)--19th century--Biography. 4. Journalists--Ontario--Biography. 5. Publishers and publishing--Ontario--Biography. 6. Scottish Canadians--Biography. I. McLean, Scott A. (Scott Alan), 1963- II. Vance, Michael E. (Michael Easton), 1959- III. Title.

PS8487.M6Z477 2008   C811'.4   C2008-900706-9

1   2   3   4   5   12   11   10   09   08

Conseil des Arts du Canada   Canada Council for the Arts   Canadä   ONTARIO ARTS COUNCIL CONSEIL DES ARTS DE L'ONTARIO

We acknowledge the support of the **Canada Council for the Arts** and the **Ontario Arts Council** for our publishing program. We also acknowledge the financial support of the **Government of Canada** through the **Book Publishing Industry Development Program** and **The Association for the Export of Canadian Books** and the **Government of Canada** through the **Ontario Book Publishers Tax Credit Program** and the **Ontario Media Development Corporation**.

Front cover image: An artist's rendition of Inglis Falls, just south of Owen Sound. Courtesy of Archival and Special Collections, McLaughlin Library, University of Guelph.

Cover design by Erin Mallory
Text design by Jennifer Scott
Edited by Jane Gibson
Printed and bound in Canada by Marquis

Published by Natural Heritage Books
A Member of The Dundurn Group

Dundurn Press
3 Church Street, Suite 500
Toronto, Ontario, Canada
M5E 1M2

Gazelle Book Services Limited
White Cross Mills
High Town, Lancaster, England
LA1 4XS

Dundurn Press
2250 Military Road
Tonawanda, NY
U.S.A. 14150

Contents

Acknowledgements

While we have been editing William Wye Smith's manuscript we have had the assistance of a great many individuals who deserve our thanks. In particular, we wish to express our appreciation to Barry Penhale and Jane Gibson at Natural Heritage Books for their interest and enthusiasm for this project. We would also like to acknowledge the help provided by the staff of the Archives of Ontario, the Toronto Public Library, University of Guelph Library, Special Collections, the Library and Archives Canada, the Owen Sound Public Library, the Special Collections at the Killam Library, Dalhousie Library, and the Interlibrary Loan Service of the Patrick Power Library at Saint Mary's University. Dr. H. Amani Whitfield, University of Vermont, and Dr. Heather Murray, University of Toronto, were particularly helpful with their suggestions for secondary sources relating to Black History and Canadian Literary History, while Dr. Renee Hulan, Saint Mary's University, kindly read early drafts and provided very helpful critical comments. Except for the mistakes made by Reverend Smith himself, we are responsible for any errors or omissions in this edited text.

Editors' Note on the Text

Several years ago, during the course of our research on the history of Scottish settlement in Ontario, we came across Reverend William Wye Smith's unpublished manuscript, "Canadian Reminiscences," in the Archives of Ontario.[1] There does not appear to be any record of how the manuscript ended up in the archives, but it is clear from the first page of his draft, dated 1900, that Reverend Smith intended to submit his book to the Toronto Methodist publisher, William Briggs. Smith had previously published volumes with the Toronto Baptist publishers Dudley and Burns, but he appears to have decided to switch to Briggs around the time he composed his "Reminiscences." Although we have not been able to determine if Briggs ever saw the manuscript, we do know that the firm did publish a collection of Smith's poetry in 1908.

Smith's desire to publish with Briggs was understandable since the firm was one of the most successful Canadian publishers of the late nineteenth century. Briggs had established a secure financial base by publishing Methodist religious tracts and supplemented its catalogue with educational works as well as poetry and fiction. Some of the most well-known figures in nineteenth-century Canadian writing, including Charles G.D. Roberts, William Wilfred Campbell and Catharine Parr Traill, had works published by Briggs and several of the company's volumes, such as Robina and Kathleen Lizars' *In the Days of the Canada Company*, were, like Smith's manuscript, concerned with the pioneer phase of Ontario settlement.[2]

The original manuscript was handwritten on half sheets of paper and appears to have been assembled over an extended period of time, with Smith jotting down his stories as he recalled them. As a consequence, the manuscript has a tendency to ramble and repeat stories. This may account for its failure to be published when Smith wrote it. For this first published version of Smith's "Reminiscences," we have selected eleven of his original sixteen chapters. We have excluded from Smith's original manuscript chapters six through ten. The chapters entitled "Unconscious Humorists," "A Few Early Glimpses," and "Backwoods Proverbs and Wisdom," we considered repetitious in both theme and content, while the chapter entitled "Of Many Dialects a New One," an exercise in amateur etymology, we considered too specialized. Similarly, we excluded the chapter entitled "About Preachers" since it dealt primarily with Reverend Smith's personal acquaintances in the Congregational church.[3] The remaining eleven chapters in this volume are, we believe, of greater interest since they treat the broader history of pioneer settlement and community development.

In producing this version of William Smith's manuscript, we have relied heavily on the typescript version held by the Archives of Ontario.[4] We discovered a number of typographical errors in that version and have corrected those errors here without indication. In several places we have inserted words to provide clarification, for example to indicate the county of a place mentioned in the text. These insertions are indicated by square brackets, "[ ]." We have also tried to retain the flavour of Smith's original manuscript by reproducing his sub-headings but have altered much of his punctuation, spelling, and use of numerals to bring them more in line with the expectations of today's reader, while keeping the author's original intentions and much of his style intact. In keeping with the time period, all imperial measurements have been maintained in the main text: miles, feet, inches … Repetitious material has been edited out. In places where Smith indicates emphasis by underlining words, we have retained that emphasis by placing those words in *italics*.

Reading William Wye Smith:

An Introduction to Background Influences and Stereotypes

Many writers of the late nineteenth and early twentieth centuries attempted to celebrate the virtues of early rural pioneers and life on the land as a general criticism of what they perceived to be the negative, alienating influence of Ontario's rapidly expanding urban industrial towns and cities.[1] From the opening chapter of his "Canadian Reminiscences," Reverend William Wye Smith signals his intention to contribute to this pioneer genre by recording personal anecdotes and stories drawn from his memories of early settlement life. Smith's version of the pioneer celebration is, however, deeply influenced by his Scottish background and his literary aspirations. As a consequence, his manuscript reveals a great deal about the Scottish immigrant community and provides insight into literary influences on the earliest published authors in Upper Canada. The celebration of his Scottish homeland and the Scottish-Canadian community was a life-long preoccupation for Smith, and the literary allusions found throughout his manuscript, though at times inaccurate, are deliberate. But, what is perhaps most intriguing about the manuscript as we read it now is the unwitting testimony that Smith provides on the interaction between Scottish-Canadians like himself and the various other ethnic groups that settled Upper Canada. In particular, "Canadian Reminiscences" reveals that, for Smith, nineteenth-century notions of national and racial characteristics ordered Ontario society.

Smith's personal history provided the starting point for his understanding of Upper-Canadian settler life. He was born

Reverend William Wye Smith, teacher, Congregationalist minister, author, poet, and publisher was born in Scotland in 1827. His parents emigrated first to New York. When William was ten years old, the family left the United States and moved to the community of St. George in Dumfries Township, Brant County, Upper Canada. His remarkable career found him involved in a variety of activities across the southwestern portion of the province as well as some time spent in the Eastern Townships of Quebec. Very little escaped his observant eye.

in Jedburgh in the Scottish Borders in 1827 and as an infant emigrated with his parents, first to New York in 1830, and then to St. George, Dumfries Township, in 1837. The extended Smith family encouraged both migrations. Smith's uncles were the first to settle in New York, and they supported the migration of the rest of the family. When his father's only brother moved to Upper Canada, Smith's family again followed. It is clear from his manuscript that Smith's father, John (1796–1889), helped his eldest son to maintain his interest in his birthplace by repeating stories about the Scottish homeland. Smith's mother, Sara Veitch (1799–1877), appears in the text far less often and his sisters Sara (b. 1839) and Jenny (1842–1881) are not mentioned at all. Indeed, Smith generally paid little attention to women in his accounts. He does refer to having two younger brothers, but names only one of them, John Anderson Smith (b. 1832) who shared William's literary interests and indeed published a collection of humourous stories, many of which featured caricatures of Scottish settlers based on the Smith family's neighbours in Dumfries Township. The township was an area of intense Lowland Scottish settlement, and, as Smith's stories make clear, shared ethnicity was important in early community relations. In this context, Smith's own Scottish birth no doubt provided a link with the elder immigrant community leaders, like his father, and unlike his siblings who were all born in North America.

In addition to highlighting his Scottish connections, William Smith's "Reminiscences" also reflect the variety of vocations that he pursued. These included early work in Dumfries Township as a storekeeper and as a teacher in the local schools at St. George and Maus's Plains, just north of Paris, Ontario. Smith clearly took pride in the latter occupation and much of his manuscript maintains a didactic quality. Aware of the respectability such positions conferred, Smith includes several stories about his early teaching experiences yet fails to mention that his sister Jenny was also a teacher, having received her diploma in 1858. By that time Smith had moved to Owen Sound and was working as a clerk in the local division court, another equally respectable, if low paying, career. In 1863, in what at first appears to be a departure from his career path, Smith bought the *Owen Sound Times* and served as editor of the paper until he sold it again in 1865.

An advertisement for the Metropolitan Permanent Building Society of Toronto. This society was one of a number of savings and insurance organizations that helped people save for a home. W.W. Smith's role, listed as "valuer," would have been much like that of an insurance salesperson.

A career in journalism was not held in as high esteem as teaching or civil service, but Smith's "Reminiscences" indicate that he had been interested in publishing from a young age when he submitted his early poems to fellow Scot and editor of the *Dumfries Courier*, Peter Jaffray. After selling the *Times*, Smith worked on and off as a journalist for the rest of his life, submitting articles to periodicals such as the *Globe*, *The Scottish Canadian*, *The New Dominion Monthly*, and the *Canadian Independent*.[2] Smith served as the editor of the latter, which was published by the Congregational Church from 1888 to 1894, and as editor of the *Congregational Church Year Book* to 1900. Earlier, Smith had published the *Sunday School Dial*, an illustrated paper for children, and during the time he was editing the *Canadian Independent*, ran a Congregational Church bookstore, at first located in Newmarket and then later in St. Catharines, Ontario.[3]

An advertisement for the *Owen Sound Times,* published every Friday from the printing office on Poulette Street. Along with the news and market reports, note the featuring of "local intelligence."

Aside from the brief periods when he edited the *Owen Sound Times* and the *Canadian Independent*, Smith does not appear to have made his living from journalism. Indeed, when he sold the *Times* in 1865, Smith embarked on a new vocation that influenced both his subsequent journalism and ultimately his "Reminiscences." In that year, Smith was ordained as a minister in the Congregational Church and began a long career of church ministry, starting at Listowel in Perth County, Ontario, and ending in St. Catharines in 1907. In the intervening years, Reverend Smith also served as Congregational minister at Pine Grove, Vaughan Township, Ontario; at Eaton in Quebec's Eastern Townships, and at Newmarket.[4] As a consequence, Smith's "Reminiscences" often refer to fellow clergymen and recount tales that were clearly intended to provide moral lessons. Smith's sermonizing is particularly evident in the parts of the manuscript where he deals with the deleterious affects of alcohol, a reflection of his life-long advocacy of temperance. Indeed, one of Smith's earliest pieces of writing was an essay advocating prohibition in Canada that received a hundred dollar prize from the Sons of Temperance.[5]

The mingling of moral and religious themes with more secular topics evident in the "Reminiscences" was also evident in Smith's poetry, starting with his first volume *Alazon and Other Poems* (1850). This collection included many poems that had been published in the New York *Saturday Emporium* between 1846 and 1849 when Smith returned to the city in order to study at the University Grammar School. After being ordained, Smith continued to write and publish poetry, producing two collected works in his lifetime, *The Poems of William Wye Smith* (1888) and *The Selected Poems of William Wye Smith* (1908), both of which contained poems inspired by his faith. Such poetry was far from uncommon in Victorian Canada; indeed, Edward Hartley Dewart's first anthology of Canadian poetry began with a section of "Sacred and Reflective" pieces which included one of Smith's religious poems, "I Come to the Well."[6]

As a clergyman author, Reverend Smith fits an established nineteenth-century Canadian pattern. Carole Gerson has shown that, in the second half of the century, literary writers were overwhelmingly

Protestant, male, middle-class professionals of either English or Scottish descent and that during the first half of the century just under half of these creative writers were either lawyers or clergyman. Rather than producing cheap popular work to satisfy the increasing demand for pulp fiction, these Canadian authors tended to produce works designed to be morally uplifting.[7] Smith's desire to produce edifying literature was, therefore, part of a broader cultural trend, but in his case, it was also reinforced by his self-conscious attempt to demonstrate his learning by connecting his work to a wider body of literature.

While studying in New York at the University Grammar School, Smith acquired some understanding of the European classics, which he displays in his "Canadian Reminiscences" by referring to texts such as Aesop's *Fables*, Froissart's *Chronicles*, and Cervantes *Don Quixote*, among others. Smith's American experience, however, is also reflected in his favourable references to the work of Harriet Elizabeth Beecher Stowe, the famous American anti-slavery advocate and novelist, as well as the work of the leading American historians, George Bancroft and Francis Parkman. In addition, Smith's manuscript demonstrates an awareness of American popular periodical literature, in particular *Harper's* and *Scribner's* magazines, which he may have first encountered as a student. Nevertheless, modern British and Canadian authors are referred to most often in the "Reminiscences."

Given his pride in his Scottish background, it is not surprising that Smith refers most frequently to Scots writers. In the manuscript, Smith alludes to contemporary Scottish novelists and playwrights such as George MacDonald, Dr. John Brown, and J.M. Barrie, and even more frequently to the Scots poets of the late eighteenth and early nineteenth century. The Scottish Border poet and novelist, James Hogg, is discussed with regard to the settlement of Dumfries Township while Thomas Campbell's poetry is quoted to illustrate Romantic parallels with Smith's own Canadian tales.

However, Robert Burns receives the most attention in the "Reminiscences." Burns was celebrated by the Scottish immigrant community from a very early date in Ontario, and Smith shared this enthusiasm, writing his own Scots dialect poetry and retracing Burns's "Border" travels when he returned to Scotland for a visit in 1862.[8] Nevertheless, leading poets and authors from elsewhere in Britain, including Samuel Coleridge, Tom Moore, and Laurence Sterne, are quoted in Smith's manuscript as are less well-known figures, such as the English historian and memoir writer, William Hutton, and the contemporary English children's novelist Jean Ingelow.

Although Smith generally pays far less attention to female authors than to male authors, he does refer to the published writing of female English visitors and immigrants to Upper Canada, including Anna Jameson, Susanna Moodie, and Catharine Parr Traill. Since these women had produced volumes that resembled both the form and content of Smith's own manuscript, it is not surprising that he compares his work to theirs. It is clear from Chapter 10, "Literature in the Bush," that Smith sought to record the first contributions to literature in Canada, including the work of Jameson, Moodie and Traill, as an indirect way of highlighting his own contribution. But, as a consequence, the authors who in Smith's view contributed to the development of Canadian poetry rather than Canadian prose, receive the most attention in his "Reminiscences." In Chapter 10, Smith produces a catalogue of all the poets he can recall that published in Canada during the first half of the nineteenth century. These include authors such as Charles Sangster, Thomas D'Arcy McGee, Charles Heavysege and Alexander McLachlan, who continue to be perennial favourites in Canadian poetry anthologies, as well as lesser known individuals such as fellow Scots, Evan MacColl and John Fraser. Most of these authors were, like Smith himself, immigrants from the British Isles. Since they were credited with bringing to Canada the poetic form, which was widely viewed in the nineteenth century as the highest form of literary expression, Smith clearly wished to be considered part of this pioneering immigrant group.

While Smith's attempts to edify the reader reflect his career as a poet, clergyman, and teacher, "Canadian Reminiscences" was also intended to entertain and in this regard pointed to his role as a journalist. Before writing the "Reminiscences," Smith successfully published many pieces in periodicals, and his manuscript draws heavily on this previously published work. In addition to his poetry, this work included a series of fictionalized tales of pioneer life, entitled "John Kanack's Experiences," published in *The New Dominion Monthly*, articles on Owen Sound local history published in the Toronto *Globe* and a series of biographical sketches published in *The Scottish Canadian* and the *Canadian Independent*. Smith's shift from publishing poetry to prose fiction and then to sketches purporting to portray actual people and events was reflected in the careers of other early writers in Canada. Susanna Moodie commenced her literary career in Canada in the 1830s by publishing patriotic poetry in Upper Canadian journals such as the *Canadian Literary Magazine* and the *Literary Garland*. In the 1840s, she shifted to prose stories with her fictionalized "Canadian Scenes" before switching to her autobiographical "Canadian Sketches." These sketches, like Smith's tales, included verifiable details, but were made to conform to accepted conventional forms for short fiction.[9] It would appear that Smith was attempting to replicate Moodie's strategy in her highly successful *Roughing It in the Bush* (1852), which organized her previously published sketches into a compilation. By entitling his manuscript "Canadian Reminiscences," Smith was also aligning the work with the large body of similarly titled publications that had appeared during the second half of the nineteenth century, which included volumes from former civil servants, politicians, sportsmen, clergymen, and literary figures. Indeed, there were several volumes recounting early pioneer experiences published in Toronto just before Smith's completion of his manuscript, including, among others, Samuel Thompson's *Reminiscences of a Canadian Pioneer* (1884), Caniff Haight's, *Country Life in Canada Fifty Years Ago: Personal Recollections and Reminiscences of a Sexagenarian* (1885), and Alexander Sinclair's, *Pioneer Reminiscences* (1898).[10] As a consequence, Smith's manuscript, both in its form and in its title, was shaped by his career in journalism and his awareness that his work needed to fit into an established genre to order to get published.

The contents of "Canadian Reminiscences," however, are revealing in ways that William Smith probably did not intend. Despite his manuscript's title, Smith includes a considerable amount of material on the United States. This is not only reflected in his literary references, but also in the incidents he reports, including his visit to the Centennial Exhibition in Philadelphia in 1876 and his attendance at the International Sunday School Convention in Pittsburgh in 1890. Americans living in Upper Canada also feature in Smith's manuscript and include those who came to Canada on their own, such as the Stimson family of physicians in Dumfries Township, as well as those who belonged to American group settlements like the Quakers and the Pennsylvania Dutch. These American references reflect both the importance of American settlement for the early history of Upper Canada and the influence that American connections continued to have on Canada throughout the nineteenth century. American references also reflect Smith's early life in the United States and the impressions that he derived from that experience. In Chapter 9, Smith recalls an exchange between his father and a slave when they were en route from Baltimore to Ohio.[11] This early encounter appears to have influenced Smith's abolitionist views, although it did not mean that he was able to escape the racist attitudes that accompanied slavery.

Indeed, Smith's Chapter 9, "The Negroes," provides the clearest illustration of his unselfconscious acceptance of racist literary conventions found on both sides of the border. Although Smith, like his contemporaries, emphasized Upper Canada's role as a refuge for escaped slaves, his manuscript reproduces well-worn stereotypes depicting African-Americans as musical, happy-go-lucky, and lazy. These caricatures had originated in the American Music Hall tradition, but were also found in the American periodicals and Upper Canadian newspapers that Smith read.[12] Although he makes a point of condemning discriminatory employment practices in his "Reminiscences" by recalling encounters with African Americans in the form of stereotypical anecdotes, Smith reinforces the very attitude that allowed racial discrimination to persist in Ontario. By downplaying Upper Canada's racism and ignoring its own history of slavery, Smith tries to take the high moral ground, chastising the United States for slavery while highlighting the activities of White clergymen, like himself, who had called for the abolition of the institution and sought to provide a refuge for escaped slaves in Canada. However, his adherence to the conventional racist representations of Black inferiority do not allow Smith to recognize the African American's own contributions in a positive light. Except for the appreciative attention paid to the Congregational clergyman, Reverend Samuel Ringgold Ward, Smith largely ignores the role that African Americans played in both the anti-slavery movement and in the creation and maintenance of their communities in Upper Canada.

As in the rest of the manuscript, the tales recounted in Smith's chapter on African Americans were intended to be amusing, and his reproduction of conventional racist stereotypes to achieve this effect demonstrates the extent to which such representations were easily accepted. Indeed, Smith employs stereotypes to create humour throughout the manuscript, particularly in his chapters dealing with the various ethnic groups who settled Upper Canada. These range from stock figures, when dealing with English and Scottish pioneers, to blatantly racist caricatures, when dealing with Irish or African-American immigrants. In Chapters 5 and 6, Smith reproduces the stereotype of the aristocratic Englishman as a means of poking fun at the aspirations of those who sought to establish themselves as colonial gentlemen. The stereotype of the dour, stolid Highlander is employed by Smith to poke fun at Gaelic-speaking immigrants and the thrifty Scot caricature is also used in recounting tales about his fellow Lowland settlers. Nevertheless, Lowland Scots are generally portrayed by Smith as individual characters rather than as representations of supposed ethnic or national characteristics.

The Irish and German immigrants in Chapter 7 are not treated as favourably. While Smith expresses admiration for some clergymen from the community, he tells tales that depict German settlers as a wooden-shoe-wearing, slightly thick-headed group inclined to superstition. In addition, his tales of the Irish settlers feature the "Paddy" caricature that represented the Irish as musical but illiterate, dim-witted yet sly, as well as religious and superstitious. Except for his discussion of David Willson, the founder of the Children of Peace community, Smith does not refer to the Irish unless it is to tell a joke that fits these stereotypes and, as several scholars have shown, such caricatures were easily translated into anti-Irish bigotry during the nineteenth century.[13] Overall, the order and content of Smith's chapters dealing with ethnic groups appear to set up a hierarchy of racial categories with the Scots and the English on top and the Blacks on the bottom.

Although "Canadian Reminiscences" sets out to recall the days of pioneering in general, Smith's organization of his material through conventional caricatures results in the image of an Upper Canadian rural society constructed along ethnic and racial lines. In this way, he unintentionally corroborates the recent findings of historical geographers who have noted the tendency for ethnic groups to settle in enclaves during the first phase of settlement in Ontario.[14] Smith's manuscript, however, also highlights the fact that these pioneers shared one experience in common: they were all settlers on land formerly occupied by First Nations. As a narrative, Smith's manuscript reflects the activity of colonization, and his characterizations of Native Peoples, in Chapter 8, "The Indians," serve to reinforce that process. While he demonstrates concern for the Natives he encountered, and, in particular, a clergyman's desire to have them accept Christianity, Smith consistently portrays the First Nations as dependent upon the settler society for support. Smith does not mention that the advance of settlement had dispossessed the Natives of their traditional hunting and fishing territories or that their attempts to introduce a new economy based on agriculture had been thwarted by that same process. Instead, starting from a restatement of the common nineteenth-century assumption that the Native populations of North America were dying out, Smith recounts tales reflecting conventional caricatures of First Nations people that range from the "noble savage" to the "drunken Indian," all of which serve to suggest an incompatibility between the settler and the Native way of life.[15]

As with the rest of his manuscript, Smith's chapter on the "Indians" contains a great deal of specific information. His tales, which focus on the First Nations of the Saugeen Peninsula, touch on Native fishing and hunting, forms of government, and encounters with Christianity. What is particularly revealing is the detail that Smith provides on Native resistance to land surrenders in the Owen Sound region, which included interferring with survey crews and petitioning the Prince of Wales during the Royal Tour of 1860. Smith gained a good deal of this specific knowledge as a consequence of his career as a clerk at the district court, his friendship with Christian missionaries such as the fellow Congregationalist, Reverend Ludwick Kribs, as well as the investigations he undertook while he was compiling his *Gazetteer and Directory of Grey County*, which he published in 1865.[16] Indeed, much of the specific information provided on people and events in the "Canadian Reminiscences" can be corroborated by other sources and, as a consequence, Smith's manuscript is particularly valuable as a source. It is also remarkable because of its focus on groups like the African Canadians and the First Nations who often only receive passing attention in the accounts of Smith's contemporaries.

Nevertheless, Smith understood and recounted his stories using contemporary stereotypes and literary conventions. His literary pretensions, reinforced by his journalism and ethnic pride, resulted in the packaging of his experiences into one particular form of writing, the settler narrative, a literary form that served not only to record the deeds of pioneers, but also to participate in the process of dispossession and marginalization of Upper Canada's first inhabitants. Through the employment of conventional caricatures in his narrative, Smith is able to blame the Natives themselves for the conditions that he and his fellow immigrant settlers had created by pioneering, the very subject that "Canadian Reminiscences" recalls and celebrates.

Michael Vance
Saint Mary's University
Halifax, Nova Scotia

Abbreviations

AO	Archives of Ontario
CBD	*Chambers Biographical Dictionary*
CHR	*Canadian Historical Review*
CSD	*Concise Scots Dictionary*
DAB	*Dictionary of American Biography*
DCB	*Dictionary of Canadian Biography*
DNB	*Dictionary of National Biography*
JCS	*Journal of Canadian Studies*
JIH	*Journal of Interdisciplinary History*
LAC	Library and Archives Canada
NDM	*New Dominion Monthly*
OED	*Oxford English Dictionary*
OH	*Ontario History*
SESH	*Scottish Economic and Social History*
SH	*Social History*

Chapter 1

The Bygone Age

In a few centuries, or even in a few generations, the first fifty years of Canadian life, the ways and means — the makeshifts of the men who took hold of the bush and made it into an inhabited and cultivated country — will be an interesting study. Then people will regret that so few materials remain for the illustration of the formative period of the country. I am glad that now in this year 1900, there are several local Historical Societies — most of them newly begun — to do something toward preserving a memory of our "olden times."

The coming of a family from Europe to America, will always with us be the beginning of the family history. It is not possible, frequently, to go back farther: but there is a solid beginning, that, "in the year 18_, my ancestor, Mr. ____ ____, from such a place in the old world, emigrated to these shores." And it is difficult for us to realize the fact, that we ourselves have been living, and are living, in the formative period of our country's history.

Every country has its "heroic age." The first dwellers in most European lands were the veriest barbarians, with little else than their bare hands to begin the battle of life, and, until touched by some influence from without, with little or no apparent desire to improve their surroundings. Their "heroic age" lasted for centuries, and has left many memorials. We, in Canada, began under different conditions. Civilized and enterprising men came to a howling wilderness it is true, yet with the ambitions and feelings of free men, and determined to conquer the circumstances of their surroundings. Their "heroic age" lasted more than a generation — till the old log house gave place to a dwelling of painted clapboard — or perchance to that of brick or stone; till the "woods" had melted away, even to the stumps that had been left behind; till the church and the school, and the Agricultural Society, the town, the fair, the railway, and lastly, the daily paper, took their places everywhere.[1]

Perhaps for Canada within the Lakes, that is the region bounded by the three great lakes of Ontario, Erie, and Huron — the garden of the New Dominion — the bygone age may be said to have ended with the coming of the railways, say 1855. As long as the "first settlers" remained in a township, that township was still under the influence of their ideas and habits — it was still for them in its "golden age" — yet more golden now to look back upon, through the vista of fifty years, than when it was reality!

Mosquitoes

A well-to-do, hale and pleasant old gentleman of Danville, Quebec, Mr. Goodhue,[2] told me that when he was a boy there, sleeping in the "chamber" of a small log house, close up under the shingles, with the "bush" all around them, the torment of the mosquitoes was something not to be imagined by people of the present day. I am reminded of a night I once passed, sleeping on the ground, up the Spanish River in Algoma. The heavy sultry air was vocal with them, and the Scotch plaid, inside which I sweltered and rolled about, was punctured everywhere with their barbs. They were certainly the perfection of skirmishers! I once called at the house of a German settler, in Brant Township, Huron [County], just as he came in for his dinner, begrimmed with "logging" on a new clearing. The day was very hot, and I asked him if he did not often wish that some of those numerous and useless Grand Dukes of his fatherland could be made to take their turn at logging? "Yaas!" said he, with a grin of anticipated satisfaction, "and let dem fight der mosquitos!"

When we were little boys — my brothers and I — our necks, and feet and hands were well-blistered by the mosquitoes, and on one occasion my father said that he would have to get another barrel of salt: "Yes," said one of the younger boys, "we must have another barrel, to *salt the bites!*" For we had found some alleviate in rubbing salt on the wounds made by the mosquitoes.

Hardships

Bush life became a dread reality when there was nothing to eat in the house, and none of the neighbours had anything to lend, and there was no money to go off and buy. Mr. Gilmour, of Muskoka, told me of his dragging a bag of flour fifteen miles over the snow in a deerskin; the hair lies back with so strong a "pile," that Norwegian settlers put a patch of it on the bottom of their "scoots," or long wooden snow-shoes, to prevent slipping back in ascending hills. John Brown, of Caledon, told me of "backing" flour, *carrying* it on his back — twenty miles across from "Yonge Street," where was the nearest mill.

One poor fellow, an English settler named Barnes, whose widow I have often seen, actually died of starvation, in the Township of Sullivan, thirteen miles south of Owen Sound.[3] The little handful of flour or meal in the house was painfully doled out to the children, and he tried, for two weeks, to support his own life on cow-cabbage and dandelion, boiled into greens. Failing to support life thus, after a bitter struggle, he lay down and died.

A farmer's wife in Caledon, Mrs. McArthur, told me that she had gathered the young leaves of the basswood, and boiled them for greens, in dire distress for bread. But for the aid of potatoes, it is difficult to see how families could have lived at all. And even then, the old-fashioned species of potatoes were so late in ripening, that the crop was of little use till the summer was well-nigh over. The man who introduced the "Early Rose" potato, a number of years ago, was a greater benefactor than he knew. The old "Merinos," and "Meshannocks," and "Kidneys," and "Cups" were all good enough potatoes, but we don't want to wait till well into August, before we can begin using them! With the Indians, the Spring is the starving time, and I thought one spring, as I was vainly endeavoring to exterminate a bed of Jerusalem artichokes[4] from my garden, what a blessing it was that the Government could bring their improvident wards the Indians, at the slight expense of sending an agent with a few bushels of artichokes, to plant a few of the rocky islands of Lake Huron. Once there, they would be always there, and it would tide the Indians over till their earlier potatoes were ready to dig.[5]

A Potato Story

An adventure of the lads of Inverness, Megantic County, Quebec, will illustrate the raising of potatoes. I had it [the story] from Mrs. Joseph Wallis of Etobicoke. The Inverness settlement was made, fifty or sixty years ago, by a large immigration of Highlanders from the Island of Arran,[6] under the leadership of "Captain" McKillop.[7] They lived under blanket tents for two months, till they got up houses for shelter. At last, such fortune as a very stony and ungrateful land — but plenty of it — could give them, began to smile on their prospects; and they were anxious to have a regular minister of the Gospel to settle among them — Captain McKillop having till this time led their public devotions.[8] They induced a good man to come out from the Highlands, and to cast in his lot with them, promising him that though they could not give him much money, they would get him a hundred acres of land, and help him clear it up and cultivate it.[9]

This arrangement had gone on for some years; the minister's farm was gradually getting cleared up, and his crop, principally potatoes, was regularly "put in" by the flock. But, one spring, some of the young men demurred to this imposed task. They said "such and such families, with sons, had so many days' work to do at the minister's, while other families, where there were only girls, escaped the impost, and it was not fair!" The girls, however, heard of it, and the reason assigned. Soon they plotted together, and two or three mornings after,

28

twelve of them with hoes over their shoulders, marched two and two, to put in the minister's crop! "And were you one of them?" I asked the elderly lady who told me. "No," she said, "I was not then old enough, but my eldest sister was one of the number." "And did they finish the work?" I enquired. "Oh," she said, "it was never so quickly nor so well done! And there never was any trouble again, as long as the minister lived. As soon as the word got round the settlement that the girls were at work, all the young men turned out to help them!"[10]

Makeshifts

When a boy, I heard William Kyle, an old storekeeper in St. George, tell of a man named Jackson, who, nearly half a century before that had married against the wishes of his friends, "and," as the story was told, "just took his wife under his arm, with his gun and his axe, and went back into the Bush." He camped at the forks of a river, forty miles back from the St. Lawrence. When winter came, he brought a fat deer in from the forest, strapped a good pack of furs upon a light sled he had made, kissed his wife, and started for Montreal on the ice of the river. There, he exchanged his pelts for "store goods," and he returned much heavier laden than when he went. His troubles were now over. He had plenty to eat and wear, and his clearing yearly got larger. Some other settlers began to find him out, and to squat down beside him, and when my old friend knew him, he was the "Squire" of the place with large mills, and other property.

No wonder, considering the tools they had to work with, and the frequent lack of skill in those who used them, that the log huts were sometimes of the roughest and smallest. I remember riding southward from Owen Sound, down the "Garafraxa Road,"[11] and seeing the axe, every time it was uplifted, of a settler who was chopping on his woodpile at the back door — I saw the axe, over the roof of the house!

I have seen the floors made of thick-hewn basswood — and basswood *will warp!* Doors, also, of split cedar, with creaking wooden

From the *Historical Atlas of Oxford & Brant Counties* (1875) 89.

Detail from a map of South Dumfries Township, Brant County, showing the location of St. George.

hinges. I have myself made both hinges and latches of wood. But of all the contrivances of those days, the most comical appurtenance to a log house was a "one-legged bedstead." It will be seen, that if stout green poles from the woods are inserted in holes bored in the house logs, at one corner of the house, so as to answer as bed rails, there is only one corner of the bed which needs support of a leg! Often the two farther corners of the house are thus occupied; for a log house with up-and-down board partitions, [it] is the first stage toward opulence and luxury, not always obtainable by the poor settler. Reverend John Wood told me of once, with a brother minister, sleeping in the house of a Scotch settler, in whose improved house of after years I myself have more than once spent the night. There was then but one room for both family and guests. The housewife, on their expressing a desire to retire for the night, remembered that there was something *outside* she had to see about, and the clergymen made use of the opportunity thus purposely afforded them, to hastily unrobe. One, however, hesitated and fumbled, and the other had to come to his rescue. "*Now*, Brother!" he said, in a vigorous whisper, as he held up a quilt at arm's length in front of the bed. The screen satisfied the demands of civilization, and all was quiet in the corner before the reappearance of the honest matron.

Schoolmasters

In those days, people had the desire to educate their children, but the opportunities were few. The elder sons and daughters of many a family had little education to fall to their share, though it was always considered a disgrace to be unable to read and write. I, myself, was only at school for two "quarters," from the age of ten to eighteen. In many cases it was that the work of the elder children was needed to build up the family fortunes, when with justice to themselves they should have been at school. And so it came about, that in the winter many young men and young women would get a "quarter's 'schoolin,'" who would not think, nowadays, to be seen at school.[12]

I have often thought of the justness of the old Hebrew rule of inheritance, that the oldest son should have a "double portion," and the younger son's single portions from their father. The elder son had often, as in our own land, borne hardships along with the parents, for the benefit of the younger children. Often in our Canadian families, as above situated, the younger children were, at a somewhat later date, given an excellent education. I am sorry to say that it was not infrequently accompanied with an overweening conceit on the part of those thus exceptionally favoured. Today it may be said, however, that there is no country where the bulk of the native-born population of middle age have so good an education. The log schoolhouse of the bush gave a partial training to the few, but the better one of modern days has given a thoroughly good training to the many.[13]

The little old schoolhouse at the crossroads was generally occupied about half the year. When three months were completed, the teacher could draw a dole from the "Government Fund." I taught at the village school in St. George when I was nineteen. The scholars

From *The Old Log School* (1992) 22.

The dilapidated remains shown in this photo are of an early old log school located in Huron County. This one was a "free school" that opened in 1856.

paid a quarter dollar a month, and I think I got fifty or sixty dollars of "public money" for the year.[14]

Sometimes big, rough fellows would make trouble for the "master." I once saw what we little boys called "a fight," between a master and scholar. At another time, the rivalry between two teachers about the "Governor's Road,"[15] south of St. George, assumed almost a belligerent character and agitated the whole neighbourhood. They had quarrelled over the pronunciation of a word proverbial for its *coolness* — "cucumber." One said it was pronounced *Kew-cumber*, and his opponent was an ignoramus not to know it. The other upheld the pronunciation of *Cow-cumber*, and thought little indeed of the scholarship of the man who pronounced it otherwise. And the whole neighbourhood took sides with one or the other! Happening in at one of these very schools (some years after the *cow-cumber* teacher), and glancing over the copybooks at the writing of the scholars, I saw something in the copy lines about "an evil toung." The master knew there was a "u" somewhere in "tongue," but had not got it in the right place![16]

Warming Houses

There is nothing warmer than a log house, when it is new, and well "daubed." I have myself wrought up the clay, and patched up the old daubing on my father's house. The first log schoolhouses were frequently built with open fireplaces, and "stick-chimneys." In these there were no "jambs" to the fireplaces, and logs of variable lengths could be flung on the fire. Indeed, the cosiest seat in the school — so the little boys always thought — was on the end of one of the logs burning on the hearth. In the schoolhouse, the boys next the fire would be too hot, and the ones next the door too cold. But it was easy to say, "Please, Master, may I warm myself?" and then the caloric equilibrium was restored.

The desks were boards fastened against the walls on each side, and the benches were "slabs" from the sawmill, raised on four legs.

The slabs *would* shrink, and one or two of the legs *would* get loose, and stick up through! And if, as sometimes happened, the bench had the extra refinement of a middle pair of pins, it was so easy to get the middle pins a little long, and the end ones a trifle short, so as to get a little "teetering" on it!

The next improvement was the short neck of a brick chimney, and "a Van Norman stove." An enterprise, which to our modern eyes will soon become prehistoric, was the iron foundry at Long Point, Lake Erie.[17] And it was really a "long point," which adjoined the vicinity I speak of, and not what it is now, an island. But, forty years ago, the "sea" broke through the land, and it will probably now always remain an island. So with the peninsula at Toronto, which, by way of unconscious prophecy, was always called "The Island." A good many years since, the lake broke through a wide gap, (much to the consternation of the city, which feared for its harbour) and made of the peninsula a veritable island.

The "bog-ore" strewn over the Long Point country in small boulders, kept the works going for several years until the supply ran out. The "Van Norman" stoves, manufactured by a gentleman of that name, were noted for their honest thickness and their endurance. The cookstoves were flat-topped; and Mother Powers, of the Governor's Road, a neighbour of ours, had one of them, and was said to bake her "buckwheats" on the top of it. When the cakes needed turning (so it is said), she had one of her girls at each corner to flop them over. So mammoth were they in their proportions [that] a funny fellow said, "about the size of an Indian blanket!" I had rather a mathematical turn for a boy, but I never could quite believe the details of this cake-turning — the parabolic curves were too intricate for me!

Ovens and Chimneys

Very few cookstoves were in use before 1840. In 1842, we moved from one farm to another and in our new house were no fireplaces. So we rented a cookstove, at the hire of a dollar a month, for a short time. But, getting rid of the healthy, cheering open fire, was not all clear gain, though certainly it was a great convenience to the women to have a stove for cooking and baking.

Once I built my mother a mud oven, and it made capital bread, but had I been acquainted with the mysteries of brick-making, I should not have made the mistake I fell into. The oven was about three feet wide, and three-and-a-half long, inside measure. The bottom was a big flat stove, bedded in a foundation of clay and supported by short posts. The walls and top were of wrought clay. The front was of stones and old bricks. The inside was of pine bark, neatly rounded off, to support the arched clay of the oven.

Now, I reasoned, "If I leave that till it is dry, it will crack and crumble; if I burn it out while it is soft, it will be tougher and better." So I fired it next morning, before going a couple of miles distant, on an errand for my father. Alas for my calculations! When I returned, my oven was down — a shapeless mass of wet and half-burned clay! But speedily I went to work again, as many a good man has done before, to repair the disaster, and in a week or two my mother was baking bread and pies in my oven.

The Jerhart Man's Chumla

Appropos of chimneys, my friend, Reverend Robert Brown,[18] told me the story of a neighbour of his, an old Jedburgh Scotsman, in the County of Lanark. It is in most part, one of the storiest counties of Upper Canada. The "Jerhart" man arrived in the autumn, after snow had fallen. He got up a log shanty, in some sort of way, but was determined when spring came, to have a good roof put on and a proper chimney built.

But his great trouble was "Wull there be stanes aneuch on ma lot to bigg a *chumla?*" The neighbours all assured him there would be plenty of stones! Still his anxiety all winter was continually expressed in the phrase, "I hope I may find stanes eneuch on ma lot to bigg a chumla!" When spring was near, and the three feet of snow began to melt, the green mossy tops of some of the boulders in the bush began to appear. The old man was now in high spirits. "Aw'm gaun to get stanes eneuch on ma lot to bigg a *chumla!* Aw can sey that!" he exclaimed. But when spring fairly opened and the oceans of boulders appeared — "Man!" he said, "Aw could have gotten stanes eneuch on ma lot to bigg a 'Jerhart!"[19]

Beverley Swamp

When I was young I read that in a drinking brawl in a New York saloon, a man was killed. Well, the man charged with the murder escaped. The police kept secret watch on his wife, and two months afterward she removed from the city, and a detective followed. He traced her to a new clearing in one of our western Ontario townships — he having a Hamilton constable with him, and a Canadian warrant of arrest — and secured the man. It was before the days of railways, and the parties were coming Hamilton-way in a waggon, and stopped for supper in Galt [now part of Cambridge].

The prisoner was full of jokes and fun, and among other things said that he understood the "Beverley Swamp was a good place for a man to run away in!" Now "Beverley Swamp" was along a certain five miles — unimproved — on the Macadamized[20] road from Galt to Hamilton — flat, and covered with pines. It was autumn, and the mud was *very* deep there. The prisoner, after a good supper, acted as if he were *very* sleepy, and, as he sat with a constable on each side of him, would lean up heavily against one and the other of them, as the waggon jolted slowly along. In the middle of this dark five miles, he made a sudden spring over the side of the waggon, into the darkness, and disappeared!

News travelled slowly in those days. Next morning, after sleeping all night in somebody's "Sugar bush," he presented himself at a blacksmith's shop, two or three miles east of the Macadamized road, and told of his arrest up west and supper at Galt, and the American detective, but skillfully put in his offence as "desertion from the American Army." His story was so plausible that the honest blacksmith soon cut off the handcuffs, and let him free. The man was never heard of more.

The Young Bloods

Fifty years ago, the young "bloods" all rode on horseback. Now they go in covered buggies. A favourite "badge," as it might be called, of the young bloods in the olden days, was in winter a red worsted "muffler" 'round the neck, worn quite loose, with the long ends hanging down in front. Sunday afternoon was the chosen time for their Knight-errantry. And as they went by on their creaking saddles, with horse curvetting and prancing, (obedient to a little touch of the spur on the side furthest from the spectator), it was easy to see that pride and conceit could grow in the woods, as well as in the populous city!

I remember meeting, in a new township, twenty years after, one of the most exquisite of the "Exquisites" of my boyhood. But what a difference! To see him in the nearest village, with flannel shirt sleeves, and not even a collar on — and his general careless "old farmer" air — one would never suppose him to have been a "young blood" in his day! Such are some of the revenges of Time! Indeed, when a young man cares nothing about improving his mind in the golden days, he is wasting what remains for him in [the] afterlife. Just the plodding, unintellectual fate that naturally follows a mentally-wasted youth![21]

Haying and Harvest

Nothing is more interesting for elderly people to look back upon, than the old arrangements for "Haying and Harvest." From Fergus and Elora, north and northwest, was a large district known as "The Queen's Bush,"[22] which, fifty or sixty years ago, was only beginning to be settled. The poor fellows would come down to us in Dumfries Township by scores, seeking for harvest work, quite sure that they

Painting of a harvest scene, titled *Barley Harvest*. From George Monro, *Picturesque Canada*, vol. II (1882) 649.

could go back in a month and find their little fields of spring wheat only just ready for cutting. They got 75¢ a day for haying, and a dollar for wheat harvesting, in both cases being boarded also.

I remember an old man we had more than once — Mr. Butcher — originally from about Aberdeen, in Scotland. He had been decoyed by some of [Simon] Bolivar's agents into emigrating to South America, about 1830 — one of Bolivar's schemes for improving his new Republic [was] by getting British settlers.[23] The old man planted "taties," instead of indigo and coffee, and his tubers got dead ripe when as large as peas! He had for his principal crop barley, instead of maize or sugar cane and his barley got "ripe" in the shot-balde! He had got into quarrels, too, with the "Spaniards," whom "he laid round his feet like mice!" Whether with a sword or a stick, I forget; let us hope it was only a stick! Then he became disgusted with that tropical country, and about Caracas in particular, and came to Canada. Scarcely [was he] more than settled in the Bush, than Mackenzie's Rebellion of 1837 broke out; our old friend — belligerent, if not "patriotic" — began shaping and boring a big dry elm log into a cannon to help to achieve Canadian Independence! Some of his neighbours got wind of it, and threatened to "inform" on him, and he desisted in time to save trouble to himself.[24]

Providing Whisky

When I got older, we sometimes did our own mowing. And I remember the sore bones the first day's mowing always gave me! I learned afterwards, especially from the Eastern Townships farmers of Quebec, that (before they had mowing machines) it was a common habit with them only to mow half a day to begin on, thus escaping the sore bones a first whole day's mowing gave me.

Once we engaged two fellows to mow. Scarcely had they made a beginning, when they begged, in the most abject way, for some whisky. They "were always furnished with whisky and they couldn't work without it," etc.[25] My father was angry, "Willie, I suppose you'll have to go to the village, and get these fellows a quart of whisky!" "What will I carry it in?" "Oh, I don't know! Ask Sam Stanton to lend you one of his *old boots!*"

However, a jug was searched out, and I started. On the way back, I saw I was going to meet a man on horseback. Had I known who it was, I should have dodged under a little bridge I was passing. But just where the great Railway viaduct now stands, south of St. George, I met the late Senator Christie,[26] then a young man, who was my Sunday School teacher. I remember I wished the jug were small enough to go into my pocket, in default of which I squeezed it close to me, on the side opposite to him as I passed, hoping he would not see it. But I am glad to say it was the first and the last whisky ever provided for "hands" on my father's farm!

Bushing

In the old days harvest hands talked of being "bushed." It literally meant that when a man was overcome with fatigue, he took to the bush, and threw himself under the shade of the trees to recover. And from the proximity of the bush everywhere, it often thus literally happened. And the oftener that in a field bounded on two or three sides by thick woods [where] the heat was most suffocating, the extreme point of exhaustion would more likely be reached. Besides, the men were often getting up strife among themselves — which the farmers were not averse to encourage — and trying [to see] who could "cut round" another, and who could "bush" one another.

I remember a man complaining of one of our neighbours in this way:

> "It ain't quite fair, the way Friend Dayton uses his harvest-hands! He comes down from the house, and takes the foremost cradle, [a scythe for cutting hay or grain], and leads us such a dicker, for about an hour. Of course, we're bound to keep up with him, and he gets about double work out of us while it lasts. And then he goes up to the house, and sits on the porch, smoking his pipe, and watching us, and resting, for about two hours; and then, just before dinner, he'll come down, and give us another hour. It ain't fair!"

The Girl That Drove the Reaper

Things fit beautifully into one another, for just about the time that the "Queen's Bush," etc, was getting cleared up, and men could not so well leave their own places to cut wheat and hay for us in Dumfries, the Reaping-machine began to come in. In 1851, Mr. John Shupe, an original partner in the now eminent firm of Bell & Son, Agricultural

An advertisement for a new reaper, called the "Victor," is described as a medium machine (weight 700 lbs.) that is superior to any of the light models before the public.

An artist's rendition of the new "Reaper with Forsyth's Johnson Self Rake," manufactured in Dundas, Ontario.

Implement Manufacturer, St. George, came up to my father's wheat field more than once to experiment with a new "Reaper" he was inventing and improving.[27]

And in the years intervening, it has not been altogether a rare thing, to see a brisk young woman (with perhaps a riding skirt) driving the reaper, perhaps her two brothers binding, and the "auld guidman" setting up the shocks — a purely family harvest party![28]

Twenty Buggies Through

In 1851, I went up to Owen Sound, with a party of four, over the "Owen Sound Road," through Fergus, Arthur, [no Mount Forest then!] and Durham. Stopping overnight at Clark's Hotel in Arthur, I asked the host if he "thought I could get safely through with my light, two-horse "rig"?[29]

A view of Owen Sound, 1873.

Courtesy of Special Collections, Killam Library, Dalhousie University.

"Oh yes," he thought so. There had been a great many buggies gone through to Owen Sound that year — as many as *twenty!* Thus re-assured, I went on. But think of twenty buggies passing up, from April to October?

Poor Houses

Remembering the houses that even well-to-do farmers lived in fifty years ago, we are amazed at the changes, and at the fact that those changes were not sooner thought of. The rooms were generally large, but the ceilings very low. And closets for hanging away clothes, were seldom seen. I have seen ceilings only 6 1/2 feet ; and 7 1/2 was considered "quite high enough for anything!" and the bedrooms were universally small — mere closets. The window glass was 7x9 or 8x10 inches. I remember a blacksmith building a house and it was considered a little "stylish" of him to have glass 10x12 inches in his windows. I myself built a house, and the glass in the window, 10x14 inches, I thought a touch above common!

Things go by comparisons. Our neighbour John Lebourveau, in Eaton,[30] Lower Canada, who, as a carpenter made window sashes, used to recommend the larger glass, to replace the "seven-by-nine." He would put in a sash [for you] with two panes. He said that he, "wanted to have the glass in a window big enough to see with *both eyes through one pane!*"[31]

Arnold's Land

It may not be generally known that Benedict Arnold, so heartily hated by the Americans for his treachery to their cause in the Revolution, drew from the British Government, large allotments of land in the County of York, Ontario.[32]

I had heard something of "Arnold's land" in north Gwillimbury, when I lived at Newmarket, and [when] speaking of it to Mr. J.J. Pearson, registrar for North York, he said, "If you'll come to the Registry Office, I'll let you see copies of his will and those of some of his sons — for the land being in this Riding, it was necessary the wills should be here, in legally certified copies." From these wills I learned the exact location of the lands, and afterwards saw them.

Some of Arnold's sons and grandsons were in the church; and some in the army, doing good service. He himself was always pestering the British Government for pension and land for "his services." I don't suppose poor Andre's relatives thought his "services" of much value![33]

The wills I examined (in copies) being pretty democratic, and the subdivisions multiplying, it came to be that the wild land (and excellent rich soil it was!) was all cut up into narrow strips among the heirs. So much cut up, that if so surveyed and actually, divided, the strips would be of an impossible narrowness. So somebody bought out, for a certain lump sum, all the heirs, and, though it was impossible to divide the land into so many equal portions, it was quite feasible to divide the money!

Chapter 2

The Pioneers

Many of the first settlers in the bush are of a class by themselves, quite distinct from the general population of the country. They do not take kindly to refined life, even the modified type of it we find in the somewhat new townships. They think "people get stuck-up," when they are able to supplant the log house with a better one, and to put on good clothes and ride in a buggy to church. And so, we find the pioneers continually selling out, and "going into the bush again."

As I never exactly lived "in the bush" myself, I may not have had as good opportunities as some, for studying this phase of character. My "pioneers" are rather those who had outlived their bush life, and found themselves — perhaps both unwittingly and unwillingly — in established settlements. And it is some of these who must sit for their portraits.

Shingle Weavers

One class of pioneers, either too lazy or too unfortunate to have acquired anything of their own, might be found in every township. They lived in old log houses, for which they paid no rent. They had a little patch of corn and potatoes, the cultivating of which was too often left to "the old woman." A pig was generally kept, and often a cow. These pastured on the roadsides and the yet unenclosed woodlands. They were "handymen," [who] made axe handles and butter ladles and had always a bunch of shingles to "trade" at the store. They were variously spoken of as being engaged in "shingle-weaving," coon hunting, axe-handle making, horse doctoring, sucker spearing, or "loafing." Mrs. Stowe's "Sam Lawson" is a good example of the class.[1]

Can You Run?

My friend, Dr. Mainwaring of St. George, once met one of this class, who had fallen below the general level of the axe-handle fraternity, and had gotten into petty crime. It was a very hot day, and the Doctor was driving slowly along the Galt and Dundas macadamized road, a few miles above the latter place. First he met two young men, whom he knew — Beverley [area] men. They were on foot, and carried guns. Behind them at a distance, was a man they were taking to a magistrate to be committed for theft. Behind him again, was his slatternly wife and some children, and the latter group were crying.

When the Doctor met the man he stopped him for a parley: "What have you been doing?" "Well, they say I've been stealin." "Where are you going?" " 'Spose I'm goin to a Magistrate, and there to gaol." "Why don't you run away?" "O, I dass'nt! They'd shoot me!" "No they won't! They are about as sick of the whole business as you are! I was talking to them. Can you run?" "Yaas!" said the unfortunate, with a knowing look. "Well now, clear! And let us see how fast you can run! Only let me past a little, so they won't think I put you up to it."

The Doctor drove on, keeping an eye on the proceedings behind him. Soon the old fellow made a dash for the woods, his old boots clattering as he went, and the brushwood snapping beneath his feet. The young men made a great deal of shouting, but never stirred off the road. There was no "commitment," but the neighbourhood got rid of a nuisance, which was of quite as much importance to them.[2]

The Wedding Guest

I once met a specimen of another variety of pioneer at Spanish River, in Algoma. He was employed at the sawmills at the mouth of the river, and we were on a tug going up a few miles. I don't know how he singled me out to listen to his story, except on the principle of Coleridge's "Ancient Mariner," who seemed always to know who had to hear his tale; and who singled out the unwilling wedding guest, and "held him by his glittering eye" till he had told him all. So this poor fellow held me.[3]

He said he had taken up a lot facing the river, in the Township of Salter [Sudbury District], and made a clearing and put up a house. We could see his clearing, on the left, fifteen miles up, and if there were any potatoes or onions in his garden fit to use, we were welcome to them — as we went up to our canoe. (We found his old-fashioned "cup" potatoes only as big as peas; so they were of no use to us).

He said he was a New Brunswicker. Some years ago, he was "engaged" to a fine young woman of nineteen years of age and was going to "settle down." But his parents objected to the match and "set the young woman's folks against him," and he went off to British Columbia and remained there twelve years.[4] The neighbours all told him, when he came back, that "It was too bad! Here the poor girl had been waiting for him all this time!" But his father and mother were just as opposed to the match as ever.

"Well," said I, to this ancient mariner, "You were now of mature years, and if she was a respectable girl, you ought to have done what was honourable and right, no matter what your father and mother might say."

"And so I determined to do," he said, with some feeling. "I didn't want to have a quarrel with my relations, and so I came up here, and took up a lot, and made a beginning — you'll see my place as you go up; it's the only house away up the river."

"And didn't you marry the girl after all?" I asked. "No," the poor fellow replied, with a husky voice, "My girl died of fever, a year ago last Christmas, when I was up here. And" he added after a pause, "I'm not going back to the settlements any more. I'm going to stay here in the woods."

The Eastern Townships

Having once spent three years in the "Eastern Townships" of Quebec, where the population is all of New England descent, I could not help hearing many stories of the early pioneers who came in over the line, beginning about the year 1800. As these stories nearly all relate to the earlier period of the settlements, I will give such as I have, in one connection. The most of them were told me by Mr. Hiram French of Eaton, and his son Mr. Levi R. French[5] of the same place.

An Owl Story

When the International Boundary Commission [men] were at work, in pursuance of the Ashburton Treaty,[6] about 1845, many of their axemen, and other workers, were from the Eastern Townships. People who are acquainted only with the woods of Ontario can have little idea of the density of the spruce and balsam woods of Quebec. A poor Frenchman told Levi French, when pathetically describing the kind of woods he had recently been lost in, held up the spread-out fingers of one hand, "and," said he, in broken English, "trees were as tick as dat!"

Several times, when trout fishing, once within a couple of miles of the New Hampshire boundary, I had good examples of what the settlers call "the black timber," that is the evergreen poles, growing so closely together — sometimes over hundreds of acres at a time — that a man, if trout fishing, is very thankful indeed to have the choice of wading the bed of a rocky stream.

Well, a poor Irishman, engaged on the survey of the Boundary, had for his "pack" — for everything had to be carried — a grindstone, continually needed for the pioneers' axes. When I lived within sight of the "Height of Land" between the countries, we could see a yellow streak, running N.E. and S.W., where the boundary was. There was a solid "bush" of twenty miles between the Canadian and American settlements, and in the following, according to their instructions, the "Height of Land," the Commissioners ordered a wide streak of timber to be felled, where the line was determined; and every hundred yards, a square hollow iron pillar, about three feet above the ground, was planted. It is a curious fact, that timber, entirely cut down and left to itself, never grows up in the same varieties again, and so this boundary streak grew up — not with maple and beech, and black birch nor with spruce and balsum, as the case might be — but with popular and other soft stuff. And we could see, at a distance of perhaps fourteen miles, the yellow streak of the autumn poplar leaves, amid the dark evergreen forest, along the line of hills that formed our southern horizon.

The Irishman and his "grind-stone," for thus he accented it, got separated from the rest in the thick spruce woods, and was "lost." After the rest had encamped, his absence was discovered and men were sent off in search of him. In the meantime, Pat had had a conversation with an owl. He never once suspected it was a bird! But when he sang out, "Hirru, there! A man lost!" he was startled and pleased to hear somebody call out, "Who? Who?" Pat bawled out. "It's I, sur! One of Captain Lawley's men, lost in the woods, wid a grind-stone!" This short conversation was repeated several times, and though the poor fellow no doubt wondered why his yet unseen friend did not do something more for him than merely enquire "who" he was — yet the sound of his "Hirru there!" brought the men who were searching for him to the spot and "Captain Lawley's man," as well as the "grind-stone," was recovered.

My brother, John Anderson Smith, in his "Humorous Sketches and Poems," has a story somewhat similar to this — "Jimmy Butler and the Owl," the locality being in Burford,[7] his own township — which has become one of the humorous "classics" of the day. It is easy to embellish stories, but I got the story of this "conversation" within sight of the mountains where it took place, and I have no doubt of the literal correctness of the anecdote.[8]

Freedom in Prayer

The same friend from whom I got the "owl," told me of a neighbour whose extraordinary noise in prayer was sometimes complained of by his brethren in the church. The good man did not intend to be noisy, but when he "let himself out," as he phrased it, he became unconscious of the volume of voice he was using.

So one day he was some distance off in the tangled spruce woods, and he bethought himself that he could have "a comfortable time in prayer" and annoy nobody, and began praying aloud. But "praying aloud" meant, with him, such a vehemence of utterance, as suggested to anyone a mile away, the idea of a man in some dire extremity of danger. And a hunter steered his way to the brother so engaged, directed by the sound. He himself was a religious man, and when he came to the place, took off his hat and stood quietly by.

At length the petitioner ended, and opening his eyes, beheld a neighbour standing beside him! "Well!" he said, "it does beat all! I can't get away out into the woods to pray, where I think I won't annoy anybody, and can holler as much as I like, but somebody will hear me a mile away, and come!" The neighbour, however, suggested that he was not annoyed, but would be glad to join with him in having a "prayer meeting" then and there, which they had.[9]

Incidents

The first settlers in Eaton and Newport townships came over the mountains from the Vermont settlements. Everything had to be carried on men's backs. One of these settlers (thus a very aged man told me), was toiling on from the nearest settlement on the Connecticut River, with a side of sole leather. It was heavy and what was worse, it was exceedingly bulky. He had evidently never read Aesop's account of the tricky ass, and his load of sponges,[10] for when he "camped" at night, he put his leather in a little stream to soak, and so that next morning he could roll it up in a small solid roll, [making it] much more convenient to "shoulder." His having made it twice as heavy as it was before, he only thought of when too late!

Mr. Hiram French, probably about 1820, had spent a year or two in Upper Canada, in the vicinity of Oshawa. On one occasion, speaking to "Squire Labaree,"[11] of Eaton, of what he had seen, he received this very philosophical reply: "Well," said the Squire, (Everybody, in the country parts, begins an observation with "well," a sort of a deliberative starting point for a discourse.) "Well, there are advantages and disadvantages in every place. And if a man knows enough to make good use of the advantages, and to let the disadvantages alone, in the place where he is, he will do well anywhere!"

On one occasion, they were celebrating the King's Birthday, (4th June), by having a township militia muster, where the men were merely ranked-up and answered to their names. Then the "boys" went down to the "flats" for a good game of ball, while the older men sat down to a grand dinner at Squire Labaree's at a dollar each.[12] Captain Powers, another of the old pioneers, who was just as "shiftless" as the Squire was provident and thrifty, was going home for want of funds to attend the dinner, but the others made up a dollar for him and insisted on his company. The dinner was a grand "success," no doubt washed down by the cider the Squire was so famous for making. Among other remarks made, the Squire said [of himself], "He owed nobody, and everybody owed him!" Captain Powers, in his speech, rejoined, "Well, nobody owes me, and I owe everybody!" — which was pretty correctly the state of the case.

Three Other Stories

I give three other stories of Mr. Hiram French:

(1) Captain Sawyer was one of the "Associates," or junta to whom the Township of Newport was granted by the Government, (about the year 1800).[13] The Captain's nose was, from some accident or other, much bent to one side. I have observed that almost half the men I meet either have the nose set on at a variation of the "ninety degrees" with the line of the eyebrows, or else have it bent sideways at the end. But the working of the Captain's nose was more noticeable in this latter respect than ordinarily. Calling one day at a settler's, the woman of the house happened to ask him "where he was going?" He did not want to tell her, and affected to laugh, as he said "he was going after his nose!" "Oh," said the woman, who looked at his nose, but did not relish the rebuff he intended for her. "I'm sorry for that for you'll be back here again, before night!" And surely enough — having lost his way in the woods, he came round, unconsciously, in a circle (people generally do that, and almost always in a circle to the left), and actually got back to the same little clearing at nightfall!

(2) Mr. French, when a young man was teaching school, a young fellow tapped at the schoolhouse door, and desired the young "Master" to send him out one of the young-lady scholars, as he wanted her to go to a party with him that night. The Master went in, and did so, and as there were no windows in the front of the log schoolhouse, the youngsters could not see who was outside. When the girl came in, some of the others, in a loud whisper, asked her, "Who it was?" "Deacon Alger," she replied, with the utmost promptness and gravity.

Now the Deacon was a very aged man, the "father" of the Newport Baptist church,[14] and it put an entirely different face on the visit to the door!

(3) A young man came into one of the country stores of the settlement. The "Trader" was a very bustling man, "What do you want today?" "Nothing, Sir!" promptly replied he. "And what have you brought to carry it in?" demanded the trader. "My hat!" said the young man, snatching off his "thatch." The storekeeper thought his ready wit deserved a reward, and dropped a handful of raisins into the proffered receptacle!

Experiences and Memories

These men had much of self-respect. After they got through the first trying years of their bush life, they developed into liberal and genial citizens and looked back with something of astonishment at the enforced narrowness of their former life. "You must not think," said honest John Ryder of Listowel, referring to a visit he had made into the "Queen's Bush" north of Fergus, "You must not think that the people who live away up North in the woods are savages, with bristles on their backs, and living on rusty pork!"

Yet the pioneers — many of them such from necessity, rather than from choice — are not all thoughtful or prudent. One of them, a Glasgow weaver, took up a lot two or three miles inland from where my friend William Bull lived, on Colpoy's Bay.[15] The town of Wiarton [then] was as yet only a "name" on a survey. Mr. Bull told me the story.

The man left his wife in the settlement, and went boldly into the wilderness, to put up a house — all alone. He got a number of small logs rolled together, and was slowly getting a house built. The walls were finished and daubed, and he was working at the door and window, but had not yet reached the roof — though he had been two weeks at work. He camped at night under a booth of hemlock branches, but woke up nearly smothered one morning, with the branches pressing heavy upon him, weighed down with eight inches of snow that had fallen through the night! He was alarmed and came out for Mr. Bull's help. He told the weaver that he should have "covered in" his house as soon as he had the walls up. However, the two went to work and prepared "basswood troughs," and with the help of a yoke of oxen, got them in, and a roof, such as the troughs made — clumsy but watertight — was on before night.

The pioneers and their families did not at all display the "fashions." If they followed them at all, it was toiling behind at such an immense distance, that the likeness was lost! I have seen them, often, at church, in their shirt sleeves. Indeed, as a boy, I have gone thus, myself. And more, I have seen a backwoods minister, "Elder" Smith of St. George, strip off his coat in a hot day, and hang it over the side of the pulpit, and, folding back his wristbands, begin vigorously at his sermon.[16]

The women mostly wore gowns of homespun and home-coloured flannel. Their bonnets — well, a handy woman can arrange a "bonnet" out of almost anything — only they were very much larger in those days, and not so easily extemporized. The boys, even big boys, and occasionally an old man, would be barefooted. Felt hats had not come in; we owe them to Kossuth's visit to America in 1850.[17] The headgear was either a cap of some sort, or a straw or "chip" hat,[18] or (on some grand occasion) a "beaver" hat. Nobody thought of colouring a straw hat, and the "chip" hats, made of wood fibre, were in shape an imitation of the tall "stove-pipe" hat. But the backwoods farmers, when they brought chip hats for Sunday wear, cut them down in height. I have thus worn them, about 1840. In those days boys did not wear overcoats, and seldom wore the long boots then universal among grown men.

The pioneer had no friction matches. The first I ever saw offered for sale, was in 1842.[19] The single small box, of which we now get three dozen for ten cents, were then four coppers each. Before that, it was a matter of some importance to "keep in" the fire. I have been sent to a neighbour's to bring a coal between two pieces of bark, though generally we managed with flint and tinder. I remember, in 1840, kindling a fire with my flintlock gun and a bit of cotton rag for wadding.

A man was supposed to aim at full dress, if he had a folded, yard-square black silk neckerchief, and a coloured silk handkerchief. But often a compromise was made, with a coloured cotton handkerchief, instead of a silk one.

Raspberry Hay

I have had many pleasant visits to Alton, and hope to have yet more. On one of those occasions, in the hospitable house of Mr. James McClellan, he told me the following, of a pioneer he knew in that region.

A man had settled on a new lot, where a "slashing" had been made. And fearing that he was going to be scarce of hay when winter came, determined to mow a nice patch of raspberry bushes — just in "the bloom" — hoping his cattle would not object to them when winter came on. But when snow fell, they wouldn't touch his "raspberry hay!" and one old cow would get a lot of it on her horns, and run scattering it round the barnyard! So he pretended, "he wasn't going to let them have that 'ere hay!" and fenced it in with a few rails, and set the dog on them whenever he found they had broken down the fence, and were stealing the "hay." The ruse succeeded. "Them 'ere cattle," he said, "had just enough of human natur' in them, to want that hay, just because I tried to keep it from them, and they ate it up, every bit of it, slick and clean!"[20]

A Primitive Mill

What with the "Hungarian process" of milling,[21] and all that, the backwoods gristmill is disappearing. But I once had the privilege

"Sketches of Meaford." From George Monro, *Picturesque Canada,* vol. II (1882) 583.

of seeing a genuine specimen of the pioneer mill, on the shores of Georgian Bay, between Meaford and Owen Sound.

By the way, "Lake Manitou" (the Lake of the Great Spirit) is the old name for that beautiful little inland sea. When Canada was ceded to Britain in 1763,[22] George III was a handsome and popular young King,[23] and was complimented by having this lake called after his name, "Georgian Bay." But it was a pity, and a mistake — but one that it is not yet too late to remedy. If the old name were used as an alternative name, the newer name would soon go out — just as "Ontario" has superseded "Frontenac."[24] The mill I speak of was owned by Robert Carson,[25] and consisted of a sawmill and gristmill, all under one roof. The millstones were granite, not "burr," and therefore more liable to get "gummed over," when the wheat was damp. And spring wheat, in those days and in that region kept in poor log barns with the snow drifting in between the logs, was very apt to be damp when it came to be threshed. Carson always asked them if their "wheat was dry?" and they always said "yes," but he was sometimes deceived and had been known to be so exasperated as to throw a damp grist out to the pigs! So he had chalked up, as I myself saw, in large shapely Roman characters, over his "bolt," this legend:[26]

Wet wheat makes men to lie;
Avoid that sin, and bring it dry!

Old Veterans

In my boyhood in Dumfries [Township], a few veterans of a former age were still lingering — as for instance, Grandfather Vanevery, a relic of Butler's Rangers in the American Revolution. He was "down" on the Americans and on President Madison[27] in particular, and he was never tired of telling anecdotes and exploits of the Revolutionary War, and of "Captain Mac-don-ald," as he would shake the words out, with his palsied voice.[28] I remember one of his shorter stories — on one occasion, he found one of his comrades rating and scolding at his mother, just as if she had been present.

"I said to him," repeated the garrulous old man. "Your mother must be dead long ago, for you are an old man, and why do you talk about your mother in that way?"

"Well," said the man, "she used to caution me, when I was a boy, not to cut my fingers, but she never told me not to cut my thumbs! And there, I've gone and cut my thumb!"

That Ancient River, Kishon

Many years ago, I came across an old man, who lived in the woods in the County of Grey, who had been at the Defense of Acre, under Sydney Smith, when besieged by Bonaparte, in 1800.[29] He said that when there — I suppose after the French had left — he and a companion got "leave" for a day, and rambled south on the seashore as far as Mount Carmel.

"Then you crossed the Kishon, at the foot of the mountain," I said.

"No; there was a little river, just after we left Acre, [Belus] but no other river all round the Bay, to Mount Carmel!"

We could not agree on the point at all, and it rather shook the old man's credibility, in my mind. But I discovered afterwards that the Kishon — "that Ancient River, the Prime Kishon" — gets so low in the summer (at least in modern times), that no mouth is visible. It merely percolates through bars of gravel and sand washed up by the sea.

Changes Going On

It is only those who have been away from a neighbourhood, and come back again to visit it, who can rightly estimate the improvements that go on in a somewhat new township. With one it may be a new gate, for another, a neglected corner cleared up; for one, a bit of new and better fence, for another, a new barn, a house, or a young orchard set out, or a garden enclosed, or some shade trees planted in front. Such items, aggregated and continued from year to year, soon make a wonderful change in the face of the landscape.

My friend, Mr. Thomas Lunn,[30] of Owen Sound, told me of pursuing (on a visit he made to Scotland), a certain fifteen miles [twenty-four kilometres] into the Border country that Burns spoke of, when he was looking for a farm to rent. And Burns remarked in his journal that he would not like a farm there — they were "too stony." That would be in 1787.[31] "And," said Mr. Lunn, "I was thinking, as I passed along, of what Burns said, "and I could not see a single stone, or a single field, all the fifteen miles !"

"How was that?" I asked. "Oh, two generations of industrious farmers had improved the land; the stones were all in "dykes" and under drains! The County had improved!"

The Cow Up the Stair!

Some men's humour takes the form of practical joking, a dangerous plaything, and one that is generally and wisely laid aside after early youth is past. If not, then a man must beware! For a man who is all the time planning practical jokes, alienates good friends, and is seldom good for much else. But here is a famous and now historical practical joke, played by students, in the very earliest years of Toronto University. It must have been about 1850; I got it from Mr. McCann, the janitor, about 1859.[32]

I had been up the corkscrew stair of the main tower, as many another visitor had been, and wondered whether it could be true that the students, one dark night, had persuaded a cow up that stair, and left her 130 feet from the ground? The janitor was very chatty and so I asked him about the story.

"Indeed, it's perfectly true, Sir!" he said.

And then I got the whole story, as far as it can be known. Sometime we may have the full confession of the plot, from some of the actors! One Saturday night, an unknown number of young men, students — unknown to principal, professor or janitor — kidnapped a cow, persuaded her inside the winding stairway, and with the tower door closed behind them, would not be much heard. But how all the scuffing and pushing up the main stair could be done, without

"University of Toronto." From J. Ross Robertson, *Landmarks of Toronto* (1894) 35.

Courtesy of Archival and Special Collections, McLaughlin Library, University of Guelph.

somebody beyond the plotters knowing it, I cannot understand. I only know it was a "grand success!" Then came the tug of war! By some stout rope on her horns, and vigorous propulsion behind, she was landed in some kind of fatigued and excited state, on the top "deck" of the tower, with a parapet four-feet high and the gravel walk 130 feet below!

Like flitting ghosts the students slipped down the stair and to their rooms, having first knotted up the bell rope in the tower. At the hour for prayers on Sunday morning, the janitor could not find his bell rope, and went up the tower to see what was the matter? There "he heard something rampaging over his head," and going up, he found the indignant cow!

"And," said he, "we had such a job — four of us — to get her down!"

"Surely, it must have been but a small cow?"

"No, indeed! She was a good fair-sized cow; Professor Buckland's cow"[33]

"And were the actors in this business ever discovered?"

"Well, I'll tell you, Sir. If anything of that kind is brought home to a student, he is liable to be rusticated. There was one student — oh! but he was a smooth fellow! You'd think butter wouldn't melt in his mouth! Sam _____; (It is perhaps scarcely fair to give the name in full, as the janitor gave it to me) he is now teaching Grammar School at Kingston. Well, when the time was coming near for his taking his degree, he thought it would be safer to confess, than have the matter found out against him. So he told Dr. McCaul,[34] the principal, that he had had a hand in the cow business, but he took good care not to name anyone else! And that's all any of us know about it!"

A good many years ago, I put this story, among some other recollections, in the *London Advertiser*, then under the editorship of Hon. Davis Mills.[35] The editor remarked in a note, "Our correspondent might just as well have given the name in full. The man is a Londoner, and well-known here!" I wondered then, and wonder now, if some of those editors and legislators, who know all about it, won't tell us the whole story soon?

Signs

On a visit to great London, many years ago, I used to read the signs and take a note of any oddities I saw, Posthethwaite, and Prettijohn, and I know not how many more strange names, but I have lost the memorandums then made.

At Portsmouth, England, some of the sailor's taverns and alehouses bore strange signs — "The Lame Duck," "The Little George," "The Glorious Apollo" — were some of them.

In our Canadian village of Hanover, I saw a sign, over the store of two very agreeable young men — who explained the literal meaning of the names — Kalbfleisch & Lautenschlager" — "calf-flesh" (veal); and "loud-slayer" or "loud-striker."[36]

A Sixth Sense

I have the following story from Dean Harris, of the R[oman] C[atholic] Church, St. Catharines, who said it was related to him by Colonel Gorham of Newmarket, Ontario, some years before. I knew Colonel Gorham, and was aware of his wonderful memory, and his stores of historical and antiquarian learning and research.

The Dean began by saying, "Some men hold that there is a 'sixth sense.' It is largely exemplified sometimes in the lower creation. You take some pigeons in a bag, and carry them far out to sea, and let them loose. They will rise up and circle around a little — till they get their bearings; we know not how — and then shoot off in a direct line for home. Or you take a dog in a box, and set him down forty miles from home and in three days he is back again! Now there are men who seem to have this sixth sense and who never lose themselves, whenever they go. They can't explain it, but they are aware of the power they possess. Such a man was the one of whom Col. Gorham told me."

Governor Simcoe founded York (now Toronto) in 1792; almost immediately he wanted to connect Lake Ontario with the Lake named "Simcoe" after himself — a distance of forty miles — with a good road and had started out a surveying party under Mr. Miller, to go "as straight as a crow would fly" to Lake Simcoe.

A man named Rogers had come from Pennsylvania to explore for good land. [There was afterwards a large immigration from that State to the County of York.][37] He had been north of the "Oak Ridges" and, about where Aurora now is, came across a trapper. The trapper said he had that morning left a surveying party, several miles to the west, who were striking out a line, "as the crow would fly," from York to Lake Simcoe. Rogers told him that they must be out of their course, for, judging by the number of hours the Trapper had been coming east, the party must have been about where Schomberg is now.

The two men parted; Rogers came on south, directly to York. He had this sixth sense and could go anywhere through the trackless

"Castle Frank," along the banks of the Don River in Toronto, was the home of Lieutenant-Governor John Graves Simcoe and his family. From J. Ross Robertson, *Landmarks of Toronto* (1894) 4.

woods. At a tavern a little north of York, he put up for the night. In the barroom he had been discussing the news he had heard at Aurora. At 9 o'clock — for he had retired early — the landlord roused him, and he found a messenger from Governor Simcoe, who wanted to see him.[38]

He was soon at "Castle Frank," on the banks of the Don, where the governor lived. A gentlemen, connected with Government House came in, whom he recognized as one of those he had conversed with at the tavern. The governor wanted to know "how he knew the surveyors were wrong?" He said he was one of those men — he did not know how it was — who never went wrong or got lost in the woods. He could go anywhere, and always come out where he intended. He himself had come in a straight line to York, and he knew, from what the Trapper told him, that the Surveyors were quite too far west. He was employed by parties in Pennsylvania, to explore for them and must now return and make his report, and though he could not remain and be a guide to the Surveyors to the north, he could remain two or three days.

So the Governor sent off a messenger to bring back Mr. Miller,[39] whom he found about where Newton Robinson [in West Gwillimbury, along today's Tauton Road] now stands. He was surprised at the order, but complied. And Mr. Rogers convinced him something was wrong. The blame was put upon their compasses, but however that might be, the survey was begun *de noveau*, and this time they went "as the crow flies," straight north to Holland Landing; thirty-four miles from York. Such, by Colonel Gorham's account, was the beginning of "Yonge Street."

Chapter 3

ODD CHARACTERS AND CUSTOMS

Once, when riding down beside the river Humber, below Wood-bridge, with my friend John McCallum,[1] my attention was drawn to a circle of stunted trees on the flats of the opposite side of the stream. They were small, spreading and crooked, alder and hawthorn trees, standing in an irregular circle and leaning out and in.

"See," my friend exclaimed, "does not that remind you of an Indian war dance?" And the ludicrous idea seemed not inappropriate. There were other and nobler trees, scattered over the flats and above our heads, and on our left, a forest of giant growth, but we took more notice of the "Bear dance," because of the oddity of those low-browed trees, spinning round — as we tried to imagine — in a circle, in the contortions of an Indian war dance.[2]

So the reader must not conclude there were no sober-minded, sensible men among the settlers I knew in my boyhood, because I choose those who formed the "bear dance." In point of fact, the majority of them were steady, moral, sensible men, but to speak of them would perhaps afford little of entertainment. They are to be found in every settlement, and their best memorial is the influence for good they leave behind them. For the first settlers of a locality determine, to a great degree, the character of the place for generations after. I think I can always tell what the first settlers were from the moral tone of the neighbourhood as it now is.

I have set myself to the task of describing the odd characters of a generation ago — those who composed the "bear dance" — for the amused spectators around. Nor yet must it be supposed that my own part of the country had more odd characters than other parts. Others may describe *their* "bear dances" — I describe the one I knew!

Wanted a Road!

Certainly the greatest oddity we had in our part of the township was John Loree.[3] He was a New Jersey man and had probably come to Canada when he was young. The Honorable William Dickson,[4] of Niagara, who originally bought the Township of Dumfries, had sold the South Concession to Samuel Street,[5] who in turn sold the wild land to settlers. Loree had a fifty-acre lot on Street's land. But it fronted nowhere, having a "fifty" in front, and a hundred behind it. This did not matter much, as long as the township was but half-cleared, but when the neighbours began to fence in their farms, and the open "bush" disappeared, Loree found he had no legal road out!

In the Eastern Townships of Quebec, they manage better. Every man who owns land in the township, can legally claim from the Township Council "a road *out*." In order that such slices off a man's land may not wrong him, the original surveys (which did not include roads laid off, as in Ontario) gave every lot two or three acres extra, to make up for contingencies.

Loree took a journey to Niagara, to make sure that when all the deeds should be granted, *his* should specify a "right of way" through the lot in front. He often wished "some *White man* would buy out Atkinson" for he denied to his Scotch neighbour, whom we have called "Atkinson," the proper standing of a White man, seeing he would not give him a way out![6] What promises Mr. Street gave him I don't know, but Loree's details of his journey were exceedingly entertaining to the neighbours. Among other things, he told us of his being invited to tea by the great man. "And I swow," he would say, "there wa'nt bread and butter enough on the table, more'n 'nough fur one man! And it was cut so thin! I tell ye, a feller had to be keerful there!"

Buy You A Coffin!

It was amusement for all the men and boys of the neighbourhood, at the time of the annual road work,[7] to set Loree on Atkinson — perhaps by repeating some mythical gossip of Atkinson's about him.

"Atkinson!" he said, on one such occasion, "we're thinkin' of gittin'up a *subscription* fur you, Sir!"

"What are ye gaun to get up a *supperscription* for mey for?"

"Well, Sir, we're goin'to buy a *coffin* for you, Sir — hev it *ready* for you beforehand. You'd feel auful bad if you thought any of your money would go to buy a coffin, after you was dead; and so we're goin'to hev it ready for you, Sir."

All this was said with the most outlandish *twang*, which he had brought with him from the pine barrens of New Jersey. And then he would sometimes end his attack, by adding, "Atkinson, you're [too] stingy to live! Ye sell all ye kin sell, and what ye can't sell, ye feed to yer hogs, and what yer hogs won't eat, ye eat yerself!"

On the Safe Side

The first time I saw him was in December 1837, the month Mackenzie was on Navy Island, when his sky was lowering.[8] Loree was in our barn, threshing some oats he had bought from the owner of the place. First, his boy came in to warm himself. "Well, Captain!" said my father, "what has happened to your *coat tail?*" for he had a little frock coat of homespun cloth, with one half of the skirt gone! "I was sowing, once in the spring," he said, with the same drawling elongation of the accented vowels: "I was sowing once in the spring, and the wind caught it, and tuck it off!"

This colloquial [exchange] occurred during one of those "cold snaps" we sometime have, and the father soon came in to warm his fingers. "Well, neighbour!" was my father's salutation, "and what side do you take in these troublous times?" His answer was sublime in its diplomacy! "Well, Sir," said Loree, "I'll join the side that *takes the country!*" He was resolved not to have his fifty acres confiscated, however matters might go![9]

He Smoked It On!

Once he came round, inviting "hands" to a "dung frolic." My father asked him what that was? He explained that it was a "bee," to get his barnyard manure hauled out to the fields. As my father was of the opinion that each farmer should haul out the contents of his own barnyard, we missed the "dung frolic" and the pumpkin pies "Mirandy" knew so well how to make! But I thought my vocabulary was enriched by the term!

The "bee," however, left John still some of the accumulation of years to have to out himself. He was hard at work at it one day — and he did not like that kind of work — when he bethought himself that his son "Abe" (his three elder boys were Abraham, Isaac and Jacob) should be there to help him. But Abe was off with his gun, for it was the time for black squirrels. At last Abe came sauntering along, with his gun on his shoulder. He rated Abe for his idleness and said he had "a great mind to give him a *hoss-whipping.*" Abe incautiously and undutifully muttered, "Better take care! Maybe gunpowder's stronger than you are! "Intimating, that as he was armed it might be dangerous to interfere with him. "With that," said Loree, "I just tuck his gun, and I chucked it about *two rod, and* I did *smoke* the hosswhip on to him; *I smoked it on to him,* Sir!"[10]

Loree and the Lawyers

He went round, for years, with an old beaver hat, whose crown would no longer stay in it, and so his wife sewed it up to a pyramidal point. My father called it a "hail-splitter," and it was probably in that hat that Loree came to the first railway meeting ever held in

Dumfries. It was at St. George, in the year 1849–50. Mr. Gilkison, a lawyer from Hamilton,[11] was the principal speaker. Dr. Stimson,[12] of St. George, supported him. The proposition was, for the ratepayers to sanction the township council taking $10,000 stock in the Great Western Railway.[13]

The farmers, generally, were averse to the proposal and someone put up Loree to oppose the lawyer. In a few doleful words, he painted the loss and risk to the township, and wound up by saying, "Mr. Cheerman, I've knowed that 'ere lawyer and sence he was kneehigh to a grasshopper, and I wouldn't believe a word he says, no further than I could throw a two-year-old *bull* by the tail! The best thing some lawyers could do, would be to go home, and stick to the plough-tail! *And some Doctors, too!*" he added, with a bow to Dr. Stimson.

The applause was unbounded; the motion was declared to be negatived, and Loree was complimented as the man who had defeated the lawyers and saved the public treasury! The poor fellow appropriated it all, and the next day hitched up his ponies and drove in his waggon to Brantford, to give the lawyers another "settling" at a county meeting in the interest of the railway. But alas! — he was not now among his friends and neighbours! On the contrary, he was among strangers and no sooner had he begun to open fire in his own peculiar style, on "the lawyers," than the audience fairly hooted him off the platform!

Financeering

In the ten or twelve years that succeeded the Rebellion of 1837, times were "hard." The farmers were not then, as now, the victims of Loan Agents and Societies, but they were continually getting "accommodation notes" discounted at the Banks. Loree wanted to get $200, probably to pay on his land, and went to his neighbour, Andreas Vanevery,[14] to ask for his name as endorser. Some Dutch[15] neighbour had, at sometime, called him by an abbreviation of Andreas, "Dreas," and by this name he was known. Dreas cautiously asked John what his prospects were for repayment? "Well," said he, "when it is due, I mean to get it out of the Gore, and pay it into the commercial, and when *that* comes due, I'll get it out of the Commercial and pay it into the Gore!"[16] He hoped by such financeering, to gain a year and to have the benefit of another crop. But Dreas wouldn't sign the note, though he was not disinclined to recount John's scheme to the first neighbour he met.

The Grasshoppers

Solomon Markle of West Dumfries, when I was a youth, sometimes entertained us with tales of the old War times. He told us as he was in the Battle of Queenston Heights in 1812. Markle had a peculiar voice, and spoke as if he had a bad "cold" in his head. "Gedderal Brock," he would say, "charged right up the hill, he did. And the Abericads picked hib off, they did!"[17]

And then he would branch off on other subjects — once, when on the subject of the depredations of the grasshoppers, he related to us how he, his wife, and all the children, armed themselves with green branches to drive them out of his clover. He told us how they formed a line, "and got the hoppers started" and then pressed them hard! "And, oh man!" said he, "before we got them to the other fence, how they did *loll out their tongues!*"

Will They No Droon?

A Scotch artisan I knew, (one of those who afterward turn out [to be] "farmers," being bantered about the various things he would be expected to do in the backwoods — among others, pig-killing) — asked, in all seriousness, "Will they no droon?" A river, which flowed past his proposed location, seemed to offer a solution of *that* difficulty, at least!

The same settler once held a conversation with a little pine tree, about as high as his head. It may be premised that his lot had many pines on it. "Ah," said he, "if I had only come to Canada when they were all *as small as you*, I could have managed better!"

Yankee Saddles

Another Scotch mechanic who had turned farmer, Mr. Robert King, of Vaughan,[18] by way of showing me how little he knew when he came to Canada, and how much he had learned since, told me that on one occasion he borrowed a saddle and started out on horseback for Toronto, twenty miles distant. He had got four or five miles on his way, with the saddle strapped wrong side foremost on the beast's back! He had been muttering objurgations all the way, about "thae Yankee saddles!" He was sure "they" did not ride half as easy as the saddles they made in Scotland!" Soon, however, a blacksmith, at whose shop he had to stop to get a shoe fastened, insisted on putting the saddle right for him.

After all, many of our best farmers have been mechanics. And it had a steadying and encouraging effect to have a trade, so that if farming does not seem to succeed, the man can always fall back on the manual arts.[19]

Daft!

Whether, because we have them mostly gathered into asylums, or whether there are fewer of them, I know not, but we have not in Canada, as in Britain, imbeciles and idiots — "daft folk" — in every little neighbourhood. One incident of the unfortunates was mentioned to my father, a few years ago, in Windsor, Ontario, which I have never seen in print.

The landlord of a hotel, at which my father lodged overnight, told him of a "crazy man" he had for a few days to do odd jobs about the house and stables. "But," said the landlord, "another crazy man came to town and mine left at once! When the other man came on his *beat*, he disappeared! And you will always find it so — two crazy men, if they have their own way, will never stay in one place. They don't seem to like one another."[20]

A Lingual Test

Somebody told my father, many years ago, that he had discovered an infallible test for the inebriation of any one. As this is often a *desideratum*, it may be worth while to give this man's formula. He held that drunkenness affected a man's speech. If he were but slightly intoxicated, his utterance would be but little affected. With deeper potations, it would be more so. But a man who was even only moderately overcome with drink, could never properly and distinctly pronounce the words "truly rural." He would offer to do so, indeed was quite certain that he could pronounce the phrase, but would be sure to say "Too-ral-loo-ral!"

Laugh At Him, Boys!

The unconsciousness of an intoxicated man is sometimes amusing. At the Sydenham Township Show, held in a field near Owen Sound, I saw a drunken man sitting by the gap, afraid to try to walk any farther. Soon along came another drunken man, who, however, could walk, though like a bicycle he could not stand still.

"Ain't you ashamed of yourself, to be sitting there, and everybody laughing at you?" And having pointed his finger at him, and "shamed" him several times, he staggered on. A few boys near, set up a merry laugh. The man veered round cautiously, and called out, "That's right" Laugh at him, boys! He ought to be ashamed of himself!"[21]

An Admirable Crichton

James Dobie, a young Scotchman when I was a lad, was the most versatile man I ever saw. He was well-educated, strong in body, and had a healthy conceit of himself — a modern "Admirable Crichton,"[22] for he seemed to be able to do anything. And always ready to embark in anything — it did not seem to matter what — that could yield him either fame or profit.

When I first knew him, he was a salesman in a dry goods store, and a polite, good salesman he made. Not long after, he had a small contract on a macadamized road, with a few labourers under him. Then, some rumours betting abroad, he wrote to the adjutant-general offering to raise a troop of volunteer horse. He showed me his letter, before he sent it. It read very "military" like, indeed. But this came to nothing.

Once I heard of him underground, mining gypsum at Paris, Ontario. There, he taught a school, for a term or two, on the Governor's Road, and was well-spoken-of as a teacher. Later on, he was "clerking" in a store, this time in Waterloo Township [in Waterloo County] where an acquaintance with German was, at that time, necessary, and he began to sputter "Dutch" among the natives.

Next I found him coming to St. George with his butcher's waggon, he having begun business with a partner in Paris. It is impossible for a man to know everything though some of the "Admirable Crichtons" attempt it, and a storekeeper, James Kyle, whose clerk I was at the time, played a practical joke on Dobie. Kyle had a carcass of very lean mutton in the storehouse, and he asked Dobie "if he would exchange beef for *venison*, pound for pound?" "Yes," he answered, he would do that. So the dealer ran out and hastily removed the *head* from the mutton (the better to pass it off for venison) before the "butcher" came in. The trick succeeded. Thirty or forty pounds of good beef were exchanged for a whole like weight of the thinnest mutton I ever saw, and the *venison* was offered at a hotel in Paris before the joke was discovered. Dobie never referred to it afterwards.

Not long after, having forgiven him for the *venison* trick, Dobie served the same storekeeper, as assistant, for a few months. I had then begun to teach school. Then he took a contract for excavating a huge barn cellar and made double wages by doing the work of two men at it, working all alone. After this, he was engineer in a steam sawmill "over the creek" in Buffalo. I called on him, at work there. Finally, he disappeared from my sight, as a travelling agent or inspector for some great bridge-building firm in New York, and was, when last I heard of him (now many years ago), overseeing the building of some iron bridges in Virginia, being respectably married, and likely, at last, to "make his mark."

The Charivari

Habits and customs change, perhaps all the sooner now, that there is more education abroad than in former days. The loss of a few of these customs we regret — of more, we applaud. Among the latter is the "Charivari." Both the thing and the name seem to have come from the French. The original intention, doubtless, was a mock serenade for some ill-assorted couple — as for instance, an old woman and a young man. But, half a century ago, the custom was so prevalent, in some parts of Upper Canada that no couple whatever could hope to escape the infliction of a *charivari* at their marriage. When the custom began to decay a little, I heard a bride say: "No, they didn't think enough of us to give a *shiveree!*"[23] And I remember two men in Dumfries, Purvis Lawrason and Sam Vanevery, who had been, before my remembrance, the acknowledged "Captains" of all the *charivaries* for years in that neighbourhood and who had led their forces through many a perilous adventure.[24]

The unearthly noise of a country *charivari*, once heard, is something never to be forgotten! A dozen strings of sleigh-bells — the old-fashioned kind, of graduated sizes and tones, half a dozen cow bells, a number of old tin pans to rattle, two or three guns, two or three tin horns, and all, except the performers on the tin horns, shouting at the top of their voices — such was the backwoods music. It came in bursts, lasting for about five minutes. Human lungs could not stand it longer. They generally took care not to "trespass," but kept on the highway.

A party, of at least fifty — as I knew, *from a close and particular estimate* — serenaded a widower, Dan Starnaman, who had (as we thought) rather hastily changed his solitary position. At an earlier date, a "treat" would have been demanded, but Temperance had made strides in the meantime, and the serenaders were content when the groom and bride came out on the "stoop," and sang them a duet in the moonlight. The whole party then moved off, led by Andrew Kyle playing on a fife, and came past my father's house, bound for another place, a mile or two away, to serenade a Methodist minister, who had just got married. This gentleman, afterward a leading Doctor of Divinity in his church, no doubt ever remembered the evening of his wedding, on the second concession of Dumfries and the astonishing music made by his volunteer "choir!"

"Meeting of the Toronto Temperance Reformation Society." The meeting had taken place on June 28, 1875, possibly in the St. Lawrence Hall at the corner of King and Jarvis streets. From the *Canadian Illustrated News*, vol. XII, no. 4 (1875) 52.

In this case, legal proceedings were threatened, but nothing occurred. Sometimes, however, legal proceedings did follow the demonstration. Within half a mile of where the old widower was serenaded, there had been, a few years before, an unfortunate *Charivari*. When William Wilber[25] was married, some of the family pretended to fraternize with the roisterers, and found out who they were, and twenty or thirty of them were arrested for "riot." They were all bound over to appear at the Quarter Sessions, in Hamilton, except one, who being a stranger in the neighbourhood, had to bear a weary two-months in gaol.[26]

The cases were tried before Judge Miles O'Reilly, and all were fined. One of the number, Colin Keir, of the Governor's Road, a Scotsman from Falkirk, had a rich Lothian brogue. He had prepared himself for this undesirable occasion, by a grand bowse[27] — a not unfrequent proceeding on his part — and when he sat in the prisoner's box, became very thirsty. "I want a drink o'*watter!*" rejoined Colin. "Can some o'ye not bring a man a drink o'*watter?*" and then, seeing they still hesitated about supplying his demand, sung out "There's not a decent man in the house, but myself, and the little man there [the Judge] with the *fence round him!*"

No doubt Judge O'Reilly, the most urbane man I ever saw on the bench — and who always managed to put everyone, even defeated suitors, into good humor — ordered Colin his "*drink o'watter!*"[28]

Peter McNaughton

With a little of the flavor of antiquarianism in my "make-up," I could not hear of the pretty little village of Belfountain having been once known to the settlers as "Tub-town," without trying to find out "the why and the wherefore?" And I found the worthy blacksmith of the place, William McDonald,[29] the very man to tell me. Belfountain has the clearest of running water running past it — the upper waters of the "Credit" — no doubt full of trout in primeval times.

But we found good trout still, in the lake near by. And here let me say to all gentle fishermen, that if they want to find fish in a small lake, find *where the lake is fed;* it may be ever so small a stream, but where the lake received its waters, *there* is where the fish gather (expecting also that something in the shape of "feed" for them, will come into the lake at that point). So we anchored a rude raft off the mouth of the small run — invisible to us, in the grass and weeds — at the "head" of the lake and found our trout in twelve feet of water. No doubt the Apostles wrought on the same lines for the same principle would make the mouth of the upper Jordan, about Bethsaida, the best fishing ground on the lake.

And Mr. McDonald told me about "Tub-town." Peter McNaughton, a bachelor fellow, a cooper, bargained for a quarter-acre lot in the new village in the woods, and would build his own house and shop. He knew a barrel wouldn't stand without hoops, and seemed to think the same principle might be good for a house. So he erected an immense *tub*, of inch-and-a-half flooring stuff, twelve feet long, and his tub was twelve feet in diameter. He had two hoops on it, one just a few inches narrower at the top, just enough to make the hoops "grip." The hoops were each composed of two elm poles, clamped together in a wonderful way with iron clamps, which he instructed Mr. McDonald how to make for him. I am afraid there is no model of the invention of those clamps at Ottawa. More's the pity! The lower part was used for a cooper shop and the upper part, surmounted with a conical roof, was his sleeping apartment. As it was one of the first buildings, the neighbours laughed about it, and called the place "Tub-Town."[30]

Peter was a kind of a universal genius. Once he was coming along the road that skirts the brow of the precipice, overlooking the Forks of the Credit, when he came upon some men, doing their "road work," and who were trying in vain to oust a big boulder from the roadway. They had dug round the stone and had an immense green elm lever in position, but there were not enough men to weigh it down. The boulder was bigger and heavier than they had thought.

"Hold on, boys!" says Peter, and, lifting a sharp axe near by, he went at the elm tree standing just behind him, and felled the tree with such mathematical precision that it struck the end of the "pry" and jerked the stone clean out of its hole! "Which way did you come?" asked the blacksmith, and I told him. "Well," said he, "you passed the stone, lying beside the road, as you came from John Brown's; we call it *Peter McNaughton's stone* and it is there to this day!"

No Place Like Home![31]

"There is no place like home!" sang the wandering and well-nigh homeless John Howard Payne, and so an old neighbour of ours in Dumfries thought. He was an old man when I was a little boy, but his story was well-known in the neighbourhood. In his old age, he would retire from his farm (the "boys" could manage that!), and from his wife (she could "get along!"), and from Canada (it could do without him!) and join the Shaker Community in Lebanon, New York State.[32]

Our neighbour was a strong, raw-boned old man, and handy with an axe, and as a preliminary means of grace, they kept him pretty closely sawing and splitting stove wood in the cellar all winter. In the spring, all the winter's experiences seemed to veer to the one point of home, and he came back again; henceforth repudiating Shakerism and all its deeds — especially its wood splitting.[33]

Fishing in the Big Head River

Meaford,[34] a pretty little town of itself, stands on a very pretty little river, the "Big Head River." It got its name thus: the mouth of the river always was a good shelter for small boats, coasting along in the old days. And some one camping there, had discovered a very large Indian skull, washed out of a sandy bank of the river and the somewhat enigmatical name of "The Big Head River," was given, thus, to the stream. Its spring come out from the base of the great "Niagara Ridge" that runs up so far north, and winds along, south and east, till it falls into "Lake Manitou" at Meaford.

I have some very pleasant memories connected with trout fishing in the bush, and occasionally these experiences were a little exciting. About 1860, I made one of a party of six, to fish in the upper waters of the Big Head River.[35] We were to leave Owen Sound at midnight, and the calculations were that we would be on the ground, and make the horses comfortable, and have our hot coffee prepared and disposed of, and be all ready to "throw in," at the first streak of day. We went eight or ten miles toward Meaford and then turned off southward. Mr. Richard Doyle,[36] of Owen Sound, was the leader of the party, and the owner and driver of the team.

Immediately on leaving the new gravel road, in descending a rough though not steep slope, the neck yoke of the spring-waggon gave way and the "tongue" dropped to the ground and snapped off; and the horses were powerless to stop the vehicle. Three of us were sitting on a high seat in front, and three were asleep on an armful of hay behind. I made up my mind "there was a broken leg" for any one who jumped out among the boulders piled up on each side of the track, and we must hang on and see what would happen! Doyle knew there was a small log bridge over a narrow gully at the bottom and hoped the waggon would strike it, and stop at the "rise" beyond. I could see nothing distinctly.

Down we went, not very far, but with gathering force. The right wheels struck the bridge, the left wheels went over the edge, and away we all went in the darkness! I had a sensation of shooting down obliquely into the darkness — the green branches giving a "whoosh!" as I went through them — and then I landed somewhat heavily on my left shoulder. I was up in a moment, for I thought of the waggon and horses coming down after us, and it was very dark in the bottom.

"Are you hurt, Sir?" I said to Reverend Mr. Hooper,[37] whom I found on his back.

"I don't know; help me up!" He was all right. Tucker was holding his ribs and groaning, "Oh!" But I thought, from the explosions of breath he used, that both lungs and ribs were sound. It had been a sudden awakening! He knew nothing till he found himself flying through the air. The two boys were scrambling about, and I now gave my attention to Doyle, who was up on the bridge, shouting for help. One horse had not gone over, but the reins were pulling his head heavily over the edge of the bridge. Doyle had sprung to the right, as the waggon went over. We soon liberated the horse and gave him to one of the boys, while we descended to grope for the other animal.

In the black darkness, we found a horse's *head*, but his body was out of reach! There had been an older log bridge, at a lower end, which was still there, two or three of the logs only having been removed. Through the opening in this second bridge, the horse had slipped into the small trickling stream that ran beneath. How the horse ever got there, and how he ever got out again with four sound legs beneath him, was a mystery to me! But we got him out and felt him all over, and there was not a drop of blood nor a scratch!

The waggon had been caught by a hemlock that had fallen across the gully, and had not followed us all the way; if it had it must have killed some of us. We took the horses back to a tavern we had passed and got a lantern, and set the boys to gather up the provisions, and at last started to walk the remaining two miles. We had our hot coffee, and got "in" our lines at daybreak and had a good day's fishing — very glad to find all our men, after their rough experience, able to handle the rod.

I never believed in the heretical theory of fishing upstream nor did we practise it there. We waded down the little river and when we silently came to a promising pool, stirred up the sand with our feet and made the water cloudy. We fished along, a mile or two down the stream, and when we got hungry — sometime in the afternoon — came back to our camping ground, and had luncheon and coffee and got safely home at night with the waggon tongue temporarily "spliced." Doyle was far ahead of me in the "count." But I was a good "second," with considerably more than any of the others.

Coon Hunting

Raccoon hunting has gone out of use, and no wonder, considering the freedom that was made with other men's timber trees! But, as a boy, I have assisted at "coon hunts" in the old style.

It was not every dog that made a good "coon dog." Hairy, bushy-tailed fellows, with small muzzles and something of the "collie" in them — were best. The men would sit round, silently, on the fences of the corn field, while the dogs were searching the field — for a raccoon dearly loves "green corn" — but it was very seldom indeed the hunters could get a shot at him. The first intimation of any success would be, a little piece in the woods — not on the very margin — the dogs barking furiously. "He *has* one! He's *treed* him!" the hunters would say and go to the place. The Blacks in the South have it, that:

> The very smallest possum
> Climbs the biggest kind of tree!

And it is equally true of the raccoon.

I remember one such run we had, at Andrew Kyle's in Dumfries in 1849. The coon took up a red oak, a monstrous tree, in the bush of genial Philip Kelly[38] — who came out to see what was going on, but made no objections. There were five or six of us and we had three axes and we would not give it up, just because the tree was big! In these days, it would land a man in the County Court, with a big bill for trespass and damages, but it was considered "all right" then.

Lanterns were lighted and three axes used at once, and after a good while the tree went over. The dogs had to be held while the tree was falling. *Then* — as soon as possible — *into the top!* For the coon might scramble up another tree! The dogs soon had him. He would weigh 25 or 30 pounds. His pelt would be worth "three York shillings," and the farmer would get a quart or two of harness oil. Raccoons were not hunted at a profit![39]

Suckers

Spearing fish at night was rough, splashing work though the boys enjoyed it very much. Some "fat pine" is split fine. The Indians use birchbark. An assistant carries a bagful of the pine on his shoulder. Another carries the light "jack" — a cap of hoop-iron at the end of a pole. A third carries a bag for the fish, and a fourth handles the spear.[40] When through for the night, the fish were equally divided into four heaps. Then one of the men turned his back, while he answered the question, "Whose lot is this?" till they were all allotted.

Where pork had been eaten all winter, any kind of fish would be welcomed in the Spring — even *suckers*, which were the main product of the Spring fishing in the interior parts.

Spruce Gum

In the Eastern Townships, Quebec, nearly all the people are descended from those New England settlers who came in the early years of the century, and when a young couple set up for themselves, it is very apt to be in one of the western States, rather than in newer Canada. So there were plenty of letters received about Eaton, where we lived, from former residents of Eaton, then in Minnesota and Dakota. And, very often, they would add a postscript — "Next time you write send us some bits of *Spruce Gum!*"

Of course, not much could be sent in a half-ounce letter. In later years, when the weight [of a letter] was extended to a whole ounce, more could find its way thus. No doubt also newspapers were made to carry "gum." The aromatic, slightly-acrid gum of the Canadian spruce was something to remind them of home and childhood, just like a Scotch settler here, getting a sprig of heather in a letter "frae hame!" And, childish as the practice might seem, in the eyes of many, the material, at least, was healthful, and in the case of the Minnesota emigrants, it reminded them of "home!"[41]

Skunks

Many tales used to be told of settlers being wheedled by the innocent-looking skunk, into too close an acquaintance. To see a skunk looking at you through the fence, as you go along some country road, it seems like some pretty little gentle beast you want to talk to, as you go along, gentle like a rabbit only not the long ears, nor the scared jerky way a rabbit has. And rather too black.

And then you think of a cat, but when you call "pussy!" it does not mew, as a cat would almost be sure to do. A stranger would almost be sure to go to that fence to investigate the matter. The little fine-furred black beast with a little white strip on its head or back, would shyly trot away, and it would not be difficult to overtake it! The unwary stranger attempts it, when, just as he is about to lay hold of the pretty little animal — "phitz" and, blinded and choked with the horrible mephitis discharge — with an odour about him it will take weeks to overcome, and in the case of his clothing, never can be overcome — he learns more than he ever knew before, about skunks!

A neighbour of ours ran down a skunk one night, with his horse and sleigh, not seeing it. And the cutter, and the horse, and the cushions and the buffalo robes, all testified to the fact, for all the winter after.

I myself overtook one, one night near Woodbridge,[42] in deep snow. It was trotting along in the sleigh track, in front. I let the horse walk, hoping my friend the skunk would soon leave the sleigh track. But the snowbanks were high and he did not care to try the side of the road. At length I let my beast jog along, to hurry up the little fellow in front. Alas! It would have been better to be patient. For he took to a high snowbank, at the level of my head — and at twenty feet distance, gave me a broadside as I passed! One little speck of the discharge struck my cheek and it stung like the prick of a pin. I had trouble all the rest of that winter, with my overcoat and my buffalo robe. A few feet nearer and the articles would have been ruined for future use.

My friend, Mr. Urquhart, of Newmarket, told me of his picking one up, near Sharon. He put it into a box and brought home with him in his waggon. When he entered Newmarket, he called two or three men he knew, who were standing chatting at a corner, to "come and see what this is!" A very slight glance was enough; they all ran off for safety, crying out "*Skunk!*"

He had not been long in the country, and did not know what "skunk" was, but supposing it was a beast, that for some unknown reason he had better be rid of, he took it by the neck and crop, and dropped it over the side of his waggon, whence it trotted away into Dr. Nash's field. There never was a more thankful man, when he afterwards found what an escape he had had!

A Good Man For a Sunday School

When I was at Philadelphia, in the autumn of 1876, at the "Centennial Exhibition,"[43] it came the time for the quadrennial election of President. [Rutherford] Hayes and [Samuel] Tilden were the candidates. In the house on 11th Street, where I boarded, "the old man," Mr. Engel, was a fierce "Democrat," and a supporter of Tilden. A young New Brunswick doctor, he often had a political bout, over the breakfast table.

"Now, Mr. Engel, do you believe all those stories the Democrat papers tell you about Governor Hayes?"

"No, I don't! Mister Hayes is a nice man! He'd be a real good man for a *Sunday School* or a splendid man for a *Young Men's Christian Association!* But he'd be no good for president. Wouldn't be any better than *old Grant!* He'd just do what them ere fellows told him! Now, Samuel J. Tilden has a head on his shoulders! That man's born to rule!"

The night before the election, at an outdoor "demonstration," I heard a "Republican" orator hold forth:

> Fellow-citizens! Our opponents in this contest are anxious to make it a personal matter, between the *two men.* We would conduct a political campaign with reference to principle, rather than to man! But if they will make it a personal issue, we have nothing to fear. Look, if you will, at the two men. Governor Hayes, when the War broke out, left a lucrative legal

practice, left a wife and a young family, buckled on his sword — and left behind him a good record when the War was done!

And the other man — with neither chick nor child to miss him — stayed at home; and *made money, and* with that money is now seeking to corrupt the electorate! If it's *got to be* a personal issue, judge between the men!"[44]

Can't You Let a Feller Sleep?

About 1863 or '64, when I was "running" the *Owen Sound Times*,[45] we almost always had once each week to work all night. On such occasions, the "boys" would get very sleepy about the "turn" of the night, at twelve o'clock, and would set up some roistering songs, as the (hand) cylinder-press was thumping on. Their great ambition seemed to be to get our neighbour, John Davis, waked up! To sing loud enough to "wake up old John!" was the way they described it.

I was afraid Davis, who was an unoffensive man, a teamster, would come in some day, and make a formal complaint. But he did nothing about it. Only at night, after a great many rousing choruses, we would hear (it was a big "double" frame house, with many partitions) away up, through ever so many partitions, a wearied-out expostulating voice, with a staccato-point between each word, "Can't-you-let-a-fellow-sleep?" This was always greeted with a great shout and the "boys" having done what they set out to do — "waked up old John!" — were much quieter for the rest of the night, for now they were wide awake, themselves.

Chapter 4

MAKESHIFTS OF BUSH LIFE

L ife in the new townships was largely an existence of makeshifts. A man had not what he wanted and he made something else, of his own contrivance, suit the purpose. My mother once repeated, to our nearest neighbour, Mrs. Charles Vanevery,[1] the old Scottish proverb, "There was once a woman who always took what she had, and she never wanted!"

"Yes," said our Canadian neighbour, "I have heard of *her!* She had no *kittle* and she hung over a patent pail, and burnt the bottom out!"

I once met a man, half way between Guelph and Owen Sound, who evidently was taking "such as he had," that he might not "want." He was leading a large cow, with a bag of flour strapped across her back, and that it should not be displaced going down hill, the cow was graced with a crupper![2]

At the very time I met this man, I myself was riding from Georgian Bay, southward a hundred and twenty miles in a rude box on a rude "hand-sleigh" sitting on a bag of oats, with my saddle hanging on the side of the box and my "harness" only some thongs cut from fifty cents worth of moccasin leather from a tannery — eked out with the saddle girths. No one seemed to think there was any oddity about my turnout, till I got to Guelph, and then the boys began to shout after me a little. But neither the man with the cow, nor myself, took either blame or credit for making people laugh, if laugh they did; it was necessity. And the necessity only became ludicrous in the after-light!

I am not old enough to have seen the plows the blacksmiths used to make for the farmers, but John Brown, blacksmith of Burwick (now Woodbridge),³ told me about them. He said "a Dutchman from Yonge Street" came once to his shop to get a plow made. "And," said he, "I want it made good and broad! One to turn a good broad furrow so that I can *get my hip against it*, if it doesn't go over!" The Wilkinson Company of Toronto Junction would wonder at such an order now!

By the way, I saw a Wilkinson steel plow (the works then at Aurora) at the Philadelphia Centennial Exhibition. Now, the United States *plows* are nearly a century behind ours — short, stumpy things, with almost perpendicular handles. You might get round a stump a little better with them — but when you got them in the open! Well, an American got hold of the stilts of the Wilkinson polished steel plow. He just imagined he was working with it — and didn't know a Newmarket man was looking on!

"Call that 'ere a plaow?" he exclaimed, "Why, you'd hev to be in a ten-acre field to *turn round!*"

I have seen harrows with wooden teeth — because the settler had no money to get iron teeth. And I have seen a woman harrowing in fall wheat with oxen, for the simple reason that her husband was pushed with other farm work, and her little boys were yet too young. But the same man, (in the Township of Elma) [Perth County], told me about overhearing his four little boys, planning for the future. One was to drive the oxen; one was to chop and carry in the wood; one was to bring home the cows and milk them. "And what will *Daddy* do?" sung out the youngest.

"Oh," said the oldest boy, with the approving nod from the others, "Daddy shall sit by the stove, and read the *Weekly Globe!*"⁴ The man was getting old — his wife was younger — and there was a quiver in his voice as he told me of the little fellows and their plotting together. They must be middle-aged men now and I hope the father did get the comfort planned for him.

I have seen those astonishing carts, made with wheels sawn from the end of a big oak log. I am told they are still to be seen in some parts of Europe. And I have seen ox-sleds habitually used in summer, because the settler had nothing "on wheels." I have myself helped to haul in wheat from the harvest field on a sled.

I have seen girls' dresses of red-and-blue checked flannel cut out with sheep shears and sewed with darning needle and woollen thread, and fastened down the back with a row of shining brass buttons, which had first graced a man's coat. And, thirty years afterward, one of those very girls was telling me about her son who was in the University! There *is* progress!

The Doos!

Self-protection often led to strange shifts in the backwoods as when an old Scotsman in Beverly Township, a few miles from us, invented an immense "craik,"⁵ to frighten the wild pigeons from his crops. They would swoop down on his newly sown grain in thousands, and the old man would leave his work and run to the house, calling to his daughter, "The doos! The doos! The ricketty! The ricketty! The doos!" The "doos" did not like the sound of his horse-fiddle,⁶ and with a noise like thunder would betake themselves away!

A Balky Horse

Perhaps there is nothing in all the experience of a farmer or country resident more exasperating than a "balky horse." I could write a whole chapter on the subject, but as I could not give a cure for the disease, we should be none the better. And such a horse generally makes a great pretence of extraordinary zeal.

> When near the hill, how keen he gets,
> With snorting and with blowing;
> And, like a screw propellor sets
> His whisking tail a-goin.⁷

I had a horse once that was so "balky" that he would only *trot* when he pleased. Once I had him under the saddle, intending to join a funeral, and as it had already started when I came in sight, I urged him forward, in order to overtake the procession. It was all in vain; so I tied him to the fence, and ran on a-foot and took my place among the mourners.

Alick Gibson, an honest blacksmith, did better, as related to me by my brother, Mr. John Anderson Smith. Alick had a balky mare, and she stopped with him one cold winter night, when yet half a mile from home. He sat in the cutter and tried various persuasions, but it was too cold to waste very much time — and still the mare would not stir! Always equal to any emergency, the stout fellow jumped out, and slipped the cutter from behind her, and drew it home over the snow, leaving her standing in the road. Next morning his mare was standing at the door of her stable with (Alick thought) *a very penitent look!*

Fine, Fine!

When Dumfries was first settled, there came a scarce year, and an old Scotsman, (they were all Scotch in the northern half of Dumfries) named Hogg,[8] having an eye to "pease-bannocks,"[9] in the scarcity of wheat, took a bag of peas to the mill at Galt and told the miller that he wanted them "grund *fine!*"

"I suppose it's for the hogs," said the miller.

"Aye, it's just for the Hoggs! But I want it grund fine, fine!"

Them Petaters

Reverend Solomon Snider[10] told me of a charcoal-burner,[11] in the Township of Norwich [Oxford County], who came to him, with his "bride," to be married; the parson had not the courage to suggest to the man more than a single dollar as his fee. The man was poor, but independent; [he was] barefooted — but then the weather was warm and he "hadn't got his fall boots yet." He hadn't any money, but he wanted to know of the minister if he'd "take *petaters* fur it?" Oh yes, he would take potatoes. They did not come, but every time Mr. Snider met him, he was always promising "to bring them *petaters!*" At last the parson told him, "My friend! If you'll never say another word about those potatoes, I won't!" Both parties agreed.

When Mr. Snider told me that story, I thought of a man, who once addressed my father, in southern Ohio,[12] and speaking of himself — "I'm a poor man, and I'm a ragged man, and I'm a *sassy* man! But I'm an honest man; I owe no man and I've got money comin' to me, and I own a good fifty-dollar *hoss!*"

Meat For the Table

It was often a difficult (and sometimes an impossible) thing, for the bush farmers to get meat for their tables. Something could be done at first with "game," sometimes with fish, but a farmer busy chopping or logging had no time for hunting. We found a very pretty custom, in Dumfries — that of a farmer always sending a quarter of mutton, or lamb, or veal, to his nearest neighbour. And of course, he would get the same again, by and by.

There was a secret, which I did not find out for years and years, in fact it never was told me at all; it was this. We three boys[13] (on the Grand River, in my first summer in Canada) were very fond of fishing; it was all "sport" to us, and we were in dread, sometimes, that our mother would think we were spending too much time fishing. But the fish we brought in every day were a most welcome addition to the scanty larder. But we knew nothing of that; we merely ate what was set before us, and then off to our fishing or plank-sailing again!

A Typical English Immigrant

Mr. Stapleton,[14] of Uxbridge [township] was a pioneer immigrant in the north part of Ontario County. Uxbridge was very new then. A Scotch settler, going into that same region of big trees and rich soil, in his family devotions thanked the Lord, "who had brought them safely, three thousand miles from their native land, and *seventy miles from anywhere!*" There seemed to be no place with a name, nearer than "York," now Toronto.

Stapleton was a Devonshire man — poor, with a large family [and] would gladly emigrate. He went to the parish authorities: "Would they send him out to Canada? And when he had found a home for his family, and had earned a little money, he would send for them?" "No, they wouldn't do that! He might leave his family for a permanent burden on the parish." "Well, could they send the *whole family* out?" "No; too much expense on the parish!"

What could he do? By some means or other — I suppose, hard work and poor living, and every penny saved — he managed to pay his passage over, and came to Quebec, and Montreal, and up the St. Lawrence on a "Durham boat,"[15] towed up the rapids by oxen. He got to Toronto and walked up Yonge Street to about Richmond Hill. Here he fell in with work.

The next spring, the parish officials, who would do nothing when he was there, bundled off the whole remaining family to Quebec. His wife only knew that her husband was "back of Toronto," and her heart sank within her, on the wharf at Quebec, when she found that Toronto was still five hundred miles in the interior! And she had no money! She did what many a woman had done before, and has done since — she sat down and had a good cry![16]

Mr. Wheeler, of Stouffville[17] (who told me the story), happened to be a passenger on the same ship, and learning that she was bound for his own part of Upper Canada, was interested in her case, and loaned her four pounds sterling — saying that Mr. Stapleton "could repay him when he was able."

When she got to Toronto, she did not know what to do, but two of her sturdy little boys said they "would go back into the country, and find Father!" And off they started. They thought they had obtained a clue, and turned east above Richmond Hill. Passing a strip of forest, one boy said, "I hear Father's voice!" and they dashed through the trees, and came out on a new clearing where some men were logging and shouting to the oxen — and one of them was the man they sought!

He soon "took up" a lot in Uxbridge. Two or three years after, some of Mr. Wheeler's family called on them in the winter. Stapleton made them welcome and said, "I've neither beef, pork, nor mutton in the house, but we'll get you some meat!" They wondered if he had veal, so early in the year. His meat was some good venison. And he told them, "his children had neither boots nor shoes, but none of them was barefoot!" He had them shod with deerskin moccasins, of his own making. He has numerous descendants in those neighbourhoods. I had a letter from a grandson, this very winter (1897).

Horse Trading

When people have no money and something is needed, they cast about whether there is not some article they can exchange for the wanted one. And this they call "trading." John Frost,[18] of Owen Sound, told me that all his boys had chickens and what not of their own property, and he was continually "trading" with them — just to teach them practically "how to do business."

A man wants a yoke of oxen. He has no money, but he has a three-year-old colt he has raised, and he perhaps "turns out" the colt and a small heifer, for a good yoke of oxen. A man wants a horse and he gets somebody (who desires such) to accept a yoke of unbroken steers for the nag. And perhaps one of the above parties knows how a "turn can be made," where everybody *owes* everybody and everybody is *creditor* to *everybody!*" And it was wonderful sometimes, how a few bits of paper, passed from hand to hand — a "note," a receipt, or an "order" — would settle ever so many debts!

From Broken Shackles: Old Man Henson from Slavery to Freedom (2001, 2007) xv–xvi. Photo of John Frost Jr., courtesy of Grey Roots Archival Collection

John Frost was the eldest son of Mary and John Frost Sr. His father, after moving to Sydenham (later Owen Sound) became a very successful and prosperous businessman, and was elected mayor in 1868. John Jr. opened a law practice and became very involved in public and municipal affairs, becoming mayor in 1892 and 1893. It is said that the Frost family provided shelter for many fugitive African Americans on property surrounding their home, known as Sheldon Place. In 1889, the book, *Broken Shackles*, was published under the pseudonym of Gleneg — the author was John Frost Jr.

Sheldon Place. Photograph by Ruth Cathcart.

There were certain "ethics" in horse trading: some good and some *not* so good! One rule was "No recanting!" You must not come back to undo your bargain! A man who "recanted" on a horse trade, lost caste among the farmers. Another rule — with much less of righteousness in it — was, that you were not obliged to speak of defects in your horse, the other man must find all that out for himself.

Seth Holcomb,[19] of Sheffield, was a noted horse trader. He "knew" a horse. He had, in some way become possessed of the mill and water privilege in St. George. He wanted to sell it. Robert Snowball, the famous waggon-maker would buy it, but had not the money.[20] "If he could turn out waggons for it, he'd be glad to buy it!" Oh yes, Mr. Holcomb would take a certain number of "Snowball Waggons," which had a good name in the country. So the bargain was made that was good for all parties. Snowball improved the property and built a new mill — and so benefited the village.[21] Holcomb "traded" off the waggons among the farmers, for horses — and so benefited the farmers — who often had horses and no money. Then he gathered these horses together and sent them off to the United States, and got cash for them — and so benefited himself.

Reverend John G. Sanderson, then of Oro, County of Simcoe,[22] told me, with satisfaction, of a horse trade one of "his members" made:

> Mr. Locke of Oro,[23] drove a brown and a grey horse together. Another farmer had a similar "unmatched" team. One day they met on the road and one farmer said to the other, "We ought to *trade* and then we'd each have a matched team!"
>
> "Very well; how will you trade?"
>
> So they agreed to trade "even," and one had a brown team and one a grey.
>
> Three weeks after, they met again. "Oh, Mr. Locke," said the other man, "you got the best of that bargain! The horse I got from you is a good enough horse, but he isn't equal to the mare you got from me!"
>
> "Well, I do like the mare and the longer the better. She is a good beast. I'll let you have her back, if you want her!"
>
> "No. Nobody shall say *I recanted* in a horse trade!"
>
> "Well, what do you think is the difference in the value of the two?"
>
> "Honestly, and between man and man, I think there is fifteen dollars difference"

"Well, I'll give you fifteen dollars. I haven't the money on me, but I'll send it to you pretty soon."

"And," said Mr. Sanderson, "I'm *proud* of my member! That was like an honest and honourable man!"

You Pay the Bill!

Storekeepers in the backwoods had sometimes to resort to makeshifts, as well as the farmers. Here is how old Willie Kyle, in St. George, managed without a detective or a search warrant. He was more accomplished at playing " 'ower the moor, among the heather," on his fiddle, than in driving a hard bargain or keeping a close eye on his goods. Through the winter he missed several things: among the rest, several yards of print, of a certain pattern. He had made a careful list of all the things he missed — including a bad half dollar somebody had given him. And he determined that the first person he found stealing, should pay the whole bill!

At last he came to know that a certain woman living on the Governor's Road was wearing a dress of the identical pattern of that that had been stolen. He put the "bill" in his pocket and started off. I knew the man quite well, to whose house he went. The good woman knew nothing of any wrongdoing about the print; [she] supposed her husband had bought it and paid for it, and said so. The slinky fellow, the husband, did not try to deny the pilfering of the print, but urgently declared he had taken nothing else, and as for the bad half dollar, he knew nothing at all of *that!*

"Well!" said old Willie, "you just *pey the bill*, or else you pack off to *Hamilton jeyl!*" The fellow "pey'd the bill!"[24]

A Backwoods Riddle

Newspapers were scarce and dear in those days. My father sent me once or twice, to borrow the *Hamilton Gazette*,[25] a small weekly, and I remember that the subscription rate was one pound (four dollars) a year. Jim Macpherson, a tavern *habitué* in St. George, liked to borrow and read newspapers, and a big "blue bonnet" he wore, was generally stuffed out like the dome of a Mohammedan mosque with them. It reminds me of what R.A. Smith, the composer,[26] said about Burns. An old man told Smith that he was a neighbour of Burns and his father. Said he, "I knew Burns very well — a decent man. He was a better man than his son Rab. I mind Rab as a wild colt, wearing a big blue bonnet, wi'a *hole* in it, and his hair sticking out o'the hole!"

Scenes of the Saengerfest, a German cultural festival focused on singing and dancing, held in Berlin on August 18, 1875. In recognition of the large number of German settlers, the settlement was named Berlin in 1833. W.W. Smith's *Gazetteer* noted that, by 1846, the town had around six hundred residents. The name was changed to Kitchener in 1916 when animosities towards the use of the German language and German practices came to a head during the First World War. Illustration from the *Canadian Illustrated News*, vol. XII, no. 10, 152.

Courtesy of Special Collections, Killam Library, Dalhousie University.

Once Jim wanted a "drop" and thought he might get the offer of it by putting out a riddle. "I was up at Woodstock last week," said Jim, "and saw a woman churning, and none of you will guess what she was churning in!" They guessed till they were tired — pail, tub, crock, barrel — everything was exhausted. At last "they would treat," if he would tell himself. "She was churning in a *churn!*" he quietly remarked, as he came forward to the "bar." Poor Jim died in the poorhouse at Berlin [now Kitchener], at last.[27]

The Tenth to the Miller

When Reverend Ludwick Kribs[28] moved from Owen Sound to Colpoy's Bay in 1857, there was no "Wiarton" (except on paper) and there was no flour mill nearer than Owen Sound — thirty miles by water, and no road "across the country." He had a small, clear stream on his lot and put up a shed to do for a "mill." He had a small "overshot" wheel, and a pair of three-foot granite stones he got from an old distillery in Owen Sound. He showed me through his backwoods mill once. The sifting apparatus — the "bolt" — took my eye. A trough, made of boards with a bolting-cloth bottom, and hung at each end by a rope, was his bolt. He could give it as vigorous a shake as he liked, by pushing it and drawing it, but it would not "go" of itself, and I suppose the flour would not pass through it unless it *were* shaken. He said he was not a *miller*, under the Statute. They are restricted to the one-twelfth.[29] He said he had *one-tenth* from the neighbours.

Chapter 5

BURIED FORTUNES

It must be one of the most annoying things in the world to have pretensions and "claims" without the surroundings of wealth or station to give them power. Such people, on the ebb of their fortunes, sometimes emigrate. If, as happens somewhat rarely, they throw pretensions to the winds and take their place among respectable, educated people who have nothing of wealth and more of the pride that often accompanies it — well and happy for them. But if they bring the pride and exclusiveness of their former pretensions with them, they find many mortifications, for our Canadian rural society has always refused to take a man on any other grounds than what it found him to be. If he was a good neighbour and an obliging man, and especially if he had also public spirit and a "good head for business," he was much thought of, but if he had nothing about him but some "Old County" genteel associations, he became "a nobody" in the settlement.[1]

As Poor as a Rat

About the year 1840, in the (undivided) Township of Dumfries, a Mr. Henderson was the "tax-gatherer." The poor fellow hopped round on a wooden leg, which was probably the reason of his appointment as he was less able to make his living otherwise. He was a "decent Scotsman," and full of anecdote and always stayed at my father's house overnight, in making his annual rounds.[2]

I had often heard my parents tell of a certain haughty farmer on the Scottish Borders, who was a petty tyrant over his work people. My father had seen him in the harvest field, on his well-groomed "hunter" with a creaking saddle, kick over a "stook"[3] that did not stand as *plumb* as his aristocratic eye demanded. He would call out to a man in the distance, "Hey, you! Come back here, and set up that stook properly!"

His name became a byword in the neighbourhood. Well, it seemed he had lost his money and had then emigrated, and as my father had heard that he was in the vicinity of Galt, he asked Henderson about him. "Oh yes, I know him very well," said the tax-gatherer, "he lives above Galt a little. He is as poor as a rat. I saw him two or three days ago — the last time I went past — bareheaded, chopping on his woodpile." I don't think my father ever spoke of his tyranny afterwards; there was a feeling of "Don't hit a man when he's down!" in his mind and the events of Providence had sufficiently avenged the old offence.

I was a little boy then, and perhaps this first suggested the thing to me, but I have noticed so many instances of it since that I can almost give it as a sure "sign" of a "gentleman" broken-in to work, when you see him working bareheaded, and especially if he is very slovenly about keeping his hands and face clean!

Had to be a Doctor

There are quite too many professional men, in proportion to the population. Dr. Stimson, of St. George, once said, in a speech, in my hearing, "When I was young, and was going through college, I used to consider what profession I would be? I thought I was *not good enough* for a minister, and that I was *too good* for a lawyer, and so I had to be a doctor!"[4] And a doctor he was, and two of his sons after him.[5]

Old Jim Maitland!

I gently veil his identity [Jim Maitland] under the above name, but he was, about 1838 and '39, one of the gilded youth of Brantford, the only son (as I think) of an aristocratic widow lady in the place. The post office, a small one-story wooden building a little back from the street, with a little spruce tree growing in each front corner of the dooryard, stood on the site long afterward occupied by Leeming & Patterson, Bakers and Confectioners,[6] only on a level equal to the second story of the present buildings. The street has been cut down. The eastward slope of Colborne Street continued to Dumfries Street.

Two or three times every day, Maitland would skip out of the post office, stuffing imaginary letters into the rear pockets of his swallow-tail coat, and spring on his pony, (the gilded youth ride in buggies now; they rode horseback then) and down the gentle grade of Colborne Street, the admired of all the ladies! I never saw a pony that could lift its feet so fast as his! It was a wonderful little beast. Then, all of a sudden, he would stop at the "Mansion House," a big wooden hotel on the corner of Market Street, with a two-storey verandah in front, and skip in to enjoy the company of other young idlers, who were ruining themselves for want of something useful to do. We could have given them plenty of work on farms in Dumfries, with such wages as their services entitled them to!

Well, some eighteen or nineteen years passed away and I was in Brantford, to give evidence in a suit before the County Court. Judge Jones presided.[7] There was nothing that interested the public and further than the jury and officials, and parties to the suit, so there were no more than perhaps two or three on the empty seats of the Court House.

Somebody had lain down on one of the backbenches and fallen asleep. His dreams had been unfortunate, for he gave a distinct and very startling bellow! "Put that man out!" very quietly said the judge, but not so quietly did the constable execute the order. "Come out o'here!" he said to the unfortunate, as he got him by the collar.

The County Court House in Brantford, Ontario. The elegant structure still stands on Market Square and, although it no longer serves as the court house, it is still in use.

The poor fellow was again sound asleep. He pushed him out at the door with — I thought — unnecessary roughness. "Who is that?" I whispered to a Brantford man sitting next to me. "*Old Jim Maitland!*" he said, with evident contempt in his words.

I was struck. "The aristocratic dandy of twenty years ago!" I said to myself. And I have often thought since, if the young fellows "having *ther* good time" now, would but ask and answer to themselves the question, "Where will my present life and habits naturally land me, *twenty years* from now?" Many of them might save themselves from a miserable doom. Two or three years after, poor Jim Maitland was, one morning, found dead, in a disreputable den over "Vinegar Hill," in the east of Brantford.[8]

Rob Roy MacGregor[9]

Two aristocratic young fellows, sent out by their friends in Scotland in the vain hope that being "in the Colonies" and among new scenes and people, they might be "steadier," came to the neighbourhood of Owen Sound. They rented a fair average farm, and with steady hard work might have done well enough. But no, each of them had an expensive Highland costume, and each of them had a set of "pipes" — one of which, they assured me, "had been at Killiecrankie,"[10] in 1689; and I had no reason to doubt it — and on every gala day, and at each steamboat excursion, these two "braw fellows," in kilts, were sure to be on hand!

Of course, their farming suffered and by and by their remittances from Scotland became spasmodic; their drinking habits were growing on them and finally there was a great collapse! One went off to British Columbia; I don't know what became of the other. This was before any Pacific railways, and John Boyd of Owen Sound, going out a year or two after by way of Panama to British Columbia, met, at Aspinwall [Panama], with Stewart, the younger of the two who was on his way back, and "dead broke."[11] He had missed getting on board the steamer in time, and his baggage had gone on to New York, and he was "putting in" the time, he said, till the next fortnight steamer would be "up" for New York. He had not a cent, had not even a coat, but he had the precious Killiecrankie pipes with him and affected to be perfectly happy. He was going about from one liquor den to another, bartering Scotch airs for a "drink," and any number of "Strathspeys" for a "square meal."[12]

Number Fifty-One

An old lady in Lucknow [Bruce County], Ontario, told me of their emigrating to this country. Her husband's brother had come out and sent them good accounts of this new country, and they determined to better their prospects by crossing the sea. They were to come to "number fifty-one" — or some such number — "Elora and Saugeen Road," and there they would find the brother, who would give them advice about getting land for themselves. They were Londoners; and knew all about "City Road" and "Tottenham Court Road" and "Old

Kent Road" and other "roads," and she told me she was thinking all the way across, of some pleasant suburban residence with "No. 51" on the door, and there they would alight from the conveyance that took them out.

But when, after a weary journey from Hamilton to Guelph, and then to Elora, they began jolting over the "crossways" and toiling up the muddy hills of the "Saugeen Road," her heart began to fail her![13] Still, she looked for "51" above some door, but never saw a "number" at all. At last the teamster drew up at the bottom of a stony ridge, covered with dead and burnt hemlocks, in front of a long, low log house, and sung out "Here's number 51." Her romance was all gone!

But, nevertheless, a good Providence, she said, had been over them. Her children were all grown up and doing well. She was living in a comfortable brick house and I sat chatting with her, before a cheerful wood fire. She said she liked the open fire; she had become accustomed to it and wood was not so dear but they could afford it. Her husband and the family were well-respected, and she was content and thankful, and "would stay here till the way opened into the Better Land!"

Passable Soup

Mrs. Jameson, the authoress,[14] who passed some years in "York" (now Toronto since 1834) as the wife of the Chancellor, either failed to estimate the scions of the old Family Compact at anything like their own valuation or had had some quarrel with them, for she writes thus about York — I quote from memory — "York is noted for *two things*: a marsh that produces turtles, which make very passable soup — and an aristocracy, founded upon nothing!"[15]

I did not know of the passage then — perhaps it was not written — or I might have quoted it to a big mud turtle I found on the bank of a long-vanished mill pond in Brantford, about where the "Y" on the railway is, and which pond stored the water for Wilkes' gristmill at the foot of Vinegar Hill,[16] opposite to the present Waterworks.

One of our Dumfries neighbours prepared a "mud turtle" one day for the pot — I saw it, when dressed; it looked very tempting — but she "wasn't *sure* about it!" and threw it away. I never heard of anyone using them, that seemed to have been reserved for the aristocratic folks of "York," who found them to "make a very passable soup!"

Decaying Schoolmasters!

Our municipal institutions — "Sucking Republics," as Ex-Governor Sir Francis Head called them in one of his books — began in 1841 or '42. They were first "District Councils," then "County Councils," and, some years later, "Township Councils." Dumfries Township sent two councillors to the "Gore District Council," at Hamilton.[17] What else they did, I don't remember, but I do remember they passed some resolutions encouraging Immigration, and among other things they said, "immigrants of education, whose decaying faculties unfitted them for more active pursuits, could find remunerative employment as Teachers." I wonder much what the present Ontario Minister of Education would say, if he, at this day, received some such resolution as that from any of our County Councils?

Purchased Experience

When immigrants first try this county, they are often very much disappointed. Their expectations have been visionary, and their disappointment so much the greater. Many would go back, at the end of the first few months; fortunately for them, they have not the money! A Scotsman, when I was a lad, and whose name I have never been able to learn, wrote a clever dialect poem, for one of the Galt papers, expressing his disappointment and regrets, but I always thought that "some of the agony" was put on! I remember two or three stanzas:

I was weel, and wad be better,
Like a fule, I sell't my gear,
Took a passage ower the water,
And a month syne I cam here.

Mercy on us! Sic a country,
Nocht but wuds, where'er ane gaes!
Wuds wad fright our British gentry,
Tho' sae fond o'muckle trees!

O for hills o'lofty grandeur!
O for "Cheviot" at my heels!
Many the doited yowes to wander,
Where the whistling plover wheels!

"Split sticks like an izzet" *i.e:* our rail fences, the mosquitoes and all other Canadian crudities and disadvantages, came in for castigation.[18]

But, in a year or two, these very men become acquainted with their neighbours, and become reconciled, and after a time, quite enthusiastic in praise of their new home! And it is strange, but perfectly true — and has often been remarked upon — that one who has lived a few years in Canada, cannot content himself in the Old Land again. He imagines "the people have changed!" never suspecting that the change is in himself. This "going back" is frequently tried, but generally with the same result — a return to Canada.

My friend, the Reverend Robert Robinson, told me of an English gentleman who settled between London and Chatham, Ontario, and bought several hundred acres of improved land, and would "farm it" in the old English style, with house and farm "servants," and so forth. After about two years, he became disgusted with the "free and easy" style of Canadian "farm servants." When he got a man who had some enterprise and "push" in him, he would find that the man did not like the exclusiveness of his house arrangements; when he had a man who would always touch his cap, and say "Sir," and who (as the farmer would put it) "knew his place," he generally found he was not worth much in the field.[19]

In the meantime, he was becoming known in the country, as an "eminent agriculturalist," and at Fairs he was in demand as a "Judge," and Sheriffs, and Judges, and members of Parliament made quite an *equal* of him; in fact, he was becoming a *Canadian*, very fast and did not know it! But he could not put up with "servants" thinking they were "as good as their master!" and sold out and returned to England. There, he could find any number of house and farm servants, who "knew their place," but alas! he had to "know *his* place," and had nearly forgotten how! The titled people and the great landowners would have nothing to do with him, as an *equal*. And now recalling how it had been in Canada, after *another* two-years' probation, he returned to Canada and once more settled down in western Ontario.

Lousy Tories!

The Hon. Adam Ferguson, of Fergus, once in a political speech at Guelph, used the scarcely polite term "lousy Tories."[20] Bob Britton, an English "gentleman" in distress, was very irate over this slip of the tongue of the Honorable Adam, and averred. "Now, if it had been a Scotchman, it might have been allowed to pass: but the idea of calling an English Gentleman a *lousy Tory!*"

A son of the Honorable Adam Ferguson, known as Ferguson Blair,[21] on his first canvass for Parliamentary honours, came to our village, when I was a boy. In his public speaking, he had an annoying stammer, not at all of the palate, but entirely of the lips. Jim Macpherson, a "character" of the village, said, "Why, that man will never do to send to Parliament! He is all the time fixing his mouth to speak, and *it won't go off!*"

Uncle Stitt

There were several stranded "gentlemen" at St. George in the old time. The two Brittons, Richard B. Stitt, and one or two others. They had been in Jamaica and then found their way to Canada.[22] I knew Stitt very well; nobody could be round St. George and not know him. He managed to make the "two ends meet," on $80 a year, the proceeds of the sale of a fifty-acre lot. He was very saving and penurious, and if his skill in gaining money had equalled his care in saving it, he should have been very rich.

It seemed suddenly to have dawned upon him that he was (as he himself expressed it), "on the shady side of fifty," and that it would be well to marry, especially if he could find a wife with a little money. It would be impossible, even if I should attempt it, to describe the adventures he had. It was Don Quixote (minus the old lean charger) over again![23] I was clerk in James Kyle's general store, and Kyle professed the greatest interest in Stitt's welfare and prospects, and often sent him on fool's errands

But what troubled him more than any one thing else, was the effusive friendliness of Purvis Lawrason,[24] who used to offer his hand to him, and call him "Uncle Stitt." "I'm *not* your uncle!" he would indignantly exclaim. "Well," Purvis would mildly say, "it isn't *your fault* you wanted to marry my aunt and, of course, then you would have been my uncle! It isn't your fault."

I regret now, that in any small degree. I was an abettor of all this practical joking on a man, who, absurd as he was in many of his notions and in much of his conduct, was harmless and polite, and with much of his original refinement about him. He finally married a middle-aged spinster in Ayr, Ontario, who had a very little means of her own and lived some years in comparative peace.

Studying Human Nature

A Mr. Morrison, a cultivated, educated man, was teaching at a school a mile south of St. George. He was one of the most accomplished penmen that I ever met. I was very young at the time, but I remember wondering if there was not *something* that accounted for his burying himself, as it were, as an obscure country schoolmaster. He was unmarried. Soon it leaked out; he was a slave to drink! The Trustees bore with him pretty well, but at the end of the year he failed to obtain a re-engagement. He went rapidly down and soon disappeared from the neighbourhood.

My father saw him the next October at Galt Fair. He was miserably clad and had a strap round his neck, from which depended in front a *raisin-box*, filled with gingerbread and cakes, which he was selling to the crowd. "*Man, Morrison!*" said my father, with startled emphasis, "is this you?"

"Oh, man!" said he, with a sickly attempt at cheerfulness. "I can study human nature this way!"

Poor Morrison! Another of those whose day broke brightly, only to set in self-wrought gloom![25]

Roughing It in the Bush

We have all read Mrs. Susannah Moodie's "Roughing It in the Bush," among the lakes of Peterboro.[26] People are not wise in this going into the wilderness, unless prepared to intermit almost everything else than the hardest and toughest of rough work with the hands, and it is a high price to pay for enough to eat and wear, that the intellect should be starved in the process. Mr. Moodie and his wife could not consent to pay that price, and their bush farming did not succeed very well. For many years, in the latter part of their life, they lived in Belleville, where Mr. Moodie was the Sheriff of the County of Hastings.[27]

They lived in a very plain though comfortable-looking brick cottage where I once called to see them. Unfortunately, Mrs. Moodie was out, but the Sheriff was very pleasant and interesting. Mrs. Moodie was one of the brilliant Strickland sisters, so widely and appreciatingly known in literature. Only one now remains at this date (1897), Mrs. Traill, now in extreme old age.[28]

My brother-in-law, Mr. James Kyle of Stratford, tells of an interesting reconnoitre with Sheriff Moodie, now many years ago.

Mr. Kyle was settling up an insolvent estate, and among the assets was a tract of wild land in the Township of Madoc. Having been acquainted with Sheriff Moodie, he asked him if he could direct him as to the best way of reaching such a "range" and "lot" in Madoc as he wanted to be able to set a value on the land. The Sheriff said that as to the last part of the journey he would not be able to give him very correct information.

"But," said he, "You see the Assizes are going on, and there is a Constable from that township coming in on duty, and he can tell you all about it. I'll let you know when he comes." Sometime through the day the man came in, and the Sheriff introduced Mr. Kyle to him. When he heard the township range and lot — "Well," said the man, "You take the *stage* out to" such a point, naming it; "then you hire a *horse and buggy*" to such another place, "after that, you can go on *horseback*" to a third point," and after that, you'll have to go the rest of the way in a canoe!" Mr. Kyle thought he would put merely a nominal value on the land, without insisting on seeing it![29]

Chapter 6

ENGLISH AND SCOTCH IMMIGRANTS

In the old days, almost *every* settler was an immigrant in the country. And nobody had any relation (with here and there an exception) to anybody else. It is different now, where our new settlements — as in Algoma and Manitoba — are largely made up of young beginners from the "old settlements." Indeed, I am told, that the first question of one settler to another, in Manitoba, is, *"What part of Ontario* did you come from?"[1]

In twenty or thirty years this feeling of isolation entirely disappears. By that time the children have grown up and married into neighbours' families and connections and links wonderfully multiply. In some places now — as an old friend used to say to me — "You couldn't throw a stick, but you'd hit somebody's brother-in-law, or cousin, or uncle." Railways help to "missus" the people, but before the railways, young men in the country seldom went beyond their own township for a wife. Nay, a young man was rather thought to be "despising our own girls" if he went into the foreign territory of another township to get a wife![2]

All of One Kind

Some townships were settled almost exclusively by people of one nationality. I have known townships entirely Irish; nay, some of themselves told me that they were all "North of Ireland" men, and that they put up a board on a tree, saying, "No Catholics allowed to settle here!"[3]

Some townships were entirely "Pennsylvania Dutch,"[4] others filled with Scotch Highlanders, who spoke only the Gaelic.[5] And now, after fifty years, you will scarcely credit — from anything you see or hear, that such was the case. The young and middle-aged are all native born; all speak good English; all are "Canadians." A county judge said to me forty years ago respecting an appointment as clerk of a Division Court, that he favoured such a one, among other things, that he was a "native Canadian." Now, the vast majority of our population is "native Canadian."

The "New" Presbyterian Church at Galt. By now the congregation had withdrawn from the General Assembly of the Church of Scotland, the "Auld" Church, and established its own "Free" church. Illustration from George Monro, *Picturesque Canada,* vol. II (1882) 467.

When I was a boy, nobody went to a Presbyterian Church in the country but Scotch folks. Now the distinction of being "a Scotch Church" has passed; the sons and grandsons of the first settlers (who are just as "Canadian" as any others) are the supporters. A mayor of Galt said to me, a few years ago, "We are too much of one kind here. Too "Scotch." Better, if we had more of a mixture!"[6]

In a "Highland" Settlement

A former pastor in Toronto told me of two of them being left at a settler's house, in a Highland settlement, in the neighbourhood of which they were to hold a Home Missionary Meeting in the evening.[7] The men (who could speak English) came in from the fields by and by, but in the meantime there were only two women in the house, who could only speak Gaelic. They wanted to be hospitable, however, and the only English words they dared venture to their guests, was "*Good Bye!*" very pleasantly said.

A Highland Tea

Once, when living at Eaton in the Quebec Eastern Townships, and making a visit to the Township of Bury,[8] I was invited by my host to accompany him to the foot of Lake Megantic[9] to an annual tea there, in connection with the Presbyterian Church of the place. The railway that now is continued across the State of Maine to Saint John then stopped at the lake, this side of the Maine boundary.[10] It was considerably after dark when the train got there, but the people were not only all waiting for us at the meeting, but also to operate a "magic lantern" he had brought with him. They were all Highlanders and the women and the babies were all out — whole "families" on ox sleds from everywhere in the woods. Then came the tea, and about ten o'clock some "speeches," more or less entertaining. By this time the babies were all sound asleep, carefully laid away in corners of the pews. Then the steriopticon[11] "slides," another hour or two and still there seemed no move or desire for adjournment. I privately asked the Chairman if, "it was not time to let the people away?"

"Oh, no," he replied. "This only comes once a year and (the women especially) never hear or see anything, except coming to Church on Sundays and they have — some of them — come a good many miles through the woods, on their ox sleds — and they are all Highland people — and they are determined to *make a night* of it!"

So we *made a night of it* till two o'clock. And then to a bedroom at a half-finished respectable hotel in the city at the outlet of the lake — the town is said to stand precisely on the track of Arnold's invasion of 1775[12] — and we were ready for the one west-bound train at 6:00 A.M. People do have a hunger for human society, even if it does take shape of a tea-meeting kept up till two in the morning!

Ojibway and Gaelic

More than twenty years ago, in going down by steamer to Montreal, on the *Banshee,* the captain told me of his father, who was an officer in the British service, and stationed, a little before the War of 1812, at Sandwich, [now part of Windsor] Upper Canada. The Indians came from far and near to Sandwich for their annual presents and his father had the oversight of the distribution.[13] He had a Welsh servant, who, during the week or two the Indians were encamping there, often went among their wigwams and came to his master with the wonderful news that the Indians spoke Welsh. The officer, to test the matter, went with the Welshman, and pausing at one of the tents, asked his servant, "What was that Indian was saying to his squaw?"[14] The man said that though he could not understand it all, the man was giving some orders about water. And, sure enough, the woman took up a pail, and went to the river for water. They went to another tent and the master asked his servant to address them in Welsh. He did so, and the Indians evidently understood a good deal of what he said, as was shown when they catechised on the subject.

Mr. Archibald McKillop, the blind Poet of Megantic,[15] held very tenaciously to the belief that the Gaelic was the mother of many languages, and — as agreeing with the Welshman, whose tongue is a branch of the Gaelic — mother also of the Ojibway and gave me a list of about twenty words, whose sound and meaning — so he affirmed — were identical in Gaelic and Ojibway![16]

Mr. McKillop wrote a Scottish patriotic poem — which he cut out of the *Sarnia Observer* and sent to me — the concluding stanzas of which were highly complimentary of Professor Blackie of Edinburgh, and his efforts to establish a Celtic Chair in Edinburgh University.[17] Mr. McKillop asked me to send the Professor the poem. In my letter to Professor Blackie, I mentioned my friend's theory about the Ojibway and gave two of the words I remembered. In reply to this part of the letter, Blackie said, "With respect to his Gaelic and Indian words, I would like to see the list, though by no means prepared to swear by it. *Et[y]mologies* are very slippery things — especially in the hands of a half-trained Highlandman!"[18]

The English Settler

"Land-hunger" is a natural feeling. Many a man is an agitator in politics, and a shiftless "nobody" in his social position, till he gets a piece of land of his own.[19] Then, having put a stake in the ground, he is *anchored*, in many more ways than one. And all immigrants aim at land owning at once. Mr. James Watson, of St. George, our next neighbour and a tenant farmer, told me this story of an English family he knew:

> The worthy couple were discussing the prospect of an early start for America. "John" said the wife, "when we gets to America, we shall be *farmers*, shant us?"
>
> "Yes," replied the good man.
>
> "Well, John, when you gets a farm, be sure and get one with a *sugar tree* on."
>
> "La" said the woman, many years after, to Mr. Watson, "I thought we could just *scrape the sugar out!*"

A "Squatter"

Joe Davidson was an English immigrant, who "squatted" on a lot in the Indian Peninsula [now the Bruce Peninsula], a few miles from Owen Sound. It was in 1856 and the "Indian Department" had given official notice that no squatting claims would be recognized.[20]

Four of us had been "exploring" the year before and had slept at the lee of an upturned elm, probably the largest tree in the township. We found it such a capital *windbreak*, that we penciled a notice on the nearest corner stake, directing explorers to this very comfortable *hotel!* Well, Joe squatted on that lot, which he identified to me by the "big elm" — and was very anxious not to have speculators run up the price on him, or buy it over his head. He wanted to know if I could help him? I told him I would stand by the government, and help him all I could. So when the number of Joe's lot was announced, I said to the auctioneer, "This man lives on this lot, and he wants to say a word. Joe pulled off his hat and the perspiration was already breaking over his forehead:

> "Gentlemen!" said he, "I am a poor man, and I have *squatted* on this lot and built a house, and have two or three acres of crop on it."
>
> "Have you any *other land?*" sang out a speculator.
>
> "No, Gentlemen! I own no other land! It's my home; I'm living on the lot, and am willing to give the up-set price for it!"
>
> "Yes, and a son born," I suggested, in a low voice, to Joe.
>
> He caught at the word; for he had nearly forgotten what I had before impressed upon him as the best part of his speech — and called out "Yes; and I have a young son, *born on the lot.*"
>
> A shout recognized Joe's felicity, and in the shout were cries of "*Let him have it!*" And Joe putting

on his hat, was stepping down from the rostrum, saying "Thank you, Gentlemen! Thank you! Having forgotten in his excitement to "bid" for the lot.

"Well, do you bid the upset price?" asked the auctioneer.

"Yes Sir! Yes, yes, yes,!" said Joe excitedly.

He got the lot.[21]

The Wind Tempered

The Reverend William Burgess came, many years ago, from some rural village in England, where he had been a humble pastor.[22] He had seven sons and no daughters. After being two or three years in the country, he would "take up" some wild land and get his boys at work for they were now beginning to put out their hand to work, "Canadian fashion."

There was rather a "boom" in land at the time — though that word for it had not yet been applied. He got some advertising *map* of land in Tilbury, and, asking Divine guidance and shutting his eyes, put his finger on some lot and sent off a payment and secured that lot. Wiser, of course, to have *opened* his eyes, and gone and *looked* at the lot.

Yet, a kind Providence that "tempers (as Sterne says) the wind to the shorn lamb,"[23] overruled even his childish simplicity for good at the last. He moved to his lot, and his heart must have sunk within him when he saw it. The most immense trees, elm, basswood, red oak — *had been* some walnut, but now all stolen;[24] I never saw so many immense trees on one acre of ground as there! However, all his little English savings were sunk there and stay he must! And he did!

I visited him, seven or eight years after, and stayed over Sunday and preached for him. He had then sixty acres cleared. The land was still liable to be overflowed in a wet spring, but the government a year or two after, cut a big drain through the township and carried off the surplus water to Lake Erie. He had got up a log "chapel" to preach in, and quite a number of English families had settled round him, encouraged by his being there — for the others in the township were French Canadians. And a railway has since been carried through the township. His seven sons (when I visited him) were nearly all grown up — the youngest being "mother's helper" in the kitchen. They were all musical, and when I preached there was a family "choir" of four of his sons, taking the different parts — two with voices and two with large soft flutes. The boys all turned out well and the settlement prospered.[25]

Hairin' the Butter!

Mr. Thomas, of Oro, near Barrie, was a model English immigrant. His boys and girls grew up, intelligent and reliable, God-fearing people like himself. His daughter, Mrs. Sanderson of Quebec Province, is one of the executives of the World's "W.C.T.U.,"[26] a trusted coadjutor of Lady Henry Somerset.[27] He told me once, in his own house, how often he was called upon by his neighbours to settle differences among them. I supposed he meant as one of three friendly arbitrators, mutually chosen, and he saw I took it in that light.

"No," he said, "that was not it. They just agreed between themselves that they would leave the matter wholly to my decision, just as a magistrate might decide a case. And," he said, with the greatest humility and thankfulness, "I have settled a great many disputes that way. They generally agree to what I decide and advise." I thought it was a beautiful tribute to his Christian spirit and wisdom.

One of his sons (I have this from Mrs. Sanderson) was riding across the prairies of Kansas on a pony. He became aware of a "shack" in the distance and rode toward it. Soon he espied a woman outside the house, working at something on a bench. He drew slowly near and saw that she had a mass of butter before her, through which she was drawing a large knife, and then narrowly observing the knife. She did not seem to notice him at all but kept on.

"What on earth are you doing?" he asked, in a low and impressive voice, full of puzzled amusement.

"Well, stranger, don't you see I'm *hairin'the butter?*[28] Did you never see that done before?"

"No, I've seen a good deal of butter made, but I never saw that done before!"

"Well! What dirty folks they must be where you come from!"

This very year (1897) one of the brothers Thomas is "running" and extending a large "creamery" in Barrie and it seems irresistibly comic that any of them needed to go to Kansas to learn how to "hair the butter!"[29]

"She Made Good Bread!"

Reverend Dr. Caldicott of Toronto was a good specimen of a transplanted Englishman.[30] Mr. Booker[31] of Hamilton told me the following, which he heard from the Doctor himself. In revisiting England, he pulled away the grass and moss from a tombstone, and told to a friend who was with him, the story of "the poor inhabitant below":

> She was a great "scold" — there was not such another one in the county. When she died, her husband, standing beside the open grave, looked down, and tried to think of something good to say of her, and said, "Well, she baked good bread!"
>
> After the funeral, the husband went to order the customary tombstone. (In England I noticed these were seldom of marble, but generally of grey stone).
>
> "What will you have put on it, beside the name and dates," asked the stonecutter.
>
> "Oh, nothing," replied the husband.
>
> "But," persisted the worker, "it is customary to put some verse or text on a tombstone!"
>
> "Well, put whatever you think best, on it."

So the stone had this inscription —
"All that she was, as woman, wife and mother —
Search where you will, you'll not find such another."

The Doctor always left the "application" to the penetration of the listener.

Hauling Wood

Mr. Levi French, of Eaton, Quebec,[32] told me of two Englishmen, who afterwards learn woodlore, but were much "at sea" in their first bush experiences. They were out in the woods with a team of horses and a waggon, to bring home some firewood. The descent of a small steep hill was before them, and they feared to take the load down with the horses! So they unhitched the team. One took the *tongue* to guide the waggon down; the other was to hold on by the wheel, to retard its progress! The wheel flung the man off, and by some good Providence the other man got down without falling under the wheels or breaking the tongue! *How*, he did not know. But they were two badly scared men!

Teague and Pat [33]

The Reverend William Millard, of Toronto,[34] a typical English immigrant, used to tell me of crossing Lake Simcoe on the ice. He wished to cross from east to west, across the broadest part. The farmer with whom he had lodged, came with him in his cutter and told him to "follow those tracks" and they would take him over. Mr. Millard was short-sighted, and wore glasses. A bright sun shining and all went well. His horse "spanked" along, always following some sleigh track, *but* — he came out, after a while, at exactly the place he had entered! The fact was, there were tracks everywhere, and he had failed to look at the direction of the sun!

The same farmer friend again started him. "Do you see something away out there?"

"Yes, I see some black specks."

"Well, when you get to them, you'll find they are two men, driving a cow and a calf. You keep by them, till you get to the cracks in the ice; and they'll help you over. And by that time you'll be able to see the other shore."

With these directions he started. He kept the men in sight, and in due time overtook them. He kept close to them for a while, but they went [too] slow. And he asked *Teague* to let *Pat* ride forward with him, and see him safely over the *cracks* (which were sometimes dangerous). But *Teague* wouldn't part with *Pat*. He had hired him to help, and he couldn't manage along!" So Mr. Millard proposed to take the tired *calf* in his cutter,[35] "and" said he, "the cow will follow, them."

As long as the calf stood up, and the mother could see it, the cow trotted along by the side of the cutter, nicely. And he let the horse go freely — for "he felt like giving *Teague* a run," he said, "for his unfriendliness." But when the calf got tired and lay down, the cow was not sure about it, and bolted here and there; Mr. Millard imitated the bawling of the calf with moderate success to keep the cow following, and the men and the cow pretty well out of breath when they came to the cracks. They were not so bad as at some other places perhaps, and they got the cutter over, and by that time he could make out the woods on the western shore, and got safely over.

Scottish Immigrants

An unfounded claim is sometimes made, that the brightest and most "pushing" of the population emigrate from the British Isles. The fact is, most of them come "by consequence." Some of their relations are in America, and then *they* come. I had two uncles who came to New York, probably induced by friends who had gone before — and so we came here. Then, my father's only brother settled in Canada — his wife's relatives having gone there, and by and bye my father followed.[36]

John Telfer, a Selkirk man, induced many Scotchmen to come out to Dumfries Township, and settle between Galt and Paris — somewhere about the year 1825.[37] Among others he angled for was James Hogg, the Ettrick Shepherd.[38] Telfer thought he "had" him: but [he] finally "reist it."[39]

"Oh man!" said he, "*The Ettrick couldna want me!*"

Some of these Scottish fellows are immense readers, and what they know they learn chiefly from books, rather than from mingling with men. These men are full of odd fancies and strange uses of words. Thus, one such Scottish exile I knew would say *centrical, financical, and* the like, and once probably astonished a rather well-informed man, whom he wanted to induce to come to my preaching, by saying apologetically, "Now, I don't want to *apostatize* you to *my* church!"

Little Willie

I once sat down, well-pleased in the Township of Wallace, [Perth County] to hear Mrs. Campbell tell me of her family's experiences as pioneers in the bush. They had potatoes and turnips (but the potatoes then were late in maturing), but they had no bread, except what was made of flour carried on the men's backs, thirty miles through the bush. Bread, therefore, was very precious. She made the "boys" eat potatoes and turnips, and gave them each the smallest portion of bread to finish with. The "boys" compared it to corking a bottle. "Now, Mother" they would say, "give us the *cork!*"

The youngest was the pet of the house, a darling boy of five years old. The older boys had run down a fawn of the fallow deer, in the deep snows of spring, and brought it home and gave it to little Willie. It soon grew very tame and evinced a great affection for its young master. He would, with a little rod, "gee" and "haw" it round the house, as the older boys did with their steers. And when Willie lay down for his midday sleep, on a sheepskin on the floor, the deer would come and lie down beside him, perfectly content if it could only have the smallest patch of the soft sheepskin to rest its *knees* on — and the two would sleep together. As the deer grew bigger, it had to sleep in the woodshed and when winter began, it got frightened one night at the near howling of the wolves, and fled to the woods, where, no doubt, in a few minutes it became a prey to the hungry prowlers.

Willie wept for his fawn but before another year was out he lay down his beautiful head and died, and from the time of his death his mother never seemed to smile again! There were no churches nor burying grounds near, and Willie's grave was made in their own little clearing in sight of the windows (as they showed me), and surrounded by a small rude fence. And at that window the mother often sat, and nursed her inconsolable grief. The husband told me that "she had never been quite like herself, since the boy died!"[40]

A Scotch "Raising"

The pioneers did like whisky, but they could be induced to do without it. My friend Robert McLean, of Toronto, long and well-known in Galt, was in the year 1841 teaching at a school in the Township of Blenheim.[41] Blenheim was full of *pines* then and little of anything else. *Shingles* were often spoken of as "Blenheim *wheat*." He was paid by *fees, and* found difficulty in *getting in* the fees — for the people had no money.

"Now," said one of his patrons, "if you could do anything with shingles, or lumber of any kind, we could pay you easily." So, to make things come round rightly, he took a contract to build a barn and hired a carpenter. He fixed the "Raising" for a Saturday — and invited his "hands." The schools were only "out" each second Saturday then. During the forenoon, a few men came — but sufficient for what was needed — and got the "bents" together. But in the afternoon, when the larger number came, and the heavy lifts were to come, the men (as he expressed it) "grew *balky!*" for there was no whisky! He saw them talking, by twos and threes together, and at last it dawned on him that it was "no whisky" that was the trouble! So he mounted a "bent" and addressed the crowd:

Gentlemen!" said he, "I have invited you here to help me in getting up this barn, as we do have to help one another as neighbours. And you know that I am a Teetotaller, and you *know* I don't drink behind the door, or use Teetotalism as a cloak of hypocrisy. I'll give you a good supper, do anything I can for you, but you know, that on principle, I neither drink whisky nor give it to others. And if you fail me now, because I don't provide whisky and go back on my Temperance principles, see what a loss I shall be at, having to hire a gang of men to raise the building!

Some of the men flung off their coats, "Come, boys! Let's go to work!" And the barn went up all right, and without "hitch" or accident, and a good supper wound up the day. "And," said Mr. McLean to me, many years after, "as far as I know, that was the very first barn that ever was "raised" without whisky in the County of Oxford!"[42]

A Thrifty Immigrant

In 1843, my father hired a Galloway Scotsman, just "out" to help us with our farm work. We did not need a man in the winter. He had two brothers in Ohio and they had advised him to spend his first summer in Canada, so as to get gradually acclimated. John was a fine, honest, quiet fellow. He never would come in to supper when there was company. We tried to laugh him out of it, but he would have his own way.

It was before the days of railways, and at the end of his term, my father left him (and his big chest) at a hotel in Dundas, waiting for the Hamilton stage, bound for Ohio.

We heard no more of him for twenty years, and then learned that while waiting at the hotel, a man from Ancaster had got into conversation with him, and engaged him to work the farm of a widow; this man being one of the "Executors." He was a good careful fellow; and at length he and the widow married. She had two young children, and had the use of the farm till the youngest was of age. John made a kind stepfather, and by the time that the farm was to pass to the children, he had paid for another good farm near by, to which he removed.

When I first heard the sequel of this story, I said to my father, "Now, if you had used John as Old Country masters often use their men, you would hardly like to meet him now, since he has become a well-to-do farmer — perhaps better-off than yourself!"

"No," said my father, "but then we did not use him so! And I have sent word by his stepson, that he and his wife must be sure to come and make us a visit."

The Tryst O'Falkirk

James Easton, was one of those bright fellows — "no man's enemy but his own!" He was well-educated. I used to admire, as a boy, his beautiful handwriting. I never saw a man that could swing an axe as Easton could. He cut us twenty cords of wood, one fall and then went off (as I suppose) and drank the money! He often left the neighbourhood of St. George, and we always understood that he was then in Scarboro. Doubtless, old settlers will remember him there. He was full of anecdotes. Here is one of them — about the Battle of Waterloo:

> A Falkirk man — and therefore a townsman of Easton's — was wounded in the battle; and ran to the rear to have his wound dressed — which was bleeding dangerously. "Dress me quick, Doctor!" he cried, "and let me win back again! But Doctor! Man! Dina this mind ye o'the *Tryst O'Falkirk?*" The *"Doctor"* was also a Falkirk man and the "Tryst" was the great Cattle-fair of those days, to which all the cattle from the Highlands were brought for sale; and

at which the noise and confusion of men and animals was not unlike the roar of the great battle.[43]

Very Scotch!

I once, when a boy, came across two Scotsmen, who were felling a basswood tree — leaving a bend near the root — to make sleigh runners! I told them the wood was utterly useless for that purpose. They said they thought — from the grain of the wood — that "it was *hickory!*"

In the same township, a bachelor friend of mine listened with some patience to a mother who (he thought) was "recommending" one of her daughters to him by saying "Annie is a gude *worker!*"

"Aye," very quietly said the Scotsman, "that is a good quality in a *horse!*"

And So Would I!

The Reverend John Climie, whom Sir John MacDonald — as elsewhere narrated — called "The Political Parson of Bowmanville," was an immigrant from Cambuslang — one of those suburban villages, now (I suppose) all swallowed up in Glasgow.[44] His mother told me of his running away, bareheaded, when four years old, and trotting across the intervening hollow to Kirkintilloch, another suburban village. On the way he was overtaken by two English drovers, clad in those wonderful "smock-frocks," dazzling white, with squares of such wonderful needlework on breast and back. The boy had never seen such a garb before, and "Angels" with white robes came into his infant mind, but he got the wrong word, and said "prophets." They talked to him, and learning that "he was gaun till his auntie's in Kirkintilloch," one of them swung him on his shoulder and carried him to his aunt's door.

She knew he had run away, and knew that his mother would soon be after him, but in the meantime gave him a "piece."[45] Like all the rest of the human race, no sooner did he begin to eat, than he began to talk.

"Auntie," he said, "hae ye any *propheets* in this town?"

"Na, we've nae prophets here! Hae ye any in *Cam'slang?*"

"Aye, I saw twa this mornin,' a big one and a little one. And the little one took me on his back."

In days long after, Mr. Climie was a spiritually-minded and diligent pastor as well as a wise man of affairs, and, in 1867 he presided at the Congregational Union held that year in Kingston. We had Prof. Stowe of Andover as a visitor, and who preached before the Union on the Sunday evening of the session. When Dr. Stowe was introduced to the Chairman of the Union (Mr. Climie) the latter said, in his friendly, impulsive way —

"I am happy to see you, Professor Stowe, and would be happier still to see your wife!"

"*And so would I!*" archly returned the Doctor. (Mrs. Beecher Stowe was just then in Florida.)

Sketch of a fugitive slave family escaping to Canada. From Harriet Beecher Stowe, *Uncle Tom's Cabin; or, Life Among the Lowly* (1852).

In telling on Monday about this private introduction, Dr. Stowe burst out into a merry laugh. "Well," said he, "I suppose it is better to be celebrated on one's wife account, than not to be celebrated at all! Ho! Ho! Ho!"[46]

Jerusalem Kail

We often remark that the world is too small nowadays, and if we wanted to hide ourselves there would sure to be some upstart to identify us! One of Reverend Dr. Lachlan Taylor's stories illustrated this.[47] What is supposed to be the "mandrake," mentioned in the book of Genesis,[48] grows in Palestine with a most sweet and aromatic white waxen-like flower. A Scotsman, living in Jerusalem, found that its root was very large and "fleshy" and argued to himself that if the flower were so sweet, the root must be edible and delicious. Here was a gastronomical discovery! He would dig some of it.

But, (however it may be now) there was not a decent spade nor pick in all Jerusalem, that he could borrow! So he armed himself with a large carving knife or butcher knife — "a gullie," as he would doubtless himself call it — and marched out to seek mandrakes. He made a famous stew of it, for the Jerusalem vegetable market was a poor affair. He ate heartily of his "stew," but woeful to tell, it had some deleterious effects, and the man almost died — and the story of the Scotsman and the *Jerusalem Kail* became a standing joke in the little English-speaking colony there.

And after getting thus far, Dr. Taylor added, "I was lecturing in Ottawa about two months ago (1859), and I told this story there and after the lecture was over a man came up the aisle, and said, "You were telling that story of the *Jerusalem kail. I am the man!*"

Dr. Taylor came to lecture in my Church at Pine Grove;[49] and Mr. W. Wallis of Etobicoke brought him from Weston in a cutter.[50] They came round my house; but did not alight. In trying to turn round in the somewhat deep snow, Mr. Wallis backed his horse a few steps, the runners caught a little, and the cutter went up at the front and down at the back, in the fashion of a coal cart dumping a load, and laid the two gentlemen on their backs in the quietest, softest manner imaginable in the clean snow! They were so muffled up in wraps and robes that it was not easy to get up, and the more so as the ludicrousness of the situation suddenly seemed to burst upon "Lachlan!"

"Ha, ha, ha!" he exclaimed, as he slowly scrambled up, and began shaking off his abundant coating of snow. "Oh, the Warden of York! To think he would use me thus! And that I've been all over the world, to be laid down in the snow this way! And by my friend the Warden! Oh, oh, oh!"

My little boy was looking through the window. Seeing Dr. Taylor so demonstrative, the child jumped to his own conclusion, "Ma!" said he, with a voice full of apprehension, "that man's *drunk!*"

Pulling Stumps!

My friend Thomas Kyle,[51] near Ayr, told me of a worthy neighbour, whom I had often seen, Mr. Rodgers, a Scotch settler, who had the misfortune to be obliged to put up with a wooden leg. I have seen him often moving with considerable activity, about his fields. One day he was jerking out stumps in a plowed field by means of a well-trained yoke of oxen. Both man and beasts find that a quick jerk accomplishes the object better than a slow pull, and so, as soon as the chain is fastened and a single word given, off they go!

Now on one occasion he quickly threw the chain round the stump, and gave the word to start, not noticing that in so fixing the chain, he had put his wooden leg inside it! The stump came out and Mr. Rodgers had a grand tussle in the plowed ground before he got on his "pins" again.

"Like a Coat!"

A Scotch neighbour, Mr. Cargill, a farmer, thought he would save a little money by making up a coat for each of his sons himself, after he had the garments "cut" by a tailor. My father met him at an auction sale; the two "boys" also being there.

"Well," said Mr. Cargill, "now didn't I do pretty well?" pointing to the boys.

"Yes," replied my father, "a good deal better than I heard you were doing!"

"What did you hear?"

"Why, I heard you sewed the sleeves into the pocket holes, and then said you thought it began to *look something like a coat* now!"

"Who told you that?"

My father felt he must either acknowledge the invention, or *carry on* the joke, so, seeing a merry fellow in the crowd, Andrew Graham, he answered, with a perfectly straight face, "Andrew Graham!"

And the last he saw of Cargill, he was looking among the crowd to find Graham![52]

Highland Mary

On the first day of January 1886, I found my way across the Township of Caledon, to the home of Mr. Anderson, close by the C.P. Railway to Owen Sound. The father, Mr. William Anderson, was deceased a few years and two sons and a daughter now occupied the old place.[53] The father was a nephew of Burns's "Highland Mary," a son of Annie Campbell, her only sister.[54] The dislike that the father of *Mary* had to Burns, has not come down to his descendants, for these estimable young people doted on Burns, and they told me all they knew, and got from all I knew, on the subject. But I found I was on the threshold of my researches. They put me in communication with Mr. Matthew Turnbull, of Rothesay on the Clyde, an uncle of theirs

127

by marriage, his wife being a sister of their father's and a daughter of Annie Campbell.

Putting together all the information from all these parties, I found that *Mary Campbell* was of a good height, with a reddish, high-colored complexion with flaxen hair — of a retiring disposition and forever spoken of by her mother for her sincerity and truth. Her mother's cousin in Greenock, in whose house she died, spoke of her as "an Angel in the home."

Annie Campbell, Mary's only sister, was twelve years old when Mary died. Mary must have been twenty-two. No record of her birth has been found — nor the exact day of her death, which would be at the close of the month of October 1786. Burns and Mary parted on the 14th of May. During all that summer, Burns wrote often, and sent her many snatches of songs. These *sister Annie* got and used to sing them to her children. A few months before his death, Motherwell called on one of the Anderson's then married, and asked "What Mary's hair looked like?" (The precious lock of hair now at Doon, was then in Caledon, near Orangeville). The mother replied, "Just like that bairn's!" Asking the mother's leave, he took out a little pair of Editmal scissors from his vest pocket, and gently severed a little lock from the child's head, and put it in his pocket.

Courtesy of Archival and Special Collections, McLaughlin Library, University of Guelph.

"Highland Mary." From John D. Ross, *Highland Mary* (1894).

I had that relation from the child herself, now a widowed lady in Chicago. At the same visit, Motherwell copied down all those snatches of songs Annie Campbell used to sing to her children, as having been sent to *Mary* by Burns. Motherwell died a few months afterward and whether any of those snatches of song ever saw the light, no man can now tell! I tried in vain, through the *Glasgow Mail* to find some clue, in any possible papers of Motherwell.

When Mary died, the father *burned everything* connected with Burns among his daughter's belongings. And Mrs. Turnbull, a daughter of Connie Campbell, told her husband, "there were a great many things burned!" He spared the pocket Bible in two volumes, Burns had given Mary at parting; a Scotsman will not burn a Bible![55]

The father never relented, but the old woman did. She used to sing "Highland Mary" to her children and grandchildren. Burns once — and only once — visited the family, shortly after Mary's death, and begged — with tears running down his face — that the mother would give him a handkerchief or something of Mary's as a keepsake. She refused him, but she used afterwards to say of him — after saying he was "wild and profane" — but he was a *rale warn-heartit-chiel!*"

Now Mary's mother could sing and Mary's sister was a singer and there is no doubt but *Mary* would be a singer. And the name "Highland Mary" would not be an invention of Burns, but a name given her in Ayrshire — from her Highland intonation. George MacDonald puts in the mouth of one of his characters the expression — concerning a Highland woman, who spoke Lowland Scotch — "Your mother could hae wiled [a] maukin frae its lair in that bonnie Hieland speech o'hers!"[56]

The old woman had kept Burns's Bibles, with a long lock of Mary's golden hair in one of them, and more than thirty years after Mary's death, she said to her two granddaughters, Mary and Annie Anderson (Annie's daughters) as she gave each of them one of the volumes, "Here, lassies! Whan ye come to be marriet, ye can sell thae for as muckle as will get ilk o'ye a *chest o'drawers!*"

When William Anderson, the Canadian immigrant, came out, he bought the precious Bibles from his sisters, giving each of them five pounds and promising "they should never go out of the family." But in Canada, he got "to his last half-crown" — so he put it — and wrote to his brother-in-law John C. Beckett,[57] printer, Montreal, "If he thought it would be wrong for him to sell the Bibles?" Beckett went to Mr. Weir of the *Montreal Herald*,[58] Mr. Rollo Campbell,[59] and a few other Scotsmen and they made up $100, and sent it to Anderson and sent the Bibles — for the use of the public forever — to the Provost of Ayr, and they were placed — the Bibles and the Lock of Hair — where they now are, at Doon, Ayrshire, on Burns's birthday in 1841.

One of Annie Campbell's children, Mary, was the exact resemblance of Highland Mary. The other daughter, Annie, was not. Mary (Mrs. Robertson) in her turn, had two daughters, one the perfect resemblance of herself, and — two generations away — a likeness of *Highland Mary*. A copy of it is in the monument lately erected in Burns's honour at Kilmarnock — placed there by the late Dr. Charles Rogers. Another reproduction is a frontispiece to Mr. John D. Ross's volume "Highland Mary." It is all the world will ever know, in answer to the question, "What did Highland Mary look like?"[60]

Slap a Scotch Girl in the Mouth

In a tin shop in Newmarket, I was waiting for a little "job" that was getting done, when a young man began telling some reminiscences. Fixing stovepipes was the burden of his tale — a terrible trial of temper to many persons. Here, he was volunteering to help two girls in Newmarket to put together some stovepipe. It "wouldn't go" and he got only vexed and thought if the girls would only let it alone, he could "fix" it better, and at last was so incautious and unreasonable as to mutter, "If you don't let that alone, I'll slap you in the mouth!"

One of the girls, a Miss Campbell, whom I very well remembered, bristled up to him, and said, very firmly —

"Did you ever slap a Scotch girl in the mouth?"

"No," he said, in an apologetic tone, "I don't know as ever I did!" He had particular reasons for not desiring to quarrel with her.

"Well," she rejoiced, "if ever you want to have a *picnic*, whether summer or winter, you just try it!"

And, turning to me with a sly smile — "That girl's my wife now!" he said.

"Sow's Creesh!"[61]

My father liked to get off a little bit of romance, once in a while. I remember an old *townsman* of his, Willie Gray, living in rooms above us, in the same house, in Carmine Street, New York, in 1834 or '35. Willie (who was an elderly man) had, like many other Scotsmen, a tremendous prejudice against pork. "Sandy-camel" was what he sometimes called the pig, with contempt. And, not eating pork, he would have nothing to do with *lard*, which he termed "sow's-creesh."

One day my father met Mrs. Gray coming in from the grocers, with a plate of *lard*. "Ah!" said he, "you are going to cheat my townsman, by putting "sow's-creesh" in his pie! Now, what will you give me if I don't tell him?"

I'll give you *a piece of the pie!*" innocently replied Mrs. Gray.

Now, how much truth, and how much romance, is in the following, I don't know: but my father — confessing to having *romanced it a little* used to tell it to Scotch folks that came to our house — amid roars of laughter.

Willie Gray, who will not touch pork or lard, suspected the shortening in his pie was not all butter and demanded of his info, "Is there ony *sow's-creesh* in that pie? If I thocht there *was*, I'd thraw it oot the window — *dish* and all! *Tell the truth now!* Ye canna cheat me! If it wasna that I had a *cauld in my heid*, I could smell't er ever I cam to the door!"

Another of his romances, was about old Willie Kyle, who was keeping store in St. George in 1842.[62] He had lived in Lower Canada, and seen the moccasins the *habitants* wore there and had some for sale. They did not take "very well," but my father bought a pair. They needed a great deal of softening with oil, to persuade them not to hurt his feet. He only wore two pairs of socks with them. Perhaps he should have got a larger pair — and, wearing two or three more pairs of old stocking feet, they might not have needed so much softening.

Old Mr. Kyle went about his store with a well-worn old black coat with long "swallow-tails." My father pretended that he and Willie Kyle were greasing their moccasins in company, in the latter's store, and that he slyly wiped off his greasy hands when he had finished, on *Willie's coattails!* Willie at last made the discovery, just as the other was disappearing out the door. When he got fairly out into the middle of the street, (opposite David Reid's shop) he shaded his eyes (as Willie had a way of doing) from the afternoon sun, and exclaimed, "It's no use pursuing him now; he's up as far as the Doctor's!"

The Lighting of the Beacons

My father, the late John Smith, so long of St. George, County of Brant, told me once more, so late as 1889, of the "Lighting of the Beacons" in Scotland. He told me "he could not recall what year it was," but I gave him the date — 31st of January, 1804. He said the Beacons, which were intended to rouse the country, and be a gathering — signed to the militia, if the French should land — were suddenly lighted up one night before people had gone to bed. At once, there was the greatest commotion. Men were hastily bidding their mothers and wives farewell and rushing off to Kelso, to report themselves ready for service. And all the women were crying and wailing that all these poor fellows "would be killed by the French!" and never come back again. He said he stood, his father holding one hand, and his mother the other, and they gazed on the Beacon on Penielheugh, and sympathized with the excitement around them.[63]

"But did not your father have to go with the rest?" I asked.

"No, my mother was his second wife and he was a good deal older than she was, and had just passed his sixtieth year, and was exempt." My father was then seven years old.

I never had anybody, before nor since, tell me something which they saw and heard, and distinctly remembered — *eighty-five years* after the event!

Skylarks

It may seem strange for a Scotsman to say he never heard a skylark, yet such is the case with myself — as far as my memory goes. In a visit I made to the dear old land in 1862, it was the middle of July before I got there, and I proceeded almost immediately to London — spending a couple of the autumn months in Scotland and was, I suppose, too late to hear the *laverocks*.[64]

My father used to tell me of a Border farmer, whom he knew long ago. The poor man had become bankrupt, and bankruptcy was a terrible thing in those days! He was footing it from Jedburgh to Edinburgh — a distance of forty-five miles — to meet the lawyers and on the way, among the Lammermoor wastes, a lark rose at his feet and went up singing towards heaven. The farmer stopped, and with his hand shading his eyes, followed the bird as he ascended, the tears coursing down his face.

"Aye!" said he, "weel may ye sing! Ye hae nae debt aboon yer heid!"

Courtesy of Archival and Special Collections, McLaughlin Library, University of Guelph.

Sitting under the vines on the verandah, on a summer evening, at the house of my friend, Mr. James Goldie,[65] of Guelph, he told me of a visit he had made to his native place, on the banks of the Doon, in Ayrshire. "Did you notice, from "the auld brig d'Doon," up the stream a short distance, a mill?" he asked. I could

A photograph of James Goldie of Guelph, Ontario. From the *Historical Atlas of Wellington County* (1906).

Courtesy of Dalhousie University Library Special Collections.

View of Guelph, Ontario, 1879. From *Canadian Illustrated News*, vol. XIX (1879) 296.

not remember having seen it. "Well," he said, "there is a mill there and when I was over, two young men were out there, shooting rooks, which had become troublesome. In conversation with them, they told me of an American coming along, when the larks were singing, and he said 'Ah, we have no skylarks in America.'"

"Why, yes, you have," said one of the young men for I was reading in a late number of *Harper's Magazine*, what John Burroughs said, about a lark rising at his feet, on the banks of the Hudson. "Well," said he, "*I am John Burroughs!* But the lark had been an imported one. We have none as natives!"[66]

And then I told my friend of a correspondence I had, about 1875, with Julius Dexter of Cincinnati, president of a little Acclimatization Society there, about larks and other singing birds.[67] They had been importing them, and setting them free in hopes they would take root in America. He said, "It was only, as yet, an experiment." But evidently, the same kind of experiment had been made near New York. Mr. Dexter wrote that they sometimes had letters from people fifty or one hundred miles away, describing some strange bird seen, and asking what it was? And it would turn out to be "one of their birds."

So there is a possibility of the "laverock," so celebrated in Scottish song, being heard in Canada, after all!

I once drove nine miles to Weston to hear a lark an Englishman had in a cage. But the bird was dead — had perhaps a broken heart at his captivity.

Chapter 7

IRISH AND GERMAN SETTLERS

No more thrifty settlers are among us, than the second generation in an Irish settlement. The first generation have had no Colonial experience, and do not always learn it with facility and are apt to have a weakness for long reminiscences over the whisky flask and the pipe — not promotive of good husbandry. But the "b'ys" grow up, full of energy and determination and develop into our best citizens. I had much to do with Irish settlers when acting for some years as clerk of the Division Court in Owen Sound, and though many of them could not read nor write, yet every one of such men would tell me with pride what "good scholars" their children were! I became aware of their illiteracy by having to "witness" their "marks," when they could not write their names. Many of them promised to try and learn to read and write; but I am afraid the effort was too great for accomplishment![1]

Laying On Promiscuously

One of this class of original settlers, Henry Brown of Arran Township,[2] who was in great demand at all "sprees" and dances, as a fiddler, and who was not by any means a teetotaller in those days — was once instructing a young friend, John Kilbourn, as to playing on the fiddle. It may be premised that Brown knew nothing of "notes," and played entirely by "the ear."

"Jack!" said he — the fiddler's tongue well loosened by recent potations — "Jack, when you're playing the fiddle, and you're afraid the tune's going to *stick*, just *think of the words, and lay on the bow promiscuously!*"

To the Head Offis

One of the wittiest men I ever met — and indeed apparently quite unconscious of his wit, was "Captain" Nathaniel E. Wallace of Woodbridge. The captain, however, had "Burwick" on the front of his brick house, and refused to patronize the newer name of "Woodbridge." When the narrow-gauge railway (now standard-gauge, and a part of the "CPR") was opened as far as Mount Forest, the captain who was a hotel keeper at Woodbridge, went with the directors' party as a kind of "Generalissimo," to manage all details of the excursion. At Mount Forest he was ordering carriages for the party, and stepping round with his big-headed cane, where an Irishman, enquiring for "the President of the Road," was directed, as a good joke — by Mr. Alfred Gooderham — to Captain Wallace![3]

"Sir," said the poor fellow, lifting his hat, and addressing the Captain as *President*, "I've been working on the line with my team, and I can't get my pay!"

"Do ye tell me, now? And I give orders to pay every man, and they tell me everything is squared up, and here, when I come to Mount Forest, I find there are men not paid. Have ye sent in yer *bill?*"

"No; but I've asked for my money a good many times, and I can't get it!"

"Well, you just make out yer bill; and take it to the offis, and tell them to *pay that bill* — that I said so! And if they don't pay it, just send it to me, at the head Offis!"

And the man touched his hat, and bowed ever so many times, and was so thankful for the satisfactory state of his prospects and went off to his woman at the outskirts of the crowd, to tell of his success.

"Now, wasn't that too bad, Captain?" said Mr. Gooderham, "making that poor fellow believe all that!"

"Och!" said the Captain, "you don't know them as well as I do! He's a countryman of mine, and it takes very little to plaze him — and don't ye see — he's gone away *perfectly happy!*"[4]

Some Cooking

An Irishman, at Aurora, kept a number of ministers in good humor on one occasion, for the rest of the day. I have the story from the Reverend John Wood,[5] one of the party. A mistake of half an hour had been made at Toronto, and the party of six, who were bound for Newmarket, were sitting on a bench in an empty box car of a freight train as there was no other way of getting up in time for their appointment. At Aurora they shunted off to let a train pass. While on the *switch* they overheard the following conversation among the railway employees:

> "Jim!" says one, "do ye know what kind of *freight* we've got this marnin?"
>
> "No, what have ye got?"
>
> "We've got six *live ministers!* And they're all goin' to Newmarket."
>
> "Och, and sure! But won't there be *some cookin'* when they get there!"

The popular idea that there is always some extra "cookin" when ministers are guests, kept the clericals in the lightest spirits for an hour longer, when, no doubt, they *were* set down to a good dinner![6]

A Lad of a Man

The Reverend W.W. Shepherd[7] told me of calling once on an Irish settler on his circuit, and found the faithful fellow taking a quiet lesson to himself, with a big Bible on his knee. After the first greetings were over — "I was just noticing," said he, "what a skilful way Paul had, of raising money for the poor saints of Jerusalem. Here he would go to Macedonia, and tell them they mustn't let the people in Corinth get ahead of them! And then he would tell the members in Corinth what he had told about them in Macedonia! Wasn't he *a lad of a man* for raising money![8]

Taking the Ghost With Him!

An Irishman I knew, who had built with his own hands, a shanty in the outskirts of one of our small towns, had, after his mother-in-law had died in his house, some apprehension of spirits being about. Some mischievous neighbour boys probably helped the fright. At any rate, Pat would build on the other end of his town lot and leave this for a cow stable, and would be careful — so as to be rid of the "ghose" — not to take a single board from the old house over the creek.

"It is all in vain!" I said to the neighbour who told me the story. The "ghose" will go with the first wheelbarrow full of household stuff that he takes to the new house. It will be like the story Froissart tells us of the French Count he knew.[9]

This French Count owned two *chateaux;* one of which he liked better than the other, but it was *haunted.* So he determined to move to his other mansion. The great man, on horseback, was escorting a load of his household stuff, when he met a friend.

"You are moving!" said the friend.

"Yes, we're moving!" piped out *something,* from among the *stuff,* on the cart!

"Oh, if you are there," said the Count, "I may as well go back!" And back he went, to settle it with the *ghost* as best he might — for he found the *ghost* was going with him!

Cornaylius

"Yes," said Mrs. Reid, our next-door neighbour in Newmarket, "Cyrus had a good many stories to tell, when he was out taking orders for tombstones for us."[10] And then she narrated to me the following:

> Once the Agent was after a man away up in Mariposa and didn't find him at home. His wife said he would be home some time in the evening; but Cyrus could not stop. So, along the road, in the dark, he hailed every man he met, for fear of losing his expected customer, and asked him, "Are you Mr. Hogan?" Meeting thus a man in a waggon, the man replied, "No, I am not. But what would yez be wanting of Mr. Hogan?"
>
> "Why, I want to sell him a headstone!" said Cyrus.
>
> "And sure, and I want a headstone meself!"
>
> "Well," replied the agent, "we'll just go back to that little *grocery, and* I'll take your order." So back they went, and after selecting the style of headstone, from the *photos* Cyrus had with him, he was asked, "What was this boy's *name?*"
>
> "Sure, he had no name at all!"
>
> "Well, we'll have to put *some* name on!"
>
> "Well then, we'll call him *Cornaylius*" (which was his own name).
>
> "And what *age* was he?" asked Cyrus, pencil in hand.
>
> "Sure, he was *no age* at all! He never breathed."
>
> And so the headstone was sent up, according to order.
>
> "Sure," said the man, "I won't *have* that! I'll have a *monyment!*"

"Why," said his wife, "what are you going to have a monument for? Isn't that just what you ordered?"

"Och yes!" he said, with a sigh — "That'd what I ordered, but it isn't *good enough*. I'll have a *monyment!*"

"Och," said his wife, "that's good enough for a bit of a *bairn!*" And so the matter was settled.[11]

Sharon

The name of David Willson is spoken of with reveration by some, and with interest by all, in the central portion of Ontario. He was a North-country Irishman, at first among the Society of Friends, then he seceded from them and formed a religious community of his own, in the first years of this century, "Sharon" — so named by him — in the County of York.[12] He was preacher, teacher and patriarch of the flock. He "married" them, buried them and read poetical tributes over their graves, settled their incipient disputes — did everything!

After a time he got the "Temple" built, and a "Meeting House." They are of wood, of a peculiar plan.[13] He was his own architect and largely his own builder. What his peculiar doctrines were, I do not well make out — though I have several of his books and had several conversations with his son. I imagine his preaching was more on moral practice, then on dogmatic theology. He was musical and somewhat poetic. I have a volume of his Hymns. I preached once to his followers, on a Christmas Day, in their great "Meeting House." The cause was then much decayed.

In the flourishing days of the "Children of Peace," there was an Instrumental Band and a Choir of Virgins, and a good deal of their worship was in Song.[14] His Band and Choir at a certain time of the year would visit Toronto, and in June and September, the "Sharon Feast" was thronged with visitors from all over the province. The September "Feast" was the principal one and was preceded by an Illumination of the Sacred buildings the night before. The admission to the feast was 25 cents.

David has been dead many years. His remains lie in the little cemetery by the roadside, among the dust of so many of his followers — all laid with their heads to the north. I mentioned this peculiarity to the late John D. Willson, his son. "Yes!" said the old man, "Well, it don't make any difference when a man's dead, which way his head lies!"[15]

Plenty of Gold

Willie Young, of St. George, used to tell us of a farmer near by that he was working with one day, and they were packing away the sheaves in the big barn as they came in. There were eight or ten thousand sheaves in the "bag," and the farmer looked up.

"I say, Willie! I wish this *bag* was just as full of gold, as it is of sheaves!"

"And what would you do with it?"

"Well, I know what I'd do with some of it! I'd give *you half* a *bushel!*"

The offer was perhaps liberal in itself, the more so that it never needed to be fulfilled. But Young thought it was a very small percentage of the barn full the farmer himself dreamed of!

Dutch Settlers

It is misleading — and perhaps annoying to the people thus denominated — to call (as we often do) all Germans of every kind "Dutch." It probably comes to us from New York State, which *was* settled with Dutch, and belonged to the Netherlands. We have Germans of two kinds: those from Germany and elsewhere in Europe — such as the *Russian* Menonites in Manitoba — and the descendants of the Pennsylvania Germans, who came immediately after the peace of 1815. These latter are found chiefly in two large settlements: one in Waterloo in Wilmot and Woolwich townships, and the other in the County of York, including Markham and a part of Vaughan Township. These again, have branched out as in Bruce County [Hanover and Neustadt] [and] a large migration from Waterloo can be found in Brant Township.[16]

Courtesy of Archival and Special Collections, McLaughlin Library, University of Guelph.

Christian Hassenyager and William Johnston were the first two settlers to take up land in Brant Township, Bruce County. Ilustrations are from the *Illustrated Atlas of the Dominion of Canada*, Toronto (1880).

You know at once when you get into a Pennsylvania German settlement. The wooden houses are very large and roomy, and the barns correspondingly large. Everything seems comfortable about them. They generally settle on *good soil*; a few farms in Waterloo are very sandy, but it is only a little "exception."

Under a Feather Bed

Once, when a young lad, I was collecting accounts and notes for a tradesman and was storm-stayed at the house of an honest German in the Township of Waterloo. When it was time for retiring, my host took a candle and I followed, away upstairs, far out of reach of any fire on that bitter cold night, into a very big room with a very low ceiling and a painted floor — in one corner of the room there being a bed. He flung down the bedclothes, and then I saw brown-and-yellow striped sheets and pillow cases, homespun and home-woven, no doubt. He "hoped I would be comfortable!" and left me. When I got between the sheets, I thought I should have been frozen! It was a big feather bed below, and a lighter feather bed above, but there seemed to be no substance nor weight about it that promised any heat!

However, the voyager may praise the boat that carries him through! And the sleeper the bed that keeps him warm! For in a minute or two I began to feel comfortable, and never slept warmer nor better.

Them is Hogs!

The Reverend Mr. Fishburn, Lutheran Minister, in a German settlement in Vaughan,[17] and for some years my esteemed neighbour, told me the following story.

I had myself noticed, at the Philadelphia Exposition of 1876, two stuffed Tennessee "hogs." And they *were* hogs! Had weighed 1,200 lbs. each, with a body as big and long as a horse. On the side was attached the "card" of the man who had stuffed them. It was about as big as a page of foolscap and in the largest type was the word "Taxidermist."

Well, Mr. Fishburn saw it too, and while looking on, a rustic couple came along. "I say, Mariar! Come here and see these hogs!" The old lady came and sidled round, and began to space out the placard. "These ain't hogs!" she said, "These is t-a-x, *tax*, i-d-e-r, these is *taxidermists!*"

The old man came round, and read it too, and "seeing was believing!" But he did not feel satisfied; he got round to where he faced the snouts of the two animals. He studied their physiognomy; he knew hogs! He couldn't be mistaken. And while Mr. Fishburn looked on, amused, he slapped his leg and exclaimed, "I say them *is* hogs!"

Stout Shoes

Once in the Township of Brant,[18] in Bruce County, I saw a blacksmith working in his shop, in a pair of wooden shoes. He wore a pair of cloth slippers over his stockings — it was winter — and then the wooden shoes, and he said they were warm and dry. An old German (so another man told me) in the same township, made them for his neighbours, out of the native poplar, and sold them for "three York shillings" a pair.

A Sly Teuton

My friend John McCallum of Kleinburg [Vaughan Township][19] told me of a German who was with the other men, in for an early supper — at a farmer's — and who were going out again. Hans had had a good meal and did not want to go out again, and professed that he had sprained his thumb.

"See dare! I can't move it more dan dat!" he said, showing them how stiff it was. Then, forgetting which hand he had experimented on, in a few moments he held up the *same hand*.

"See," he added, "how I can move *dis one!*"

The Body of a Dutchman

My friend, the Reverend Solomon Snider was of "Dutch" descent. He used to dream of human perfection in this rise. Said he, "If I could but have the *head* of a Scotchman — the *tongue* of an Irishman — the *heart* of an Englishman — the *body* of a *Dutchman*, I would be a perfect man. And then he would expatiate on their national characteristics — the cool head, the eloquent tongue, the warm heart and the enduring body — of this ideal man.[20]

Witches!

Mr. Snider told me about some superstitions he had found in the western part of the province. He had lived long in Norwich Township, and I suppose he referred to that region.[21] I condense his statements.

Witches were a terror of old and young and not without reason when it was found what they could do! What quantities of soap grease were wasted, in the vain attempt to make soap! How many hours were spent on the churn, while the butter *wouldn't come!* (I am afraid the "Thermometer Churn" has a good deal to answer for, in the way of snuffing out the superstition about "bewitched butter!")

My friend continues: How much *bread-sponge* had to be thrown into the swill barrel because it wouldn't *rise!* Manes and tails of horses would be found in the morning braided up and fastened together for stirrups for the witches, or fairies, who had ridden them through the night!

A man's cows got lean, lost relish for food, and would yield no milk. But when an old woman *marked crosses* on their horns and foreheads, they were themselves again! They were held to have been "witched." Again, a man declared he was taken out every night by the witches, and bridled and ridden like a horse! And he would be completely exhausted when morning came. He showed the *sores* at the corner of his mouth where he had been "jerked" by the bit! He so firmly believed all this, that he walked fifty miles, to consult a witch doctor, who delivered him from his tormentors!

Again, an old soldier, who lived alone in a little cabin, died very suddenly, in the presence of some young men whom he had been diverting with tales of his former exploits. One of them ran to the house of Mrs. S., who was found with a pot fiercely boiling in which were three pigs' livers, all stuck full of pins and needles! In reply to the news that "old uncle Simon was dead!" she said, "Served him right! Why didn't he *let my pigs alone?*" It was a case of "tit for tat," he had bewitched her pigs, and she (with the help of the murdered pigs' livers) had compassed, by witchcraft, his death!

Once more: An old woman told her husband, one day, "My butter won't *come!*" He at once cast a *silver bullet* for his rifle (lead will not kill a witch!), and fired it into the churn! The butter was all right! — but not so an old woman of the neighbourhood, who had bewitched the butter! She went hobbling round for months, suffering from a concealed bullet wound!

After giving me these examples from his own former neighbourhood, and from the recollections of his older neighbours, Mr. Snider added, "If you do not believe in *witches*, after all I have told you — then all I can say is, *What is the use* of witches at all if people are so perverse and rebellious that they will not believe?"[22]

A Bright German

John was a young German who came to Owen Sound when I lived there. He had come from Germany without a word of English and had been but four years in America, yet his English was as perfect as the native Canadians among whom he moved. He lived by sign-painting, but was fast drifting into artistic work and decorating. I last heard of him near Lake Scugog.[23] I wish I knew what became of him. One likes sometimes to strike on a genius, and he was one.

Chapter 8

The Indians[1]

The Indians will gradually disappear as a distinct race and be absorbed in the general population of North America. The Blacks will probably maintain their distinct position. In the meantime, they form classes in our population, which are not to be overlooked. In his natural state, the Indian is something like the dog "Rab," celebrated by Dr. John Brown ... But the Negro would rather live in peace, and eat and drink, and rejoice! And as a converted wolf would make an excellent sheep dog — and is, I verily believe, the progenitor of that useful race — so an Indian, once tamed and civilized, takes things very seriously, and gives his whole mind to his circumstances. Where to get his bread and pork for today, engrosses his utmost stretch of attention.[2]

"There are but a very few of us here," said a college-bred Indian to me, once, "who try to *do* anything in the way of improving ourselves!" And I do believe that the poor fellow, who died a year or two afterwards, just pined away with disappointed hopes. Poor Charles Keeshick![3] Improvements come, but they seem to be forced upon them from without.

"I don't know," said William Walker, an Ojibway, in a speech at Brantford, "how you White men get so ahead of us. We have the same *moving powers* as you — the same hands and feet — but you seem always *to get ahead of us!*"[4]

The Negro has within live ambition, vigour and a latent intelligence that will bear a good deal of polishing.[5] We know not how heavy-browed, clumsy and unintelligent were our own ancestors, as seen by the Romans nor how much the mental acumen we so much prize has been merely the result of ages of gradual training.[6]

Indian Maps

A man up the Lakes once asked me, "if I had ever seen an Indian Map?" He said an Indian would draw you a chart of your proposed voyage and put down correctly the islands and headlands on each side. But they paid no attention to the "direction," and the course marked out for you would be always perfectly straight! It was Davy Crockett's motto reduced to practice — "Be sure you're right, then straight ahead!" An Indian probably imagines he is going straight but it seems impossible for him — as I have seen, when canoeing with them — to steer from one headland to another as a White man would! The Indian must follow the bend of the shore, and never likes to be very far from it. And bold as he is, in navigating his canoe, he does not like to make a thirty-mile stretch across the Lake at any time.[7]

A Modern Jonah [8]

My friend, the Reverend Ludwick Kribs[9] gave me an Indian story of some adventurers of more than a century ago. Before the American Revolution, when Sir William Johnson was all in all among the Indians of the Province of New York, a deputation of braves from the North West Lakes was proceeding to some great gathering, to meet Johnson.[10] They had come down from the North, and were now ready to cross "Lake Manitou" from Cape Commodore, or Cape Rido, to the Christian Islands, thirty miles distant, the highlands of which were in sight. They intended to ascend the Severn River to Lake Simcoe and take the portage from where Beaverton is now, to Balsam Lake (where, when this was told me, and perhaps now, a road exists, called the "Portage Road") and once there, they could descend through the Trent River system and its many lakes, to the Bay of Quinte, then across the Oswego River and so up among the lakes of New York.

A White man was with them, and while preparing their dinner on shore, the White man had killed a snake — for which he had been reprimanded by the Indians — "it was unlucky!" Half way across, a breeze arose and the Lake got dangerous. Had it lasted a little longer, they would have thrown the White man — the "Jonah" of the voyage — overboard, for he heard them discussing the step. Fortunately, a little more hard paddling (and it is hard to upset a canoe when urged swiftly forward!) soon brought them past danger.[11]

A Canoe Maker

In company with the Reverend Robert Robinson,[12] some fifteen miles up the Spanish River, in Algoma, I once had an interview with a dignified Indian, who was just finishing a batch of three canoes, which he would bring down to sell to White visitors at the steamboat landings. A "two-fathom" canoe is for one man. A "three-fathom" canoe will carry two or three persons. And they will measure it with their outstretched arms in the original fashion of "fathoming." My friend, who was acting for a Missionary Society, asked a good many questions about his tribe: "who was chief?" and so on, and then told him he was anxious — if they would only build themselves houses and settle down in a village, like many of the other Indians — to send them a teacher so that their children might know about the Great Spirit, and learn to read His Book and know about a great many things that were good to learn.[13]

The Indian, whose name was "Green Feather," had lighted his pipe and sat down to smoke, but he was so interested he forgot to continue his smoking, and sat listening with the greatest attention as the interpreter told him what the White man said, emitting, at the end of every sentence or two, a grunt of satisfaction. His brother was the "Second Chief" of the tribe — the vice-president of their very small Republic.

"He would tell his brother, and the others, when they came back to camp. It was good. They would hold council and let us know!"

Having succeeded so well, the missionary next began explaining to him the Christian religion, and urged it upon his attention. He was still very courteous in his attention. Determined to know something of his mind, the missionary asked him the direct question, "What he thought about it? And if he did not think it would be well for him to be a Christian, and worship only the Great Spirit?"

Now Green Feather's diplomacy came in! "He didn't think it was best for him *to say anything about that!* His brother was Second-Chief; if his brother were here, perhaps he would say something about it. But when his brother was not here, he did not think it best to say anything about it!"[14]

The Serpents' River

Two or three days after we saw "Green Feather" we were at the mouth of Serpents' River. Enquiring of our Indian boatman, James Nawa-geeshick, *why* it was so called? "Were there any rattlesnakes there?"[15]

"No, there were no rattlesnakes west of the French River, the outlet of Lake Nipissing. It was from some great figures of *serpents* on the rocks, near the mouth of the River — Indian landmarks."

So on our way back, we landed at the pictured rocks. The Indian said somebody professed to have seen a great sea serpent,[16] not far off, sporting in the water and there were representations of it. The rocks ran up, smooth and steep, like the steep roof of a house, from the water; and two wriggling serpents were traced — by merely *scraping off* the dark moss and lichens to make the figures. They were a foot or more in breadth, and must have been a hundred feet long — with their tails in the water! Each had *horns* on his head, about three feet long. The figures were only three or four feet apart. They seemed to have been neglected and are probably effaced by this time. This was in 1874. I crept up the rocks, as high as the figures reached and had a good look at them.

Indian Politeness

An Indian has his own ideas of politeness. He does not trouble a settler by knocking at his door. He does not want to disturb the good man, and so comes softly in with his moccasined feet, without any signal at the door.[17] He has learned to shake hands and he says, "Bu-zu," which he seems to think is a part of a universal language. He gets it from the uneducated French trader, who says "Beau jous" instead of *Bon jour.* He has also got hold of the Gaelic name for whisky from the Montreal traders, and calls it "Squibby."[18] But he uses the word chiefly as denoting the condition of himself and his compatriots when under the influence of the *fire water.*

When the Prince of Wales visited Collingwood in 1860, I was one of an excursion party from Owen Sound. John Thomas Wahbatick, the drunken son of a chief, was anxious to protest to the Prince against some doings of the Indian Department of the Government.[19] Some one called out, "Oh, you're *Squibby!*" It startled John Thomas a little, but he tried to throw off the imputation by pointing to this one and that one around him — "me not *squib-bae!* That man's *squib-bae!*"

I met his father, the old chief, some four years after that, and had a talk with him on the road. The old man could speak English imperfectly. Among other things I asked him:

"Where — John Thomas?"

"Fergus."

"John Thomas — *drink?*" going through the pantomime of tipping up the little finger.

"Oh!" said the old man, with unutterable disgust, "Oh, all-time! Ten year!"[20]

Giving Names

They have an original way of giving names to everything. In Ojibway, the name of a horse signifies "a one-toed animal." They had observed, when horses were first brought in by the Whites, that their hoofs were not divided like the deer or the buffalo. And though they knew all about turkeys, they knew nothing of peacocks, till the Whites brought them in. They were something like the turkey, but so much grander in their feathers, that they called them "the Great Spirit's turkey."

If a man has a limp, or a squint, or any disability about him, they will be pretty sure to take it off in some Indian nickname. One acquaintance of mine they called "Glass eyes" — he wore spectacles. Another was "Big Bluebird." Another was "White Swan," and when he asked why he was so called, they said "White Swans come from the South and you came to us from the South." Another still, whose impetuous manner had challenged their admiration and awe, they called "Thunder-from-a-clear-sky." Me they called shining hair — *Mahkatae-Wangue.* Very many of their names of animals and the like, have a descriptive meaning — our names have not.

A Gaelic friend insisted on my taking notice of the fact, that wherever a language gives a *name* that has an understood *meaning* in it, that language may be set down as an original one — not one derived from some other tongue. Of course, his conclusion was that as this was pre-eminently so with the Gaelic, it showed that it was an ancient and original language. I said it was the same with the Ojibway, and it might, if pushed too far, indicate that they were descended from the Indians! "No," he said, "but it proved that the Gaelic was a very ancient language: and was itself doubtless, the mother of many languages."[21]

Poetry and Music

I have never heard of an Indian Poet,[22] though an old Indian, forty years ago, told me that in his boyhood, in the old pagan times, they were regularly taught to chant "hymns" by the high priest of the tribe, the "Medicine Man," or "Mystery Man." An Indian friend of mine, William Walker, tried his hand at some of our popular hymns. I am not an expert in the Ojibway, but I carefully transcribe two stanzas — the first the chorus of the gospel song "Hold the Fort!" and the second chorus of "Shall We Gather at the River":

Soongegahbowh ninpeezhah mah
Jesus ekedo
Howh! Nuhquatowh, ningahneebowh
Wahdookuhweyun

A ke gah mah wun jee de min suh,
Kwa nau je wung, kwa nau je wung see beeng,
See be uh puh na wan je je wung
Ke zha muh ne doo uh yaud.

Others have had success in a larger scale, in translating hymns. I thought it was a curious thing that my friend did not try (nor stumble on) *rhyme!* And told him so. But he did not seem to consider that rhyme was of any special consequence. And indeed it seemed to have been so with the ancients. Not a single *rhymed* poem of antiquity is in existence! The monks, in the early middle ages, first introduced it.[23]

In the music of their war dances (which I have heard), there is not the least rhythm or cadence; it is simply "tom! tom! tom! tom!" with the same regular beat and the same tone, throughout.[24] The Christian Ojibway have a few hymns translated, but as far as I have seen, without rhyme. They learn the notes of the musical scale readily and make good and correct singers. Nor does an Indian choir put on any "airs" at a concert. They come to *sing* and they just begin, as impassive and matter-of-fact like, as if embarrassment and shyness were mere matters of the imagination!

Theirs is an unusual language to the ear. Any language is necessarily so, that lacks the sound of *l, f,* and *r,* as is the case with the Ojibway.[25]

Keeping House in English

I once visited a house on the Saugeen Reserve, where the husband was Ojibway and the wife Mohawk, and they could not understand each other's language. But they could each speak English moderately well and "kept house" in English. Their son, Matthew, was an intelligent little fellow of nine or ten, and already had plans to "make a home" for himself, (and it was to be "a big *brick* house! Oh yes!") and to have plenty of horses and cows. I wonder if he really *did* have any of the enterprise of the White man, when he grew up?[26]

An Indian "makes" a wigwam — does not "build" it — and so he never speaks of "building" a house; he "makes" it. The bark of the white birch is all in all to him. He makes his house of it, his canoe of it, burns it for lights, and when he makes maple sugar, he has birchbark vessels (very like an old-fashioned "cocket hat,")[27] for holding the sap. He does not seem to have discovered (not having such need for it) that pieces of birchbark packed in an old iron tea kettle, and all the cracks and openings luted with moist clay, will emit from its spout — when over a good fire and no longer — the most beautiful *gas!*

The Ojibway term for birchbark is "Wigwass" — "bark," *par excellence*. So a "wigwam" means simply a "bark house." Others of their words we may trace: "squaw" is a corruption of their word "e-quac," a woman (or wife, for an Indian is like a Greek; his wife is his "woman.") And they do not like "squaw"; they prefer to be called "Indian woman."[28]

Indian Sport

An Indian has very little idea of "sport." Fishing and hunting are to him a very serious business. As an Indian said to me, when I offered him a dollar for a very big fish he had speared under the ice — being disappointed in not getting one myself out of Lake Huron — he wants to "eat — um!" And I never happened to see an Indian fishing with a baited hook! It is too slow; he uses the spear or the net.[29]

Once, four of us came across four Indians at Boat Lake,[30] County of Huron, before the region was settled, and camped for the night near them. One shock-headed Indian we called "The Wild Man," because he never wore a hat, sang out to us as we approached, "No bread, no potatoes, plenty *fish*, plenty *duck!*"

We had a loaf of bread with us and some butter. So we bought a pike from them, and cut it in pieces to boil, and borrowed a tin pail to boil it in, and a little salt. We had no plates, and they grinned and laughed to the outer verge of Indian politeness when they saw me, with an axe, taking out four of the very largest *chips*, from a cedar near by, to serve for plates! They had been there four days and had carried two canoes three or four miles through the woods from Colpoy's Bay — and would stay there till they got tired of eating fish and wild ducks without bread or potatoes. Frederick Wahbazee, of Saugeen, told me that he had taken forty barrels of lake herring the spring before.[31]

To Fry Their Fish!

The Indians have unbounded faith in medicine. Dr. Cameron of Owen Sound told me that he never could satisfy them, even in the smallest ailment, without giving them big doses of *something, and* magnesia and other harmless ingredients answered many purposes![32]

But another medical friend, Dr. W.S. Francis,[33] of Manitowahning,[34] on the Manitoulin Island, was much worse off. He was "frozen in" with little communication with older settlements for several months, and had to lay in supplies in the fall. His big carboys[35] of Castor Oil astonished a young friend, up there looking for land, to whom I had given a letter of introduction to the Doctor. But the good-natured physician explained that in his Indian practice (he had medical charge of the Reserve opposite), he used large quantities of castor oil — and he regretted to say that sometimes they so forgot propriety and good faith toward the Indian Department, as to use this medical supply *to fry their fish!*[36]

Indian Speech

The speech of an Indian, when we get a literal translation of it, seems always to us to be most fanciful and romantic in its illustrations and epithets. But that is largely due to the poverty of their language. They have never cultivated abstract thought and know nothing of the great affairs or interests of the world, and they have never constructed terms, or expanded their vocabulary to take in such things. So an Indian, anxious to tell you of his high esteem, and the deep respect he feels for you, says, "his heart is *big* toward his white brother!" Or, if he wishes to express his sincerity, he says "his heart is *white*."[37]

I once drew up a memorial for an Indian Church at Colpoy's Bay, addressed to a Missionary Committee, and put a little of the romantic in it, and, in a printed report in which it was mentioned, the Children of the Forest were complimented on their touching and original simplicity![38]

"Manito-wahning," the "deep water of the Spirit," seems robbed of half its meaning and more than half its beauty, when an old fur trader, a friend of mine — as we looked at the beautiful blue-green depths so near the shore — declared to me in the most positive terms, as a thing he knew to a certainty that it was not the Great Spirit, but a *spirit-beaver* that gave his name to the place![39] The Indians greatly admire the wisdom of the beaver, and always speak of him as if, in many respects, he were an equal of themselves. And a beaver that no man could trap, and that only came up to revisit the glimpses of the moon when he pleased, had from time immemorial haunted the spot![40]

A Native Milliner

Mrs. Hodge of Birchton,[41] who had returned from a sojourn at the Sanitarium at St. Leon Springs in Lower Canada, showed me a dress hat she had brought home with her, made in a wigwam by an Indian woman. It was a dark drab, of a pleasing shade, with band, rosette and plume — all of the same colour and of the same material — and that material was simply fine "splints" of *ash wood!* I never saw anything of the kind more beautiful or more suggestive of what *might* be done with industry and skill. The Iroquois himself prepared the simple meals of the household, and beat out the splints, and his "squaw" made from rough — finished — and dyed *two hats* in a day, thus earning about two dollars. Unfortunately for her, the "season" for visitors at the Springs ended with the fine weather. Their imitation is most wonderful, and so at school, the boys and girls become expert at penmanship, but the same expertness does not follow them in arithmetic. The one is by imitation — the other needs thought. I have often seen them examining with great care various articles of household and personal adornment, for the purpose, no doubt, of trying their skill on copies of the same.[42]

Indian Dogs

Indians keep but few animals; though every Indian keeps a dog, and one of his high aspirations is to keep a horse. And if an Indian has a horse, he will not walk. Someway, it seems *infra dig.*[43] I once saw three Indians come into a White man's house, almost frozen. They had come seven miles on a bitter cold day, on a sled behind a horse. To jump out, and run behind, to get warmed up by the exertion, as a White man would do, was out of the question with them. It was more dignified to ride! We had just finished dinner, and there was plenty of potatoes and beef left for the poor fellows. And how they did enjoy the meal! "Thanks," they all said, in their own tongue and one of them added in English — patting his stomach — "feel better now!"

Why an Indian keeps a dog, I never could make out, probably for company. For I never knew an Indian dog good for hunting or "retrieving." They don't seem to train them; perhaps they are of a kind that could not be trained. But an Indian has no end of time on his hands, and *might* train a dog to many useful exercises. But oh, what *raiders* they are! If there's a hunter's or a tourist's camp within two miles, an Indian dog will find it out, and watch his chance to eat up all that can be eaten — even to the soap! I was once at a religious meeting among the Indians, when two dogs got up a friendly tussle below the benches. A tall Indian rose, and peering under the seats, at last got hold of the hind leg of one of the combatants! The door was open, and he slung the dog out a dozen feet from the door! I thought there were many better fates in the world than being an *Indian's dog!*[44]

Little Joseph

I must not forget to tell the story of "Little Joseph." Joseph was an Ojibway, of the Saugeen Reserve. When I was introduced to him on the road, as it was growing dark, I thought in the dim light, and from his appearance and his diminutive size, that he was a boy not yet full grown, but he was a man of fifty. He was lame and came to church (it was winter) in a little sleigh, drawn by two faithful dogs. He turned them loose and when our service was over, whistled for his team, and was soon off again like the wind.

Joseph had been only a few years a Christian — kept up paganism after all the others had deserted it. Yet no doubt he had often — if it were merely for curiosity and for company's sake — been at the preaching and perhaps knew much more than he practised. He took sick, and at last was so far gone, that the Indians around him said, "Joseph is dead!" He, however, gradually came to and as soon as he had strength to speak, he quietly said, "*I am not going to be a pagan any more!*" And he kept his word. He was a man without a family and lived alone in a little log hut. He had his faithful dogs, and his Ojibway New Testament, and thirty dollars a year "Indian money" from the Government; and probably not an unfulfilled wish in the world! "This is Little Joseph — *he is a good man!*" said my Indian friend, in introducing us to one another.[45]

An Indian Saddle

In Tilbury, a young man told me of a visit they had had from a very dignified Indian not long before, where the visitor was mounted on a pony, on a wooden saddle of his own making. First was a folded blanket on the beast's back, and then a small saddle, carved out of solid maple, with a girth over all to keep it in place. It was brand new, and he was giving it what the Scotch call a "handsel," by first using it to visit the White man.[46]

An Indian Orpheus[47]

I have sometimes thought I got little glimpses of Arcadia once in a while! They did not last long, but they were sweet! Once I passed along by the Bay Shore, on the Indian side, in sight of the town of Owen Sound, on a beautiful day, in the loveliest part of the year, and saw a young Indian, lying on the green grass, under a little tent made of a boat sail — playing to himself some little tunes on an accordion. And I thought, like Tom Moore, "if there's peace to be found in the world thy heart that is humble may hope for it here."[48]

But very likely he was wishing he were a White man! Like the little soft-eyed daughter of an Indian friend when he had received a "box" from some friends in Toronto, which contained among other things a bright blue coat for her with large white buttons. She could not be persuaded to put it off at bedtime, but slept in it the first night. And she laid her chubby cheek on her father's arm, and wanted to know (so the fond father told me) "If she was not a *Soggonosh E-quae-Sis*, now?" (A White man's little girl.)[49]

Indian Sugar Making

Whether — or to what extent — the Indians made sugar from the maple, before the Whites came to America, I begin to despair of reliably finding out. I once saw a statement that "Maple Sugar was first made in New England in 1737." Appleton's *American Encyclopedia*[50] says it was first made (in New England) in 1751, and from thence spread into New York and the other provinces. Parkman, the historian,[51] wrote me that "he thought *Appleton* was wrong," but he did not give me his own theory. George Bancroft,[52] historian, wrote me that "he knew nothing of it, farther back than his childhood recollections in New England." The *Savans* of the Smithsonian Institution at Washington incline to the theory that the Whites got the art from the Indians, but neither they nor any other of my correspondents explain — if this were so — how the pilgrims were dying of scurvy in the spring of 1621 — with their Indian friend Squando beside them — when maple syrup is such a specific for the blood, and they made none — nor for (as far as we can learn) a hundred years later![53]

An Indian at Saugeen explained to me how their communism wrought in spring, when they wanted to make maple sugar. An Indian will go out on his snowshoes to "prospect." Having come across some good dry upland ridge, with good maples, he will dress off a square patch on the trunks of four beech trees, at the four corners of his "claim," and thereon — if he can write — put his name or initials. If not, then his "totem." And his claim is respected by all the other Indians, but only for that sugar season. Next year it is open to "preemption" in the same manner, and whoever marks it first, to him it belongs. And I never heard of their quarrelling over it.[54]

Indian Memorials

Campbell writes about — speaking of the beech:

On my trunk's enduring frame,
Carved many a long-forgotten name.[55]

And many of us have left memorials in the beech. It is likewise the memorial and monument of the Indian. I remember when a boy, visiting the yet smoking encampment of some Mohawk Indians on the Grand River, a few miles below Galt. They had left on a tree their "totem." I knew nothing of *totems* then, and did not try to identify it with any animal or creature — but I remember it seemed to me like a rude figure *eight*.

A portrait of Reverend Peter Jones, 1932, by the English miniaturist, Matilda Jones. He was the second son of a daughter of Chief Wahbanosay, a Mississauga, and Augustus Jones, the land surveyor involved in the clearing of Yonge Street. A much-respected Methodist missionary, Peter Jones lived in Brantford and served communities along the Grand and the Credit rivers. His book, *History of the Ojebway Indians: With Special Reference to their Conversion to Christianity*, was published in England in 1861. Portrait taken from *A Guide to Provincial Plaques* (1989) 11.

They are all in clans or families, according to their "totems," or crests. For instance, there will be the totem of the Otter, the Beaver, the Eagle, and the like. Now their personal names will be all derived from the same, within the family circle of the "totem." Thus, the Otter —there will be Big Otter, Creeping Otter, etc., and so of all the others. And they claim "cousinship" — ever to the twentieth degree — with one of the same totem. In fact, in a "Reserve," an industrious and well-to-do Indian is liable to be almost "eaten out" by hosts of "poor relations."[56]

A Writ of Ejectment

Charles Rankin,[57] District Surveyor, Owen Sound, told me that in 1833 he laid out Collingwood and St. Vincent townships on the south shore of Georgian Bay. His party came across from Penetanguishene, then a Naval Station, in a *batteau*.[58] The government had bought up the Indian title to the lands as far west as the perpendicular line between the townships of St. Vincent and Sydenham. But Chief Wahbatick, mentioned elsewhere, did not seem to have been a party to the "surrender," and, calling upon Mr. Rankin, ordered the surveying party to desist "and to leave his land!" Mr. Rankin reasoned with him, showing him that the government did not claim the land further west than "Vail's Point," but that up to that headland, they had bought out the Indian rights.[59]

He still threatened the party, but having implicit faith in his "Great Father" at York (Toronto), Sir John Colborne,[60] he would first try peaceful means. He departed and within the short space of ten days he re-appeared, having been, by canoe and on foot, to the Seat of Government in the meantime!

The clerks at the Crown Lands Office had imposed on the fiery little Chief, and, giving him a paper to "serve" on any unauthorized trespasses, got rid of him. The paper, which he imagined had all the virtue of a "Writ of Ejectment," was nothing but a printed Notice of "Lands for Sale." This he carried over a hundred miles in his bosom and "served" it with all due gravity! But seeing no immediate effect, grew more confidential, and admitted that he was "buckatae," (hungry) got something to eat and drink, and made peace with the party.[61]

Twenty or thirty years after, he was in my house at Owen Sound, with a most wonderful *club* in his hand. I asked him "what was that for?" He said "Kill — um! *bear!*" The handle was three feet long and the head was round, the size of a man's fist, of some dark, heavy wood, and with several vicious-looking *spikes* in it, three inches long. A formidable weapon, either in hunting or war.

With respect to the survey above, Mr. Rankin said, he called the first township "Alta," from the "Blue Mountains" in it, and the other "Zero" because it bounded the extremity of the Crown lands at that time — all the rest to Lake Huron was "Indian Land." But some influences at the Crown Lands Department caused the names to compliment some of the British Navel heroes and *Alta* was named "Collingwood," and *Zero* was called "St. Vincent."[62] He had left a town plot at the mouth of the Big Head River, unnamed; this was called, after Lord St. Vincent's country seat, "Meaford."[63]

How Two Names?

Francis Wahbazee, of Saugeen, once asked me, in his own house (through an interpreter) "Who the Romans were and the Corinthians" and various peoples whom he found mentioned in his Ojibway Testament. And so I sat down, and we had an interesting talk for two hours. His wife was squatted on the floor, sewing a corn-husk mat, but she stopped her work, put her forearm on her husband's knee, and looked up at us — drinking in every word.

I don't know that I ever "preached" to any company, large or small, with more comfort — or more appreciation — than to that noble old Indian and his wife. His totem was "The Swan," which was imbedded in his name, "Francis," being prefixed by the missionary who baptized him.[64] He was born in what he had learned to call "Westconsin," at the headwaters of the Mississippi. He told me, many years before, that he never heard the name of God (Keeshi-Manitou) in his own language, till he was ten years old. Then he heard a French trader say something about "Keeshi-Manitou." He ran home, and asked his mother *"Who Keeshi-Manitou was?"* She was either unable or unwilling to tell him and merely said, "Go away, and don't trouble your mother with your foolish questions!"

It was probably an unwillingness on the part of the poor Indian woman to enter upon serious questions. Like an old chief, north of Georgian Bay, who was addressed by my friend the Reverend Robert Robinson, and advised and solicited to "pray to the Great Spirit." "No," said the Chief, "I *don't want* to pray to the Great Spirit! If I should speak to the Great Spirit, he would look down, and say, "Who is that speaking to *me?*" And he would take notice of me and see my bad heart!"[65]

So Wahbazee never heard a word more on the subject, for ten years more, till he crossed over into Canada. Being somewhat satisfied with the information I could give him, of these ancient New Testament peoples, he next wanted to know, "How it comes that White people have *two names, and* the Indians only *one?*" I therefore had to branch out into history again, and told him of our rude ancestors, and their conversion by "Missionaries," and of their adopting in many cases, Bible names. And how some eight hundred years ago, they got into the fashion of adding a second name. And then he wanted to know *"Where they got* these second names?" I said, some of these names were from their trades, as *Mason, Carpenter, Weaver, and* the like; some were from the lands or villages where they lived, as *Milton, Cobham;* some were from animals, as "Mr. Lyon," "Mr. Wolfe" and so forth. Here he stopped me, in a little apparent excitement — as much as an Indian ever allows to himself — and asked, "If a White Minister *would ever baptize a child* by the name of *wolf?*"

"Oh yes," I replied, "It is so long ago, and if I had a nice young lady friend named — Miss Wolfe — I would never think of the animal of that name when I met her. My grandmother's name was Fox, but when I think of my grandmother, I never think of a fox with a long tail, running in the woods!"

He still repeated his wonder "that a Minister would ever baptize a child with such a name as *wolf!*" Animals to them are "characters," and I suppose a wolf, for cruelty and treachery, bears a very bad name.[66]

A One-Sided Bargain

A storekeeper at a lumbering station on the edge of civilization told me about a rather handsome Indian girl I saw "trading" there, in company with her mother; and of a White man who wanted to marry her. The girl's name was, in English, "Long Face." The suitor, in accordance with Indian usages, carried on the negotiations with the parents.

"And what did Long Face think of the proposition?"

"Oh, she left it all — Indian fashion — to her parents."

"And how did the affair end?"

"Very unfortunately for the would-be groom! *He* was anxious to impress the parents with the idea that he was a man of consequence, and *means* — spoke of his farm — and so forth, till at last the old Indian and his wife said he might have Long Face, *if he would "keep" them, as long as they lived!* Not feeling able to support the whole Indian family in idleness — and looking upon it as rather a one-sided bargain — the affair was broken off, at which my informant added, "Long Face was rather pleased."[67]

Pinching Times

An Indian is generally a poor provider. He has sometimes a pinching time in spring. When things come to the worst, he takes to the road, and by basket-making and various kindred arts, manages to supply present wants, and come home with a bag or two of good provisions.

At Newash, opposite Owen Sound, the Government gave the Indians, in 1842, some oxen to work a large clearing made at Government expense, and also some cows. But as the Indians had

Courtesy of the Owen Sound Public Library, Local History Collection.

A very old photograph of the school that the children of the Newash Reserve attended. The reserve was just north of Owen Sound.

forgotten to make any provision for fodder for the animals, they killed them for "beef" when the snow fell![68]

Indian Legends

Some of the Indian legends are not devoid of humour. William Walker, of Saugeen, told me the following — "as the old women told *him*," so he said:

> The Indians thought the sun at night tumbled into a hole — some long burrow — and rolled under the ground, and came up in the East next morning![69] A sharp Indian boy noticed, as he saw the sun blazing among the trees, one evening, the *very spot* where he disappeared — between two certain trees! So next day he set a snare there and in the evening actually trapped the sun! He remained, blazing among the

trees, but could not get into his *hole*, being held by the boy's snares! The animals of the forest held a meeting to see what was to be done — for they must have *night* as well as *day!* They resolved that some of their number must go forward, and gnaw through the snares that held the sun. The bear, the beaver, the otter, and all the sharp-teethed animals tried it in vain. They could not get near enough, for the heat!

At last, one of the smaller animals determined to sacrifice himself, if need be, for the good of the whole. He crept forward resolutely and actually gnawed the thongs and let free the imprisoned sun, who quickly dropped into his hole! But the poor little creature was very badly singed and scorched, and has had *a bad smell ever since!* And the Indians call him "*Skunk!*"

Another legend my Indian friend told me, must have been concocted since the Whites came to America:

Nanaboosh, or Nana-boozoo — the same demigod known to the more Southern Indians as "Hiawatha" — began, like Prometheus to make man out of clay. The Grecian demi-god stole fire from Heaven to animate them; Nanaboosh used *fire* in another way — he baked them in an oven! He tempered the heat of the oven carefully, and put in his first clay man. But he came out "white" — only half-baked! He was the progenitor of the White men. He said to himself, "I must fire-up better!" And so he made his oven very hot, and behold, the second specimen came out, burnt quite *black!* He was the father of the Negroes.

"Now," said Nanaboosh, "I *must* take more care! I must have that oven just right!" So he tempered the oven very carefully, and was sure to have all things right this time, after *two* partial failures! And the third man came out just right! *Just the colour of a nice crust of bread!* And *he* was the ancestor of the Indians.[70]

Indians Like Credit!

Like with some people borrowing money — so is an Indian about getting credit — the great thing is to *get* it! The repayment is a distant contingency, which need not trouble anybody! I was told that the pretty little river that empties into Lake Ontario a few miles west of Toronto, was called the "Credit," because some trader established himself at its mouth, and would give "credit" to the Indians, even as he did to the Whites. The rumour spread far and wide through the woods, that such and such a storekeeper gave the Indians *"credit"* and the place and the river got the name — from this fortunate and happy fact![71]

In the first years of the history of Owen Sound, some disreputable people would sometimes take money from the Indians for whisky. But a beautiful retribution followed! The Indian's money soon was gone, but not so his thirst — and he would go back to the liquor seller next day and want more "fire-water."

"Where's your money?" the dealer would demand.

"Oh, pay by and by; Indian-money come!"

Driven from the premises by the irate dealer, the Indian would go straight to a magistrate.

"Mr. ___ sell Indian whisky!"

"Whom did he sell to?"

"Me! Injun!"

And then the dealer was fined twenty dollars. This happened two or three times and closed, very happily, the hopes of the Indians for getting whisky — either on credit or otherwise; though sometimes they would still get it by the connivance of disreputable Whites. But when I lived at Owen Sound, with an Indian settlement within one or two miles, there was very little drinking among them.[72]

An Indian Dandy

I was once at an Indian "Council" at Colpoy's Bay. An Indian had put away his wife, and taken another (pagan fashion), and the Christian Indians were greatly scandalized. The Indians do not make "motions" and take "a show of hands" but they talk and confer — with sometimes a great waste of time — till the opposition is silenced, and then the matter is concluded. So every man had to make a speech, and I learned afterward that the man was brought to his senses, and confessed and repaired his evil conduct, as far as he could.

But at the Council, though the man had nothing to say, he evidently desired to impress them with the idea that he was a man of consequence, and they must be careful how they handled his case! He was, that day, the highest style of an Indian "dandy!" He had on blue broadcloth pantaloons and they met his bright yellow buckskin moccasins, and the blue and the bright yellow "set" each other off, beautifully. He had no coat; it was summer. But he had a blue cloth vest, to match the trousers. And he had a white shirt, just from the "store," elaborately finished and laundered, and this he wore *in the style of a frock coat!* He was a great "gentleman!"[73]

A Noble Indian

Of these later years, I paid another visit to the Indian, Wahbazee, already mentioned. During the four days I stayed at his house, he told me a good deal of his life and adventures, for he had learned a little English since I first met him thirty years before.

The first night I was there, a rap came to the door, and a signal, "How, how!" He answered, "How! how!" and got up. A conversation in Ojibway was held in the dark, but next morning there was light bread on the table, for his wife, like the majority of half-civilized Indian women, had failed to get into the mysteries of *yeast.* Some kind neighbouring Indian family — more advanced — had sent a loaf for the White man.[74]

He told me he had lately made two important journeys. One was to "west-consin," to see his relations, for he belonged to a tribe of Pottawatamies there. But he was disgusted with their remaining barbarism. They put on their war-paint-daubs on their cheekbones, as he made me understand by pantomime — all in his honour — but he added, "No *tea!*" This was a convincing sign of their want of civilization! The old man would pour his saucer full, and take it up in both hands to his lips; he did enjoy his "*tea!*" They could give him roasted raccoon, and all the delicacies of the hunting "season," but no *tea!* On the whole, he did not think much of the United States. He said, "Every man — Yankee man — *little gun*" (making a motion toward an imaginary hip pocket) a boy — fifteen year — little *gun!* Me — Canada — Queen Victoria good!"[75]

His other visit had been to the French River and Lake Nipissing. He had lived long enough in civilization to know that a territory could be put to other uses than merely hunted over, and to know good land from bad. When I asked him what kind of a country it was, he dismissed it with one short sentence, "Oh, all too much *stone!*"

On Sunday he went with me twice to church, and sent his granddaughter to the Sunday School, and at the tea hour was teaching her the "Apostles Creed" in Ojibway. He made her say it over from his dictation several times, till she pleased him.

He had a hickory cane, he had cut near Brantford, and he had steamed it and bent it. I carved an eagle's head on the end of the bend. And though he was pleased at this small courtesy, yet I could see that a little spice of dissatisfaction mingled with it — for had I not done something that was far more in his line than my own? For the White man had done something — with merely a sharp penknife — that it had never occurred to him to do![76]

Improvement

On this visit, I was in a large number of Indian houses. In every house I found a cookstove and a coal-oil lamp, in four I found sewing machines and in two, cabinet organs; in all, bedsteads and chairs, and *some* kind of curtain or blind for the windows — sometimes only scalloped newspaper.

Thirty years before, when I first visited the Saugeen Reserve, *none* of these things were found, with the exception of some kind of cookstove, generally. They are improving — slowly, yet improving. Laziness, which seems to them "dignified leisure," has been bred in their bones for so many generations, that like the salt-rheum or the scrofula, it will take three or four generations to breed it out of them; let us have patience. Our British ancestors were pretty stupid fellows, and it took ever so much of warm Saxon blood and ever so long training in activity, to make us the queer, domineering, overturning, exacting hotch-potch we are![77]

A sketch by Anna Jameson of some Indian Lodges along the shore of Lake Huron, dated 1837.

From *Pearls and Pebbles* (1999) 134.

The Indian at Home

I remember visiting the encampment of some Indians near Listowel.[78] The wigwam was of bark and cotton cloth, seven or eight feet in diameter. A small fir was in the centre, where the old man — whom I had known at Saugeen — was carving out something for sale, and at the same time watching the pot in which was boiling his dinner.

I admired the way he kept that pot boiling, without making a fire so big as to make it too warm in the tent. He would take two bits of dry hemlock bark, scarcely as large each as a human hand, and set them upright in the hot ashes under the pot, and the little blaze would lick round the bottom of the pot, without making too big a fire, and keep it nicely going.

Chapter 9

The Negroes[1]

In former days there was a considerable traffic on the "Under-ground Railroad," that brought many slaves to Canada. Strange how they all knew that to "go far enough North" would bring them to freedom. My father, newly arrived from Scotland, asked a mid-dle-aged man, a slave at a country tavern, where we had stopped on our journey from Baltimore to Ohio, "Are you *for life?*" The poor fellow looked round, to see that no one else could hear him, and then said with infinite pathos, in a confidential voice — "*I have no other hope!*"[2]

Settlements of them in the country and "quarters" in the towns often show a good deal of squalor, and always improvidence. I once complained to Sammy Barnes, of Owen Sound, that the Black people there — and there were about twenty families of them — were indolent and lacking in resources and application.

"Well, now," said Barnes, "there's a reason for that, boss." In the South, the slaves are very religious — most of 'em Methodes and Baptises — and their preachers tell 'em it isn't right to run away. But the good-for-nothing fellows — them that won't work, and are all the time quarrelling with the overseers — *they* are the kind that run away! And you don't see the *best kind* of 'em here!"[3]

Good Humour

Nothing can exceed the general good humour of the race. It is said by an American poet:

> Negroes and boys do whistle on the street!
> The boys for lack of better sense,
> And Afric's sons because kind Providence
> Has gifted them with whistling-pipes complete[4]

An African's light heart is the one thing that keeps him up, amid all the discouraging facts of his situation, the chief discouragement being one for which he is not at all responsible — the unchristian prejudice of the Whites. I always feel like giving a Black man an extra warm "Good morning!" or a warmer shake of the hand than anybody else as a kind of acknowledgement and restitution on behalf of my nation![5]

Sell Me for Pay!

A Negro came to me once, to ask my advice about a debt for which he feared he should be sued at Court. After telling what I thought he had better do, I observed, "Ah, John! You were better off in Missouri!" (for he was a runaway slave). "You couldn't be sued for debt there!"

"Yes, but they's sue my master and *sell me* for pay! And that would be *wuss* yet!"[6]

A Nice Young Man!

A Black woman used to tell my wife about her escape to Canada. They had been very foolish in their attempt as they started in a large party of about twenty. The whole county nearly, was up in pursuit, and soon they heard the baying of the bloodhounds. It was now "each one for himself!" She, with a single companion, stood in a great swamp, all night, up to the waist in water. By and by, she got into the hands of the Quakers of Pennsylvania and in due time reached London, Ontario, where, by a singular good Providence, she found her mother who had escaped some years before. She had been married and her husband was one of the original party of twenty. Some of the other fugitives afterwards told her that he was overtaken and *torn to pieces by the dogs.* And she always ended her pathetic story by saying, with much feeling — *"He was such a nice young man!"*[7]

Misplaced Sympathy

I once saw a Black boy — "Jack Clark" — come into a store in Owen Sound, walking on the sides of his feet, in the most helpless, bandy-legged condition; he bought a stick or two of candy and wobbled out again and out of sight, in such a way as to enlist the sympathies of a farmer's wife, who looked after him, exclaiming, "the *poor boy!*" Yet it was all pretense; he had as good a pair of legs as any boy in town! His father laughed at his escapades. "Ha! ha!" he would say, "dat boy's too much for me!" And I am afraid his influence over him was not good for the boy turned out badly.[8]

Henry Clay

We had a Black neighbour near Woodbridge, who professed to have been a slave of Henry Clay's.[9] I never questioned Levi about it for I took it for one of their frequent lapses of memory.[10] A man may tell a certain thing so often, that he imagines at last it is true. We have all seen so many slaves born and reared on the estates of Washington, Jefferson and Clay, that we grow skeptical.

But Levi had certain anniversaries, and "days," he kept up. And on such occasions he would have his breast all decorated with strings of beads and ribbons and his *beaver hat* on! And why not? He had been a slave, and was now a free man and felt the exhilaration of "doing as he pleased!"

He, as well as all other Blacks I have met with, was very particular in putting "Mister" before the name of any man he spoke to, or spoke of with an especial care — so I thought — to put the "handle" to the name of every Black man. And again, why not?[11]

The One-Wheeled Velocipede

In 1868, a former (and exploded) "craze" about velocipedes was revived. This time it was the "evolution" of the "bicycle," but just then it was a wooden-wheeled velocipede, the four wheels turned with a crank by the feet.[12] During the winter the young fellows were all getting velocipedes ready, and wishing for Spring. On the first of April, 1869, two Negroes in Hamilton, as related in the papers, had a hand in the best April joke ever known in that city. Taking advantage of the "craze," some wags (who kept their own council well) inserted in the Hamilton papers an announcement that Professor so-and-so, from Buffalo would, on "Thursday Evening" (they took good care *not* to say 1st April) hold a meeting in a certain hall, to form a class for instruction on the velocipede and that on the same day, at twelve o'clock he would give an exhibition of a "one-wheeled velocipede" of his own invention, on King Street.[13]

At the ringing of the noon bell, all the men hurried from the factories, and the citizens were out in shoals and both sides of King Street were full of people. A very few minutes elapsed, and then, from a hotel yard on James Street, and round the corner, and down King Street, appeared a big Negro, fluttering with ribbons, with a *wheelbarrow* before him, and in the wheelbarrow a little Negro, likewise decked with ribbons, scraping Negro melodies on a fiddle! Hamilton has had many "ovations," but probably never such a cheer greeted Prince or Governor, as rose from the whole length of that street, to greet the *One-Wheeler Velocipede!*[14]

A Black Preacher

I have the following story of a Black preacher, from Reverend George Willett.[15] Some twenty years ago, an honest Black man from the South, who had been a preacher, came to Montreal. The Reverend John McKillican,[16] Sunday School missionary, got hold of him and advised him to go up the Ottawa Valley, and said to one of the steamboat captains, "Take this poor fellow along and set him down at some of the stopping-places, as he may wish! He is a *good man!*" So the captain set him down at Carrillon, or Point Fortune, and he found his way to Vankleek Hill, [Prescott County] where Mr. Willett preached.

Sam wanted to make a home for his daughter and himself (his daughter being pretty well-educated), but he scarcely knew what it was best for him to do. However, Mr. Willett introduced him to Mrs. Wells, the widow of the sheriff of the county, and she employed him as out-door servant and "man of all work."[17]

He said to Mr. Willett that he had "always been a preacher, and he would like to serve the Lord *now*. But he supposed the White folks wouldn't care to have a Black man preach to them." However, he wanted to do something: "Would they let him attend the fires in the church? He didn't want pay for it, but he wanted to do something!" So it was agreed that Sam should mind the fires and they never were so well attended to! The only fault ever found with his administration of the fire department was that on mild days he would have the stoves unconscionably hot and be sitting in the corner close by, in perfect enjoyment of the heat, while the rest of the congregation were likely to melt!

In the prayer meetings, the young people at first were amused at the oddity of some of his expressions, but they soon got accustomed to his ways, and learned to value the man for his honest fervor and originality. Finding no right opening for himself, and for his daughter (who had remained in Montreal), he determined, in spring, to go west to St. Catharines, where (he learned) was a large settlement of

Blacks. So Mr. Willett brought him down to Hawkesbury, on the Ottawa from whence he could cross over and get the cars.

Now Sam was not a handsome man! And the French-Canadian boys, who had scarcely ever seen a Black man, trotted along the sidewalks of the village, staring at Sam. "Sam," said Mr. Willett, "couldn't you *make* a face at those boys, and start them off?" And Sam turned his head a little, and showed his teeth and the whites of his eyes in such a way, and made a face so unspeakably frightful and hideous, that the boys all scampered off and left them! Mr. Willett parted from him with many expressions of interest and good will and heard from him afterwards that he and his daughter were in St. Catharines; and that he was regularly ministering to a little religious community of Blacks there.[18]

Sammy Barnes

My friend Sammy Barnes, of Owen Sound, sometimes preached. I dropped in at one of his services on Sunday afternoon. He was speaking of Christ's conversation with Nicodemus and remarked that many things Nicodemus heard that evening, "must have been a great *surprisation* to him!" which was undoubtedly the case.

Sammy had been a slave in Maryland, but from an overheard conversation, finding he was to be sold, to relieve a *chattel-mortgage* on himself, he escaped.[19]

Buxton

The Reverend William King, whom I once heard preach at Ayr, Ontario, had (through his wife) become the owner of a number of slaves. Resolving to set them free, they found they could only effectually do it by bringing them to Canada, which they did. And he settled down among them at Buxton, near Lake Erie, as a "friend, philosopher and guide" among them.

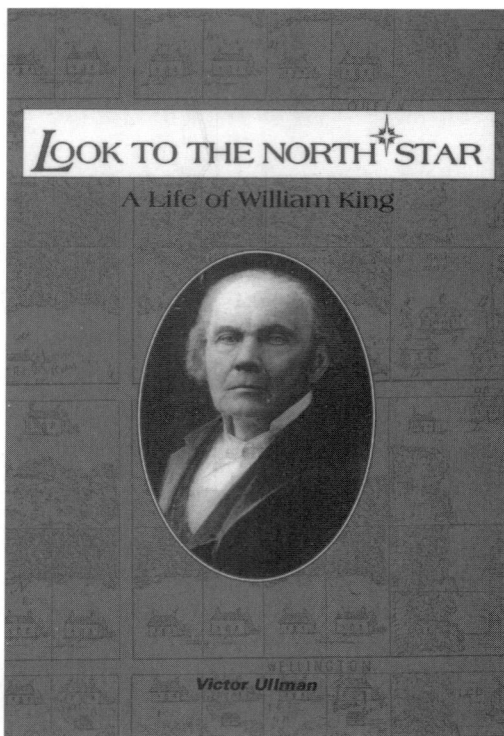

LOOK TO THE NORTH STAR

A Life of William King

Victor Ullman

Reverend William King left Louisiana with his fifteen slaves and arrived in Raleigh Township, Kent County, in 1849. They formed the nucleus of the community of Buxton, which fifteen years later had a population of about one thousand freed and fugitive slaves.

Photograph from *Look to the North Star* (1994) cover.

I remember sending him twenty copies of the "Sunday School Dial,"[20] when I was publishing it for distribution among his people: but I never had the opportunity of visiting Buxton — though I often thought about it. I hope the experiment of the settlement was, in fair measure, successful.[21]

John Wesley

Jack Clark, of Owen Sound, then a smart-looking coloured lad of fourteen, was employed for the day, on board the little twin-screw Steamer *Rescue*[22] on which the Prince of Wales took a sail out of Collingwood harbour in September 1860, when visiting that town. Jack was cabin boy. And, bringing in a pitcher of water for the Prince to wash his hands and face — for it was a hot dusty day — was addressed by the Prince.

"Well, my boy! And what's *your* name?"

"John Wesley Clark, Sir."

"John Wesley? And do you think you'll ever be as good a man as John Wesley?"[23]

"*I hope so, Sir.*"

A view of Collingwood Harbour in the early 1880s, showing the significance of the timber trade to the region's early development. From George Monro, *Picturesque Canada*, vol. III (1882).

The rascal! It was not but a few months afterward, that he and another coloured lad were convicted of rifling an old woman's bureau drawer of a few dollars in her absence, and Jack must go to the Reformatory at Penetanguishene.[24] The only way to get there was by steamer to Collingwood, rail to Barrie, and then on an acute angle from Barrie to "Penetang."

On the cars from Collingwood to Barrie, there were but a few in the car, and Jack was sitting by himself, with his hands free, but shackles on his feet. The Deputy-Sheriff (who told me the story), merely kept his eye on him from a distance. Soon an English gentleman, evidently a stranger in the country — noticing this bright-looking, well-dressed Black boy, came and sat down beside him. Jack winked at the Sheriff, to let him understand he was taking some fancy *role*. His feet he kept carefully under his seat! In answer to many friendly enquiries of the stranger, concerning his parentage, his education, and prospects, etc., Jack told him he was from Owen Sound, where his parents lived, that he had a fair education, and that now he was "going down, where some friends had *got a situation* for him!" The man was ever so much interested and Jack winked to the Sheriff whenever he got a safe chance, to let him know that "he was laying it on pretty thick!"

When they came to Allandale, however, where Jack had to change cars, he was so interested in looking out the window, that he forgot about his feet and as the fetters made a *clank*, the man looked down. The murder was out! His philanthropic friend slipped away, without even bidding him "good-bya," and Jack winked at the Sheriff harder than ever!

Ashamed of Him!

The Reverend Dr. [Ringgold] Ward, a Black preacher, of whom a number of friends have informed me — a man of considerable eloquence and power — was, many years ago — preaching at Kleinburg. My friend, John McCallum, was present. A drunk man, fresh from the village tavern, staggered up to the open door, and looked in to see who was preaching. Having satisfied his curiosity, he was moving off, making some contemptuous remark about a "nigger!"

Dr. Ward effectually extinguished him, by calling out, in his most stentorian tones, "What is the disturbance at the doah? Now, if that had been a *Black man*, I would have *been ashamed* of him!"[25]

Courtesy of Toronto Public Library, Special Collections, Genealogy and Maps Centre.

Samuel Ringgold Ward, a celebrated and eloquent Congregationalist minister, came to Canada and served as an agent for the Anti-Slavery Society, touring the province of Canada West and giving speeches on anti-slavery. This photograph was the frontispiece of his book, *Autobiography of a Fugitive Negro: His Anti-Slavery Labors in the United States, Canada and England* (1855).

Wouldn't Have Believed It!

A number of years ago, when at the International Sunday School Convention at Pittsburgh, Pennnsyalvania, I was pleased with the address, and the general hearing, of Bishop Arnett of the Colored Methodist Church of the South. The governor of the State of Pennsylvania, General Beaver,[26] had just given the convention a rousing and eloquent Address of Welcome and Bishop Arnett was to respond. He spoke about being himself born and reared in slavery and said, "If anybody, twenty years ago, had told me, that I should stand on such a platform — an honoured member of such a Convention as this — and that the governor of the great State of Pennsylvania would come all the way from Harrisburgh to welcome *me* ..." and then he seemed perfectly at a loss how to get the words to express himself, and finally added, with deep-toned emphasis, "Well, I *wouldn't have believed it!*"[27]

Mary Taylor

Mary Taylor was a "character" for many years in the early history of Owen Sound. Her husband, John Taylor, was a blacksmith, doing a small business for himself.[28] It has often been remarked, that among us, we very seldom see a Black man a mechanic. It is to some extent a mistake that the Blacks make, but much more largely a reprehensible prejudice on the part of the Whites. I do not know whether the Labor Unions exclude Blacks from membership — but I do know that I never see or hear of Black apprentices and Black journeymen working in any of the large "shops." I suppose they cease to seek such places, knowing they would be refused, but in very many of our villages and towns, a Black carpenter, or a Black mason, or a Black iron-worker, doing for himself, would find his fair share of custom. They should think of it, and aim more for it in such directions.[29]

Mary Taylor, known affectionately as "Granny," once kept a store in the vicinity of the Eighth Street Bridge over the Sydenham River. A very devout person, she worked hard to raise money for the first Black church, "Little Zion," a log shanty near the present Market Square. She was a familiar sight on the streets of Owen Sound for many years.

Courtesy of Grey Roots Archival Collection.

Well, John Taylor was a blacksmith. But John wasted a good deal of time, and something of money, over the delusive "glass o'grog" that has impoverished so many. And John would get in debt, and be sued in the Division Court. John Mills, the bailiff,[30] never could find anything to seize, to satisfy these small "judgements." So, rather than return the writ "no good," (the tools of his craft being exempt from seizure), he would go to Mary — nobody ever thought of calling her "Mrs. Taylor" and coax two or three, or four dollars out of her, for "poor John." She "never could see what possessed John to get into debt! *She* kept the house and what she had was her own! She'd help him this once, but she would never promise to help him any more!"

Mary could make good pies and was always on hand on great occasions, with a stand for fruit and refreshments. When the County Council met or when the Assizes were held at the Court House were great field-days for Mary. She had no children and was quite free to attend to "business." [She was s]carcely five-feet high, of great breadth of form and as "strong as a horse." The boys would sometimes "plague" her a little, but the "dudes" were afraid of her, and were generally on their good behaviour with her. Strange tales were told of her encounters with conceited young fellows, who were incautious enough to make too free use of their tongues, of how Mary would grasp them round the waist, and carry them despite all struggles, out of the building! She was just as efficient with the whitewash brush and the mop pail, as she was in defending herself against impertinence. Honest, alert, obliging with a poor neighbour, independent to the verge of rashness — "Mary Taylor" is a name and a character impressed on the memories of all old-time citizens of Owen Sound.[31]

The Story of a Cookstove

A young Negro, whose name I have forgotten, went about Owen Sound in the old days with the most wonderful head of hair. Men wore their hair longer then, but this man never trimmed his at all. Of course it became "frizzled" into a wonderful knot on the back of his head. He apparently took as much pains to "cultivate" this headdress of his, as those natives in the Upper White-Nile region, since discovered by Sir Samuel Baker,[32] who took several years, and an unconscionable number of cowrie-shells, to establish a proper *coiffure!* By and by, he had to wear his silk hat well-tipped over his eyes! John Edwards, another coloured man observed to me one day, "Why, that man never cuts his *har!*"[33]

The man had a "lot" and a shanty up near the bend of the Sydenham River. He had bought a cookstove of George Butchart,[34] and never paid for it, for the price of which, in due time, Butchart got a "judgement" of the Court. While a cookstove was exempt from general seizure for debt, it could be seized when the judgement was for the price of itself, and Bailiff Paul Dunn[35] wanted to seize "*that*" stove! But the house was always locked, and he must not "break into" a house! The debtor slept at home — living all alone.

So the Bailiff went one morning, (as he related the story to me) and softly stationed himself under the low eaves of the little log house, leaning a heavy cordwood stick against the door, just where it opened, and patiently waited. When at last the door opened, the firewood stick fell in, and prevented the man shutting the door. The bailiff got one leg in, and the two men struggled — the one to get in, the other to shut the door. However Dunn's English "wind" was better than that of the Black man, and the latter fell back panting against the rear wall.

"What do you want? Mr. Dunn."

"I want to seize that stove, on Butchart's suit."

"Oh, I thought yo wanted to eject me from this house and lot! I'd a let yo in, if I'd knowed it was the stove yo wanted!"

And so it ended peaceably, and when Dunn's son arrived with a horse and waggon at daylight — as pre-arranged — the Black man with the wonderful top knot helped them in with the stove![36]

African Dutifulness

At a Temperance meeting in Owen Sound,[37] at which I was present, and of which my friend Mr. William Bull was chairman, the Reverend Walter Inglis,[38] afterwards for many years a Presbyterian pastor at Ayr, Ontario, but then newly arrived in the country, made a few remarks. He had just come from South Africa where he had been associated with Livingstone[39] and Moffat, and was full of African experiences. Some young fellows in the back seats were rather demonstrative in their applause, and Mr. Inglis — despite polite disclaimers on the part of the chairman — took it as a discourtesy to himself and gave the young fellows a "talking to."

An artist's rendition of Inglis Falls, just south of Owen Sound. Peter Inglis, an enterprising Scottish millwright, purchased the land and a small existing mill. In 1862, a new, much grander four-storey gristmill was constructed that produced flour and feed for livestock. In 1945, after years of service, the mill was destroyed by fire. Today, the falls are part of the Inglis Falls Conservation Area, a destination for many tourists and local visitors. From *the Illustrated Historical Atlas of Grey County* (1880) 51.

"I have come from South Africa" he said, "where, even among the savages, age is honored by the young. I have seen a man of forty, stand and *take a whipping from his father!*" The young men, who had intended no insult, but had been amused at his quaintness of manner, and intonation of voice, were effectually silenced.[40]

When afterwards he lived at Kincardine — where I was once in his house — a man of that vicinity told me of Mr. Inglis relating some African stories at a tea meeting in a schoolhouse at Pine River. Anxious to have them understand what a lion's roar sounded like, he got down on all fours and put his mouth close to the floor, and *roared!* Such a shout of applause went up, that my informant said, with mock gravity, "We looked up to see whether *the roof* had not been lifted off!"

Chapter 10

LITERATURE IN THE BUSH

I t becomes an enticing piece of antiquarian research to go back sixty years, and take a survey of the literature of our country from 1837 down. At that time there was not a daily paper in this province. The first was in 1851, in Toronto. If anybody published a book — and there were a few — he paid the printer out of his own pocket and never got any considerable part of his outlay back. None of the weekly papers were less than three dollars a year — many four dollars. Payment in "advance" was thought unreasonable and half the subscriptions, probably, were never collected. You had to pay down your one (or two) "coppers" as you received your paper from the hands of the postmaster. I remember paying four coppers a week, for a couple of years, on a New York paper.[1]

The Ragged Followers of the Nine[2]

I have, piled on my desk before me at this moment, fourteen volumes of the earlier Canadian poets — as specimens of the poetry, and printing and binding of those days. The oldest I have is *Hamilton and Other Poems* by Rogers & Thompson, 1840. I knew Mr. Stephens well.[3] He told me that he visited most parts of Upper Canada, selling his book, and in this way, I suppose, managed to make it "pay." It is in 12 mo. of 180 pages, plainly bound in brown cloth. The paper is poor. Stephens had a knack of rhyming, and in later days was often in request at Owen Sound, in public gatherings, for "an Impromptu." This was generally forthcoming, and if the fame acquired thereby was not very lofty, the immediate applause was very prompt and hearty. Many years after he issued a larger volume and included "Hamilton" in it. I advised him to rewrite, remodel, and rename the poem — its descriptions and many of its allusions having become obsolete. But it was not remodelled. I have not found any older volumes of verse than Stephens, but I have not searched any large library to see.

The next, in point of date, is a small 16 mo. of 125 pages, of my own, printed by Hugh Scobie of Toronto in 1850 — imp cloth, "agate" type. It allowed a young fellow to get "into print" — I don't know that anything else was accomplished by it.[4]

About this time Alexander McLachlan had come to Canada, and, in 1856, he issued a decently printed (though on poor paper), but very shabbily bound edition of his "Poems." Two years after he issued his "Lyrics."[5] The first was a 12 mo. of 192 pages, cloth back, paper boards, and the publisher, and from whom personally I bought the book, was "John C. Geikie" — so printed on the title page — the now celebrated British author, Dr. Cunningham Geikie.[6] He was then keeping a Book & Stationary Store on 70 Yonge Street. McLachlan afterwards issued his fourth (and larger) volume, comprising all he cared to publish, up to that date. Some of his poems show wonderful strength, and if he had been critical enough to leave out the weaker poems, the volume would have been still better than it was.[7]

Next comes Charles Sangster, the most classical, the sweetest, the most polished, of our early bards. He polished too much — sacrificed strength to it, sometimes! The volume before me, *The St. Lawrence and the Saguenay*, is a well-printed, well-bound 12 mo. of 262 pages, published at Kingston (where he lived), and New York. It was printed at Auburn, New York. Another volume of Sangster's, from the press of John Lovell, Montreal, dated "1860," is *Hesperus, and Other Poems and Lyrics*, a 12 mo. of 186 pages. Mr. Sangster told me once, that he "intended henceforth, to publish only in the smallest possible editions; just to *register his claims.*" He had no doubt found disappointment and loss (in a money-sense) in publishing. He deserved a better appreciation than he has received.[8]

Sangster's friend (and mine) Evan MacColl, of Kingston, though he was known and admired in Scotland for a volume of Gaelic poems, and one in English (partly in Scotch-dialect), *The Mountain Minstrel*, did not publish a Canadian volume that I am aware of, till after the period to which I confine myself — 1860. He excels in rugged strength.[9]

Charles Heavysege, whom I remember meeting in Montreal — a short, sharp-looking middle-aged man, with a piercing eye — published anonymously a drama, *Saul*, in 1857 in Montreal, an 8 vol., 315 pages, cloth. Notwithstanding what seems to me a forbidding subject, the drama is said by competent critics — some of them British — to show great strength. Poor Heavysege! I imagine that things went hard with him to the last. When I saw him, he was a reporter for one of the papers — I think the *Witness*.[10]

I have a little 12 mo., cloth, of 124 pages, sent me by Thomas D'Arcy McGee, 1858, *Canadian Ballads and Occasional Verses*, printed and published by John Lovell, Montreal. McGee afterwards published a larger volume at New York. He was beginning to take a high place in literature, as already he was doing in statesmanship, when the tragic end came! Some of his poems are elevated in language, and strong, vigorous, and musical.[11]

Oscar, and Other Poems, by Carroll Ryan is a little 16 mo. paper boards, printed at Hamilton in 1857, the first poem having its scene and hero in the Crimean War. Mr. Ryan was one of the many young men, who write well and with facility, and then in more mature life hew their way through the world in plain prose and "business."[12]

An ambitious young fellow in Hamilton, Mr. John R. Ramsay, got out *The Canadian Lyre*, a 16 mo. of 128 pages in 1859. Afterwards, a second and a third volume. I notice one of his poems, "The Spinning Wheel," I had marked for quotation or recitation, more than thirty years ago.[13] He wrote irregularly, but his best pieces were fine!

There are others, whose volumes — once possessed — I cannot

now lay my hands on: Isidore G. Ascher of Montreal, a liberal-minded, sweet-voiced Hebrew, some of whose poems greatly took with Miss Jean Ingelow, whom he met in England.[14] And then there was John Fraser, poor fellow, drowned at Ottawa, whose *Tale of a Tub* was a well-drawn poem, touching on the burlesque.[15]

A volume, 12 mo. of 163 pages, from the press of John Lovell, Montreal, is before me, 1859, the author Augusta Baldwin [Baldwyn]. Very sweet — perhaps that is the one word to describe Miss Baldwin's book. But it is a pity the world will not buy — and pay for — sweetness![16]

"Harriet Arnie" — the name representing a lady of Hamilton — published *The Acacia*, a little collection of poems in 1860, 16 mo., cloth, 130 pages, at Hamilton. As sometimes thus found, there are several martial and patriotic pieces in the tasty little volume, in equally tasty verse.[17]

Callow Authors

I have elsewhere spoken, in connection with Galt, of the first paper there, *The Dumfries Courier*,[18] which must have been started early in the year 1844. In the autumn of that year, a "poem," painfully elaborated and dreadfully sentimental, was secretly copied out, and mailed (postage 4–1/2d) by me to that paper, and in due time appeared. I don't know whether my parents saw it, I cannot remember that they did. My only confidant was Joseph Caldwell Brown, about my own age. He too was fame-struck, only he affected the heroic in prose. He had a "story" of the Ages of Chivalry, in the *Brantford Courier*,[19] which ran through four weeks' issues. He told me "he got dreadfully sick of it" before he got through. The fact was, as he told me, he had introduced so many characters, that he did not know at last what to do with them, and determined that the story should not run beyond four weeks, he made his hero tumble off his horse and break his neck, and by some such summary process or other got rid of the others and wound up the story.

"That story wasn't quite as good, Brown, at the end, as it was at the beginning!" said Mr. Lemon, of the *Courier*.

"No," said Brown, demurely.[20]

I have been an editor myself since and have learned that it is always safest to have the whole of a "story" in hand, before inserting the first part of it!

We all meet with unappreciated poets. On one occasion, when acting as editorial writer on a country paper, the read editor (to get rid of him), sent a disappointed poet to me. His effusion, I had recommended to be thrown aside, and now he wanted to convince me it "was good." He pulled off his cowhide long boots, and "spouted" his piece in his stocking feet. He did not want, in the energy of his declamation, to make stamping that would be heard in other parts of the building. I had all the elocution to myself, but remained hard-hearted and unconvinced.[21]

A Woodbridge Poet

The late Robert King, of Vaughan, said once to me. "Man! If I had had an *eedication*, the poetry would hae rolled oot o'my mooth in a perfect stream!" The only specimen with which he ever favoured me, however, was once when he crossed the street in Woodbridge, with his finger uplifted for emphasis, and began — at the distance of ten feet — to repeat an elegy on his then lately deceased old friend, John Elliott:

> Honest John is gone at last;
> And all his toils and troubles past!
> He has not left his like in Vaughan —
> An honest, sterling, upright man![22]

"Now, what do you think of *that?*" exclaimed the unappreciated poet.

A Hornbook

About 1840, I made my youngest brother a veritable "Hornbook"[23] — made from a sound pine shingle, cut to proper shape, with a "handle" at the bottom, and on it the alphabet, in large and small letters. I remember I made one mistake in making the "printing letters" with the pen. I made the small-letters "p" open at the bottom, like an "h." The alphabet was pasted on the shingle, and the little boy marched off to a kind of "hedge school," kept by Mr. Hoag, in Dumfries Township.[24]

When I taught at the village school in St. George, in 1846, I took two of the "A.B.C. — darians," and taught them to read, without teaching the alphabet. Began the first day to teach them to remember the looks of certain words of two letters. I am told that (this) plan is often tried now, but it was a new thing then. One of the two was Mr. John Batchelor, lately of Brantford.

In those days we had a Spelling book by Alex Davidson of Niagara. One chapter gave words of the same sound but different spelling, and he had grouped together: "weather" and "whether," "weal" and "wheel," "*were*" and *where*. Cockney, but scarcely "English."[25]

A Fiery Young Highlander

The *British Colonist* newspaper, was founded by Hugh Scobie, in 1839 or '40. In 1850, I had a small volume, *Alazon and Other Poems*, printed at that office, and, not at all unnaturally, Mr. Scobie applied to me near the New Year, 1851, to "write them a New Year's Address for the Paper."[26] And he did the same for 1852, giving me on both occasions a little synopsis of public events, as suggestions for me. The late W.W. Copp,[27] Publisher, was then a young man behind the counter in Mr. Scobie's bookstore, which occupied one of the numbers now comprised in the establishment of W.A. Murray & Co. on King Street [Toronto]. That was my first acquaintance with Mr. Copp. Very many years after — indeed only a year or two before he died, he said to me one day, "Do you know whom we had write our *New Year's Addresses* for the *Colonist*, before you came on the field," I professed my total ignorance of that part of ancient history.

"Senator Macdonald!" he said.

"When I looked my surprise — for I had only known the Senator as a staid solid, middle-aged man, full of business — "Oh," he said, "I tell you, he was a fiery young Highlander in those days! A number of young men of us formed a Literary Society, and he was our first president. You ought to have heard his inaugural address from the chair. It was a flowery and impassioned affair!"[28]

William Lyon Mackenzie

I never met William Lyon Mackenzie, nor am I sure that I ever read any copies of his *Advocate*, that had so much to do in stirring up the Rebellion of 1837. In after years, when he was back again, and

Courtesy of Archival and Special Collections, McLaughlin Library, University of Guelph.

LESSLIE & SONS' STORES,

Lesslie & Sons' Stores. This shop was established in York in 1822, on the north side of King Street near the corner of Frederick. One of the earliest brick buildings in York when erected, it was one of the most fashionable stores in town. From J. Ross Robertson, *Landmarks of Toronto* (1894) 236.

195

took the better and more effectual path of constitutional agitation, I sometimes saw "Mackenzie's Message." It was one of the "Curiosities of English Literature." When he wanted to be away for a week or two, on the political "stump" helping some friend toward his election, he would let the paper rest till he came back! His subscribers got a year's issues, but they did not get fifty-two numbers.[29]

Taking tea one evening, about ten years ago, with the late James Lesslie, our conversation turned on Mackenzie, and said Mr. Lesslie, "Mackenzie was bookkeeper in my father's establishment in Dundee, before ever we came to this country. He was a man of upright principles — a sincere and conscientious man. *But he was never made for a leader.* He was no leader of men!"[30]

Localize Your Stories!

Mr. Peter Jaffray was the founder and conductor of the *Galt Reporter.* This would be in the year 1845.[31] He had a number of sons — all printers — and all pushing young men who have made the family name well-known in the field of journalism, all over North America. I used to give him a poem, once in a while — sometimes a prose sketch and my brother, John Anderson Smith, still more frequently, a humorous "story." His advice to us was always — "*Localize your Stories!* Put real names and places in! People are ever so much more interested, when they see the names of persons and places they know! *Localize* them!"

My brother has no doubt been indebted to a considerable amount of the popularity of his stories, to his following Mr. Jaffray's advice. Prof. Vallance told me he had read "Jimmy Butler and the Owl" all over Ireland, and "Bill and the Widow," and "Courting in Smoky Hollow," "Jerry Jones," and "Ike Sickle's Quilting-Bee" are cropping up all the while over the country as humorous "Readings" at entertainments. Mr. Isaac Sickle, of St. George, the hero of the "Quilting-Bee," a staid bachelor of fifty or sixty when he first read the "story," exclaimed, "That's all a *get-up, I could have married that girl if I had wanted her!*"[32]

Returned Manuscripts

Nothing seems more enticing to a young writer than to "write *something*," and send it to a periodical, and nothing is more depressing to the young spirit than to have it politely returned — with a printed circular note, saying in roundabout language that they don't want it! And sometimes when they do accept a contribution, they will keep the young aspirant for literary success waiting for many months, before it appears. If it were immediately printed, the gratified author would "write again"; whereas, here they keep him back and thus, very effectually, keep down the flood of manuscripts!

In counselling a lady, a few years ago, I gave her this advice. The papers and magazines are overwhelmed with articles offered. There are only two doors standing invitingly open, just now — for anything *humorous* or *for the children*. These two departments offer by far the best — and almost the only — openings at present!"

John Dougall

There never was a more sterling man than John Dougall, founder of the Montreal *Witness*. The *Witness* was founded (I think) in 1840.[33] I remember reading his first announcement. The daily edition was begun, as experiment for the summer, during the visit of the Prince of Wales to Canada in 1860, and the venture promising well, it was continued.

In June 1869, I was in Montreal for a week, attending a Congregational Union. Mr. Dougall, who was himself a staunch "Independent," came to me, and said, "I want you to take hold of the *Witness* for three weeks! I want to go off to the White Mountains, and get the fresh air!" And then he described what my duties would be, and said, "I won't ask you to do it for nothing!" mentioning a weekly sum as *honorarium*. And then he added these weighty words, as indicating his foundation principle and that of his paper: "We don't profess to take a side in politics, though we are generally found on the side of Reform; but if a public question comes up that has a *right* side and a *wrong* side to it, we take what we believe to be the right side — *let the consequences be what they may!*"

I was engaged to preach at a new place the next Sunday — and indeed moved there in a few weeks — and did not remain in Montreal, but I often thought of his utterance, "Let the consequences be what they may!" Mr. F.E. Grafton, who was his "right-hand man" in the business office for many years at first, told me that many a time Mr. Dougall could have had his own figure for "booming" races, and theatres and the like, but would never touch them.[34]

Afterwards, when he went to New York, to establish a one-cent paper that should be clean and godly in its "news" and its advertisements, and spent $120,000 in the attempt, (my figures are reliable), and when the "reptile press" of the city would, in their references to "John Dougall's paper," end their paragraphs with a satanic *Let Us Pray!*, he was still endeavoring to carry out the same principle. The *Daily* could not be maintained, but the *Weekly* is still a power for good in that land.[35]

A Sunken Star

Mr. John Lovell, of Montreal, helped many a poor fellow into public notice, and did more patriotic work for Canada than ever Canada rewarded him for![36] He told me once of one of his *proteges*.

He had published a little volume of poems for a bright but unsteady young fellow, whose name I withhold, and the book was not likely to pay for itself, and when the young man came to Mr. Lovell and said to him, "I am going to Upper Canada, and if you will let me take 150 copies of my book with me, I think I can sell them up there, and it will be so much toward reimbursing you" — the publisher was pleased and handed the books over.

Six months afterwards, a shabby-looking young man, without a shirt collar, and with a general flavour of decay about him, came into Lovell's office. [Lovell] did not know him and he had to introduce himself. It was the same young man. He had been to Upper Canada, had existed on the proceeds of the books he had with him [and] made one prolonged "spree" of six months, and was now in the mire! A sunken star!

The "Mouse on the Arm"

In 1884, the *Globe*, Toronto, offered some prizes for "Stories" for its Christmas issue. I sent one — "The Mouse on the Arm" — and had a "third prize" of $25.00 awarded me. The story was of a boy, who had become separated from his parents, and was working in Guelph, while the parents — knowing nothing of him — had settled half way to Owen Sound. Then the Guelph Brass Band made a grand excursion (the real date was 1851) to Owen Sound, delighting the

THE OLD GLOBE OFFICE

The "Old *Globe* Office" was located at the corner of Jordan and King streets. The site had been used by the Commercial Bank, and afterwards, by a Mr. Dallas, who operated a woodenware business before selling the building to George Brown in 1850. The *Globe* occupied the west side of the building, the offices in front, and the press room attached to the rear of the building. From J. Ross Robertson, *Landmarks of Toronto* (1894) 217.

settlers, at every crossroad, with their playing. This boy played a trombone, and at one spot the mother was among the listeners. Something touched her mother instinct, and she pined and fretted, till at last she went down to Guelph, and discovered her boy by the birthmark of a *mouse* on his arm.

This might not have been worth mentioning, but for what follows. I was preaching that winter at Alton, near Orangeville. When it came out, a woman told Mr. James McClellan,[37] in whose house I was lodging, that "she knew *that boy*, and his folks! She used to live in Guelph!" And, a few days after, a middle-aged man said to him, "I used to live in Guelph. I was a carpenter and belonged to the Band. I remember very well, going to Owen Sound, and I knew all about that story!"

The excursion to Owen Sound — and the charming of the longing ears of the settlers in the bush on the way — was all true; is it not in the early history of Owen Sound? But the boy (though he sometimes seems *very real* to me now) was but one of my "dream-children." But here were two respectable persons, in *one township*, who "knew *that boy!*" How many more might there not be, elsewhere? And I begin to think — as others, and wiser, have thought before — that people can remember things that never happened! And perhaps, after all, these "happenings" of the imagination give us more real enjoyment than most of the sober facts, among which we carefully pick our daily steps!

A Backward Place!

In 1873 and '74 I wrote a serial in the *New Dominion Monthly*, Montreal, called "John Kanack's Experiences."[38] It might be called the predecessor of these "Reminiscences," for most of the incidents were real, but made to fit into the "story." Two clerical friends — one of them the Reverend Dr. Dickson,[39] now of Galt — were taking an extended holiday in Cape Breton Island, in the farthest and most out-of-the-world corner of it, opposite desolate Anticosti and

Labrador, and were reading some of my backwoods sketches to the good woman with whom they lodged, and where they brought home their sea-trout to fry. The only remark she made, was pity for the benightedness of the writer of the chapters.

"Why," she exclaimed, "what a *backward place* it must have been, where that man was brought up!"

Let the present inhabitants of St. George, in Brant (as the old Scotchman said), "Put that in their pipe, and smoke it!"

Clear Grit

As connected with Literature, I have sometimes been interested in tracing the "whereabouts" of old printing presses and "imposing-stones." In 1850 or '51, William McDougall, up to that time connected with the *Globe*, started the *North American* newspaper.[40] It was devoted to "Retrenchment" in government expenditure, and largely (though not exclusively) supported by those who had always been considered as of the "Reform" party. George Brown of the *Globe* called them "*Clear Grit*." The *North American* did not last long, and the "Cave of Adullam" was broken up, but the name "Clear Grit" — afterwards docked off to "Grit" grew up as a title for the entire Reform Party, of which George Brown was at that time the head — an example of things "coming home to roost."[41]

The "Washington" hand press on which the *North American* was run off — 1,500 to 2,000 impressions a day, and by one man with aching bones! — was, in my time, doing duty for a weekly paper in Owen Sound. In the same town, I ran the *Times* as a Reform journal for a couple of years and we had the hand press in the office on which *The Church* newspaper had been printed in Toronto long before. I remember picking up *The Church* in the St. George Post Office, about the time Lount and Matthews were executed for treason; the *Examiner* (James Lesslie, proprietor) had been in *mourning* the week of the execution, and *The Church* was raving over the matter: "If," said the *Church* editorial, "parents wish their children to grow up

EXECUTION OF LOUNT AND MATTHEWS.

From J. Ross Robertson, *Landmarks of Toronto* (1894).

Courtesy of Archival and Special Collections, McLaughlin Library, University of Guelph.

rebels and infidels, let them read the *Examiner!*"[42] When we worked that old *press* in more peaceful times, in Owen Sound, it seemed to me, sometimes, as if I could almost hear it protesting against the use it had come to!

Messrs. Dudley and Burns, Toronto,[43] have the old "imposing-stone" used by William Lyon Mackenzie, in his last newspaper enterprise, and I do not doubt that antiquarians will, from time to time, find many such old and long-enduring links with former days in printing offices.

In The Division Court

Mr. Hutton, of England, published many years ago, a very entertaining book, called *The Court of Requests*, giving reminiscences of cases that had come before him as a magistrate.[44] In like manner I could give quite a number of interesting cases in the Division Court at Owen Sound before Judge Wilkes,[45] in which I acted as Clerk of the Court and kept the records.

A very curious thing, and which I never saw mentioned by anyone, came under my notice in connection with my duties as Clerk of the Court: more accounts and notes came in for suit on *Mon-*

Judge Frederick T. Wilkes of Owen Sound. From *The Illustrated Historical Atlas of Grey County* (1880).

day, than on any other day — a decidedly greater number; and as, in Owen Sound, we had 1,200, 1,600 and once 3,000 suits annually, I had a better chance to avoid mistakes in this matter, than if an average of one suit came in per day, and often two on Mondays. Here it would be an average of four or five per day, and perhaps seven to ten on Monday, or one year, ten per day, and fifteen or twenty on Monday. John Crow had been cogitating all *Sunday*, about "that feller that owed him," and determined to "put him through, tomorrow!"

A Deep Scheme

John Lee kept a watchmaker's establishment on Poulett Street, Owen Sound. Two bachelor brothers, named Doherty, lived twenty miles away, on a farm in St. Vincent Township — "William" and "John."[46] One of them — nobody knew which — brought a silver watch to Lee to be "cleaned." It was taken in the name of "William

Doherty" and properly booked. A couple of months after — Mr. Lee not happening to be at home — one of the brothers got the watch from Mrs. Lee, and paid the $2 demanded for cleaning and "fixing" it. So far, "all right."

Two months more, and one of the brothers called on Lee for "that watch." He looked at his book. "Why, you have got it," he said. "No." So he called his wife. She could not identify the man, but as far as she could remember, this man had got the watch, and paid her the two dollars.

"No, I never got the watch. You have given it to somebody else. And I cannot afford to lose my watch!" After a time, a suit was threatened, unless Lee paid $18, the assumed value of the watch. He found there were two of them and found something of their character, and determined to fight it out in the small debt court.

The case came on, a suit for $18 damages. Lee did not bring his wife, as she could not positively identify the man who got the watch. So, under the circumstances, the judge had all the parties sworn. Their role was simple: "William" had taken his watch to Lee, and neither of them had ever seen it again. Lee admitted having received the watch and could not *prove* that he had delivered it to either of the brothers. Some evidence was given as to the value of the watch.

"Well," said the Judge, in a familiar way, "it seems to me that the only thing now to consider, is the *value* of the watch. I think fourteen dollars would be about the right amount." And he was just going to say "Judgement for Plaintiff, fourteen dollars. Fifteen days. Next case!" And I dipped my pen, to second it on the "Procedure Book," when one of the Doherty's said expostulatingly — "*Yes, but there's the Two Dollars we paid!*"

"What is that you said?" demanded the judge. "Repeat that again, please!" But the man was dumb, and red up to the roots of his hair! He had blurted out the truth, inadvertently and the "case" was spoiled!

"If," said the Judge very impressively, with uplifted hand, "*If you paid the two dollars, you got the watch!* I am sorry I have no power, in this Court, to send you to Kingston for your perjury.[47] Judgement for Defendant! Two dollars for defended hearing! Mr. Lee, what witnesses have you, to be paid?" A shout went up, in the Court, which Paul Dunn, the Bailiff, to save appearances checked — *after a few seconds* — with "Order in the Court, please!"

Stop the Execution!

In the Division Court, at St. George, where I served as "Clerk of the Court" a couple of years, a quantity of ready-made clothing had been seized for debt. The bailiff had sold one or two garments — I acting as clerk and cashier — when a man was seen galloping up the gravel road from the east, crying "Stop the Execution!" It was the debtor, a storekeeper at Harrisburgh, who "had made a raise," and was now prepared to pay judgement and costs in a good-humored way, "Wasn't it just like a novel! My coming up, in the very nick of time to *stop the executing*."[48]

At The Library

When teaching school on "Maus's Plains," three or four miles north of Paris, Ontario, in the summer of 1849, I went, every fourth Saturday, on foot to Galt — nine or ten miles — to exchange books at the Circulating Library there. A book one carries ten miles under one's arm, is apt to be valued sufficiently to be carefully read, and I read some good and useful books that year, in the domain of history and *belles lettres*.[49]

In the Township of Euphrasia, one of the newer townships of the County of Grey, I found, as long since as the year 1865, a good Public Library, established by township funds. It was divided into five sections — one for each "Ward," which were interchanged every year. In 1864, an average of three hundred books were taken out every month. A good example for richer townships.

In the town of Newmarket, where I lived for twelve years, there was, and is, a respectable library, belonging to the Mechanics

Institute. Once, in conversation with the intelligent custodian of the library, Mr. Lyman Jackson, I mentioned the "Mitchell Library" of Glasgow, where (as then recently given by the Scotch papers) out of 35,000 volumes taken out within a certain period, only 7,000 were fiction — one-fifth of the whole — and in each of the two classes of (a) Travels and Adventure and (b) Theology, and Philosophy, *more* than in the class of fiction were asked for.[50]

Said he, "We are not in Scotland here! With us, there are perhaps *eight* works of fiction taken out to *one* of all the other classes put together!"[51]

And as the Newmarket Library was only open for exchange of books for certain hours on two days of the week, I had the opportunity of observing a stream of young ladies coming in to exchange their novels, and *one* appeared to be reading them through in course, according to their catalogue numbers![52]

Growth of Words

I remember reading in an old descriptive geography my father had — title page gone, but issued about 1800 — about the United States: "After the war, the rancor of a few led them to propose the adoption of a new language, and a wit recommended the Hebrew. The English, however, has continued to be used; though with a tendency toward the introduction of new words, which will probably result in the formation of a distinct "language."

We are all pleased to testify that this tendency has *not* resulted in the formation of a new language, thanks to such publications as Webster's — and more recently of the "Century" and "Standard" dictionaries, and the ever-increasing interchange of periodical and other literature between Britain and America. But new *words* are continually springing up. A word is first slang, then colloquial, then local, then used generally and admitted into good society among established words. Some remain colloquial, as "shove," a verb meaning to push; it was used by Pope,[53] early in the eighteenth century and everyone uses it occasionally in colloquial speech, but no one uses it in polite composition.

Some words seem inventions, as "hoodlum," first used in San Francisco. "Boycott" was a Captain Boycott in Ireland, who could not get a single Irish peasant to work for him; and had to get British soldiers from Dublin to come and harvest his grain.[54] "Boss," and probably "boodle," are from the Dutch, both useful words and will, by-and-by, be considered proper words. I remember a poor Italian, for whom I got an Italian New Testament. I found him reading in *Luke* — he had begun at the beginning — and to show me he understood what he was reading, he turned a verse or two of the "Parable of The Supper" into English, and where we have "And the master of the house, being angry" etc., he had it, "And the *boss* was *mad* etc.[55]

I can remember, when living as a boy in New York, (before 1837) the "busses" were all "stages." "Omnibusses," a polite form of "Carryall," were common in London, England, but the name had not got over to America and had not been curtailed to "bus." Now, wherever the English language is spoken, it is "bus."

And there is a new tendency to simplify a class of words, as "sleeper" for sleeping-car, "mailer" for mailing-machine, and the like — a very good tendency, indeed. The farmers say "thresher" for threshing-machine — which everybody called it fifty years ago.

In the "Eastern Townships" of Lower Canada, the New England stock there used a number of archaic and peculiar words. They spoke of a "scar-bauk," a word not generally used, according to my knowledge, though allied to the Scotch "scour." They would say "footings" for stockings, and "team" for a single horse geared, "sugary" for a sugar bush, and the high-sounding "traverse-sleigh" for our colloquial *bob-sleigh*.

A good many years ago, William Cullen Bryant,[56] then and for many years before, the managing editor of the New York "*Post,*" stuck up in his office a list of new, unauthorized and slang words, which were not to be printed in the *Evening Post*, and reporters were commanded and correspondents expected, not to use them. I cannot reproduce the list from memory, but half the words are now acknowledged as proper and well-authenticated and used everywhere!

When a lad, I read an article, in which the writer exclaimed against a "brood of bastard words that had crept into the language," and blamed the British House of Commons for many of them. I remember that "inimical" was one of them.[57] But it seemed to me then, as it does now, that the chief fault in the eyes of this survival of the last century was that these had "grown" during the existing century!

Chapter 11

BACKWOODS EXPERIENCES

In this concluding chapter of my "Reminiscences," I pretend to very little of order in the way of arrangement. The materials will be "unconformable strata," resting on the others, without much character of their own. It will be something like the Monday dinners at an economical boarding-house — whatever was "left over from Sunday!" And with respect to this chapter, to tell beforehand what is going to be in it, would be as difficult a task as the Highland cook had, to make Prince Albert understand what was in a Scotch *haggis!* There was oatmeal intil't, and suet intil't, and chopped liver intil't and onions intil't — "Oh yes," said the Prince, "I think I know it all now, except *one ingredient:* what is intil't?" So, instead of describing our haggis, and trying to tell "what is intil't, we will make it and serve it up!

How Things Grow

I once got an illustration of how exaggerations, in books or elsewhere, come. When a young man I called in for a chat with Mr. Peter Jaffray, the editor and founder of the Galt *Reporter.*[1]

"Well, what is going on at St. George?"

"Oh, nothing!"

"Oh yes! There must be something! Give us an item of news or gossip, of some kind!"

So I happened to think that Pat Chambers, a few days before, had set a steel trap for a fox and a large bald eagle had been caught by the leg in it, and when Chambers came out next morning to look at his trap, the eagle in his desperation broke the small chain that fastened it, and was making off heavily through the air, with trap, chain, and all when the farmer brought it down with his rifle. It was a large specimen and measured from tip to tip of its wings, 6 feet, 9 inches. In the next *Reporter* the item appeared, but the editor had forgotten the measurement and had it "9 feet." And Charles Durand quoted it in a literary pamphlet he was conducting in Toronto and it may be in some work on Natural History by this time![2]

Dom Pedro

Dom Pedro, Emperor of Brazil, paid a flying visit to Canada in 1876.[3] Going down to Montreal on the steamer *Spartan*,[4] I was told at Kingston that the Emperor and suite had come on board and that we should have his company to Montreal.

He was rather a large figure of a man, apparently fifty, with a full grey beard, his teeth much gone, and with rather a piping voice for so large a man. He affected no dignity nor exclusiveness, and let it be understood that he desired to be addressed only as "Sir." He spoke English well, yet with a kind of "staccato" separateness in the words, and without proper emphasis. He took a great many "notes," and asked many questions, and occasionally ran into the cabin to bring out the Empress to look at some of the rapids — for she was somewhat of an invalid. One man interested him very much by telling him the story of the "Windmill," near Prescott.[5] At last the Emperor asked him the date of the affair "In 1838," said the man. "Oh, that is an old story!" said the disgusted Emperor, as he turned away.

Mr. Robertson, from the Welland Canal, formerly of Lanark, Ontario, was much in conversation with him, and gave him many lumbering adventures in the backwoods, and down the St. Lawrence, including a *wreck* on Lake St. Peter on their raft in a great storm. When

"A View of the Battle of Windmill Point, November 13, 1838." From Charles Lindsey, *Life and Times of William Lyon Mackenzie* (1862) 192.

nearing Montreal, I said to Mr. Robertson, "You have interested the Emperor much to-day. He has been very friendly with you!"

"Yes, he has been very condescending, indeed!"

"You will shake hands with him before he leaves the boat?"

"Well, I would like to, but I don't know! He might think it too familiar on my part, if I offered him my hand!"

"I'll tell you! Just bid him good-bye, with a polite wave of the hand, and most likely he'll *offer you his hand!*"

"I will!"

And I thought, "I'll be near you!" He did, just as suggested, in his homely, but warmest Scotch, and the Emperor shook his hand, warmly bidding him "Good-bye!" Two of us, standing beside Mr. Robertson, raised our hats, and the Emperor also shook hands with us, with a friendly "Good bye, sir!" Then, to avoid a general handshaking, he turned away and busied himself giving orders about the baggage.

"Yarbs"

We have not the skill, (not having the necessity to acquire it), that the first settlers in Canada had, in knowing the virtues and qualities of everything that grew in the woods. The old lady who preceded us on the first farm my father had in Canada, regretted leaving it — more than for anything else — on account of the *"yarbs"* in the garden![6]

There was a little tree grew on the oak "plains," the settlers "Tea-tree," for they sometimes infused its leaves, as a substitute for the Chinese article. Tea was for long a dollar a pound and the settlers had not always the "dollar!" The "plains" were particularly rich in botanical treasures.

Lobelia,[7] and I know not how many more medicinal herbs, grew on our old homestead in Dumfries — wild. And as for dye-stuffs — and it is good that wool, being an animal product, is so easily dyed — almost every tree that grew gave something for the dye pot. Butternut bark for brown, oak bark for a "tan" colour, elm and beech bark for shades of drab, soft maple, with iron-rust, or copperas, for black, the goldenrod for yellow and blood-root for staining red.

Sassafras was much valued.[8] Many people drank it in the Spring, for days and weeks, instead of tea, as being "good for the blood."[9] I once met a farmer, with a very large and long root of sassafras on his shoulder, taking it home for "spice." He said they washed it, and laid it up to dry, and after it was thoroughly dry, they ground the bark in a spice mill, and used it for seasoning in fruit and pastry. Sassafras — "sassifrax" all the settlers call it — has a good deal of romance about it. It likes to grow among rocks, and the old superstition was, that it would *split* rocks! For what good purpose I know not except perhaps to open up concealed mineral treasures. Sir Walter Raleigh spelled it "SARSEPHRAZE."[10]

Sarsaparilla[11] is found also in many places. And on stormy ground sometimes occurs the low bushes of the "moose-wood," (the "leatherwood" of the Upper Canadians, and the "wickopy" of the "Eastern Townships" and New England). The bark is as strong as twine, and I have seen economical millers — troubled with farmers asking for bag-strings — have a bundle of *wickopy* hung up in the mill to answer for "strings." And I have seen, on some few occasions, useful ropes made of twisted basswood bark. If we had to go back to a life in the Bush, we would become more skilful in these matters!

What a Small Hand!

Sitting in the comfortable mansion of my friend Mr. McRoberts, in Toronto, we were speaking of old times. When young, he lived in Troy, Beverley Township [in north Wentworth County] and on one occasion, got me to come down the five miles from St. George to assist at a Temperance Meeting.[12] Mr. McRoberts also made a short address himself and I could not understand the attack the chairman of the meeting made on him — spoke of his "impudence" etc. I mentioned it and my friend said, "Oh, they were a cranky family, anyway!" And then told me of one of the sons of that faraway *Chairman*.

It was years after, when McRoberts had become a magistrate, that the young man, whose name we shall call Tenderfoot, was brought up before him on a charge of theft. The evidence seemed conclusive enough and the only thing the magistrate could do, was to commit the man for trial to the Hamilton gaol. But he could not go that night, and there was no "lock-up" in that primitive village — the constable must take care of his prisoner as best he could! He took him home to his little log house and let him lie down on a bed, with handcuffs on, and lay down in front of him. The constable had no evil conscience to keep him awake, and soon was profoundly sleeping.

Every country constable carries a pair of handcuffs in his pocket. But as he generally has but one pair — and as they are used for all sorts and conditions of man — he has them of a medium size — large, rather than small. I remember my father making me laugh, when he told me of trying on a pair his next-door neighbour, Albert Huson, had, and how he slipped them off! Mr. Huson said, "I never saw anybody able to do that before!"[13] Well, Tenderfoot had been diligently working, and had got his hands slipped through the handcuffs, and was silently and cautiously working the window open, close to the bed. His boot gave a little clank as he slipped through the window. The constable sprang, just to see his foot disappearing in the darkness. He, too, sprang through the window, and the two men were dodging round Beverley pine stumps for quite a "while." But the prisoner, having a dark night to favour him, got to the woods and disappeared from the neighbourhood.

Twenty years afterwards, Mr. McRoberts came plumb face-to-face with him at the corner of a street in Toronto. Tenderfoot was so surprised, that he did not seem to know what to do. McRoberts frankly held out his hand, and grasped Tenderfoot's. As he held the man's right hand, he gave it a smooth down with his own left hand, saying "What a very *small hand* you have, Tenderfoot!" The fellow saying nothing, only looking a little scared, McRoberts added, in an friendly and impressive tone, "Tenderfoot, if you *behave yourself* nobody will trouble you!"[14]

A Beverley Choir [15]

Beverley was no more backward than other townships though the Dumfries people tried to think their neighbours in the next township were to be pitied — with their pine stumps and their rocky land. And I suppose there were just as rustic choirs elsewhere, as the one I now speak of. At a picnic in Beverley that I was at, there was a choir of six or eight voices. The choir was asked to "sing the grace" that was given out by the chairman. "Be present at our table, Lord," etc.

To my amazement — the chairman who was not much of a singer, and to the dismay of everybody who *was* — instead of striking up "Old Hundred," as they were expecting to do, struck up the good old-fashioned, common metre, repeating tune, "Ortonville!" Having settled on the tune, the words must be made to *fit*, which they accomplished by snapping off two syllables from the ends of the second and fourth lines![16]

Order-r!

Another backwoods chairman, near Owen Sound, was very nervous over "his responsibility" in the chair, and was commanding, "Order-r in that corner-r!" — putting the strongest Scotch Border accent on the *r's*. Now, in "that corner-r," were six young men of us, who after a ride of seven miles on a cold night, had come in a little late, bought our tickets, and were vainly endeavoring to get a sufficiency of tea and cakes.

At last the chairman effectually completed matters, by pronouncing, "If they'll no keep order-r, they'll just *hae to be put oot!*"

I once saw a chairman at St. George (this time it was an outdoor tea), on some breakdown of the arrangements, leave the "chair," while some long-winded speaker was amusing the wood echoes, and himself kindle the fire and get the kettles boiling for the tea!

Salt

With salt so cheap as to be used on land as a fertilizer, our children will forget how valuable and — important a thing it used to be. It all formerly came from about Syracuse, in New York State, and came in barrels of various weights. There (as now) 280 lbs. were considered a "barrel," and any excess or lack was accounted for. Every teamster going west or north, could always get a few barrels of salt for return lading. Very little Liverpool salt (that from sea water), found its way to the central and western parts of Upper Canada. And there was always the apprehension that if war should break out, we might be cut off from our supplies of salt.

In the War of 1812, salt was made at St. Catharines, from the saline spring there, but it was full of mineral "salts" of different kinds. And the discovery of salt at Goderich, about forty years ago, was due to an accident. They were boring for petroleum, and found none, but they struck salt rock — two beds of which are each thirty feet thick, and remarkably pure. Some time, when they sink a shaft down to the salt rock, it will even be cheaper than it is![17] I have heard settlers tell of using clean wood ashes, in dire distress for salt!

Lost in the Woods

Some of the old settlers told melancholy tales of being lost in the woods. An old man in Vaughan told me of his brother in Nasagaweya, an elderly man, who had wandered away, perhaps at the time a little unsettled in his mind, and had never come back or been heard of. The following account, which refers to Horning's Mills in Melancthon Township, County of Grey [the township is now in Dufferin County], I quote from my *Gazetteer* of that County, 1865, being information gathered at that time on the spot:

> A melancholy tale hangs round the early settlement of this place. Thirty years ago (about 1834), four children, one a son of Mr. Horning, and three children named Van Meer, wandered into the woods, perhaps in search of the cows and *were never more heard of!* It was supposed — it does not seem to be known on what grounds — that they were carried off by the Indians.[18] The mystery was never cleared up. No traces were discovered, nor were any remains of the little unfortunates ever found.
>
> It is easy to refer to, but impossible to describe, the desolation of the parents, the sickness of hope deferred, the catching at every atom of probability on which a hope might hand — only to be again disappointed; and at last the utter darkness and the blank despair. Twenty years after — the father was then dead — an Indian-looking young man appeared in the settlement, and gave out that he was Mr. Horning's son, but his contradictory accounts of

himself gained no credence, and he was set down as an imposter."[19]

Pumpkin Sauce

William Kyle, of St. George, used to relate how, about the time of the War of 1812, he had to cross two unsurveyed townships in Lower Canada, to reach a certain point. He had a pocket compass, and was not "lost"; but much of the land was overflowed and his progress was very slow, and being two days (instead of one) in getting across, his provisions were exhausted. Almost despairing of getting out, and nearly dead with hunger and fatigue, he at last came to the log hut of a settler. The woman had no cooked provisions, nor bread, but as she had a large pot over the fire boiling pumpkins, he could not wait, but ate a large quantity of the half-boiled "pumpkin sauce," and lay down. He afterwards thought it was very Providential, for a heavy meal of solid food might have been fatal to him.

The Village Store

One of the landmarks of the bygone age was the country "store." In Lower Canada the dealers were called "traders," in Upper Canada "storekeepers," and in legal documents, "Merchants." "After harvest" was the pay time among their customers, which meant sometime in the *winter*. And too often a good balance was left over for another "harvest" to put right. It always appeared to me a very foolish thing, to live on the proceeds of the "next" harvest, instead of spending the proceeds of the *last* one. For in the latter case, the farmer would know exactly how much he had to live on, and could keep out of debt and could also buy to so much more advantage. But I never farmed on my own account and especially I never farmed on a new place, unpaid for with a large family — as many of our old neighbours did — and perhaps made too few allowances for the pressure of circumstances.[20]

How well I can remember the old-fashioned "store!" Cow bells hung on a row of nails in the beams of the ceiling — a few ox-bows hung on the wall — a barrel full of axe handles — a spinning-wheel and reel set out as a sample of more in the "Storehouse" — a box of gun-flints on the counter — two pieces of "moleskin" trousering, two pieces of satinette, and as many of homespun flannel, for shirting, at the end of the single counter — the barrel of vinegar behind the stove, worn bright with the boys continually sitting on it — the five men and two boys continually sitting, in relays, on the counter, discussing the neighbourhood news. Yes, the *Country Store* was an institution by itself! And when, at night, the horses "hitched" to the opposite fence were headed homeward, the same effect was produced as the delivery of an individual mailbag at every house — the news was carried!

There was an unconscionable amount of "bad debts," and the merchants of those days must have succumbed as often as in later days, but that there were more chances of securing themselves, in one way or other. A merchant would take a *Note* against somebody, or "make a turn" with somebody *he* owed, or take a yoke of steers, or an "order" on a sawmill, or a lot of sawlogs, or turn out a yoke of oxen and a waggon to the debtor, and then take a "quit-claim" deed for the "place" the debtor was on — there was always *some* way of getting in a debt![21]

All horse trades and parliamentary candidates were discussed in the country stores, and when there was not room for all the local "Parliament" on the counter, the rest sat on nail kegs. There was generally a scattering at noon, when the storekeeper locked up for an hour to go to his dinner, though sometimes he left two of the most regular of the nail-keg "members" in charge till he came back again. I never knew them to do anything worse than help themselves to a fresh bit of tobacco, when their pipes ran out!

One night, in old Willie Kyle's, in St. George — there were two of these "local Parliaments" there then — the convexity of the earth, and especially of the aerial heavens, was discussed and Willie astonished some of the more unlearned of his auditory by declaring that once, in Lower Canada, "he had gone *so far north*, that he could not put a sixpence *between his head and the sky!*" He then paused, in the tuning of his fiddle, long enough to say, that "There was a very good reason for it — he hadn't a sixpence left!"

Straight Plowing

The farming of the pioneers was as rude as their adornment of dress. A man who was glad, in any shape whatever, to get a little red earth turned up and had "gee'd" and lap-furrowed around stumps for years, like a young friend of mine along the Grand River, long since dead, *poor fellow*, poetically inclined, who spoke of them as "Those odious things termed *stumps!*" — such a man would not heed much about the straightness of his furrows. He left that to his sons! I have heard my own father say that in striking out a new furrow, he managed "to *call in* at every stake!" And if we did not need to turn our team round more than once in mid-furrow, in finishing up a "landing," we looked upon it as pretty good management!

It was only after Agricultural Societies were established (about 1845), and prizes given for competition in "Plowing Matches," that the winding furrows began to be straightened out and farmers began to take pride in good plowing.[22]

Punch and Judy

One of our neighbours, "Dan" Starnaman, was going to Toronto on some business of his own and the superintendent of the Baptist Sunday School, a mile east of St. George, put a very few dollars in his hands to get a few books for the Sunday School library. Among others he brought back, was "The Diverting History of Punch and Judy." When some of the brethren objected to it as a Sunday School book, he said that he, "bought it, because he thought it was *suited to the capacities* of the children."[23]

The Old Sawmill

The old-fashioned sawmill was, in those primitive times, an indispensable institution. It sat upon some backwoods "creek" where the men and boys speared *suckers* below, in the Spring. Its saw went at a leisurely rate through far finer pine logs than one generally sees at sawmills now, and left a "stubshot" of two to four inches on the boards, which had to be "dressed off" with a sharp axe, before the boards were marketable at Dundas or elsewhere.

In Dumfries we used to pity the Beverley men, because they had such a fight with the pine trees and pine stumps. And, just about the time the first settlers there had wrestled through the worst of their difficulties, and got their really good and strong soil under good cultivation — despite the many, and large, and long-enduring pine stumps — lumber began to be a cash article at the Lake ports, and many of them wished they had their "pine" back again![24]

In my boyhood, nothing was "cash" but wheat and pork. Wheat at an average of five York shillings (62–1/24), and pork about three dollars-and-a-half per hundred pounds. Lumber and sawlogs, and fan bark, and shingles, and staves, and the like, were all "truck" — something to be "traded off" or sold on the longest possible credit. Whenever a farmer wanted some lumber, he would take in some sawlogs to the mill and the mill man would cut them "for the half." And, of all men in the world, I used to think that a sawmill man, with a quid of tobacco in his cheek, was the readiest for a practical joke!

My brother and I once went to one of these old mills, that of N.E. Mainwaring's, which, in our time, had almost outlived its usefulness, however, for a load of boards.[25] Mr. M., who was an inveterate joker, spied something odd about my brother's trousers. The fact was, they were made of blue-striped bed-ticking — a fancy of his own for nether garments.

"What will you take for your *pants*, Jack?"

"A dollar!" was the prompt reply.

"Here's your money! Off with them!" said the man of boards. But a dispute arising whether a key in the pocket went with them or not, upset the negotiation. I afterwards told Mr. M. that Jack had resolved to make a straight cut across the fields for home — about a mile. "And I should have had some fun out it too!" cried he, "for I would have *sot the dogs* on him!"

"The Forty-Niners"

There was a wonderful craze for California in '49. I was teaching school that year and kept contentedly on, and let other young fellows all around go off, without wishing to join them. But my parents — as I learned *years after* — were very much afraid I would catch the "gold fever," though they thought it best to say nothing. My brothers were too young.

Some of the most enterprising men I have met since, were returned "Californians." Some brought home gold with them, but most came as they went. And many a case of a family — estrangement arose out of the unnatural absence of husband and father — for they were not all young men. Bridegrooms going off in a pet,[26] and never returning, husbands deliberately deserting their wives, dramas of the "Enoch Arden" type — in one of which the ousted partner became the hopeless inmate of an Insane Asylum — there I could adorn with real names and dates, but I forbear.[27]

Speaking of returning from the gold regions reminds me of the experience of one of our old neighbours on the Second Concession of Dumfries, who went to California; and only stayed there three weeks. He had all the adventures of riding over the Coast Range on muleback, and of seeing a great many things he never saw before. Among other adventures, the "train" of which he and his mule formed a part, "whipped up" as fast as possible through a place where robbers were sometimes found. And he said, "Every man had just to lay on the *stick* with all his might, and follow the mule before him, and get out of it as quick as he could!" Then he contentedly came back again. He said that he had "seen enough to pay for all the money spent!" He was wiser than some others.

Retired Farmers

Farmers often "retire," sell their farms, buy or build a house in a village, and go about with their hands in their pockets. Never having addicted themselves to reading, they have no relish for books and know not how to employ themselves. A minister from Brampton, speaking to me of his town, said it was growing slowly and steadily, the principal additions being of the class of "Retired Farmers." I replied that I pitied those men; they had so few mental resources that a life of leisure was not a happy life for them.

"Perhaps so," said he, "but they have more to entertain them in a county town, than in other villages. There is the County Council three times a year for several days, and the County Court four times a year, and the Assizes twice a year and these men constantly attend all these!" And men leave the fields, the woods, the pastures, the gardens, of a country home, to gain these town privileges!

My friend Reverend Joseph Unsworth, of Georgetown,[28] told me of a worthy farmer and his wife, who thought of selling their farm, and coming to live in that beautiful little town. They consulted him about it. They confessed that the price of the farm, invested, could not yield more than $500 scant — "but they had never spent nearly that in a year" and expected to keep a horse and buggy, and educate two growing daughters and provide for an otherwise large family. He took pencil and paper and made out a list of expenses — and went on remorselessly to *$1,200* and not one item could they object to!

"Now," said he, "you *are living* at the rate of $1,200 a year; only you don't know it, because you *raise* nearly everything. But in Georgetown, all these things would be *cash!*"

"Husband!" said the startled wife, "we've got our farm yet, and we'll keep it!" And they did.[29]

Sugaring Off

Where maple sugar is made, the "Sugaring off" is quite a season of festivity. This industry has almost died out in the older parts of Ontario, the farmers having plenty of other work to do as soon as spring begins to open, and grudging the firewood necessary in sugar-making.[30] It is therefore in Lower Canada it is seen in most perfection. Not in the French country, along the St. Lawrence, but out in the "Eastern Townships" towards the New England border. And during my three-years' residence there, we saw much of it.

"Sugar houses" are built in the woods — small frame structures with a simple "arch" of brick put in. In point of fact, it is merely two small brick walls, two or three feet high, with a large sheet-iron *pan* resting on them, and the fire put underneath. The trees are tapped about an inch deep, with a small auger, and cedar buckets without handles are hung on a nail under short spouts of sheet iron. The sap is brought in a large puncheon on a sled, drawn by oxen, and every means is taken to save labour and to ensure perfect cleanliness.

Many farmers, in a long course of years, never bought a pound of sugar. They made 800, 1,000, up to 2,000 pounds. A farmer's wife said to me, "If we have a poor year, and only make three hundred pounds, we make it do, and if it is a good year and we make eight hundred pounds, we use it all!" This for a family of seven, with an occasional "hired hand." The buckets are washed out and neatly piled up in the sugar house, along with a couple of cords of firewood, for the next spring.

Courtesy of Special Collections, Killam Library, Dalhousie University.

"Making Maple Syrup." From *Canadian Illustrated News* (1874) 188.

When the sugar is ready, an Eastern Township man will go out-side his sugar-house, and "holler." Everybody within reach, who has time to spare, will come and "eat sugar." I have counted twenty-two and twenty-four, on such occasions. You have *two* "paddles." A big one, to dip into the pan, and a small one to scrape from the larger one, and put to your mouth — for it is considered unpardonable rudeness to put the paddle from your mouth into the pan.

There is always a demand for salt bacon or smoked beef at dinner after a "Sugaring" — or for the sourest pickles. These act as an antidote to nausea, and the same parties who have eaten from a half to a whole pound of sugar each, will be ready in the afternoon for another "Sugaring."

The inhabitants there, who are almost all natives of New England descent, delight in recounting humorous stories of new immigrants and their sugar experiences. One, in Eaton Township, tapped all the trees he came to and wondered why some of them gave him no sap! Old Mr. Williams, of Oro in Ontario, father of Reverend R. J. Williams,[31] had the same experience, and told a neighbour, as a strange circumstance, that "he had five trees, with their spouts all pointing into one trough, and not a drop of sap from one of them!" The fact was, he had tapped a clump of *basswoods*, mistaking them for maples.

The same old Englishman, who had spent most of his life in a Woolwich dockyard, was chopping in his cedar swamp, and "lodged" a tree. He thought he would "go up" and loosen the entanglement! So he ascended the oblique trunk of the refractory tree, till twenty or thirty feet from the ground — when down came the tree, chopper, axe, and all! The old man received such injuries in his hip, that he was lame ever after. He said that he "didn't see how it was!" He had many a time gone to the *masthead, and* he had thought surely he could go up *that!*[32]

The Eaton man who tapped *all* the trees, having been put right as to the trees that gave sap, and those that gave none, got his sugar-works going at last, and in due time had a quantity of "syrup," which he thought he would take to the house to "sugar off." So, having come out to his sugar-works on *horseback* — for the "going" is almost an impossible thing for a week or two in the spring, horses and men breaking through and floundering deep in the snow — he would take his buckets of hot syrup by horse. Behold him, then, on *horseback* with a "neck yoke" on his shoulders, at either end of which depended a pail of hot syrup! It would need be a steady horse and a good road! But it was neither of these. The horse floundered, and some of the syrup scattered over his flanks, and though *not* hot enough to scald him, was warm enough to frighten him. He bolted off, and after him the syrup was strung along, and "spun" into fine threads over the snow for half a mile; the man got home — but had nothing to "sugar off" that day!

It was popularly believed that the festivities of the sugar season were favourable to matrimonial arrangements among the young people. At least some person must have thought so, for on the end of a sugar house near Bulwer, I read, as I passed by, this warning, painted in rude letters of red:

NO SPARKING
ALOWED
HEAR[33]

Two Trades

I have always held that the average Canadian is quite capable of knowing two handicrafts. And it is a grand thing to have them. My parents used to tell me that in Scotland, many stonemasons took to weaving for winter employment. Speaking of Scotch mechanics reminds me of what Mr. John Watson, the eminent implement manufacturer of Ayr, Ontario, told me once, in his own house.[34]

He was a skillful moulder, with a specialty for the difficult moulding of "hollow-work," and landed at Boston, along with a fellow workman. They did not find employment there and came on westward, seeking work. At Troy [New Hampshire] they parted, one going south; Mr. Watson came on, west. After several disappointments, he came to Lockport [New York], where a foundryman wanted a hand to do hollow-work. "Can you do hollow-work?" asked the "boss." I'll try!" said young Watson, very confidently — knowing that was his strong point.

"Oh, if you can only *try* you'll be no better than the others that have tried it, and failed!" And he turned his back and left him.

Watson determined he would never say "try" any more. After Buffalo [New York], he came to St. Catharines, and then to Hamilton. Here one of the foundries wanted a man to cast *stoves*. "Can you make *stoves?*" asked the proprietor.

"Yes!" answered Watson — remembering his experience at Lockport. Now, he

THE CENTENNIAL GOLD MEDAL!

JOHN WATSON,
AYR, ONT., CANADA,
For Agricultural Implements

The Only Gold Medal Given for Agricultural Implements at the Great Centennial Exhibition was Awarded to John Watson, of Ayr.

An advertisement for John Watson, Agricultural Implements, of Ayr, County of Waterloo. The Watson equipment won many awards in international competitions. From *Historical Atlas of Waterloo and Wellington Counties* (1881) 31.

never had made a stove in his life, but he knew if he had a "pattern," he could make anything any other man could make! So he got work and gave good satisfaction. After three weeks, he got a letter from his "crony," who had not found steady work. He spoke to the "boss":

"I have a crony, who came out with me — just as good a workman as I am: and he would like to get work."

"Can he make *stoves?*"

"Well, he can make stoves just as well as I can. I never saw a stove made till I came here!"

"Didn't you tell me you could make stoves?"

"Well, haven't I *made them?*" And that argument settled the matter!

A plasterer told me, a short time ago, that he had a fancy of learning shoemaking, as a winter employment. And I lately advised a "handy" fellow, who had a growing family, and not much work at his trade in the winter, to take up *shoe-mending*, to keep the "pot boiling." A skillful worker at a marble yard told me he was also a good *printer*, and we all know the good use Hugh Miller made of his enforced leisure in the winter — how the sturdy stone worker became the eminent "Geologist and Author."[35]

And a printer and iron moulder I knew, told me he was unable to say *which* trade he liked best — he generally "liked best the one he was employed at for the time." I knew a tailor, near Woodbridge, who was advised by his wife to "change his trade," and in six months he had passed his novitiate in a cooper shop, and was making barrels for a livelihood.

Some More Superstitions

If a "bush lot" is left in a settlement for a number of years and then cleared and "broke up," it will be found to be full of all kinds of pestilent weeds. These seeds get into the air, and are carried by the birds — and all root themselves in that "bush!"

So with superstitions — they seem to root themselves so easily and persistently in the bush! An old neighbour in Dumfries, two concessions north of us — who was something of a beekeeper — had had a death in his family, and he said in the most serious tone, [while] in my father's house, that "he had not *told the bees* of it, and they all left him, and flew away!" And it is hard to eradicate the belief in *Water-witchery* — that a hazel twig will indicate subterranean streams of water, by bending itself down when it comes over the vein!

Another ridiculous superstition — not an old exploded one, but an apparently deep-rooted and present one — is the Lucky Horseshoe. Some — even Christian people — speak about "Luck," as if it were a divine Power or Being, instead of merely being an irreverent name for God's Providence or Spirit. I have seen old horseshoes nailed under the doors of merchant shops and over the doors of inner offices, and I have never failed to find one on the capstan or foremast of every lake vessel where I have thought of looking for it!

People will say, "Well, I can give you many instances of good luck, following such a thing, and surely that proves something!" Yes: it proves the well-known and happy tendency of human nature to remember the bright days and forget the dark ones. We trust in some lucky talisman; half our experiences are distressing and half are favourable — we credit to "good luck" that which is good, and largely forget altogether the other "unlucky" half!

I have known people who always killed their pigs when the moon was filling her "horn" — for then the pork would swell in the pot! Otherwise, and it would shrink. Others of our neighbours were careful to sow their peas in the young of the moon, for the reason that they would swell and "fill" in the pod, as well as in the kitchen pot. And when a boy, I have been warned by neighbours' children against letting the baby see its face in a glass before it was a year old because it if did, it would die![36]

Now, when I was a boy — though I believed none of these things — it was of no use for me then to say anything, for I had, as a little boy, no influence. And now, when perhaps my advice might be better heeded, these old neighbours are all dead! I am somewhat in the plight of the Scotsman, who made a walking tour through Cumberland and Yorkshire to see the country, and at every farmhouse was attacked by unmannerly dogs. A dozen years after he would make the same tour, but this time he armed himself with a heavy walking stick, remembering particularly certain places where he had an old score to pay off! But alas for his calculations! His old enemies were all dead and gone, and a new generation of house dog, wonderfully polite, he thought, (they saw his stick!) were in their place.

Going to the Bush

Most people consider it a great slander to say that "Every politician has his price!" but it is little slander to say that every Canadian farmer "has his price." He will generally sell out, if he can only get money enough for his farm. One of the commissioners sent out by the British Government in 1879, said, in Toronto, that he did not know what better thing the British farmers could do, than to come out here and buy up the cleared farms, and let the native farmers "go back and improve the western wilds, which they seemed so fond to do."[37]

But when our farmers want to sell, they seldom go about it in a very merchant-like way. I have always noticed that those dealers who mark their goods plainly and conspicuously with a selling price, do more business in consequence. And when a man advertises a farm for sale, he would be wise to put the "price" in, too. But the fact is, if a new immigrant comes to enquire, the "price" will be higher than to one of his neighbours. And under the most favourable circumstances, the two men will expect to sit on the fence, and whittle sticks for a couple of hours, before coming to an understanding!

All these difficulties surmounted, however, a farmer from an old settlement generally makes a good back woodsman. They go there to "get land for their boys," or to get rid of a mortgage, and sometimes for no reason but a restlessness that has possessed them, and sometimes to obtain a position in Society denied them at home. I have known instances of the latter. With the price of a good hundred acres in possession, a man will take up four hundred acres in a new township, get fifty acres cleared by contract the first year, take by far the lead of all his neighbours (who are poor), and, when the township is organized, he will get himself elected reeve, and then be made a magistrate and become a "man of consequence."[38]

To the North West

I do not know where the present craze for the North West will end, but in the meantime it furnishes some humour. For instance, my brother told me of a Burford farmer who was selling off his stock and implements by auction, and who was going about with a sticking-plaster on the back of his neck, to humour some boil or felon. A wag asked a friend near by:

"Is that plaster, on the North-West side of Underhill's neck, what is *drawing him* to Manitoba?"[39]

A Perilous Descent

Going once by "stage" — at night — from Hamilton to Toronto, in the "old days," before railways, the driver told me of an acquaintance of his, who was once driving some members of the old Upper Canada Parliament to Toronto, to attend the House. It was one of those great hills on "Dundas Street" — the "Sixteen-mile Creek," I think — we were going down at the time, and the driver pointed out the place to our right, where the horses had bolted over, and gone down among the stunted timber, at the immanent risk of dashing everything to destruction.

However, the driver, who could not stop his team, skillfully guided their precipitous descent, avoiding all the trees as they slid down among the snow and came out safe, with his passengers, at the foot of the descent, merely remarking, "he's a *poor driver* that can't go wherever he wants to!"[40]

"Two Days from New York"

In 1846, ten years at least before we had any Ocean telegraph, I read the *Dundas Warder* published by Mr. Robert Spence, afterwards postmaster general.[41] One week he announced that "the telegraph line was now extended as far west as Buffalo, and he would be able to give his reader news, *two days from New York!*" The foreign news reports were always then headed "Four days later from Europe!" — or whatever the number of days might be, since the last arrival of a mail steamer. In our weekly papers, we generally got the news up to within fourteen days of the time we read the paper in our country houses, and thought the despatch quite creditable.

"Lord Ullin's Daughter"

When I lived in Owen Sound, a young man had stolen a girl from her father's house and like "The Lord of Ulva's Isle" would cross the "stormy water" from Thornbury to Owen Sound (forty miles) in a small sailboat, to reach a clergyman.[42] It was fine weather and everything smiled on the voyagers. But Lake Manitou began to growl and shake its mane, and to make matters worse, a rain set in. It was not till the third day — I know not in what kind of a plight — they arrived at the manse of the Presbyterian minister, Reverend Thomas Stevenson, and were fondly tied in the knot matrimonial.[43]

Molasses?

John Loree, of Dumfries, was passing Kyle's store in St. George, where the storekeeper was drawing a quart of tar for a farmer from the barrel on the verandah — he would not have it in the store.

"Is that *molasses*, Jim?"

"Yes!" answered the dealer in jest. Whereupon the farmer with a disregard of propriety that brought its own speedy punishment, crooked his forefinger through the amber descending stream and got in his mouth — not molasses, but *tar!*

A Practical Joke

Old Mr. Mainwaring,[44] near St. George, was always watching for a chance to play practical jokes. Mr. Kyle, whom I served for a year behind the counter, "got round" him, on one occasion. Mainwaring came in with a heavy two-gallon jug of whisky, he was taking (on foot) home for his harvest hands.

"Ah, Jimmy!" he said, "would you like to have a drop? You poor teetotaller you! *You dassn't* take a drink!" So Kyle got him out to give his opinion on a pretended "horse trade" and the old gentleman set down his jug. Kyle slipped in, to tell me to "change that jug for one of water," and hurried back again.

Soon Mainwaring picked up the changed jug, and marched off home, and before he was fairly out of the village, everybody knew of the trick. He had a mile to go and the day was warm, and he thought he would "taste" it, before he took it out to the field. He duly "watered" it in his glass, then more from the jug — then the "pure stuff!" We expected him to come after his liquor, but he was too proud! The two gallons only cost him fifty cents, but he never came after it. After standing beneath the counter for a month, I was directed to pour it out in the yard.

"Tired of Hard Work"

Farmers sometimes get "tired of hard work" and become storekeepers. I remember one, who left a good little farm of fifty acres, and invested its value in village premises and stock in St. George, and began a "business." It did not succeed. He added to it an unlicensed Eclectic medical practice. Still it did not succeed. At last, all was gone and he suddenly went off.

Another in the same place, sunk a larger farm, only to become an insolvent in a few years. I could greatly multiply these instances, from my own and my friends' memories, but they do not need multiplying.[45]

An Ornamental Front

I once saw, in the then very new Township of Arran, in Bruce County, an experiment, which might be repeated anywhere in the new country. An old bachelor, in clearing up a new fifty-acre lot, had run a double fence along his front — these being a rod apart. He had not "left" the original wood, but after it was all burned over, had simply put up his double fence and left Nature to her will. When I saw it — perhaps five or six years after — it was all grown up with "soft stuff," poplar, sumach, soft-maple, etc., as high as one's head, and would make a beautiful front line to his farm.[46]

Rats

The common black rat came over to America — like other "emigrants" — in ships and, before the days of railways, were slow in reaching the more inland parts. At St. George, we were twenty-three miles from lake navigation at Hamilton — where they had rats long before we had!

We heard of them at a distance, then in Beverly, our next township, and — in 1845 — we found they had reached our own barns! No doubt they came "to stay," for the farmers have no charm or power to drive them away. But I thought it worth while to chronicle their advent in Dumfries.

"Hoo's yer Mither?"

In 1860, the Prince of Wales, on the railway from Toronto to Collingwood, stopped long enough at Newmarket to receive an "Address" from the Corporation. The reeve (it was then an incorporated "Village"), was Mr. Sutherland, an honest Scotchman. To give due emphasis to the address, somebody who posed as an "Elocutionist," was to read off the document — the reeve and council standing by. But the reeve did not want to have nothing left to him but pantomine! So when the address had been read, he made his best bow to the Prince:

"Prood to see ye! *Hoo's yer Mither?*"[47]

The Red River Men

In 1811, about twenty-five families of Highlanders, sent out by Lord Selkirk, arrived at York Factory, on Hudson Bay and penetrated to Red River, Manitoba, in the spring of 1812.[48] In August 1812, a ship-load from Kildonan, Sutherlandshire, arrived at Fort Churchill, and when winter was established, traversed the five or six hundred miles to Red River on foot, dragging after them on slender sleds ("cala-bashes"), such provisions and clothing as they could thus convey.

In the early spring of 1885, I found two of the old pioneers still living, where they finally settled in West Gwillimbury, [Simcoe County], Ontario. They were too old and feeble to give me any information, but I found the "historian" of the colony in the person of a son of one of the original emigrants. (There is always a "historian" in every family group, or colony.)

They left well-filled chests at Fort Churchill, which they never recovered. They started with a single half-breed guide,[49] and if he had by any casualty lost his life, the whole company must have perished in the icy wilderness. He would go on ahead, leaving the trail of his snowshoes, and they followed on snowshoes, dragging their "calabashes" behind them, and would camp in some thicket on the banks of some river. Among them was a babe six months old, who lived to be a patriarch in West Gwillimbury. They were thirty days on the march.

At Red River, they were considered as intruders on the domain of the North West Fur Company, and after hardships and discouragements of all kinds, determined to leave that country for Upper Canada. Captain Cameron, the head of the North West Company at Red River, helped them out of the country by furnishing them with guides, etc. to Fort William. From there they coasted along Lake Superior, and then through the islands, and down Georgian Bay and reached their final settlement.[50]

Two circumstances, as illustrating the tenacity of a Highlandman, respecting his word and his convictions, may be stated. Shortly after they got to Red River, they set up a small "still," such as are now sometimes discovered working in some lonely Highland glen. But the Fur Company did not like that. They did not allow whisky to get among the Indians — perhaps more in the interest of fur than morality — nevertheless a good rule. And they called a meeting of the settlers, and said, "If you will all sign a paper not to make any more *whiskey*, we'll bring you out a Minister in the spring!" And my informant said, "Within ten minutes, our fathers all signed the paper!" But the *Minister never came!* But they kept their word, and made no more whisky.[51]

Perhaps one-half of the total settlement remained. And after attending Episcopal service for thirty years — for there was no other — the Reverend Mr. Black came out and settled with them at "Kildonan," and every man, woman, and child of the Highlanders deserted the English Church Service and followed Mr. Black! There was not one left.[52]

The Reverend Prof. Gregg, of Knox College, Toronto, thanked me for my Red River researches — which were published in the *Globe* — as he gleaned some items for his "History of the Presbyterian Church," then in preparation; and Sir Roderick Cameron, head of a great shipping firm in New York telegraphed to the *Globe*, "Who is it writing about the Red River men? I am so pleased to find that any of them yet live. I am the son of the Captain Cameron mentioned."[53]

The Big Anchor

Penetanguishene was a Naval Station on the Lakes in the old days, and, in 1814, during the War, a war vessel was on the stocks there. "Stores" for "Penetang" were sent up Yonge Street to Holland

Landing, thence over the ice of Lake Simcoe to Orillia, then over to Coldwater, [and] then on the ice again to Penetanguishene.

Among other things, a great *anchor* for this new vessel was on the way from York (Toronto). Mr. Samuel Brock, some distant connection of General Brock, had the "contract," and it was slowly drawn up and down the hills on Yonge Street by several pairs of oxen. This was early in 1815.

They were almost at the place where they should take to the ice, when a horseman overtook them, waving a printed "Proclamation" over his head and shouting "Peace!" The news had taken three months from Europe to get that far. They tumbled the anchor off at the side of the road and returned. It lay, half-buried in sand and earth, for fifty-five years! Then, in 1870, it was put in its present position in "the Park" at Holland Landing. It is the "palladium" of the village! I measured it in 1884: length, 16 ft.; circumference of shank, 20–1/2 to 28 in.; from point to point of flukes, 9 ft. 7 in.; breadth of flukes, 28 in.; length of flukes, 34 in.; thickness of flukes, 2 in.; cable-ring, diameter, 28 in.; thickness, 3 in.; circumference of arms, 22 to 28 in.; length of each arm, 67 in. The square part of the shank, where the crossbar of wood was intended to fit, is 6 x 7 in. square, for a length of 30 inches. The villagers of Holland Landing are justly proud of their anchor, and pleased at the strange fortune that left this marine curiosity forty miles from even the nearest Great Lake![54]

Cunning Wolves

Mr. John Lebourveau, of Eaton, told me of the wolves, when he was a boy, in the "Eastern Townships." One night, he thought he heard a noise, and looked through the little window of the "chamber" (or loft) of the log house. It was winter, with a hard crust on the snow and bright moonlight. They had their sheep penned up with a high rail "fence," too high, and strong, and close, for a wolf to get through. But here was a big wolf, suddenly showing himself at one side of the enclosure, and the sheep, frightened, would rush against the other side. Then he would slip round, and show himself suddenly on the other side. He hoped, by this manoeuvre, to have the sheep break down the fence in their frightened "rushes" — and *then!*

And the boy saw *two or three others*, sitting on their haunches, at a distance in the field, under a tree! Afraid that the catastrophe might really happen at any minute, the boy raised an alarm, and the wolves disappeared.

Toast!

In stopping overnight, years ago, in a French-Canadian hotel in Lower Canada, I was coming in from seeing after my horse in the morning, and scented burning butter. "Oh," thought I, "this is Friday, and we shall have fish" — to which I felt no objections. There was no fish on the table but some very excellent buttered *toast.*

My daughter,[55] who was with me — a half-grown girl — told me, *after breakfast*, how the toast was made. She had been loitering round the kitchen, chatting with the landlady, who was the only one in the house who could speak English. And the landlady would butter two slices of bread — clap them on top of the hot stove, buttered-side down — and let them frizzle, putting a "flat-iron" on each slice to keep it flat. And when that side was done, would turn them over — putting on the flat-irons as before! It depended wholly on "how clean the top of the stove was!" In my case "Ignorance was bliss!"

Fools' Gold

Mr. McLean Purdy, the courteous postmaster of Eugenia, in the County of Grey, on the upper waters of the Beaver River, showed me, in 1865, some specimens of what he called "Fools' Gold," found below the beautiful Falls of the River at that place. And "thereby hangs a tale."

In 1852, when the country was new and wild and everybody was talking of "California Gold," someone thought he had discovered gold in the rocks below the falls. The secret at first was only known to two or three, or at most half a dozen, and they wrought like beavers, to make their "pile," before the whole country came flocking to "the diggings," and the Government perhaps interfere with "free mining."

But *murder will out*, and rumors of *gold* seemed carried by the very air, and it was not many days till another prospecting party discovered them from the brink of the gorge, hard at work below. Seeing they were discovered, they laid down their picks and held a parley. The newcomers were anxious to be assured that it was "the real stuff" — being a little doubtful on that point.

"Well!" said an old man, wiping the sweat from his brow, and sitting down a very respectable pile of the purest and most glittering *rocks* he had been able to find — "Well, if it's *gold*, I've got *enough!* And if it *ain't* gold, I've got enough!"

One adventurous waggon-maker from "Yonge Street," happening to be in the region, made a rush with the rest, to *the diggings;* and soon departed homewards, several days journey — laden as he was — through woods and bush roads, with a back-breaking load in a bag. All the way home he was revolving in his mind, what use to make of his wealth? He decided on selling his "shop," buying a good farm and living in comfort the rest of his days.

He got home, and before he slept, kindled his forge-fire, to test it by melting down a little of the "precious stuff." The catastrophe was entirely unanticipated. The sulphurous fumes and horrible stench of the vile stuff choked him, and well-nigh drove him out of the premises! The harder he blew at his bellows, the more horrible became the stifling fumes, till in despair he pitched the whole lot into the "street!" He had carried home a back-load of worthless *iron pyrites!*[56]

"Something Else to Think About"

Once, in riding from Magog to Sherbrooke, (Lower Canada) in the "stage," the driver pointed to me a spot where a bear had met him a few days before. It was a lovely, uninhabited spot, for miles — what the French call a "brûle" — a burned-over place, with a small second-growth and many raspberries. The bear had soon disappeared among the raspberry bushes, and with some trouble he had got his horses by, he having to lay his whip pretty soundly on his "near" horse, which was a "colt," to make him pass the spot. The story had got abroad, and in a few days the gossip of Sherbrooke had it that "a bear had stopped the Magog stage, and the driver had to *lash him with his whip*, to get past him!"

The celebrated Scottish Divine, Dr. Chalmers, was once thus riding in a public conveyance, when the driver began whipping one of his horses — apparently without any cause — and then explained to the Doctor, who was sitting beside him, that the horse had been frightened at that spot, and always "behaved bad" when he came to the place; and the driver said he wanted to cure him "by giving him *something else to think about!*" The principle thus suggested, was as good as a "text" to Dr. Chalmers, and he wrought it out in one of the most celebrated of his sermons, "The Expulsive Power of a New Affection!"[57]

Smoking Tunes

Mr. John McCallum, of Kleinburg, was very fanciful about his pipes, and had some grand German — *meerschaums* — with amber mouthpieces. The first time his youngest boy saw or heard the Scottish bagpipes, he noticed that they had similar mouthpieces, and somehow got the identity of the two sorts of "pipes" confused, and as he jumped round the piper with delight, he screamed out, "didn't they *smoke some nice tunes* out of those bag things!"

Would "Break the Bank!"

Mr. Thomas Blain, governor of the County Prison, St. Catharines,[58] who is a Niagara man, told me of a former resident of the town of Niagara — an example of the proverbial "rolling stone." His father had him well-educated, and in due time (as he chose the "Law"), had him duly articled. But, "It was too *slow* in this country!" so he betook himself to Ann Arbor, in Michigan, to finish his law studies. Then he turned from the Law, and thought he would be a Druggist. So he had a time in a drugstore. Soon he tired of that, and went oft, in aimless travelling or speculating.

By this time his father was dead, and Mr. Blain advised him *to hold on to the house* at any rate, for a house and lot were all he had left. But he had some "good scheme" in his head and needed money, so a few hundred dollars were raised by mortgaging the house. Then he got over to England and wrote Mr. Blain to sell his house in Niagara, and remit him the balance, after the mortgage was lifted. Times were hard and the house only brought $1,000, and a balance of $300 was sent him. He said that he was "going to *Monte Carlo;* he had a plan of making a *haul* there: he would go there, and *break the bank!*" He went, but instead of his "breaking the bank," he wrote Mr. Blain that "the Bank broke *him!*" His money was all gone, but his spirits never seemed to flag. He sent some copies of a comic paper, "*Tid-Bits,*" in which were some small contributions of his, which he had marked, and he was now "writing for the papers," in London.[59]

Any one who knows what a "Penny-a-lines" is in London, will know the straits he must have been reduced to. His only "assets" seemed to be restlessness and conceit — and a cheerful spirit. The first he will gradually (but effectively) get rid of in the mill of Adversity: the last is a good inheritance, and may see better days!

A Sabbath in the Bush

I lately gave a "Lecture" in St. Catharines, on Burns's "Highland Mary," and had occasion to speak of William Anderson, of Caledon Township, Ontario, a nephew of Mary's, who so long was the possessor of the Bible in two small volumes Burns gave to his aunt as a parting pledge, in 1786.[60] At the conclusion of the lecture, Mr. Walter McGibbon made a few remarks, and said he was brought up in the same township, within a mile of William Anderson's.

When Anderson was clearing his bush lot, a man named David Anderson, (no relation however,) worked with him, and one Sunday they chopped all day — mistaking the day. Toward evening, a neighbour thought he heard axes going, and a tree falling — and further remarked that the Andersons had not been at church, and thought "he would go over and see if all was right?" He found the two men hard at work. He told them it was the Sabbath day, and wondered to see them so employed. Then they explained the mistake they must have made. David Anderson said, "Well, it's done, and we can't help it now!" They had thought it was *Saturday!*

The next day, David was working as usual, but William Anderson as the only reparation he could make — worked none, but stayed quietly in his house all day, (there was no "church" to go to on Monday) and read his Bible: perhaps from the very volumes *Burns* had given to Highland Mary, for they were then in his possession! Like Robinson Crusoe, who kept "Sunday" for twelve years on the wrong day — it was more in the spirit in which it was kept, than the *time, and* he had, at least, thus discharged a debt on his conscience![61]

Orders for Beer

Mr. James McKee, of Garafraxa, told me some of the experiences of the late Mr. Piper, of that township,[62] who had wrought as a mason on the Court House and had at Goderich, when the County buildings were first put up. The eccentric Dr. Dunlop,[63] the founder of the town, often visited the works, and the men sometimes asked him for an order for beer. Once he scrawled an order on a huge building stone. The men carried the stone to where the beer was sold, and had the order honoured! On another occasion, when thus "dunned" for beer, he wrote the order on a stick of timber lying beside him. This too was carried off, and presented for beer!

So fond were the men of their "beer," that when Bishop Strachan[64] of Toronto came one day to see the works, the men gravely discussed locking him in a cell till he "shelled out," but lacked the nerve to do so.

"See here, boys!" said Mr. Piper, "You'll love a poor man for beer, but when a rich man comes, you're afraid to say anything to him! Now, if the Bishop goes into another cell, I'll lock him in!" And, passing the cell doors, with a plank on his shoulder, he turned the key on the Bishop, and walked on. The other men were quick enough to take advantage of the circumstance. "Eight gallons of beer, please!" said they, and the Bishop promised they would have it, and was speedily released.

Afterword

Reverend William W. Smith and Identity

At his death on January 6, 1917, Reverend William Smith was remembered by the Toronto *Globe* as "A Poet of the Pioneers." This public literary reputation had been maintained in the opening years of the twentieth century with the publication of Smith's *Collected Poems* in 1908 and in the continued reprinting of his poetry in anthologies such as Theodore Rand's *Treasury of Canadian Verse.*[1] In the interwar period, however, Smith's work along with that of many other immigrant poets was dismissed by Modernist critics as derivative and inferior. In 1924, J. Logan and Donald French identified Smith's literary limitations with the following:

> Although William Smith left Scotland in his infancy and was for almost four score years a Canadian by adoption, almost all his writings show the influence of the language, the literature, the history, the religious and philosophic spirit of his homeland ... Yet he did on occasion enter into the Canadian spirit and show an appreciative understanding of Canadian conditions, the beauties of the Canadian landscape, historic themes and national aspirations.[2]

By the time the *Oxford Companion to Canadian History and Literature* was published in 1967, Smith was recognized as a popular poet in his own day but one who belonged "to the mid-nineteenth century" and by implication was of little relevance to "modern" Canada.[3] Smith's obituary in the *Globe*, however, also highlighted the fact he had translated the New Testament into broad Scots as an important part of his legacy. Indeed, the report of Smith's burial at Newmarket in the *Canadian Congregationalist* focused on his religious rather than literary vocation.[4] The paper noted that "[b]y the will of God he served his generation nobly and well for a period of ninety years . . ." and, that at his grave, Malachi 2: 5–7 was read:

> My covenant was with him, a covenant of life and peace, and I gave them to him; this called for reverence and he revered me and stood in awe of my name. True instruction was in his mouth and nothing false was found on his lips. He walked with me in peace and uprightness and turned many from sin.

For his contemporaries then, Smith was both a pioneer poet and a devout clergyman. Smith's "Canadian Reminiscences" contain evidence of both of these identities, but his writing also reveals a more complex interplay of vocation, ethnicity, and patriotism in shaping Smith's view of himself and those he encountered.

The last chapter of "Canadian Reminiscences," for example, with its references to leading Scottish clergymen, such as Reverend John Black of Red River, Dr. William Gregg of Knox College, Toronto, or Dr. Thomas Chalmers of Glasgow, attest to both Smith's own Scottish background and his clerical vocation. As he is throughout his "Canadian Reminiscences," Smith is interested in illustrating the pioneering work of his fellow Protestant clergymen in spreading the gospel and, more particularly, the work of those ministers who shared with the Congregationalists' evangelical determination to reform society. As a consequence, his final chapter, in addition to naming leading Scottish clergymen, refers to such activities as hymn singing, temperance advocacy, and Sunday observance as well as to two Victorian institutions of reform, the asylum and the penitentiary. Indeed, Smith's criticism of superstition, also found in his eclectic last chapter, makes explicit his clergyman's desire to transform society and his dismay that "even Christian people" believed the "ridiculous" lucky horse shoe superstition. For Smith, the belief in "Luck," as if it were a divine Power or Being," had distracted his neighbours from a proper understanding of "God's Providence."

The criticisms directed toward superstition found in "Canadian Reminiscences" are also indicative of Smith's class identity. He locates superstition among the earliest pioneers in the newly settled districts or among ethnic groups such as the Germans, both of which he believed were in need of enlightenment and civilization. Such attitudes toward popular belief were shared by other evangelical clergyman who, like Smith, supported both the Home and Overseas Missionary societies of nineteenth-century Britain. Indeed, it has been recently demonstrated that missionaries often made direct comparisons to the "heathens" they had encountered overseas and the labouring population of industrial Britain, to the detriment of the latter. These comparisons allowed clergyman to elevate themselves above the common populous and supported their claims to belong to the respectable Victorian middle class.[5] The tone of Smith's "Canadian Reminiscences" reflects this heightened importance that many nineteenth-century clergymen believed they possessed by virtue of their vocation.

Smith's vocation is also reflected in the patriarchal character of his "Canadian Reminiscences." The sermons of nineteenth-century evangelicals and the biblical references in "Reminiscences" tended to highlight passages from the Old Testament with its emphasis on patriarchy and authority rather than the New Testament with its emphasis on the love of Christ. Indeed, Smith's manuscript, with its focus on the activities of men, is no different than early accounts of Congregationalism in Canada. These highlight the critical role of "founding fathers" in establishing and spreading the faith and the male comradeship of the early clerical pioneers. As with Smith's text, women are rarely referred to and when they are it is usually in supportive roles.[6]

In Smith's case, neither of his wives, Margaret Chisholm or Catherine R. Young, are mentioned by name, nor are his daughters, while his sisters are left out of his account altogether. This may have been a device to protect the privacy of his family, but Smith's willingness to name his father, John Smith, and his brother, John Anderson Smith, suggests that this was not the case but instead a reflection of deeply ingrained patriarchal attitudes. In this regard, Smith was little different than his respectable middle-class contemporaries, though these broader patriarchal tendencies were reinforced by his clerical vocation.[7]

It is also apparent from his "Reminiscences" that Smith's ethnic identity was reinforced by the number of Scots he encountered among his fellow clergymen, a fact that may well have encouraged him to publish his broad Scots version of the gospels in 1901.[8] It is, however, also clear from his manuscript that Smith's Scottish identity was first formed in his parent's household and reinforced by his childhood experiences in the South Dumfries pioneer community. Although he does not discuss this in his manuscript, the Smith siblings' marriages also appear to have reinforced these "ethnic" ties.

In Chapter 5, Smith mentions his brother-in-law, James Kyle, a Scottish merchant in Stratford, who must have been the brother of one of the women married to Smith's brothers. Smith's sisters Sarah and Jenny had married, respectively, the brothers Alexander and Murdo McLean, sons of Scottish immigrants from the Inverness region, while Smith's own first marriage to Margaret Chisholm also connected him to a Scottish immigrant family.[9]

The tales in "Canadian Reminiscences" illustrate how these familial and early community ties with fellow Scots were reinforced in Smith's early working life. He mentions two Scots, Willie Kyle and Peter Jaffray, who worked in two of Smith's earliest vocations, storekeeping and newspaper publishing. Indeed, the manuscript is full of references to Scots who were involved in writing and publishing, from John Dougall of the Montreal *Witness* to James Lesslie of the Toronto *Examiner.* Although he does not mention it in the manuscript, even Smith's brother-in-law, Murdo McLean, was involved in the newspaper business having co-founded the *Huron Expositor.* Beyond his own areas of employment, Smith identifies in the "Reminiscences" numerous Scots who held public office, including Senator John Mac-Donald, Dunbar Moodie, Adam Fergusson, William Lyon Macken-zie, and Bishop John Strachan. Overall, the manuscript reflects the fact that both Smith's private and public worlds were full of Scottish connections, and it is therefore little wonder that he was preoccupied with his own ethnic origins.

Nevertheless, despite the fascination with his birthplace and his self-conscious Scottishness, both the "Canadian Reminiscences" and Smith's published poetry demonstrate his ability to shift easily between Scottish and Canadian identities. In the Preface to his *Selected Poems*, published in 1908, Smith reflected on this dual identity:

> Having left Scotland so long ago that I cannot even recall the look of her shores, and knowing the land almost exclusively through her Songs, her literature and her People, the "Scotch," in song and expression, has greatly appealed to me in the latter half of my life, and perhaps not wholly in vain. So the Maple Tree and the Heather are here brought out into the sunshine of homely verse by one who loves them both.[10]

In "The Three Brethren," a fictionalized account of Border emigration published in his earlier collection, Smith also commented on the dual identity he and other "Canadian" Scots had embraced:

> To be a "Scot be-north the Lakes!"
> A man who gives-a man who takes —
> And finds that one can serve his God,
> And love his country, though abroad; —
> And inward croon to his dying day,
> Some Scottish Border roundelay,
> Attuned to harp *some Maple tree*
> Gave up her heart the stock to be![11]

Smith frequently elevated the Maple tree as the emblem of Canada, as he did with Heather for Scotland, and his "Merry Maple" was set to music and published as *The Maple: A Patriotic Song* by the Anglo-Canadian Music Publisher's Association in 1894. The same firm would publish his "Canadian Flag Song" as part of its *Empire Series of School Songs*:

> Fly the Old Flag!
> To the colors cling,
> Fly the Old Flag!
> Let the wel'kin ring;
> We'll fly the Flag,
> For Canada and King;
> For Canada and for King.[12]

The linking of Canada and monarchy expressed in this patriotic poem was part of the wider late nineteenth-century English Canadian celebration of the dominion's role in the British Empire, a celebration that was at its apogee between 1870 and the outbreak of the First World War.[13] Indeed, Smith's collections of poetry contained several imperial poems with Canadian settings, including "The Death of Wolfe," "The Burial of Brock" and "The Volunteer of '85" — a tribute to a fallen soldier who had been sent to suppress the North West Rebellion. In both the "The Death of Wolfe" and "The Burial of Brock" the martial prowess of the Highland Regiments, by the late nineteenth century a central Scottish feature of British imperial iconography, was dramatized by Smith linking both his Scottish and imperial preoccupations.[14] At the same time, overseas missionary activities, reflected in Chapter 9 of the "Reminiscences" with the reference to the work of David Livingston and Walter Inglis in Africa, had encouraged evangelical clergymen like Smith to enthusiastically support the British Empire as an instrument for furthering the spread of Christianity. Indeed, it has recently been suggested that the missionary movement had been a key element in popularization of the empire in nineteenth-century British society, but it has also been shown that in British culture, particularly as reflected in literature, served to legitimate imperial dispossession and colonization.[15] Therefore, as an evangelical Christian, as a man with literary ambitions, and as an immigrant colonist, Smith naturally reflected the imperial identity of his age.

Smith's imperialism allowed him to easily accommodate both his Scottish and Canadian identities — and indeed to see no conflict between the two — but British imperial attitudes also allowed him to view his assumed position at the top of Canadian society as natural. During the nineteenth century, notions of racial superiority and inferiority were increasingly employed as justification for imperial expansion and essential "race" qualities were ascribed to all peoples, including Europeans, not merely those with different skin colour. The Anglo-Saxon "race" was viewed as naturally superior and, as a consequence, as having a duty to govern others.[16] In Britain, this was demonstrated in the attitude towards the "Celtic" populations of the British Isles, especially the Irish, and became even more visible when extended beyond Britain to Asia and Africa. An elaborate racial hierarchy developed with Anglo-Saxons on top, then northern Europeans, followed by Southern Europeans, and then people of colour at the bottom. Smith's manuscript reflects this hierarchy by placing the English and Scottish immigrants first in his sequence of chapters on ethnic groups in Ontario. Similar racial classification was also apparent in the United States during the nineteenth century and American attitudes probably reinforced Smith's racial perceptions, but as a consequence of segregationist policies and the emerging civil rights movement early in the twentieth century the complex racial hierarchy was simplified in the United States into a White, or "Caucasian," race versus a Black, or "Negro," race.[17]

The Canadian racial view that developed after Smith is perhaps best exemplified by John Murray Gibbon's *Canadian Mosaic* published in 1938. Like William Smith, Gibbon, though born in Ceylon, was the child of immigrant Scottish parents. He wrote several books, including a study of the Scots in Canada, but was best known for *Canadian Mosaic*, which argued that the Canadian people should be understood as an assemblage of various European "racial groups."[18] In contrast to William Smith's "Canadian Reminiscences," Gibbon's account left Blacks and First Nations peoples out altogether, yet despite its exclusive White European focus, Gibbon's mosaic analogy was clearly a development on the hierarchy of races found in Smith's manuscript. Indeed, both Smith's conception in *Canadian Reminiscences* and Gibbon's later elaboration in the *Canadian Mosaic*, illustrate that contemporary notions of Canadian multiculturalism, promoted vigorously since the 1960s, are rooted in earlier notions of racial hierarchy adopted by imperial Scots like Reverend William Wye Smith.

Appendix A
Works of William Wye Smith

Books and Major Works

Alazon and Other Poems: Including Many of the Fugitive Pieces of Rusticus. Toronto: H. Scobie, 1850.

Gazeteer and Directory of the County of Grey for 1865–6. Toronto: Toronto Globe, 1865.

The Print of His Shoe, or, Following Christ. Boston; Chicago: Congregational Sunday School and Publishing Society, 1887.

Poems. Toronto: Dudley & Burns, 1888.

Vetulia; or, Going to the Bottom of Things. Toronto: Dudley & Burns, 1891.

The Gospel of Matthew in Broad Scotch. Toronto: Imrie, Graham & Co., 1898.

The New Testament in Braid Scots. Paisley: Alexander Gardner, 1901.

The Selected Poems of William Wye Smith. Toronto: W. Briggs, 1908.

Other Publications

"The Carrier Boy's New Year's Address," in *British Colonist*, Toronto: January 3, 1851.

"Concerning Highland Mary," *Highland Mary*. John D. Ross, ed., Paisley: Alexander Gardner, 1894.

"The Scots in Canada. II," in *The Scottish Canadian*, May 7, 1891.

Poem at the conclusion of an article by John B. Smith, "Extermination of the Mosquito Plague in New Jersey," in *OAC Review*, Vol. 18, No. 3. December 1905.

"Canadian Winter Song," in *OAC Review*, Vol. 35. No. 4. December 1922.

William Wye Smith published a series entitled "John Kanack's Experiences" in the *New Dominion Monthly*. In this series Smith drew heavily from his own experiences and the people he met for inspiration for his stories:

"Sprouting," March 1873.
"Leafing Out," May 1873.
"John Crow," June 1873 (includes the poem "Circe" by Smith.)
"Pioneers," July 1873.
"Settling Down," August 1873.
"Aristocracy," September 1873.
"Plowing Deeper," October 1873.
"Summer Time," January 1874.
"Neighbours," February 1874.
"A Trip Up West," May 1874.
"A Letter from Kitty Seagram," June 1874.
"To Pastures New," July 1874.
"Conclusion," September 1874.

Sometime around 1900 William Wye Smith wrote a series of articles on the early history of Owen Sound. These articles were later reprinted in the *Owen Sound Sun Times*. The articles are part of the Owen Sound Public Libraries Local History Collection:

"City's First Survey was Made in 1837," July 23, 1932.
"John Telfer Named Crown Land Agent, 1840," July 30, 1932.
"Early Settlement of District began 91 Years Ago," August 6, 1932.
"Owen Sound's Growth in Early Days Traced," August 13, 1932.
"Travel in Early Days of Owen Sound District," August 20, 1932.
"Government House," August 27, 1932.

"Owen Sound Named After Capt. Owens," September 3, 1932.
"First Owen Sound School Opened," September 10, 1932.
"Early Municipal War Between Townships," September 17, 1932.
"Lord Elgin's Visit to Owen Sound in 1857," September 24, 1932.
"Early Day 'Characters,'" October 1, 1932.
"Sale of Indian Land in Keppel Township," October 8, 1932.
"Earthquakes of 1663," October 15, 1932.

Smith also acted as editor of a variety of publications, including:

The Canadian Independent
The Congregational Yearbook
The Owen Sound Sun Times
The Sunday School Dial

Appendix B

POEM OF ARCHIBALD McKILLOP: "THE BLIND POET OF MEGANTIC"

Megantic More Than Forty Years Ago

Old Megantic's banks and braes, lovely lakes and balmy bowers,
Where in childhood's happy days we have culled the fairest flowers,
See that mountain's towering head, see this vale so green and low,
Mountains rise and valleys spread, just as forty years ago.

Here the silvery streamlets pour, down the dewy dell at morn,
There the mountains torrent's roar, laughs the loudest laugh to scorn,
here when young I loved to roam, nature's wildest charms to know,
here are fathers found a home, more than forty years ago.

Where the hills of Arran swell, high above Lochranza's shore,
Few there are that live to tell of the friends they saw no more,
When from Scotia's favored strand, still unstained by conquering foe,
Sailed that hopeful hardy, band, more than forty years ago.

Dark and dense the wild woods lay, gaily green for leagues around,
Here the savage beasts of prey, undisturbed asylum found;
Then with pioneering toils, stalwart arms with many a blow,
felled the woods and burned "The piles," more than forty years ago.

Now the plowman guides his steeds, where the great old woods have
  been,
See our gardens, orchards, meads, Oh what changes we have seen,
Ordered by unerring law, seasons come, and seasons go,
Gone, the rarest sights we saw, more than forty years ago.

Gone the camps and camping ground, old log meeting house and all,
Gone the schools assembled round, fires that blazed against the wall,
Gone the barns, and houses, too, roofed with bark in many a row,
Frames and shingles known to few, more than forty years ago.

Now we build our palace piles, some of wood and some of stone,
Roofed in strange, fantastic styles, bark forgotten and unknown,
Gone the simple ways of life early years were wont to know,
Less of law and less of strife, more than forty years ago.

Gone the fathers they are dead, gone their kind, endearing ways,
Worn the bibles that they read, mute their earnest songs of praise,
Gone, a generation gone, all forgotten, lying low,
Men whose noble deeds were done, more than forty years ago.

We who live in Canada, now the new Dominion styled,
Still remember when we saw Inverness a desert wild,
And Megantic all around, with the parishes below,
But an Indian hunting-ground, more than forty years ago.

I am older, so are you, growing older day by day,
Surely we are dying too. Ah! How soon to pass away;
But Megantic shall remain, mountains rise and rivers flow,
Who shall then in sweeter strain, sing of forty years ago?

This poem was composed by Archibald McKillop in 1872, and published in 1875, in the *New Dominion Monthly*. Source: Dugald McKenzie McKillop, *Annals of Megantic County Quebec*. (Lynn, MA: D. McKillop, 1902) 8.

Notes

Editors' Note on the Text

1. Archives of Ontario [henceforth A0], MU 2125.
2. Robina and Kathleen Macfarlane Lizars, *In the Days of the Canada Company: The Story of the Settlement of the Huron Tract and a View of the Social Life of the Period, 1825–1850* (Toronto: W. Briggs, 1896). For background on William Briggs, see Carl F. Klinck, ed., *Literary History of Canada, Canadian Literature in English*, Vol. 1 (Toronto: University of Toronto Press, 2nd edition 1976), 200–01.
3. This chapter does, however, contain much that would be of interest to historians examining the development of the Congregational Church in Ontario and Quebec.
4. AO, MU 2124.

Reading William Wye Smith:

An Introduction to Background, Influences, and Stereotypes

1. See Allan Smith, "Farms, Forests and Cities: The Image of the Land and the Rise of the Metropolis in Ontario, 1860–1914," in David Keane & Colin Read, eds., *Old Ontario: Essays in Honour of J.M.S. Careless* (Toronto: Dundurn Press, 1990), 71–94.
2. See Appendix A.
3. *The Congregational Church Year Book 1888–89; The Congregational Church Year Book 1899–1900; The Canadian Independent*, January 1, 1888 and November 8, 1894.

4.	Douglas Walkington, *The Congregational Churches of Canada: A Statistical and Historical Summary* (Toronto: United Church Archives, 1979); "Rev. William Smith," *The Express* [St. Catharines], October 4, 1967.

5.	Caledonian Society of Toronto, *Selections from Scottish Canadian Poets* (Toronto: Imrie, Graham & Company, 1900), 135.

6.	Henry J. Morgan, *Bibliotheca Canadensis, or, A Manual of Canadian Literature* (Ottawa: 1867), 353; E.H. Dewart, *Selections from Canadian Poets* (Montreal: John Lovell, 1864), 53.

7.	Carole Gerson, *A Purer Taste: The Writing and Reading of Fiction in English in Nineteenth-Century Canada* (Toronto: University of Toronto Press, 1989), 8.

8.	See the *Dumfries Courier*, January 31, 1846, for a description of an early Burns Society meeting in Dumfries Township; see also Elizabeth Waterston, *Rapt in Plaid: Canadian Literature and Scottish Tradition* (Toronto: University of Toronto Press, 2001), 12–42.

9.	See John Thurston, *The Work of Words: The Writing of Susanna Strickland Moodie* (Montreal: McGill-Queen's University Press, 1996), 99–103; and Carl Ballstadt, "Susanna Moodie and the English Sketch," *Canadian Literature*, 51 (1972), 32–38.

10.	This type of writing was also promoted in Upper Canada by the development of local literary and historical societies, reflected in publications such as Alexander D. Ferrier's *Reminiscences of Canada and the Early Days of Fergus: Being Three Lectures delivered to the Farmers' and Mechanics' Institute, Fergus* (Guelph: 1866) and James Young's, *Reminiscences of the Early History of Galt and the settlement of Dumfries, in the Province of Ontario* (Toronto: 1880).

11.	It appears that Smith's father briefly considered farming in Ohio before moving to Upper Canada. See "William Wye Smith," *The Express*, October 4, 1967.

12.	See Charles R. Wilson, "Racial Reservations: Indians and Blacks in American Magazines, 1865–1890," in *Journal of Popular Culture*, Vol. 10, No.1 (1976), 70–79; and Allan P. Stouffer, "'A Restless Child of Change and Accident': The Black Image in Nineteenth-Century Ontario," in *Ontario History* [henceforth OH], Vol. 76, No. 2 (June 1984), 128–50.

13.	See Donald Power, "The Paddy Image: The Stereotype of the Irishman in Cartoon and Comic," in Robert O'Driscoll and Lorna Reynolds, eds., *The Untold Story: The Irish in Canada*, Vol. 1 (Toronto: Celtic Arts of Canada, 1988); and L. Perry Curtis Jr, *Apes and Angles: The Irishman in Victorian Caricature* (Washington: Smithsonian Press, 1997), revised edition.

14. See A. Brunger, "The Distribution of the Scots and Irish in Upper Canada, 1851–71," in *The Canadian Geographer/Le Géographe canadien*, Vol. 34, No. 3, (1990), 250–58; and "The Distribution of the English in Upper Canada, 1851–71," in *The Canadian Geographer/Le Géographe canadien*, Vol. 30, No.4 (1986), 337–43, as well as John Clarke and John Buffone, "Social Regions in Mid-Nineteenth Century Ontario," in *Histoire Sociale/Social History*, Vol. 28, No. 55 (1995), 204–05.

15. For a discussion of these stereotypes, see Wilson, "Racial Reservations" and Daniel Francis, *The Imaginary Indian: The Image of the Indian in Canadian Culture* (Vancouver: Arsenal Pulp Press, 1997).

16. In publishing the *Gazetteer*, it was Smith's intention to create a useful work that would provide an accurate and informative description of Grey County. Such an undertaking involved Smith visiting "every township, village, hamlet, and Post Office" in the County. The result was a work that represents an invaluable resource on the people, places, and character of mid-nineteenth century Grey County. See W.W. Smith, *Gazetteer and Directory of the County of Grey for 1865–66* (Toronto: Toronto Globe, 1865), Preface.

Chapter 1: The Bygone Age

1. As Smith suggests, there was a tremendous growth in local historical societies between the 1880s and 1920s. See Gerald Killan, *Preserving Ontario's Heritage: A History of the Ontario Historical Society* (Toronto, Ontario Historical Society, 1976). These groups tended to celebrate Canada's rise as a "White settler" dominion of the British Empire. As a consequence, the history they produced focused on the colonization of the Native peoples, the conquest of the French, and the arrival of Anglo-American and European immigrants. In this work, as in Smith's estimation, the growth of the pioneering community became emblematic of the rise of the nation. Cecilia Morgan in "History, Nation, and Empire: Gender and Southern Ontario Historical Societies" (*Canadian Historical Review* [henceforth *CHR*], September 2001, 491–528), has pointed out that women, who comprised a large proportion of the membership of many of these middle-class societies, were able to insert themselves into this romantic narrative of progress at a time when they were excluded from the formal political life of the country. Nevertheless, the essentially masculine account of the rise

of nationhood continued to prevail and this is reflected in Smith's "Reminiscences" where women only make rare appearances.

2. Here Smith is referring to Mr. C.F.H. Goodhue, a very prominent man in the early years of the Eastern Townships. Goodhue established an axe-manufacturing business in Sherbrooke and also owned considerable lands in Ascot, Compton County. C.M. Day, *History of the Eastern Townships.* (Montreal: John Lovell, 1869; reprinted Belleville, ON: Mika Publishing Co., 1989), 371–78.

3. The Township of Sullivan (Grey County), named after Robert Baldwin Sullivan, commissioner of Crown Lands, was first surveyed by John Stoughton Dennis during the summer of 1843. Being adjacent to the Garafraxa Road and southwest of Owen Sound, Sullivan Township was well-placed as a destination for the hundreds of settlers pouring into the region each year. Sullivan Historical Society, *A History of Sullivan Township: 1850–1975.* (Desboro, ON: Richardson, Bond & Wright Ltd., 1975), 3–11.

4. Jerusalem artichokes, also known as sunchokes, are a member of the sunflower family. The plant grows throughout the United States and Canada, producing an edible potato-like tuber at the end of the stalk under ground. It is a very strong growing perennial, and as Smith indicates, can quickly become a weed problem if not properly managed. For more on Jerusalem artichokes see, *North Carolina State University Horticultural Information Leaflets* at www.ces.ncsu.edu/depts/hort/hil/hil-1-a.html, accessed on December 9, 2007.

5. The "improvident" condition of the First Nations was created in large part by the settlement of their former hunting territory by immigrants such as Smith. For the controversial history of Indian Land Treaties see Robert J. Surtees, "Land Cessions, 1763–1830," in Donald B. Smith and Edward S. Rogers, eds., *Aboriginal Ontario: Historical Perspectives on First Nations* (Toronto, Dundurn Press, 1994). For the attempt to transform the Mississauga into agriculturalists, see Olive Dickason, *Canada's First Nation: A History of Founding Peoples From earliest Times,* (Toronto: Oxford University Press, 1997), 205–12; and Donald B. Smith, *Sacred Feathers: The Reverend Peter Jones (Kahkewaquonaby) and the Mississauga Indians* (Toronto: University of Toronto Press, 1987).

6. The Arran immigration to Inverness Township in Megantic County began with the landlord-assisted emigration of eighty-six individuals in 1829 who came to Canada on-board the *Caledonia.* The community of settlers and their Canadian-born children reached a population peak of 275 in 1845 after which time out migration to other parts of

North America began to reduce their number. See J.I. Little, "From the Isle of Arran to Inverness Township: A Case Study of Highland Emigration and North American Settlement, 1829–34," in *Scottish Economic and Social History* [henceforth *SESH*], Vol. 20, part 1 (2000), 9–19. The immigrant families were given free land grants of one hundred acres each in an attempt to encourage emigrants from all parts of the United Kingdom to settle in Lower Canada. Colonial authorities were concerned about the "undiluted American element" that dominated settlement in the Eastern Townships and were also anxious to have a larger "British" population in the colony to challenge French Canadian nationalists in the Legislative Assembly. J.I. Little, *Ethno-Cultural Transition and Regional Identity in the Eastern Townships of Quebec* (Ottawa: Canadian Historical Association, 1989) 5–15. See also Lucille H.Campey, *Les Écossais: The Scottish Pioneers of Lower Canada, 1763–1855* (Toronto: Natural Heritage Books, 2005).

7. Archibald McKillop, from Lochranza on the northwestern corner of Arran, was a fish merchant and Sunday school teacher who became the leader of the families who "volunteered" to emigrate to Canada in 1829. He was well rewarded for his services obtaining eight hundred acres for himself and his family by 1831. He was appointed justice of the peace in 1830 and "Captain" of the militia in 1831. During the Lower Canadian Rebellion of 1837 he was elevated to the rank of major as a reward for raising a company of Megantic men to garrison Quebec City. Little, "From the Isle of Arran to Inverness Township," 13–14.

8. The early difficulties of the Arran settlers were well-documented in the account published by Archibald McKillop's descendant, Dugald Mckenzie McKillop, *Annals of Megantic County*. (Lynn, MA: D. McKillop, 1902). These trials are corroborated by other sources, but Smith is mistaken in characterizing the land as "ungrateful." J.I. Little has recently demonstrated that by 1831 the Arran immigrant community's agricultural productivity was considerably better than that of its neighbours, partly as a consequence of the fertility of the soil. See Little, "From the Isle of Arran," 16.

9. The minister Smith is referring to is likely the Reverend Donald Hendry (or Henry), who was actually a deacon. He had served as a missionary in various parts of the Highlands before coming to Lower Canada in 1831. The settlers were all Congregationalists and as such had been a minority on the heavily Presbyterian Arran. They had been located primarily on the northern part of the island and most

came from the Sannox farms on the northeast coast. Donald Meek has suggested that, in general, connections based on evangelical faith not only reinforced the tight-knit sense of community in the Highlands, but also encouraged such group migration across the Atlantic. See, Little, "From the Isle of Arran," 24, fn. 51; and D. Meek, "'The Fellowship of Kindred Minds': Some Religious Aspects of Kinship and Emigration from the Scottish Highlands in the Nineteenth Century," in *Hands Across the Water: Emigration from Northern Scotland to North America* (Aberdeen: Aberdeen & Northeast Scotland Family History Society, 1995).

10. The settlers came from the part of Arran that held most strongly to the traditional communal agricultural practices. It was these practices that the landlord, the Duke of Hamilton, saw as the main impediment to "improved" agriculture and had encouraged him to order the "clearances," which ultimately resulted in the settlers' assisted emigration. The majority of the "cleared" Arran tenants had migrated to other parts of Scotland and only those most determined to maintain their religious and cultural practices emigrated to Lower Canada. Ironically, their "backward" communal approach to agriculture actually allowed the colony to succeed in the early years. It did not take long, however, before individuals had to migrate out of the new settlement in search of economic opportunity. Little, "From the Isle of Arran," 3–4 and 20–22; and "Agricultural Improvement and Highland Clearance: The Isle of Arran, 1766–1829," in *SESH*, Vol. 19, part 2 (1999), 132–54. One of the few surviving pieces of evidence from the settlers themselves is a Gaelic letter in which the author describes the need for such secondary migration. Ronald I.M. Black, "An Emigrant's Letter in Arran Gaelic, 1834," in *Scottish Studies*, 31 (1992–93), 63–87.

11. The Garafraxa Road, (now Highway No. 6), which ran north from Fergus through Arthur, Mount Forest, and Durham, ending in Owen Sound, was surveyed by Charles Rankin during the summer of 1837. Great hardships and the outbreak of rebellion in 1837 meant the road would not be opened until 1840. It developed as the main artery for settlers and others venturing north into what became Grey and Bruce counties. See James Gow, "Charles Rankin's Survey of the Owen Sound Road," in *Wellington County History*, Vol. 2 (1989), 19–33.

12. The social and economic pressures leading to irregular school attendance in nineteenth century Ontario are examined in Susan E. Houston and Alison Prentice, *Schooling and Scholars in Nineteenth-*

Century Ontario. (Toronto: University of Toronto Press, 1988), 214–23.

13. Literacy rates do appear to have been remarkably high in Upper Canada. Early data from the census records suggests levels as high as 90 per cent and, as a consequence, the province was able to support thirty-eight different newspapers by 1836. It is, however, debatable if schooling became more effective as the century progressed. School attendance figures from the 1870s suggest that nearly one in five school-age children in Ontario did not attend at all, while two in five attended less than one hundred days in the school year. In addition, class sizes appear to have been smaller in rural schools of the 1830s, and the schools were kept open from eight to ten months of the year. See Harvey Graff, "Towards a Meaning of Literacy: Literacy and Social Structure in Hamilton, Ontario, 1861," in *History of Education Quarterly*, Vol.12, No. 3. (Fall, 1972), 411–31; J.G. Hodgins, *Documentary History of Education in Upper Canada*, Vol. 25, (Toronto: L.K. Cameron (1894–1910), 224; and Harry Smaller, Teachers and Schools in Early Ontario," in *OH*, Vol. 85, No. 4. (December 1993), 295–96.

14. Smith is referring to the education system initiated with the 1841 Common School Act, and developed in subsequent legislation, that provided government money, in combination with local school fees, to pay the salaries of certified teachers. These moneys were administered through local trustees. The system had a long evolution characterized by tension between those who wished to maintain local autonomy and those, such as Egerton Ryerson, the advocate of educational and religious reform, who wished to create a uniform centralized school system. Clergymen in Upper Canada often combined their parish duties with school teaching as a method of supplementing their income, while others, like Smith, began their careers with a brief period as schoolteachers. See Houston and Prentice, *Schooling and Scholars*, 97–123, 66–67; and R.D. Gidney, "Egerton Ryerson," in *Dictionary of Canadian Biography* [henceforth *DCB*], Vol. 11 (1881–1890), 783–95.

15. The Governor's Road (officially Dundas Street), was a name coined for the road proposed by Lieutenant-Governor John Graves Simcoe. The road, which ran from Burlington to the proposed site of London, and then on to Lake St. Clair, was to serve the dual role of providing security against invasion by the Americans from the south, and opening up the region to settlement. By 1794, the Governor's Road had been cut as far as the site of London on the Thames River, but

it would be another six years before the extension to Lake St. Clair would be completed. Despite its grand title, the road was treacherous, and in many places remained little more than a cart path for years. Mary Byers, *The Governor's Road* (Toronto: University of Toronto Press, 1982), 3–5.

16. Tales such as these were employed by school reformers to denigrate the quality of schooling received in the years before the creation of a standard system of education. Nevertheless, it has been shown that these criticisms were overstated and that the log schoolhouses had indeed met many of the basic needs of the local population. Part of the motive for the creation of a centralized system, advocated by reformers like the Methodist Ryerson, was to ensure that in addition to the three "Rs," proper Christian morality and socially conservative values would be inculcated into the "lower orders" of the province. This appeared particularly necessary after the tumult associated with the 1837 Rebellion. Indeed, it was suggested that some "ignorant" schoolmasters had played a significant role in inflaming the population. See R.D. Gidney, "Elementary Education in Upper Canada: A Reassessment," in Michael B. Katz and Paul H. Mattingly, eds., *Education and Social Change: Theme's from Ontario's Past* (New York: New York University Press, 1975), 3–27; and Smaller, "Teachers and Schools," 297.

17. The Van Norman brothers, Joseph and Benjamin, originally from northern New York, were the first iron founders to produce stoves in Upper Canada. At its peak in 1840 their foundry at Long Point produced 750 tons (680 tonnes) of cast and wrought iron goods. See Norman R. Ball, "Joseph Van Norman," in *DCB*, Vol. 11 (1881–1890), 897–98. For information on the early settlement of Long Point and the development of the region, see R. Robert Mutrie, *The Long Point Settlers* (Ridgeway, ON: Log Cabin Publishing, 1992). This work is invaluable to familial or genealogical studies as the author has provided detailed examinations of a wide range of relevant sources, including land transactions and marriage records.

18. Reverend Robert Brown (1833–93), was born in Caledon, Ontario. He was educated at the Congregational College in Toronto and served as Congregational minister in Garafraxa (1862–73) as well as Middleville, Hopetown, and Rosetta, Ontario (1873–82). In 1883, Brown joined the Presbyterian Church and served in Manitoba (1886–88). He later moved to Tacoma, Washington. See Douglas Walkington, *The Congregational Churches of Canada: A Statistical and Historical Summary* (Toronto: United

Church Archives, 1979); and Ibid., *Ministers of the Presbyterian Church in Canada 1875–1925* (Toronto: United Church Archives, 1987).

19. "Jerhart" is the Scots word for Jedburgh, a town in the Borders of Scotland. Smith's use of the vernacular here was anticipated in his published poetry, which contributed to the large body of such work, largely imitative of Robert Burns, that was produced in Canada during the nineteenth century. Employing Scots dialect in prose writing was also a hallmark of the popular periodical literature and the sentimental "kailyard" novels ("kailyard" simply translates to "kitchen garden" or "cabbage patch") circulating in Scotland at the time Smith was writing. The "kailyard" novelists use of Scots was part of their celebration of a mythic bygone rural ideal, but in the broader press its use can be seen as a response to the rapid expansion of the Scottish reading public. See Gillian Shepard, "The Kailyard" and William Donaldson, "Popular Literature," in Douglas Gifford, ed., *The History of Scottish Literature: Volume 3 Nineteenth Century* (Aberdeen: Aberdeen University Press, 1988). Smith's use of dialect, however, often descends into conventional contemporary caricature, particularly when he deals with other ethnic groups.

20. This term refers to the Scottish inventor John L. McAdam, born in Ayr, Scotland, who developed the process of covering a road with small broken stones compressed to form pavement. McAdam had journeyed to New York City in 1770, where he made a fortune in his uncle's counting house. Upon his return to Scotland in 1783, he began experimenting with new types of road construction. In recognition of his work he was made surveyor general of Metropolitan Roads in Great Britain in 1827. See the entry on John McAdam in *DNB*, Vol. 12, 395–97.

21. Smith uses the phrase "young bloods" to denote young men who considered themselves the "leaders of rural fashion and young society" and who rejected the leadership of local elites. As an educator and clergyman, Smith viewed such social rebellion as empty-headed time-wasting. As with several of the tales recounted in his *Reminiscences*, Smith published an earlier fictional version of this criticism in his "John Kanack's Experiences," in *NDM* (September 1873), 136. For a complete listing of these articles see Appendix A.

22. The "Queen's Bush" was a 800,000 hectare tract of land that extended west and north from Waterloo County to Lake Huron. By the 1840s, approximately 2,500 squatters, who could not afford to purchase land elsewhere, had settled in one portion of the area known as

the Queen's Bush Settlement. At the time, the settlement, which comprised portions of Peel, Woolwich, and Wellesley Townships, was home to 1,500 Black settlers, a large portion of whom were fugitive slaves and free Black immigrants from the United States, as well as a smaller number of former Canadian slaves who had been freed by the British Emancipation Act of 1834. Both Black and White settlers supplemented their subsistence livings with occasional wage labour. In 1843, the Crown began surveying and selling off land in the Queen's Bush, which forced most of the squatters to relocate. Many of the Black population moved to Grey County and north through the Owen Sound and Collingwood area. Only a few headstones remain in the Queen's Settlement today to mark what at one time was one of the largest Black communities in Upper Canada. See Linda Brown-Kubisch, "The Black Experience in the Queen's Bush Settlement," in *OH* Vol. 88, No. 2 (June 1996), 106–18; see also, Linda Brown-Kubsch, *The Queen's Bush Settlement: Black Pioneers 1839–1865* (Toronto: Natural Heritage Books, 2004); and W.M. Brown, *The Queen's Bush.* (London: John Bale, Sons & Danielson, Ltd., 1932).

23. This is a reference to Simon Bolivar (1783–1830), leader of South American independence from Spain and the first president of the Republic of Columbia. At the time, Columbia included modern day Ecuador, Panama, and Venezuela. See John J. Johnston, *Simon Bolivar and Spanish American Independence* (Princeton: Von Nostrad, 1968). Bolivar negotiated preferential relations with Britain in order to encourage trade and investment in his new republic. One consequence was the creation of the Columbia Agricultural Association in London with the mandate to create an agricultural colony in Venezuela. Several factors contributed to the failure of this scheme, but chief among them was the inability of the Scots settlers to adapt to the new climatic conditions and their reluctance to work beside former Black slaves. For a detailed account of the scheme, and the subsequent migration of 137 of the settlers to the Guelph region, see Edgar Vaughan, "Scottish Settlers for Canada from Venezuela: A Bureaucratic Problem in 1827," in *Historic Guelph: The Royal City*, Vol. 18 (April 1979), 4–112. For John Galt's role in their settlement on Canada Company land, see Robert C. Lee, *The Canada Company and the Huron Tract, 1826–1853: Personalities, Profits and Politics* (Toronto: Natural Heritage Books, 2004), 59–60.

24. Two families by the name of "Butchart" were among the Venezuelan immigrants who settled in Upper Canada. Alexander Butchart was

from Aberdeen and had served nine and a half years in the Royal Artillery before taking his family to South America. He is most likely the "Mr. Butcher" referred to by Smith. See Edgar Vaughan, "Scottish Settlers ..." and "The Guayrians at Guelph in Upper Canada: Some Additional Notes," in *Historic Guelph: The Royal City*, Vol. 19 (April 1980), 60–70. By presenting the 1837 Rebellion in this comic manner, Smith is trivializing the seriousness of the event. Although the November rising, led by the Scottish-born William Lyon Mackenzie (1795–1861), was badly organized, and the battle between rebels and soldiers in Toronto a rout, elsewhere the potential for serious unrest was readily apparent. In Lower Canada, the fighting lasted well into 1838, and there were fears that unrest could re-ignite in Upper Canada at any time. It was only in hindsight, after the successful suppression of the conflict in both provinces, that the Upper Canadian elite could afford to ridicule the pretensions of rebels. For an introduction to the scholarly work on the Rebellion in Upper Canada, see C. Reid and R. Stagg, *The Rebellion of 1837 in Upper Canada*, (Ottawa, ON: Champlain Society, Ontario Heritage Foundation, 1988). For Lower Canada, see Allan Greer, *The Patriots and the People: The Rebellion of 1837 in Lower Canada* (Toronto, University of Toronto Press, 1993). See also Greer's important article "1837–38: Rebellion Reconsidered," in *CHR*, Vol. 76, No.1 (1995), 3–18, which highlights the necessity of viewing the Rebellion in Upper and Lower Canada as a single event. For a summary of Mackenzie's career and a list of the most useful biographical works, see Frederick H. Armstrong and Ronald J. Stagg, "William Lyon Mackenzie," in *DCB*, Vol. 9 (1861–1870), 497–510. Smith was not alone in personalizing and thus trivializing the efforts made by reformers to promote radical change in Upper Canada. See M. Vance and M. Stephen, "Grits, Rebels and Radicals: Anti-Privilege Politics and the Pre-History of 1849 in Canada West," in D. Pollard and G. Martin, eds., *Canada 1849* (Edinburgh: Centre for Canadian Studies, 2001).

25.   In the early nineteenth century the supply of alcohol was customary in most workplaces and there are recorded examples of settlers refusing to contribute their labour to communal "bees," such as a barn raising, if drink was not offered. See Catharine Anne Wilson, "Reciprocal Work Bees and the Meaning of Neighbourhood," in *CHR*, Vol. 82, No. 3 (September 2001), 444.

26.   David Christie was a political reformer, school commissioner, speaker of the Senate, and prominent figure in early Dumfries Township.

The Christie family arrived from Scotland in 1833, settling in South Dumfries the following year. David Christie resided at "the Plains" between Paris and Brantford. J.M.S. Careless, "David Christie" in *DCB*, Vol. X (1871–1880), 168–71.

27. The Bell and Son Foundry was one of St. George's prominent industries. The firm was established in 1838 by Benjamin Bell, who focused primarily upon the building trade. In 1857, he went into partnership with John Shupe and began manufacturing agricultural implements. The partnership lasted for less than a year, and later Bell's son Charles joined the business. From there the business prospered, shipping farm implements throughout Canada, and to Great Britain, South Africa, New Zealand, and Australia. Jean Waldie, *Brant County*, Vol. 1 (Paris, ON: Brant Historical Society, 1984), 134.

28. Smith was clearly enthralled by this gender-crossing practice. In 1888, he published a six stanza poem on the same theme: "Then I spurred a little onward, and I doffed my ready hat; For there with royal presence On a very throne she sat, — With a riding-skirt and bodice, and the scepter of a whip; — And the girl that drove the Reaper Drove the colour from my lip …" From *The Poems of William Wye Smith* (Toronto: Dudley and Burns, 1888). Such perceived role reversal in other vocations was not always viewed so benignly. Catharine Wilson cites the extreme example of one cross-dressing Quebec girl who was sentenced to two years in jail in 1918 for participating in a logging bee. See Wilson, "Reciprocal Work Bees," 451.

29. Edwin Guillet cites one authority that claimed that there were eighteen to twenty taverns along the route at mid-century. He refers to a tavern with rooms at Arthur belonging to one John Wright. It is not certain if this is the "Clark's Hotel" referred to by Smith. See Guillet, *Pioneer Inns and Taverns*, Vol. 4 (Toronto: Ontario Publishing, 1958), 80–82.

30. Eaton Township was constituted December 4, 1800, and after a slow start developed rapidly. By 1869 there were two academies and fifteen elementary schools, six post offices, seven churches, four gristmills, and fourteen sawmills and other establishments. See Day, *History of the Eastern Townships*, 396–99.

31. The small pioneer log house would appear to have been introduced to Upper Canada by Loyalist immigrants from the United States, however, its adaptability to the wooded conditions in Upper Canada meant that it was "evidently employed by all groups entering the province." See Peter Ennals and Deryck W. Holdsworth, *Homeplace:*

The Making of the Canadian Dwelling Over Three Centuries (Toronto: University of Toronto Press, 1998), 84–90.

32. A great deal has been written on this much-maligned figure of the American Revolution. For a detailed balanced examination of the life and career of Benedict Arnold, see James Kirby Martin, *Benedict Arnold: Revolutionary Hero: An American Warrior Reconsidered* (New York: New York University Press, 1997). On July 24, 1800, the Executive Council of Upper Canada were instructed to award Arnold and his sons a large grant of land as a "mark of royal favour." A five thousand-acre block was set aside below Lake Simcoe, and a further, smaller grant, was set aside south of Renfrew in the Ottawa Valley. To meet the residency terms of the grant, three of Arnold's sons, Richard, Henry, and John, moved to Ontario and became prosperous farmers in the eastern part of the province. None of the brothers appear to have occupied the lands north of Toronto. Arnold himself remained in London where he had moved after leaving New Brunswick in 1791. He died in 1801 without ever having visited his Upper Canadian lands. See Barry Wilson, *Benedict Arnold: A Traitor in Our Midst* (Montreal: McGill-Queen's University Press, 2001), 223 and 217–36.

33. "Poor Andre" refers to Major John Andre who acted as an intermediary for Sir Henry Clinton in concluding the notorious deal for Benedict Arnold to hand over West Point to the British in return for $20,000. Andre was captured and was subsequently hanged for spying on October 2, 1780. Arnold, of course, escaped. See entry for Arnold by Curtis Fahey in *DCB*, Vol. 5 (1801–1820), 28–36.

Chapter 2: The Pioneers

1. Harriet Elizabeth Beecher Stowe (1811–96) was born in Litchfield, Connecticut, the daughter of a Congregational pastor and staunch Calvinist, Lyman Beecher. In 1836, she married Calvin Ellis Stowe, a professor of Biblical literature at Lane Theological Seminary where her father was the head. Mrs. Stowe had a long teaching career herself at Bowdoin College, Maine, but is most well known for her novels. The most famous of these being her indictment of slavery, *Uncle Tom's Cabin; or Life Among the Lowly*, first published in serial form between 1851–52. The book, along with her other anti-slavery novel *Dred* (1856), was credited by, among others, Abraham Lincoln, with giving inspiration to the Abolitionist Movement in the years leading up to the American

Civil War. Her character Sam Lawson, "The Village Do-Nothing," first appears in *Oldtown Folks* (1869), a novel that drew heavily on the New England boyhood reminiscences of both her husband and her father. He appears again as the accomplished storyteller in the follow-up volume, *Sam Lawson's Oldtown Fireside Stories* (1872). Stowe made Lawson the antidote to New England Puritanism. At least one critic has suggested that, with Lawson, Stowe was able to contrast "Puritan inwardness with Yankee realism and humor" reflecting her own evolution from strident abolitionist to sentimental recorder of bygone New England village life. C.H. Foster, *The Rungless Ladder: Harriet Beecher Stowe and New England Puritanism* (New York: Cooper Square Publishing, 1970), 202. See also the entry for Stowe in the *DAB*, Vol. 11 (New York: American Council of Learned Societies, 1935), 115–20. Despite his laziness, Lawson is clearly a sympathetic character. Stowe made him her principal storyteller — a feature that would not only make him appealing to her creator, but, given his aims with *Canadian Reminiscences*, to Smith as well.

2. Smith's suggestion of a cavalier attitude towards crime in nineteenth-century Upper Canada is challenged by recent scholarship. John C. Weaver in particular, has examined the history of crime and punishment in the Gore District, a district formed in 1816 and comprised of parts of York County, the Home District and Niagara, where Smith's incident takes place. He has pointed out that the records of the district gaol in Hamilton show that by the 1840s there was an increase in prosecutions and concern with petty crimes, especially those against property. In addition, the numbers of women incarcerated for drunken and disorderly behaviour, including prostitution, rose dramatically. An inkling of this concern with immoral behaviour is perhaps reflected in the reference to the prisoner's "slatternly wife."

Susan Lewthwaite has also recorded in the 1830s and 1840s numerous instances of impoverished rural settlers exercising their own form of justice through social violence, and their open defiance of local magistrates trying to enforce the law. Weaver argues that the increase in prosecutions was in large part a response to a perception of greater social order with the arrival of large numbers of Irish Catholics before and after the Great Famine. Peter Oliver, in contrast, has argued that Upper Canada had a very low crime rate, particularly for serious offences, when compared to Britain or the United States, and that prison developments in Upper Canada were instituted by reformers following debates in those countries. Nevertheless, both he and Weaver agree that new standards of morality and concern with the "disruptive lower orders" inspired much of the penal reforms of the second half on the nineteenth century. See John C. Weaver, "Crime, Public Order, and Repression: The Gore District in Upheaval, 1832–1851," in *OH*, Vol. 78, No. 3. (September 1986), 175–207; John C. Weaver, *Crimes, Constables, and Courts: Order and Transgression in a Canadian City, 1816–1970* (Montreal: McGill-Queen's University Press, 1995); Susan Lewthwaite, "Violence, Law, and Community in Rural Upper Canada," in Jim Phillips et al, eds., *Essays in the History of Canadian Law: Crime and Criminal Justice*, Vol. 5 (Toronto: University of Toronto Press, 1994), 353–86; and Peter Oliver, "*Terror to Evil-Doers: Prisons and Punishments in Nineteenth Century Ontario* (Toronto: University of Toronto Press, 1998), especially Chapter 11, "Terrorizing the Underclass: The Intermediate Prisons."

3. A reference to Samuel Taylor Coleridge's epic poem "The Rime of the Ancient Mariner." At the opening of the poem, an old seaman singles out one of three guests arriving at a wedding feast to tell him his tale:

> He holds him with his skinny hand,
> "There was a ship," quoth he.
> "Hold Off! Unhand me, grey beard loon!"
> Eftsoon his hand dropt he.
>
> He held him with glittering eye —
> the Wedding Guest stood still,
> And listens like a three years' child:
> The Mariner hath his will.
> *Lyrical Ballads* (Bristol: Biggs and Cottle, 1798).

4. There was a good deal of out migration from New Brunswick and Nova Scotia during the second half of the nineteenth century. Many men were attracted to the emerging fishing and lumber industries of British Columbia while others took a leading role in the development of the mercantile and political life of the colony. A few single young women also undertook the journey to work as schoolteachers. See E.R. Forbes and D.A. Muise, eds., *The Atlantic Provinces in Confederation* (Toronto: University of Toronto Press, 1993), 139–41; Jean Barman, *The West Beyond the West: A History of British Columbia* (Toronto: University of Toronto Press, 1996); and Jean Barman, *Sojourning*

Sisters: The Lives and Letters of Jessie and Annie McQueen (Toronto: University of Toronto Press, 2002).

5. A Congregational church was established at Eaton Corners (located in the Eastern Townships to the east of Sherbrooke, Quebec) in 1835. Smith was minister there from 1878 to 1880. His first congregation, however, was in Listowel, Ontario, where he served from 1865 to 1869. Commencing in 1870, Smith was minister in Pine Grove, Ontario, in Vaughan Township, until he left for Eaton. Smith returned to Ontario in 1881 to serve in New Market (now Newmarket) where he remained until 1884. From that date, he appears to have been in permanent charge of a congregation until he accepted the minister's post in St. Catharines in 1893. Smith served in St. Catharines, with a brief three-year interruption, until 1907.

    Levi French was an associate of Captain Josiah Sawyer, to whom the majority of the Township of Eaton, Lower Canada, was granted. Levi French was, therefore, a prominent landowner and one of the first men involved in the opening of the township to settlement. Douglas Walkington, *The Congregational Churches of Canada: A Statistical and Historical* Summary (Toronto: United Church Archives, 1979); *The Canadian Independent* (January 1, 1887), 11 and (May 2, 1887), 135; and "Rev. William Wye Smith," in *The Express* (October 4, 1967). See also Day, *History of the Eastern Townships*, 396–7.

6. The Ashburton Treaty was named after Alexander Baring, Lord Ashburton, who in 1842 negotiated the boundary treaty with Daniel Webster, then American secretary of state. The negotiations were undertaken as a consequence of a series of disputes, including the Aroostook War, along the Maine-New Brunswick border in the late 1830s. For a detailed discussion of the treaty and the border survey referred to by Smith, see Francis M. Carroll, *A Good and Wise Measure: The Search for the Canadian-American Boundary, 1783–1842* (Toronto, University of Toronto Press, 2001); and H. Jones, *To the Webster-Ashburton Treaty: A Study in Anglo-American Relations, 1783–1843* (Ann Arbour, MI: UMI Out-of-Print Books on Demand, 1990, c.1977).

7. J.A. Smith, "A Lost Irishman: Jimmy Butler and the Owl," in *Humourous Sketches and Poems* (Toronto: Dudley and Burns, 1875), 52–56. Burford Township, part of the Brant District, was first developed by Abraham Dayton, a native of Connecticut. Dayton and his associates began settlement in the summer of 1793, and from there the township prospered. Jean Waldie, *Brant County*, Vol. 1, 108–09.

8. It would appear that the model for the story was "Pat and the Owl,"

which was being recited at popular "penny reading" entertainments. The story was being performed in Hamilton, Ontario, as early as 1874, the year before J.A. Smith, William Wye Smith's brother, published his version. In 1875, another local orator performed his own "Jimmy Butler and the Owl" but set the tale in the woods of Ancaster. See Heather Murray, *Come, Bright Improvement: The Literary Societies of Nineteenth-Century Ontario* (Toronto: University of Toronto Press, 2002), 93–94. The use of the obvious stereotypical Irish name, Pat, and the comic stage Irish dialogue, strongly suggests that Smith's boundary tale is yet another version of the same joke. Patrick O'Sullivan has suggested that the appearance of such jokes was a reaction to the arrival of large numbers of Irish peasants to North America in the 1840s. Presenting the Irish as good-natured buffoons was one way of making their presence less threatening and maintaining their lower social status. See P. O'Sullivan, "The Irish Joke" in *The Creative Migrant* (London: Leicester University Press, 1994).

9.   Although some of the more radical evangelical sects that emerged in New England in the early nineteenth century did not gain a foothold in the Eastern Townships, there is evidence, as Smith's tale suggests, that cross-border contact did spread the influence of intense piety on an individual basis. See J.I. Little, "The Mental World of Ralph Merry: A Case Study of Popular Religion in the Lower Canadian-New England Borderland, 1798–1863," in *CHR*, Vol. 83, No. 3 (September 2002), 338–63.

10.   A reference to Aesop's fables that were first recorded in Greek in the early sixth century BCE (Before Common Era). See Aesop, *The Complete Fables*. (Harmondsworth: Penguin Books, 1998), Olivia and Robert Temple, translators.

11.   Labaree was a family name frequently found in northern New England, the likely origin of Smith's "squire." There is an early reference to a New Hampshire Labaree, perhaps an ancestor, in Susanna Johnson's eighteenth-century captivity account. See Susanna Willard Johnson Hastings, *A Narrative of the Captivity of Mrs. Johnson: Containing an Account of Her Sufferings, During Four Years With the Indians and the French* (New York: 1841).

12.   The celebration of the monarch's birthday as a popular expression of "Britishness" emerged at the end of the eighteenth century. These occasions were characterized by both elite demonstrations of loyalty and popular games. At times these celebrations were transformed

into protests with the rough play degenerating into rioting. See Linda Colley, *Britons: Forging the Nation 1707–1832* (New Haven: Yale University Press, 1992); and C.A. Whately, "Royal Day, People's Day: The Monarch's Birthday in Scotland c. 1660–1860," in R. Mason and N. MacDougall, eds., *People and Power in Scotland* (Edinburgh: John Donald, 1992), 170–88.

13. Captain Josiah Sawyer was granted lands in Newport Township (Compton County, Quebec) along with Edmund Heard, in 1793, however, Newport Township was not formally established until July 1, 1801. They chose a site well away from any other settlements and within two years had moved their families into their new homes. The settlement prospered, with Captain Sawyer playing a significant role in the regions development. One of the first villages established in Eaton Township, Sawyersville, took its name from Captain Sawyer. Day, *History of the Eastern Townships*, 396, 408–09.

14. The Baptist Church was located at a point near Newport called Grove Hill. Day, *History of the Eastern Townships*, 399.

15. Colpoy's Bay was named after a pilot in W.F.W. Owen's expedition to the region. Owen was leading a team whose task it was to survey Georgian Bay in 1815. He would name the Sound, where the City of Owen Sound now stands, after himself. By the late nineteenth century when Smith was writing, it had become a popular resort for summer holidays or picnics and could be reached by steamer from Owen Sound. William Wye Smith, *Gazetteer and Directory of the County of Grey, 1865–66* (Toronto: Globe Steam Press, 1865), 63.

16. Here the author is referring to "Elder" William Smith of St. George's Baptist Church. Elder Smith led the St. George congregation in erecting a church in 1858. Waldie, *Brant County*. 135.

17. Louis (Lajos) Kossuth (1802–94) led an abortive Hungarian republican revolution in 1849. After failing to win Hungarian independence from the Hapsburg monarchy, Kossuth fled to Turkey and subsequently made a tour of Britain and the United States to gain support to continue the struggle. The tour of the United States actually took place from December 1851 to July 1852. Kossuth's arrival in New York was greeted with great popular enthusiasm and John Nicholas Genin, a local hatter with considerable promotional skill, used the occasion to sell a large quantity of his unsold soft felt hats. He had the hats modified to resemble Kossuth's distinctive head gear and instantly created a new fashion. Wearing a Kossuth hat became a public demonstration of one's commitment to republicanism. The

fashion trend lasted long after Kossuth's visit, which failed to gain the official United States support he desired. Soldiers on both sides of the Civil War wore the Kossuth, or slouch hat, and its popularity continued long afterwards, particularly in the west. See Donald S. Spencer, *Louis Kossuth and Young America: A Study of Sectionalism and Foreign Policy, 1848–1852* (Columbia: University of Missouri Press, 1977), 59–61.

18. Chip hats were constructed from birch wood. The bark was removed, a knife was dug into the wood, and thin strips or "sheens" were pulled up. These strips were then woven into hats. See Joleen Gordon, *Handwoven Hats: A History of Straw, Wood and Rush Hats in Nova Scotia* (Halifax: Nova Scotia Museum, 1981), 50–8. For a general discussion of early clothing, see Edwin C. Guillet, *The Pioneer Farmer and Backwoodsman* (Toronto: Ontario Publishing Co., 1963), 73–85.

19. In 1827, the English chemist John Walker began selling the first struck matches, but it would be some time before such innovations would be widely available. Early matches, while highly popular, tended to self-ignite, and it was not until the late 1850s that a less volatile match using red phosphorous was available. See Fenella Saunders, "They Invented It When? The Match," in *Discover* (April 2001) 18. See also, "John Walker, 1781?–1859" in *DNB*, Vol. 20, 534–35.

20. Smith published a fictional version of this tale in "John Kanack's Experiences," in *New Dominion Monthly*, May 1874, 265–66.

21. "Hungarian Milling" was developed by Andras Mechwart (1834–1907), the technical director at the Ganz factory in Budapest. The factory produced railway wheels and Mechwart used the firm's manufacturing capability to develop a new flour mill that used steel rollers instead of stone wheels. Mechwart's mill made it easier to separate the bran from the rest of the flour and thus produced a finer end product. By 1900, as a consequence of these innovations, Budapest flour mills produced over a million tonnes of flour per annum making it, for a time, the world's leading centre of flour production. See Janos Estok, "Developing Cereals," in *Hungarian Quarterly*, Vol. 42, No. 162, (Summer 2002).

22. Canada was ceded to Britain in the Treaty of Paris at the close of the Seven Years' War in 1763.

23. George III (1738–1820) reigned during a particularly troublesome period in British history. He became king in 1760, at the height of the Seven Years' War with France, and would have to deal with both the American and French revolutions. Throughout his life he was plagued

by seizures that left him depressed, unpredictable, and unfit for rule for extended periods of time. (Today, it is known that he suffered from porphyria.) He was, however, extremely popular, and a marked contrast to his son George IV, who became king in 1820 after serving as Prince Regent for nine years. Charles Arnold-Baker, "George III" in *The Companion to British History*, (Tunbridge Wells, Kent: Longcross Press, 1996). For a detailed study of the life of George III, see Christopher Hibbert, *George III: A Personal History* (London: Viking, 1998).

24. Here, Smith seems to be confused, suggesting that "Frontenac" was an earlier name for what today is Ontario.

25. Melba Morris Croft describes Robert Carson as "an early settler who travelled through the region in search of less marshy ground." *Fourth Entrance to Huronia: The History of Owen Sound.* (Owen Sound: Stan Brown Printers Ltd., 1980), 28. Smith states that Carson's Mill was on the shore of Georgian Bay, one mile west of Cape Rich. The mill was built about 1842, and was of "primitive description, but … a great convenience to the neighborhood." William Wye Smith, *Gazetteer and Directory of the County of Grey, 1865–66*, 47.

26. Butler's Rangers were a corps of Loyalist troops raised by John Butler (1728–1796), an American veteran of the Mohawk Valley. The Rangers worked closely with the Native Six Nations, particularly the Seneca, and conducted raids deep into American territory during the Revolutionary War. They were one of the most successful British colonial fighting forces, but earned a lasting reputation for cruelty and deceit among successive generations of American historians. See R. Arthur Bowler and Bruce G. Wilson, "John Butler," in *DCB*, Vol. 6 (1771–1800), 117–20; and Mary Beacock Fryer, *King's Men: The Soldier-Founders of Ontario* (Toronto: Dundurn, 1980), 129–78.

27. James Madison (1751–1836) was president of the United States from 1809 to 1817.

28. Captain Alexander MacDonald is credited with originating the idea of raising loyal colonial veterans to fight for Britain during the American Revolution. MacDonald had had a varied military career having first seen service suppressing the Jacobite Rebellion in 1745 and then in the Caribbean and North America during the Seven Years' War. As early as 1774, he was using his Highland connections to recruit former soldiers, settled in Nova Scotia where he remained before returning to Britain in 1784 after the death of his wife Suzanna. See Christopher Moore, *The Loyalists: Revolution, Exile, Settlement* (Toronto: McClelland & Stewart, 1984) 17–23, 216; and

Alexander MacDonald, "Letterbook," in *Collections of the New York Historical Society* (New York: 1882).

29.   The Battle of Acre, which Smith mentions here, was part of Napoleon Bonaparte's Egyptian expedition in 1798–99. The fortress of Acre was a medieval stronghold held during the crusades by the Knights Hospitallers, a military and religious order that both cared for sick and injured crusaders, and distinguished themselves on the battlefield. Napoleon's siege lasted from late March until the twentieth of May, 1799, and ended with the French taking heavy losses from both battle and plague. Sydney Smith was commander of the British fleet, which played a crucial role in Napoleon's defeat. See J. Christopher Herald, *Bonaparte in Egypt* (London: Hamish Hamilton, 1963), 284–304.

30.   Mr. Thomas Lunn first arrived in Owen Sound with his wife aboard the schooner *Otter* from Toronto in 1843. Upon settling, Lunn took an active part in the town's development, acting as a councillor for Sydenham Township and the Town of Owen Sound (1856); he was also one of the first officers of the County of Grey, and in 1862 was elected mayor of Owen Sound. See Croft, *Fourth Entrance to Huronia*, 33, 48, 49, 58, 70, and 88.

31.   Burn's journal entry for Sunday, May 13, 1787, reads "come up the Tweed to Melrose — dine there and visit that far-fam'd glorious ruins — Come to Selkirk, up the Ettrick the whole country hereabout, both on the Tweed and Ettrick, remarkably stony." It does not appear that Burns visited the most picturesque part of the region, the Vale of Yarrow. The poet had undertaken the tour to escape Edinburgh and, perhaps, to seek some inspiration. Nevertheless, as Smith implies, a recently received offer from a benefactor, Patrick Miller, to lease a farm on an estate near Dumfries was another likely motive for Burns's tour. See Raymond Lamont Brown, *Robert Burns's Tour of the Borders, 5 May-1 June 1787* (Totowa, NJ: Rowan and Littlefield, 1972), 4–5, 21, 35.

32.   The incident took place on Hallowe'en in the west wing of the newly completed University College. Smith is mistaken about the date since the foundation stone for the college was not laid until 1856. University College was the first building constructed for the newly established University of Toronto that saw its male-only student population expand from thirty-five in 1853 to eighty in 1859, and to two hundred twenty-five in 1860. See Martin L. Friedland, *The University of Toronto: A History* (Toronto: University of Toronto Press, 2002), 60; and W. Stewart Wallace, *A History of the University of Toronto* (Toronto: University of Toronto Press, 1927), 77.

33. Professor George Buckland (1804–85) was appointed professor of Agriculture at the University of Toronto in 1851. A prominent English agriculturalist, Professor Buckland served as editor of *The British American Cultivator* and was instrumental in the establishment of the Ontario Agricultural College, now the University of Guelph. Ann MacKenzie, ""George Buckland," in DCB, Vol. 11 (Toronto: University of Toronto Press, 1982), 132–33.

34. Dr. John McCaul (1807–87) arrived in Toronto on January 25, 1839, to take up the post of principal of Upper Canada College. In 1842, he became vice-president, and then president, of the newly formed King's College. While McCaul opposed the transformation of the Anglican King's into the secular University of Toronto in 1849, he remained as professor of Classics and the new institution's first president. He was purportedly a reserved individual who attempted to steer clear of student controversies, but he did provide stable scholarly leadership for the fledgling institution. G.M. Craig, "John McCaul," in *DCB*, Vol. 11, 540–42.

35. David Mills (1831–1903) had a remarkable career in a wide range of fields: education, journalism, law, and politics. In addition to several terms as MP for Bothwell, which comprised parts of Kent and Lambton counties, Mills served as justice minister in Sir Wilfrid Laurier's Liberal government and then briefly as a judge on the Supreme Court. He was a consistent advocate of the separation of jurisdictions between the provincial and federal governments and this brought him into conflict with Sir John A. MacDonald, who argued for the overriding power of the federal government. While he was editor of the *London Advertiser* from 1882 to 1887, Mills wrote a series of partisan but learned editorials attacking MacDonald's policies and constitutional interpretations. As a consequence of these attacks, MacDonald dubbed Mills "The philosopher of Bothwell." See Robert C. Vipond, "David Mills," in *DCB*, Vol. 13 (1901–1910).

36. In 1848–49, the Durham Road (later Highway No. 4, now County Road 4, and western Highway 9) crossing from Durham to Kincardine, was opened and settlers began pouring in to the area. In 1849, Mr. Abraham Buck was the first to settle on the site of what would become the town of Hanover, and in the same year was followed by Mr. Christian Hassenjager, a native of Hanover, Germany. The area would attract other settlers of German descent, many of whom had originally settled in Waterloo County. Josephine Elizabeth Hahn, *Home of My Youth: Hanover* (Hanover: self-published, 1967), 9–12.

37. This would appear to be a reference to Timothy Rogers (1756–1828), who founded a Quaker settlement near what would become Newmarket in 1801. The previous year Rogers had made a tour of the land north of York and, according to his journal, went "thirty or forty" miles into the back country looking for a suitable settlement site. The pioneers who established Yonge Street Meeting, and a series of other Quaker communities in York County, were largely from the Philadelphia area. Simcoe viewed the pacifist religious dissenting groups, such as the Quakers, Mennonites, and Dunkards, as ideal settlers and had actively encouraged their migration to the colony. However, during the War of 1812, the commitment of these sects to non-violence became a divisive issue. One radical sect that emerged out of Yonge Street Meeting were the Children of Peace who also proved to be controversial, not least because they allowed women prominent public roles. See Arthur Garratt Dorland, *A History of the Society of Friends in Canada* (Toronto: Macmillan and Co., 1927), 91–9; Gerald Craig, *Upper Canada: The Formative Years 1784–1841* (Toronto, McClelland & Stewart, 1963), 44–46; Peter Brock, "Accounting for Difference: The Problem of Pacifism in early Upper Canada," in *OH*, Vol. 90, No. 1 (Spring 1998), 19–30; Kate Brennagh, "The Role of Women in the Children of Peace," in *OH*, Vol. 90, No. 1 (Spring 1998), 1–18. For a township by township listing of the early settlers of York County, see Charles Pelham Mulvany et al, *History of Toronto and County of York* (Toronto: C.B. Robinson, 1885).

38. Timothy Rogers could not have met Simcoe, since the governor left the colony in July 1796. He did, however, meet with Simcoe's successor Lieutenant-Governor Peter Hunter who agreed to grant Rogers forty farms of two hundred acres each for the Quaker community. It would appear that Smith, or his informant, may have been confusing the two governors in retelling the tale. See S.R. Mealing, "John Graves Simcoe," in *DCB*, Vol. 5 (1801–1820), 754–59; and Dorland, *A History of the Society of Friends*, 92.

39. Nicholas Miller, a New York artisan who arrived in Upper Canada in 1793, is a likely candidate for the Mr. Miller of this story. He worked on a number of government jobs associated with the construction of Yonge Street and at one point held the post of "Overseer for Highway." Colonel Gorham may have been a descendant of Eli Gorham who, in 1808, built a carding and woollen mill on Yonge Street at Newmarket, but this has yet to be established. See F.R. Beechem's detailed history

of the road, *The Yonge Street Story 1793–1860* (Toronto: Natural Heritage Books, 1996), 40, 53–57, and 153.

Chapter 3: Odd Characters and Customs

1. John McCallum was one of the founders of the Woodbridge Presbyterian Church, which was established in 1874. See G. Elmore Reaman, *A History of Vaughan Township* (Toronto: University of Toronto Press, 1971), 162.

2. A variety of "Bear Dances" were performed by First Nations peoples throughout North America, but Smith clearly had in mind the group dance performed west of the Mississippi River. This particular version of the dance, which is still performed each May by the Ute Nation in Colorado, was illustrated and described by the American ethnologist George Catlin (1796–1872) whose work was widely circulated in North America. The "Bear Dance" was part of hunting ritual and not, as Smith implies, a war dance. See George Catlin, *Letters and Notes on the Manners, Customs, and Condition of the North American Indians*, Vol. 5 (London: G. Catlin, 1841), 244. Smith also used his "Bear Dance" analogy to justify his earlier fictional depiction of eccentric pioneer characters. "John Kanack's Experiences," in *New Dominion Monthly* (September 1873)137.

3. The story of John Loree related here by Smith is typical of the anecdotal nature of much of what Smith was reminiscing upon. Often inserted by Smith for comic effect, such stories contain a wealth of information on the problems faced by many of the early pioneers attempting to establish a new life "in the bush."

4. William Dickson (1769–1846) was a native of Dumfries, Scotland. He was raised in a mercantile family, and it was his Scottish family connections in the Niagara Peninsula that enabled Dickson to establish himself as one of the leading merchants and land speculators in Upper Canada. Partly as a consequence of his legal training, Dickson acted as a land agent for other investors, but he made the colonization of Dumfries Township his own personal project and used his professional contacts in the Scottish borders to aggressively promote the settlement. As a consequence, by the 1820s the township had become a significant centre of Lowland Scottish settlement. See Bruce G. Wilson, "William Dickson," in *DCB*, Vol. 7 (1836–1850), 250–52; E.J. Cowan, "From the Southern Uplands to Southern

Ontario: Nineteenth-Century Emigration from the Scottish Borders," in T.M. Devine, ed., *Scottish Emigration and Scottish Society* (Edinburgh: John Donald, 1992), 61–83; and John David Wood, "The Historical Geography of Dumfries Township, Upper Canada: 1816–1852," University of Toronto, unpublished MA thesis, 1958.

5.   Samuel Street (1775–1844) was born in Farmington, Connecticut, and after settling in Upper Canada became one of the colony's wealthiest men. He began a milling business in the Niagara Peninsula but soon branched out into money lending and land speculation. By the 1830s he had become the leading stockholder in the Bank of Upper Canada and was a major shareholder in the Gore Bank and the Bank of Montreal. In addition, over 3,000 acres in the London district had been purchased by his firm. William Dickson had acted as his agent for many of those land sales. See Bruce A. Parker, "Samuel Street," in *DCB*, Vol. 7 (1836–1850), 832–35.

6.   John Loree's use of "White man" in this context reflects the development of the concept in the early nineteenth century and is likely related to his New Jersey origins. David Roediger has demonstrated that the term "White" was originally employed to distinguish European settlers from indigenous peoples. During the first half of the nineteenth century "Whiteness" emerged among the American labouring population as a central feature of working-class identity. The concept was linked to both notions of racial superiority and fair dealing. See David R. Roediger, *Wages of Whiteness: Race and the Making of the American Working Class* (New York: Verso, 1991).

7.   Settlers often banded together to construct roads that would increase the value of their property and ease communication. At times, pioneers would also work on land company or government road construction to supplement their incomes. Starting in 1837, the government funded the construction of a "macadamized" road from Dundas to Waterloo, and this appears to be the construction project referred to by Smith. See Edwin C. Guillet, *Early Life in Upper Canada.* (Toronto: University of Toronto Press, 1933), 504–547; and James M. Young, *Reminiscences of the Early History of Galt and the Settlement of Dumfries in the Province of Ontario* (Toronto: Rose and Company, 1880), 120–21.

8.   In early December 1837, after the defeat of the rebellion in Toronto, William Lyon Mackenzie and several others had made their way to Buffalo, New York. Once there they attempted to raise American support in order to return to Upper Canada to aid the rising that had emerged in the western part of the province under the leadership of

Dr. Charles Duncombe. The result was the invasion on December 14 of Navy Island just above Niagara Falls by a small "Patriot" force. On December 19, Mackenzie issued a proclamation on the island offering three hundred acres in Upper Canada to anyone joining the rebels' cause. Eventually, the invaders were joined by several hundred others, but they abandoned the island on January 14 after the Canadian volunteers burned the American supply boat *Caroline*.

By that time, Duncombe's rising had collapsed. Nevertheless, "Patriot" forces, largely recruited along the American border, continued to conduct raids into Upper Canada at Windsor, Niagara, and Cornwall throughout 1838, contributing to a deep sense of insecurity and anti-reform sentiment in Upper Canada. It was not until the American President Van Buren clearly stated that the United States would not protect American citizens engaged in such raids that the activity largely ceased. All the same, as late as 1840, "Patriots" were still active, one group having blown up Brock's Monument at Queenston Heights. See C. Reid and R. Stagg, *The Rebellion of 1837 in Upper Canada* (Ottawa: Champlain Society, Ontario Heritage Foundation, 1988); Edwin C. Guillet, *The Lives and Times of the Patriots* (Toronto: University of Toronto Press, 1968), 71–87. For the treatment of the American "Patriots" transported to Australia in the aftermath of the raids, see Cassandra Pybus and Hamish Maxwell-Stewart, *American Citizens, British Slaves: Yankee Political Prisoners in an Australian Penal Colony 1839–1850* (Melbourne: University of Melbourne Press, 2002).

9. Smith is again making light of the seriousness of the situation in 1837. Since the War of 1812 American settlers had been viewed as potentially disloyal by the Upper Canadian elite, but most chose the neutral position espoused by Loree. All the same, others in South Dumfries had been heavily involved in the reform movement and indeed had encouraged Duncombe to lead a rising in support of Mackenzie. Dumfries settlers had organized rebel meetings in the township and only abandoned participation in the rising when it became clear that the rebellion had been defeated in Toronto. Concern ran so deep that local leaders declined to raise and arm the local militia due to concerns over loyalty. Samuel Lount, one of two individuals executed for his role in the rebellion, was for a time hidden in the house of the South Dumfries settler, Mr. Latshaw, and the son of another, Horatio Hills, died in Kingston goal awaiting trial for his role in the rebellion. See Colin Read, *The Rising in Western Canada: The Duncombe Revolt and*

After (Toronto: University of Toronto Press, 1982), 93–4, 103, 140, 170 and 182; and *The History of the County of Brant, Ontario* (Toronto: Warner, Beers & Co., 1883), 434–42.

10. The use of corporal punishment came under sustained attack from reformers during the nineteenth century and, as a consequence, practices common at the start of the century, such as public floggings, were eliminated. Nevertheless, by the time Smith was writing, moderate physical "correction" on children was still viewed as acceptable and a means of preventing the development of criminal behaviour. See Peter Oliver, *'Terror to Evil Doers': Prisons and Punishment in Nineteenth-Century Ontario* (Toronto: University of Toronto Press, 1998), 20–42 and 225–7; Myra C. Glenn, *Campaigns Against Corporal Punishment: Prisoners, Sailors, Women, and Children in Antebellum America* (New York: State University of New York Press, 1984); and Neil Sutherland, *Children in English-Canadian Society: Framing the Twentieth-Century Consensus* (Toronto: University of Toronto Press, 1976), 101 and 107.

11. Archibald Gilkison, who practised law in Brantford, is likely the individual referred to by Smith. The Gilkison family connection with Upper Canada began when William Gilkison (1777–1833), a trader from Irvine, Scotland, settled in the colony. William founded the town of Elora in 1832, while his son David (1803–51) later became a leading merchant in Guelph. See *DCB*, Vol. 11, 935; D.E. Fitzpatrick, "William Gilkison," in *DCB*, Vol. 6 (1821–1835), 285–86; and Gilbert A. Stelter, "David Gilkison," in *DCB*, Vol. 8 (1851–1860), 327–28.

12. Dr. Elam Stimson was born in Tolland, Connecticut, and served in the United States army during the War of 1812. Although from humble circumstances, he was able to study medicine at Yale College. When Stimson arrived in Upper Canada, he first settled in St. Catharines, moved to Galt in 1824 and then to London in 1831. In London he acted as coroner and physician to the jail, but in 1833, after his wife Ann Bolles and his youngest child had died from cholera, Stimson relocated to St. George. He responded to the cholera epidemic that claimed two hundred people in Galt over a ten-day period in 1834, with his medical publication, *The Cholera Beacon*. In St. George, where he lived with his second wife, Ann's younger sister Susan, he continued to practise medicine until his death in 1869. Stimson's daughter, Rebecca, married Dr. Nathaniel Mainwaring, who was also originally from Connecticut and also established a large medical practice in South Dumfries. See C.M. Godfrey, "Elam Stimson" in *DCB*, Vol. 9 (1861–1870), 748–49; Jean Waldie, *Brant County*, Vol. 1,

132–33; and *The History of the County of Brant Ontario* (1883), 205.

13.   In an effort to encourage railway construction, the government of the Province of Canada had adopted a series of acts, starting in 1849, that would guarantee the credit of projects that were able to obtain half their funding from private or municipal funds, but ultimately the Great Western Railway (GWR) became dominated by British investors. The first railway construction commenced in Upper Canada in 1852, however while the GWR main line stopped at St. George, it missed Galt. Eventually, a branch line was constructed and opened with considerable fanfare on August 21, 1855. See Douglas McCalla, *Planting the Province: The Economic History of Upper Canada 1784–1870* (Toronto: University of Toronto, 1993), 199–216, 311; James M. Young, *Reminiscences of the Early History of Galt*, 228, 244–46.

14.   The Vanevery (or Van Every) family from New York had a long association with Dumfries Township. David Van Every is recorded as being one of the earliest settlers, having arrived in St. George in 1817, while Charles Van Every and Andrew Van Every were listed as township "Pathmasters" in 1824 and 1829 respectively. See C.M. Johnston, *Brant County: A History 1784–1945* (Toronto: Oxford University Press, 1967), 16; Young, *Reminiscences*, 138, 212–13; and *History of the County of Brant*, 205.

15.   As was the common custom, Smith is employing the term "Dutch" (a corruption of "*deutch*") to designate the group of Low German-speaking immigrants known collectively as the Pennsylvania Dutch. These devout people comprised of Swiss Mennonites and Palatine Germans originally settled in Pennsylvania in the early eighteenth century. Their pacifism during the American Revolution was, however, resented and many chose to immigrate to Upper Canada with the official encouragement of Lieutenant-Governor Simcoe. When Smith and others referred to "German" immigrants they were identifying those individuals who came out directly from Germany after 1820, thus distinguishing them from the earlier "Dutch" settlers. See Aaton Spencer Fogelman, *Hopeful Journeys: German Immigration, Settlement, and Political Culture in Colonial America, 1717–1775* (Philadelphia: University of Pennsylvania Press, 1996); and Heinz Lehmann, *The German Canadians, 1750–1937: Immigration, Settlement and Culture* (Saint John's, NL: Jesperson Press, 1986), 14–24, 66–79.

16.   The Gore Bank operated exclusively in the western part of Upper Canada, while the Commercial Bank had fourteen offices, primarily east of Toronto. Loree's predicament was far from usual during the

1840s. Indeed, the Gore Bank had to write off over 20 per cent of its capital as a consequence of discounts on overdue and bad debts. See McCalla, *Planting the Province*, 156–58.

17. The death of General Isaac Brock at Queenston Heights was quickly adopted into the heroic mythology of both Upper Canada and the British Empire. As early as 1840, John Richardson had incorporated the incident into his novel *The Canadian Brothers* (Montreal: A.H. Armour & H. Ramsay, 1840), and, in the 1880s, James McIntyre had produced an epic poem on the subject [see "Reminiscences" *Poems of James McIntyre* (Ingersoll, ON: Office of the Chronicle, 1889)]. The heroic death was also incorporated into general histories, such as *Tuttle's Popular History of the Dominion of Canada* (Montreal: Tuttle & Downie, 1877), and school textbooks, like Buckley and Robertson's *High School History of England* (Toronto: Copp Clarke, 1891). Despite such attention, in the long run General Brock's heroism on the field of battle proved to be less appealing than that of Laura Secord, who ran to warn the British Army of the American advance. See Colin M. Coates and Cecilia Morgan, *Heroines and History: Representations of Madeleine de Verchères and Laura Secord* (Toronto: University of Toronto Press, 2002).

18. Robert King was originally from Cumnock, Ayrshire. He worked as a stonecutter on the construction of Osgoode Hall before taking up his one-hundred-acre farm on lot 3, Concession 9, Vaughan Township. The farm was northeast of Woodbridge near Elder Mills. See G. Elmore Reaman, *A History of Vaughan Township*, 204; *Illustrated History of the County of York, and the Township of West Gwillimbury and Town of Bradford, in the County of Simcoe, Ontario* (Toronto: Miles & Co., 1878).

19. Although there was a great deal of artisan emigration to Upper Canada, few emigrant advice books addressed this audience directly. One obvious exception was William Thomson's, *A Tradesman's Travels in the United States and Canada in the Years 1840, 1841 and 1842* (Edinburgh: Oliver & Boyd, 1842). Thomson, a weaver from Stonehaven, Scotland, described in some detail the combination of farming and weaving in the region around Toronto. Another exception was *Chambers's Edinburgh Journal*, which actively promoted emigration to Canada. William and Robert Chambers, the editors, were great supporters of emigration as a means to alleviate the suffering of the British working class. From its inception in 1832, *Chambers's Edinburgh Journal* included a wide range of articles related

to emigration and, in particular, to the artisan class that possessed the skills needed in the colonies. See Scott A. McLean, "Literature to Instruct, Entertain and Amuse: The Cheap Literature Movement in Scotland, 1768–1845," University of Guelph, unpublished PhD. thesis, 1998), 261–81.

20.   The movement to create an asylum system in Upper Canada originally developed out of a desire to reform the gaols (jails). By the 1830s, reformers were distressed by the inclusion of the insane within the general prison population. As a consequence, an asylum was established in Kingston, and was quickly joined by institutions in Toronto, London, Guelph, and elsewhere. Historians have noted that those on the margins of Canadian society, particularly the poor Irish immigrants, were far more likely to be incarcerated in such institutions. They have also noted the increased influence of medical and moral reformers in the development of "treatments" for the insane as the century developed. Despite Smith's belief in a distinction between the two countries, similar trends were also apparent in Scotland itself. See James E. Moran, *Committed to the Asylum: Insanity and Society in Nineteenth Century Quebec and Ontario* (Montreal: McGill-Queen's University Press, 2000); Oliver, "Terror to Evil Doers," 44–48, 231–36, and 382–86; Cathy E. Kindquist, "Migration and Madness on the Upper Canadian Frontier, 1841–1850," in *Canadian Papers in Rural History*, Vol. 8 (1992), 129–61; Cheryl Krasnick (Walsh) *Moments of Unreason: The Practice of Canadian Psychiatry and the Homewood Retreat, 1883–1923* (Montreal: McGill-Queen's University Press, 1989); and "'In Charge of the Loons': A Portrait of the London, Ontario Asylum for the Insane in the Nineteenth Century," in *OH*, Vol. 74, No. 3 (1982), 138–84; Mary Orr Johnson, "The Insane in Nineteenth Century Britain: A Statistical Analysis of a Scottish Insane Asylum," in *HSR*, Vol. 17, No. 3 (1992), 3–20; and Jonathan Andrews, "Case Notes, Case Histories and the Patient's Experience of Insanity at Gartnavel Royal Asylum, Glasgow, in the Nineteenth Century," in *SHM*, Vol. 11, No. 2 (1998), 255–81.

21.   Although the excessive use of alcohol in public was common early in the nineteenth century, by the 1840s the Temperance Movement was well-established in Upper Canada. Towards the end of the century, drunkenness at community gatherings like a township agricultural fair would, as Smith suggests, be viewed as shameful by the "respectable" middle class. Indeed, Congregationalists like Smith were particularly

prevalent in the Temperance movement. See Jan Noel, *Canada Dry: Temperance Crusades Before Confederation* (Toronto: University of Toronto Press, 1995).

22. A reference to the J.M. Barrie play "The Admirable Crichton," which had just been produced when Smith was composing his *Reminiscences*. Crichton, the satirical play's central character, is a butler to an English peer who proves to be a man of limitless talent when the aristocratic family is shipwrecked on a South Pacific island. The butler's ability to perform any task required for the party's survival and comfort win him the awe and respect of his social superiors, but Crichton is forced to return to his subservient role once the party is rescued, See *The Plays of J.M. Barry* (London: Hodder and Stoughton, 1936), 159–237.

23. The popular custom of "Charivari" was imported from Europe, the first recorded examples in North America being found in Quebec. Nevertheless, the custom was widespread and practiced under various names, including "shiveree" and "serenading" from Newfoundland to the Carolinas. Its central function was to impose community norms on couples. Marriages between couples of wide age disparity were particular targets, but the practice could also be used to punish a range of transgressions from adultery to wife beating. These "Charivaris" could be extremely violent and at times end in death. Examples of such fatal treatments can be found in Ontario as late as the 1890s. At times, the targets were also chosen to ensure racial segregation. Susanna Moodie describes the death of Tom Smith, "a runaway nigger" who was subjected to a fatal Charivari because of his marriage to an Irish woman. See Susanna Moodie, *Roughing it in the Bush, or, Life in Canada* (Toronto: McClelland & Stewart, 1991, originally published in 1852), 210–11; and Brian D. Palmer, "Discordant Music: Charivaris and Whitecapping in Nineteenth Century North America," in *Labour — La Travail*, Vol. 3 (1978), 5–62.

24. In 1875, Purvis Lawrason is listed as possessing the one-hundred-acre lot 5, Concession 2 near St. George. Sam Van Every was the son of Andrew D. Van Every who arrived in South Dumfries in 1819. See *Illustrated Historical Atlas of the County of Brant; The History of the County of Brant, Ontario* (1883), 188.

25. A "Charles Wilbur" is listed, in 1875, as possessing lot 10, Concession 3, and lot 12, Concession 4, near St. George. See *Illustrated Historical Atlas of the County of Brant*.

26. The legal suppression of the "Charivari" was part of a general replace-

ment of customary policing by the "rule of law." Elites were further encouraged to suppress the custom since it was apparent that the practice had become highly political. For example, the analysis of the targets of Charivari in Lower Canada before 1837 has revealed that extent to which the popular customs were being employed to further the cause of reform. See, Allan Greer, "From Folklore to Revolution: Charivaris and the Lower Canadian Rebellion of 1837," in *Social History* [henceforth *SH*], Vol. 15, No. 1 (1990), 25–43. An intriguing consequence of the legal suppression of the rural community Charivaris was the adoption of aspects of the practice among urban artisans. In 1890, striking weavers in Hamilton, Ontario, used elements of the custom to ensure unity among strikers. See Palmer, "Discordant Music," 37.

27. "Bowse" is a version of the word "bouse" or "booze." In this context it signifies a heavy drinking session. *Oxford English Dictionary* [henceforth *OED*], Vol. 1, A-B (Oxford: Clarendon Press, 1933), 1027.

28. Miles O'Reilly (1806–90) was born in Stamford, Upper Canada, near Niagara Falls. He was called to the bar on June 22, 1830, and became chief judge of the Gore District Court in 1837, but resigned in 1854 to run, unsuccessfully, for the Conservatives in the general election. O'Reilly was deeply involved in the prosecution of the 1837 rebels and gave testimony at the trial of Charles Durand. O'Reilly was also involved in early railway development and the building of the Anglican church in Hamilton. See *DHB*, "Hamilton," Vol. 1 (1981), 160–61. A useful introduction to the various courts of Upper Canada and their function can be found in Marion MacRea and Anthony Adamson, *Cornerstones of Order: Courthouses and Town Halls of Ontario, 1784–1914* (Toronto: Clark Irwin, 1983), 254–58; see also C.K. Talbot, *Justice in Early Ontario, 1791–1840* (Ottawa: Crimcare, 1983). Smith published a version of this story in "The Scot in Canada Vol. 2," in *The Scottish Canadian* (May 7, 1891), 10.

29. William McDonald possessed one hundred acres at lot 10, Concession 4W, in Caledon Township. See *Illustrated Atlas of the County of Peel, Ontario* (Toronto: Walker & Milles, 1877).

30. Smith's version of the story can be compared with the account provided in Margaret Whiteside, *Belfountain and the Tubtown Pioneers* (Cheltenham, ON: Boston Mills Press, 1975).

31. This tale was used by Smith in his story "Sprouting" part of his series entitled "John Kanack's Experiences," which appeared in the *New Dominion Monthly*, March 1873. In the story Smith begins by stating that, "some men are naturally communists" and prefer to work with

others. His Dumfries neighbour, given the name Tyson, is said to be of a different mind and unable to adjust to the communal way of life among the Shakers.

32. The Shakers were a small branch of radical Quakers known for their "shaking, dancing and shouting" during religious ceremonies. Originally found in England, Shaker settlements were established in North America and at the height of their popularity there were approximately 6,000 members with communities in Indiana, Kentucky, Ohio, and New York, where the spiritual headquarters was established in the latter state, at Lebanon. The communities were communally oriented with members living in large "families" of men and women sharing work and living space, but maintaining a separation along gender lines and adhering to strict rules of celibacy. Studies of the Shaker community at Lebanon have revealed that many individuals who were initially attracted to the spiritual life of the religious community found it difficult to conform to the group's celibacy and strict discipline. As a consequence, membership fluctuated dramatically throughout the nineteenth century. See Stephen J. Stein, "The 'Not-So-Faithful' Believers: Conversion, Deconversion and Reconversion Among the Shakers," in *American Studies*, Vol. 38, No. 3 (1997), 5–20; Priscilla J. Brewer, "The Demographic Features of the Shaker Decline, 1787–1900," in *Journal of Interdisciplinary History* [henceforth *JIH*], Vol. 15, No. 1 (1984), 31–52; and for a general introduction to the movement, see Edward Deming Andrews, *The People Called Shakers: A Search for the Perfect Society* (New York: Dover Publications, 1963).

33. Shakers could leave the community at any time, although often without their possessions. It was common for people to join the Shaker communities during times of hardship, only to leave once times had improved. These individuals, like Smith's old neighbour, were known as "winter" or "bread-and-butter" Shakers. See "Shakers" at rebelweb.anokak12.mn.us/rebel/student4/sundvall/Home. htm, accessed on December 15, 2007.

34. The first settlers arrived at the mouth of the Big Head River in 1834, a year after Charles Rankin had begun surveying the Townships of Collingwood and St. Vincent. Originally the site was called Peggy's Landing, after Peggy Miller, one of the original settlers. However, rapid development of the region prompted the government to formally plan a village, and in 1845 the surveyor William Gibbard arrived and a village plan was established. The new village was given

the name Meaford, after Meaford Hall, the residence of Sir John Jervis, Earl St. Vincent, in whose honour the township had been named. "First Settlers Arrived at Site of Meaford," in *Owen Sound Sun Times*, Saturday, July 26, 1952.

35.   In his *Gazetteer and Directory of the County of Grey, 1865–66* (46) William Wye Smith describes the Big Head River as being one of the best trout streams of the region. Early in the twentieth century, the speckled trout, purportedly introduced by A.A. Herriman, a Hudson's Bay Company trapper, were being promoted as one of the main attractions of the region. See the promotional book designed to attract British settlers entitled, *Owen Sound on-the-Georgian-Bay, Canada* (Owen Sound: 1912), 112.

36.   Richard Doyle served as town councillor from 1869–72. He later became interested in developing a cement industry in the area, and, in April 1888, with John Corbet, William Robinson and R.P. Buthcart, formed the North American Chemical, Mining and Manufacturing Company. Eventually, cement plants were established at Shallow Lake, Durham, Wiarton, and three at Owen Sound. Melba Morris Croft, *Fourth Entrance to Huronia: The History of Owen Sound.* (Owen Sound: Stan Brown Printers Ltd., 1980), 106, 110, 119, 165, and 203. For more on R.J. Doyle's business and the early history of the cement industry in the region, see the obscure, but useful work by A.C. Tagge, *The Cement Industry in Canada.* (Montreal: 1924), 36–49.

37.   Reverend Joseph Hooper emigrated to Canada from England in 1858. He had been ordained in 1848 and resumed his clerical vocation in Ontario as Congregational minister at New Market (1858–59) and then at Owen Sound (1859–64). In 1865, Hooper moved to Ohio where he continued to serve as a Congregational minister until 1870. See Walkington, *The Congregational Churches of Canada.*

38.   In 1875, a "P. Kelly" is listed as possessing 280 acres on lots 31 & 34, Concession 4, and lot 32, Concession 5, in the western portion of South Dumfries. See the *Illustrated Historical Atlas of the County of Brant.*

39.   Raccoon hunting is frequently referred to in pioneer literature, both as a necessity and as an amusement. For example see, Catharine Parr Traill, *The Canadian Settlers Guide* (London: E. Stanford, 1860), 186; and F. Douglas Reville, *History of the County of Brant* (Brantford, ON: Hurley Printing Co., 1920), 265–66. One settler even produced a poem on the activity from the point of view of the raccoon. See Robert McBride, "The Lambton Coon Hunt," in *Poems Satirical and*

Sentimental on many Subjects connected with Canada (London, ON: 1869), 83–85.

40.   The "fire-fishing" technique was developed by the Ojibwa and then picked up by fur traders, settlers, and travelling sportsmen. The practice is described in numerous sources including Sir Richard Bonnycastle, *The Canada's in 1841* (London: H. Colburn, 1841), 5–7; N.P. Willis and W.H. Bartlet, *Canadian Scenery Illustrated* (London: G. Virtue, 1842), 90; and Anna Jameson, *Sketches in Canada: And Rambles Among the Red Men* (London: Longman, Brown, Green, and Longmans, 1852), 50. As early as 1850 the Mississauga were complaining that settlers were depriving them of their fishing grounds at the mouth of the Credit River, commencing a long history of Native displacement from their traditional food source. See Peter S. Schmalz, *The Ojibwa of Southern Ontario* (Toronto: University of Toronto Press, 1991), 150–51, 161–63, and 179; and Smith, *Sacred Feathers*, 16, 20–24.

41.   For an assessment of the social and cultural impact of westward migration from the Eastern Townships, see J.I. Little, "Watching the Frontier: English Speaking Reaction to French Canadian Colonization in the Eastern Townships, 1844–1890," in *Journal of Canadian Studies* [henceforth *JCS*], Vol. 15, No. 4 (1980–81), 93–111; and "The Bard in a Community in Transition and Decline: Oscar Dhu and the Hebridean Scots of the Upper St. Francis District, Quebec," in *Canadian Papers in Rural History*, Vol. 10 (1996), 45–79.

42.   This incident would have taken place while Smith was resident in Pine Grove, near Woodbridge, Ontario. Smith was minister of the Congregational Church in Pine Grove from 1869 to 1878 during which time he also published his "John Kanack's Experiences." Pine Grove Chapel was a sister church with the Humber Summit Congregational Community Church on Islington Avenue, north of Steele's Avenue. The ministers split the services between the two churches and frequently travelled back and forth. In 1878, a "William Smith" was listed as occupying lot 7, Concession 6, just south of Pine Grove. See Reaman, *A History of Vaughan Township*, 114–15, 141–42, and 148–49.

43.   The exhibition, which ran from May 10 to November 10, 1876, commemorated one hundred years of American independence. Exhibitors drawn from nations all over the world, including Canada, displayed both their cultural and industrial accomplishments. Historians have noted that the Exhibition saw the display of the first statue of an African-American hero, the Methodist Richard Allen, thus encouraging the promotion of Black self-respect. At the same time, the

display of traditional Chinese culture encouraged the perception of many Americans of Oriental "backwardness" supporting those who wished to restrict Asian immigration. See J.D. McCabe, *Illustrated History of the Centennial Exhibition* (Philadelphia: The National Publishing Co., 1876); *Canada at the Exhibition, 1876, Fairmount Park, Philadelphia* (Canadian Commission of the International Exhibition, 1876); Mitch Kachun, "Before the Eyes of All Nations: African-American Identity and Historical Memory at the Centennial Exposition of 1876," in *Pennsylvania History*, Vol. 65, No. 3 (1998), 300–23; and John Haddan, "The Non-Identical Chinese Twins: Traditional China and Chinese Yankees at the Centennial Exposition of 1876," in *American Nineteenth-Century History*, Vol. 1, No. 3 (2000), 51–100.

44. The Hayes-Tilden election was the most controversial in American history until the Bush-Gore election of 2000. As with the latter contest, the Democratic candidate, Samuel Tilden, won the popular vote, but the Republican candidate, Rutherford Hayes, won the election by obtaining more votes from the electoral college. In addition, it was voting irregularities in Florida that became the focus of attention in 1876 as they did in 2000. The Hayes Presidency marked the end of the "Reconstruction" era that ultimately led to institutionalized segregation in the American South. See Sanford J. Mock, "Whatever happened to President Tilden?" in *Financial History*, Vol. 69 (2000), 16–19, 35, 38; James C. Clarke, "The Fox Goes to France: Florida, Secret Codes, and the Election of 1876," in *Florida Historical Quarterly*, Vol. 69, No. 4 (1991), 430–56; Mark D. Harmon, "The New York Times and the Theft of the 1876 Presidential Election," in *Journal of American Culture*, Vol. 10, No. 2 (1987), 35–41; and Ari A. Hoogenboom, *The Presidency of Rutherford B. Hayes* (Lawrence, KA: University of Kansas Press, 1988).

45. Smith took over the operation of the *Owen Sound Times* from Edward Todd who had run the paper since 1863. In 1864, the paper was purchased by David Creighton and J. Rutherford, who later divided the newspaper and printing operations between themselves in 1869. See *Owen Sound by-the-Georgian-Bay*, 102–03.

Chapter 4: Makeshifts of Bush Life

1. In 1875, a C. Van Every was listed as occupying a fifty-acre farm on lot 11, Concession 1, in South Dumfries. The farm was a short

distance southwest of St. George. See *Illustrated Historical Atlas of the County of Brant*

2.   A crupper is a strap looped under a horse's tail, in this case a cow's tail, to keep the harness from slipping forward.

3.   John Brown was the son of James Brown, a settler from Pennsylvania. In 1826, he and his wife, Hanna Burkholder, settled on lot 5, Concession 7 of Vaughan Township, near what would become Woodbridge. Part of Brown's property was located on the Humber Flats where he established a sawmill and blacksmith shop, which produced small agricultural equipment for the Abel Agricultural Works. See Reaman, *A History of Vaughan Township*, 190.

4.   The *Toronto Globe*, founded by the Scottish Liberal George Brown, was published as a weekly from its foundation in 1844 to 1846. It was printed twice weekly from 1846 to 1849, tri-weekly from 1849 to 1853, and daily from 1853. In 1936, the *Globe* was incorporated into the *Globe and Mail*. See J. Brian Gilchrist, *Inventory of Ontario Newspapers 1793–1986* (Toronto: Micromedia, 1987) and J.M.S. Careless, *Brown of the Globe* (Toronto: Dundurn Press, 1989).

5.   In this context the Scots word "craik" refers to a "clamour." It can also refer to the loud cry of a bird, grumbling or complaining. See Mairi Robinson, ed., *The Concise Scots Dictionary* [henceforth *CSD*] (Aberdeen: Aberdeen University Press, 1985), 120.

6.   The term "horse fiddle" was coined in North America during the nineteenth century and refers to a noisemaker. It was constructed by mounting a large cogwheel on a board. At one end of the board a thin long piece of hickory, or similar wood, was attached with the free end resting on the cog. When the wheel was turned a loud ratcheting noise was created. Besides being used to frighten off crop-stealing birds, such devices were also commonly employed in Oxford and Waterloo County Charivari's during the nineteenth century. See *OED*, Vol. 11 (Oxford: Clarendon Press, 1976), 158; and Brian D. Palmer, "Discordant Music," 27.

7.   The lines are from the second stanza of Smith's published poem "The Balky Horse." See *The Selected Poems of William Wye Smith* (Toronto: William Briggs, 1908), 109–10.

8.   There were several Scots with the name Hogg among the early settlers of North Dumfries, including the niece and nephew of the celebrated author James Hogg (1730–1835). In his efforts to recruit settlers for the township, William Dickson's agent, John Telfer, had offered the "Ettrick Shepherd" a farm in Dumfries. Although

Hogg was not persuaded to emigrate himself, he did provide letters of introduction to his kinsmen. For James Hogg, a literary career, rather than emigration, provided the means to escape the hardships associated with the transformation of agricultural practice in the Borders. See Young, *Reminiscences of the Early History of Galt*, 41; Thomas Crawford, "James Hogg: The Play of Region and Nation," in *History of Scottish Literature*, Vol. 3, 89–106; and E.J. Cowan, "From Southern Uplands to Southern Ontario," in T.M. Devine, ed., (*Scottish Emigration and Scottish Society*, (Edinburgh: John Donald Ltd., 1992), 62.

9. "Pease-bannock" is a Scottish flat bread made with pease-meal, *CSD*, 480.

10. Reverend Solomon Snider was the son of German immigrants who had settled in the Thames River area. He served as an itinerant Methodist minister in Westminster Township in Middlesex County in the early 1830s, and was later transferred to Matilda Township in Dundas County in the eastern part of the province. After his marriage at the end of the decade, Snider left the Methodists in protest over their decision to unify with the British Conference. Snider's ability to both speak and read German proved to be a considerable asset when he preached in western Ontario. In 1844–45, Snider briefly returned to Methodism preaching in West Tilbury Township in Essex County following the dissolution of that union. Snider then served as the Congregational minister in Stratford (1846–48); Canso, Nova Scotia (1860–61); New Durham, New Hampshire (1861–66); and Howick Township, Huron County (1867–74). See John Carroll, *Case and his Contemporaries, or, The Canadian Itinerant's Memorial: Constituting a Biographical History of Methodism in Canada from its Introduction into the Province to the Death of Rev. Wm. Case in 1855* (Toronto: Wesleyan Conference, 1871–1877), Vol. 3, 455; Ibid., Vol. 4, 42, 253, and 426–27; Ibid., Vol. 5, 32; and Walkington, *The Congregational Churches of Canada*.

11. Charcoal-burner here refers to a person who made charcoal for a source of fuel.

12. Smith's family had lived in the United States before moving to Canada and may well have spent time in Ohio.

13. It is clear from Smith's text that one of his brothers was John A. Smith, but the identity of the other brother is not readily apparent. See William Wye Smith, *Alazon and Other Poems* (Toronto: H. Scobie, 1850), 100–01.

14. By the 1870s, a lumbering and machinist business had been established by Henry Stapleton in Uxbridge Township, lot 21, Concession 1 — a fifty-acre plot near Island Lake that he and his family had occupied since 1833. See *Illustrated Historical Atlas of the County of Ontario*, (Toronto: J.H. Beers & Co., 1877).

15. Durham boats were flat-bottomed barges eighty to ninety feet [twenty-four to twenty-seven metres] in length. They were introduced to the St. Lawrence by Americans in the year 1809, and by 1824 were regularly used on the Ottawa River. Since they were primarily used for freight they were far from comfortable for passengers, but they did offer affordable and much welcomed transportation for newly arrived emigrants. Edwin C. Guillet, *Early Life in Upper Canada*. (Toronto: University of Toronto Press, 1969), 418–19.

16. In recounting this tale of female immigrant distress, Smith was following a well-worn convention. In nineteenth-century accounts, women were frequently portrayed as being easily subject to despair as a consequence of both their experience of emigration and the hardships of pioneer life in the bush. Men, however, were consistently portrayed as determined battlers taming the wilderness. For discussion of these gendered portrayals in the Australian context, see Kay Schaffer, *Women and the Bush: Forces of Desire in the Australian Cultural Tradition* (Cambridge: Cambridge University Press, 1988). A further, unsympathetic example of the portrayal of female immigrant weakness in the Canadian context can be found in William Bell, *Hints to Immigrants: In a Series of Letters from Upper Canada* (Edinburgh: Waugh and Innes, 1824), 262.

17. Edward Wheeler occupied the one hundred acre lot 1, Concession 9, just outside of the Town of Stouffville in York County. See *Illustrated Historical Atlas of the County of York*.

18. John Frost arrived in Owen Sound from Ottawa in 1856. He brought a stock of merchandise and opened a retail store, but became disillusioned with the settlement and moved to St. Catharines. After a short stay he returned to Owen Sound and took an active part in the community's development, serving as a Sydenham Township councillor, and in 1868, as mayor of Owen Sound. Frost is mentioned as being vocal at several town meetings and also as being a great supporter of establishing better educational facilities in the community. See Croft, *Fourth Entrance*, 36, 49, and 104. His son, John Frost, Jr., wrote the book, *Broken Shackles*, published in 1889 under the pseudonym of "Glenelg" and based upon the oral history

of "Jim Henson," a resident of Owen Sound who had escaped from slavery in Maryland. See Peter Meyler, ed., *Broken Shackles: Old Man Henson From Slavery to Freedom* (Toronto: Natural Heritage Books, 2001), xiii — xvi, reprinted 2007.

19. Seth Holcombe was a prominent figure in the early history of Beverley Township. Apart from running a store and dealing in land and stock, Holcombe served as reeve in 1850, 1852, and 1853, and as councillor in 1851. He was also involved in the formation of an agricultural society in the township. John A. Cornell, *The Pioneers of Beverley.* (Dundas, ON: Roy V. Somerville, 1889), 128, 158.

20. Robert Snowball, an emigrant from Yorkshire, England, built the first carriage and waggon shop in the St. George area in 1833. His business acquired a good reputation, and by 1857 his shop was constructing one hundred waggons annually, generating an annual income of £15,000. See Douglas A. Mannon, *From Bauslaugh's Mill to the Present* (Paris, ON: J.R. Hastings Printing, 1987), 37. See also Wood, *The Historical Geography of Dumfries*, 88.

21. The new mill was built by Robert Snowball's eldest son William, who had taken over the waggon works in 1858–59. William Snowball began construction of his new mill in 1869. A cut-and-dressed stone building, the mill was erected by a Mr. Reith, a Paris stonemason. Mannon, *From Bauslaugh's Mill to the Present*, 51.

22. Reverend Sanderson was a Methodist preacher from Ireland who came to Upper Canada around 1832. See John Carroll, *Case and His Contemporaries*, Vol. 4, 295, 297. The Township of Oro, Simcoe County, is situated on the north shore of Lake Simcoe. Settlement of the township began in 1830, with offers of grants of land to half-pay officers of both the army and navy. Others soon followed. Many of the earliest settlers were from the west of England and the Scottish Highlands, primarily from the Isle of Islay. For this reason the northern and central part of the township, where the Highlanders had settled, saw the establishment of a strong Gaelic community. The early years of the township also saw the arrival of a considerable number of Black settlers, many of whom worked as field hands for the Scottish settlers. At its height, the Black community numbered no more than 150 to 200 individuals and their numbers were dramatically reduced in 1847 when Reverend R.S.W. Sorrick, a former slave, moved with many of his parishioners to Hamilton. According to 1861 census returns, the Black population of Oro Township had declined to ninety-seven by mid-century. See Lt. Col. W.E. O'Brien, "Early Days in Oro," in

Pioneer Papers. Simcoe County Pioneer and Historical Society. No. 1. (Barrie, ON: 1908; Reprint, Belleville: Mika Publishing, 1974), 22–27; Robin Winks, *The Blacks in Canada: A History* (Montreal: McGill-Queen's University Press, 1997) 147; Jason H. Silverman, *Unwelcome Guests: Canada West's Response to American Fugitive Slaves, 1800–1865* (New York: Associated Faculty Press, 1985), 24–26; and Michael Wayne, "The Black Population of Canada West on the Eve of the American Civil War: A Reassessment Based on the Manuscript Census of 1861," in *Histoire Sociale/Social History,* Vol. 28, No. 56 (1995), 465–99.

23. In 1881, one George Locke, a farmer born in Ireland in 1839 who settled in Oro Township in 1843, occupied the seventy-five-acre lot 13 on Concession 13 between Rugby and East Oro. This could be the Mr. Locke of the story or, perhaps, his son. See *Illustrated Atlas of the Dominion of Canada* (Toronto: H. Belden, 1881) "Simcoe Supplement."

24. The imprisonment of debtors was widespread in nineteenth-century Ontario, particularly in the first half of the century. In 1836, 282 out of the 510 inmates of the Gore District Gaol in Hamilton were imprisoned for debt. The poor conditions that prevailed in these facilities seriously undermined the health of these debtors, particularly as they tended to be incarcerated for longer periods than other prisoners. One notorious case in the 1850s was that of Elizabeth Hart who, despite having five children to support and no husband to assist her, was imprisoned for debt in the Gore District Gaol for a period longer than she would have served if she had stolen the sum in question. Given these circumstances, Willie Kyle's threat was far from trivial. See John Weaver, "Crime, Public Order, and Repression," 20; Peter Oliver, "Terror to Evil-Doers," 48–60.

25. The *Hamilton Gazette* was a Tory paper published by George P.B. Bull (1795–1847), a native of Drogheda, Ireland, who arrived in Upper Canada in 1831. Bull was a staunch Orangeman, Freemason, and supporter of High Church Anglicanism. His paper was published from 1835 to 1856, when it was absorbed by the equally conservative *Hamilton Spectator.* See *Dictionary of Hamilton Biography,* 37; J. Brian Gilchrist, *Inventory of Ontario Newspapers,* 56.

26. Robert Archibald Smith (1780–1829), a composer of sacred music and the musical conductor of St. George's Church in Edinburgh, was the son of an East Kilbride silk weaver. Smith was born in Reading, England, while his father was looking for work in his trade. When

the Smith family returned to Scotland, both father and son took up muslin weaving in Paisley. It was through his connection to the Paisley Abbey Church that Smith was able to give up weaving and pursue his musical career. At one point, he worked with Robert Tannahill, setting the Scottish poet's words to music. It is in one of the collections of Tannahill's works that the account of Smith's life was published. See Dictionary of National Biography [henceforth *DNB*], Vol. 53, 114–15; and Philip A Ramsay, *The Works of Robert Tannahill, with a Life of the Author, and Memoir of R.A. Smith, the Musical Composer* (London: A. Fullerton & Co., 1838).

27. In 1837, Upper Canada's first House of Industry, or "poor house" was established in York (Toronto) — ostensibly to deal with the massive influx of impoverished Irish immigrants. Similar institutions were created in a gradual, piecemeal fashion across the province, largely because taxpayers were reluctant to meet the costs associated with housing the poor. One consequence was the continued practice of confining beggars and vagrants in local gaols rather than establishing purpose-built institutions. By mid-century, however, more Houses of Industry were created to meet the need created by a rising population and to satisfy the demands of reformers that the gaols be restricted to the incarceration of criminals. See Oliver, "Terror to Evil-Doers," 59, 90, and 335. For a detailed discussion of the tensions associated with the city's renaming as Kitchener in 1912, see John English and Kenneth McLaughlin, *Kitchener: An Illustrated History.* (Waterloo: Wilfrid Laurier University Press, 1983), 107–34.

28. Reverend Ludwick Kribs (1812–87), born in Barton, Upper Canada, (Barton Township, Wentworth County) was the first minister to graduate from the Congregational College of British North America. He served as minister at the Colpoy Bay Indian Mission, near present-day Wiarton, from 1853 until 1869. In 1854, as part of his missionary activities, Kribs also preached to a small group of Mohawks on the Newash Reserve near Owen Sound and to a group of former slaves in the town itself. Kribs had received his ordination at a time when the Congregational Church Union of Canada had publicly condemned slavery and, in 1853, had called on its members to provide aid to fugitive slaves. While some of Kribs' parishioners were indeed escaped slaves, other Blacks in Owen Sound would have been freemen who had migrated from the United States or migrants from other Ontario communities. According to census returns, the Black community of Owen Sound numbered eighty-six in 1861, the majority of whom

attended the Methodist Episcopal Church founded by their own lay preachers in 1843. Kribs was minister at Owen Sound Congregational Church from its establishment in 1855 to 1857, when he moved to Colpoy Bay to concentrate on his missionary activities. See Henry J. Morgan, *Canadian Men and Women of the Time; a Handbook of Canadian Biography* (Toronto: W. Briggs, 1898), 547; Croft, *Fourth Entrance to Huronia*, 59, 93; Winks, *The Blacks in Canada*, 222; Michael Wayne, "The Black Population of Canada West," 465–99; and Brown-Kubisch, "The Black Experience in the Queen's Bush," 114. See also Chapters 8 and 9 below.

29.   Smith is possibly referring to what he could charge for "milling."

Chapter 5: Buried Fortunes

1.   By the end of the nineteenth century the pretentious gentleman immigrant had become a commonplace object of ridicule in Canadian publications. The foppish, usually English, aristocratic fool was the object of a great deal of satire and the tales Smith recounts in this chapter reinforce such characterizations. While the egalitarianism of settlement society is somewhat exaggerated by Smith, there is a great deal of evidence to suggest that most British settlers of labouring or artisan origins saw their migration to Canada as a rejection of the homeland's class hierarchy. For a more favourable account of the influence of elite immigrants on the development of Canada, as well as a discussion of the negative stereotype, see Patrick A. Dunae, *Gentleman Emigrants: From British Public Schools to the Canadian Frontier* (Vancouver: Douglas & MacIntyre, 1981), 125–27. For early artisan attitudes, see Michael E. Vance, "Advancement, Moral Worth, and Freedom: The Meaning of Independence for Early Nineteenth-Century Lowland Emigrants to Upper Canada," in Ned C. Landsman, ed., *Nation and Province in the First British Empire: Scotland and the Americas, 1600–1800* (Lewisburg: Bucknell University Press, 2001)151–80.

2.   James Young identified three men with the name Henderson — John, Thomas, and William — who emigrated from Roxburghshire and sailed on the *Sarah Mary Ann* from Mayport, England, in April 1831. All three were also original members of the Galt Circulating Library. It is possible that the Mr. Henderson in Smith's account was one of these three men. See Young, *Reminiscences*, 60, 125.

3.   "Stook" is the Scots word for an upright stack of cut sheaves of grain or corn set up in a field to dry. Robinson, *CSD*, 673.

4.   Smith used this anecdote of Dr. Stimson in his story "Settling Down" part of his series "John Kanack's Experiences," published in the *New Dominion Monthly* (August, 1973).

5.   There were six medical doctors in the Stimson family. The father Elam and his three sons, Edwin, James, and William, as well as two son-in-laws — the husbands of Elam's daughters Mary and Rebecca. See above Chapter 3 and William Caniff, *The Medical Profession in Upper Canada* (Toronto: W. Briggs, 1894), 635–6. The over-supply of physicians is corroborated by other sources. Dr. John Scott, an immigrant from the Scottish Borders who settled with his family in Dumfries Township in 1834, established his practice in nearby Berlin (now Kitchener) rather than compete for patients in the township. See Michael E. Vance [wrongly attributed to William E. Vance] "Impressions of a Berlin Pioneer: The Emigrant Letters of Dr. John Scott," in *Waterloo Historical Society*, Vol. 77 (1989), 26–37.

6.   In the spring of 1863, William Patterson and H. Leeming established a confectionary manufacturing business in Brantford, it would appear, by taking over a similar business that had been operating from the 1840s. They produced a variety of products, including cigars, where it was hoped they would weaken the hold on that industry by Hamilton's Tuckett family. By 1875, the firm was employing as many as thirty people and was an important business in the area. C.M. Johnston, *Brant County: A History 1784–1945*, 58; *Illustrated Historical Atlas of the County of Brant* (Toronto: Page & Smith, 1875), 67.

7.   Smith is referring to Judge Stephen J. Jones who was a member of a United Empire Loyalist family that had settled in Stoney Creek, Wentworth County. Jones studied law with Miles O'Reilly (see above, Chapter 3) in Hamilton and was called to the bar in 1846. He was made Brant County judge in 1853, and retired from that office in 1897. In addition to his judicial calling, Jones was an active member of the Brant Avenue Methodist Church and a keen Temperance advocate. See *The Canadian Biographical Dictionary and Portrait Gallery of Eminent and Self-made Men: Ontario Volume* (Toronto: American Biographical Pub. Co., 1880), 258–61; and Henry J. Morgan, *The Canadian Men and Women of the Time: A Handbook of Canadian Biography* (Toronto: W. Briggs, 1898), 515.

8.   "Vinegar Hill" was a piece of common ground in the eastward of the City of Brantford. Its extent roughly corresponds to the area bounded

by the modern Alfred, Murray, and Colborne streets. As early as 1841 the ward boasted two taverns. *The History of the County of Brant*, 252–53, 277.

9.   Rob Roy MacGregor (1671–1734), a notorious Highland outlaw in his own time, was transformed into a romantic hero by William Words-worth and Sir Walter Scott in the nineteenth century. The MacGregor family had a claim to Highland leadership, but Rob Roy was essen-tially a cattle thief who flirted with the plan to restore the exiled Stuart monarchy in 1715. By using this subtitle Smith may have been making an ironic gesture towards Rob Roy's dubious career or, more likely, to the costume and equipment of the Highlanders in his tale. As Michael Lynch has indicated, by the end of the nineteenth century Rob Roy had become "a convenient symbol of tartanry in Modern Scotland." See Michael Lynch, *Scotland: A New History* (London: Pimlico, 1993), xvi; Walter Scott, *Rob Roy* (Edinburgh: A. Constable, 1818); and "Rob Roy MacGregor" in *DNB*, Vol. 12, 543–46.

10.   The Battle of Killiecrankie, fought on July 27, 1689, was the first in a long series of clashes in Scotland between the supporters of the exiled Stuart monarchy and government forces. At Killiecrankie, the Stewart forces, made up largely from members of the western Highland clans and led by John Graham of Claverhouse, "Bonnie Dundee," defeated the force supporting William of Orange, the new Protestant monarch of Scotland and England. Claverhouse, who earlier had developed a reputation for cruelty in his brutal suppression of the intensely Protestant "Covenanters" in the southwest of Scotland, died at the battle. Later Jacobites (the followers of James II and his heirs) had far fewer victories. Nevertheless, "Killiecrankie" was elevated into myth, and the site itself quickly became an early tourist destination. For a general account of the battle and Claverhouse's career, see Magnus Linklater & Christian Hesketh, *Bonnie Dundee: For King and Conscience* (Edinburgh: Canongate Press, 1992). See also Edward J. Cowan, "The Covenanting Tradition," in E.J. Cowan & R.J. Finlay, eds., *Scottish History: The Power of the Past* (Edinburgh: Edinburgh University Press, 2002); Bruce Lenman, *The Jacobite Risings in Britain, 1689–1746* (London: Eyre Methuen, 1980); and Peter Womack, *Improvement and Romance: Constructing the Myth of the Highlands* (London: Macmillan, 1989), 37 and 114.

11.   Aspinwall (or Colon) was the Atlantic terminus of the Panama Railroad, built in 1855 by William Henry Aspinwall (1807–75) to facilitate travel between New York and San Francisco. In the 1860s, when Smith was in

Owen Sound, a great many men were travelling from eastern Canada along this route to the gold fields of the British Columbia interior. The land route was not practical until the CPR (Smith's Pacific Railway) was completed in 1886. By that time the North American west was a favoured destination for British "remittance men" and many did end up, like Smith's Stewart, as victims of alcoholism. Nevertheless, recent scholarship has argued that others who were supported by elite families in Britain contributed enormously to the development of both the Canadian and American West. All the same, when Smith was writing the negative image, the "remittance man" had become ingrained in the United States, Canada, and Australia — where the expression originated. See "William Henry Aspinwall," in *Dictionary of American Biography* [henceforth *DAB*] (New York: Charles Scribner's Sons, 1964), Vol. 1, 386; Barman, *The West Beyond the West: A History of British Columbia*. (Toronto: University of Toronto Press, 1996), 72–98; Larry A. Macfarlane, "British Remittance Men in Frontier America," in *Journal of the West*, Vol. 40, No.1 (2001), 41–48; Marjory Harper, "Aristocratic Adventurers: British Gentlemen Emigrants on the North American Frontier, ca 1880–1920," in *Journal of the West*, Vol. 36, No.2 (1997), 41–51; Mark Zuehlke, *Scoundrels, Dreamers and Second Sons: British Remittance Men in the Canadian West* (Vancouver: Whitecap Books, 1994); and Dunae, *Gentleman Emigrants*, 123–146. See also Scott Shipmqn, ed., *English Bloods: In the Backwoods of Muskoka, 1878* (Toronto: Natural Heritage Books, 2004).

12. These two Scottish characters and their pipes figure prominently in Smith's story "Aristocracy," part of his series "John Kanack's Experiences" published in the *New Dominion Monthly* (September, 1873).

13. The "Saugeen Road" was one of the several pioneer roads built in the 1850s to encourage settlement in Bruce County. It ran from Elora in Nichol Township, Wellington County, to Southampton in Saugeen Township, Bruce County, and passed through Peel, Maryborough, Minto, Carrick, Brant, and Elderslie townships. The Town of Lucknow, named after the city made famous during the Indian Mutiny, is located further to the west in Kinloss Township. See "Bruce Supplement" in *Illustrated Atlas of the Dominion of Canada* (Toronto: H. Belden, 1880); *Illustrated Atlas of the County of Wellington*. (Toronto: Walker & Miles, 1877), and Norman Robertson, *The History of the County of Bruce* (Toronto: William Briggs, 1906), 64–67, 494.

14. Anna Jameson (1794–1860) had a long writing career, publishing on topics as varied as Shakespeare, Fine Art, and the position of women

in European society. It was, however, her *Winter Studies and Summer Rambles in Canada* (London: Saunders and Otley, 1838) that generated the most interest among Smith's contemporaries and later Canadian scholars. The book recorded Jameson's experiences during the winter of 1836 and the summer of 1837 when she was in Upper Canada, supporting her husband's bid to become chancellor of the colony. The Jamesons were estranged, and once Robert Jameson had secured his appointment, Anna returned to Britain. See Judith Johnston, *Anna Jameson* (Aldershot, England: Scolar Press, 1997).

15. Smith appears to have confused his references since Jameson, while noting the presence of turtles on Toronto Island, does not mention soup. Smith may have got the soup reference from Sir Richard Bonnycastle who mentions it in his roughly contemporary book (*The Canadas in 1841,*52–53). Jameson's actual passage on Toronto society reads, "We have here a petty colonial oligarchy, a self-constituted aristocracy, based upon nothing real, nor even upon anything imaginary." (*Winter Studies*, 98). A great deal has been written about the Family Compact since William Lyon Mackenzie coined the term to describe the monopoly of office holding enjoyed by a close-knit group of leading Toronto families. Indeed many scholars have highlighted the regional differences in the composition of the elite within the colony, but in general these studies have tended to reinforce the claim of the reformers that the political life of the colony was concentrated in the hands of a small, interconnected group. Jameson, however, had no time for the reformers, "those scoundrels" (*Winter Studies*, 102), and literary critics have pointed out that Jameson's attack on the local elite can be read, instead, as part of a broader criticism of the position of women in elite British society. In *Winter Studies and Summer Rambles,* Jameson contrasted her winter in the stifling environment of Toronto society with the freedom and joy of travelling among the Anishinabe in the summer. Indeed, Jameson made an explicit comparison between the restraints placed upon women in "civilized" European society with the personal autonomy enjoyed by Native women. See S.J.R. Noel, *Patrons, Clients, Brokers: Ontario Society and Politics 1791–1896* (Toronto: University of Toronto Press, 1990), 83–93; Donald H. Acheson, *The Irish in Ontario: A Study in Rural History* (Montreal: McGill-Queen's University Press, 2nd ed. 1999), 191, Fn 108; Susan Birkwood, "True or False: Anna Jameson on the Position of Women in Anishinaubae Society," in *Nineteenth-Century Feminisms*, No. 2, Spring/Summer (2000), 32–47; Adele E. Ernstrom,

"The Afterlife of Mary Wollstonecraft and Anna Jameson's *Winter Studies and Summer Rambles in Canada*," in *Women's Writing*, Vol. 4, No. 2, (1997), 277–96; and Thomas M.F. Gerry, "'I am Translated': Anna Jameson's Sketches and *Winter Studies and Summer Rambles in Canada*," in *JCS*, Vol. 25, No. 4 (1990–91), 34–49.

16. It is likely that Smith is referring to the "Y" formed by the link between the spur line that fronted the town and the Brantford, Norfolk and Port Burwell Railway main line. The Wilkes family had a prominent place in the early history of Brantford and played a key role in founding the Brantford Congregational Church. The family had emigrated from Birmingham where they had also been heavily involved in the church and its missionary work. In the early 1820s, John Aston Wilkes founded a general goods business in York and in 1823 had his sons, John Jr. and James, establish a branch of the business in Brantford. James Wilkes built the "White Mill" to grind flour beside the Brantford Canal, near Vinegar Hill. Another son, Dr. Henry Wilkes, who was educated in Glasgow, was an important member of the Congregational College in Toronto, and was responsible for encouraging several Scots ministers to come to Upper Canada during the 1840s. See the *Illustrated Historical Atlas of Brant County; The History of the County of Brant*, 266 and 279–281; John Robertson, *History of the Brantford Congregational Church, 1820–1920* (Renfrew, ON: Renfrew Mercury Print, 1920), 23–30; F.H. Marling, *The Congregational College of British North America: The Story of Fifty Years, 1839–1889* (Montreal: Witness, 1889); and John Wood, *Memoir of Henry Wilkes, D.D. LLD.; His Life and Times* (Montreal: F.E. Grafton, 1887).

17. Sir Francis Bond Head (1793–1875) was governor of Upper Canada at the time of the 1837 Rebellion. He wrote his *Narrative of Recent Events in Canada* (London: J. Murray, 1839) to answer charges that his conduct had precipitated the conflict, but the passage to which Smith refers is from Head's later book, *The Emigrant* (London: J. Murray, 1846), 332. Since Head believed that his own misfortunes were caused by Upper Canadian reformers, he was distressed to see the move to create responsible government in the Canadas in the 1840s. Head saw all measures to develop local autonomy as an encouragement to republicanism, but studies of local government in Upper Canada have suggested that rather than promoting radicalism, bodies like the District Councils tended to reinforce the power of the elite in the colony. See S.F. Wise, "Sir Francis Bond Head,"

in *DCB*, Vol. 10 (1871–1880), 342–45; Kathleen Ann Hayer Burke, "Local Government and the Nature of Local Prominence in a New Settlement Area: Upper Canada 1788–1812," University of Waterloo, unpublished PhD dissertation, 1993; and Colin Read, "The London District Oligarchy in the Rebellion Era," in *OH*, 74 (4) (1980), 195–209.

18. The reference to the Cheviot breed of sheep as well as the dialect of the poem suggest a Scottish Border origin for Smith's anonymous poet. This is also in keeping with the reference to the gentry's fondness for trees since the early nineteenth century saw the vigorous implementation of protective forest law on Border estates, although this trend was also apparent elsewhere in Scotland and England. See Cowan, "From Southern Uplands," 66–67; and Bob Bushway, *By Rite: Custom, Ceremony and Community in England 1700–1880* (London: Junction Books, 1982). Scholars have tended to agree with Smith that the disappointment with emigration was exaggerated in literary works. Peter Womack has shown that as early as the 1780s, Scottish emigration was being represented as a romantic tragedy in the poetry written in English. In addition, Michael Kennedy has pointed out that despite the existence of many nineteenth-century Gaelic songs celebrating immigration to the New World, only those that lamented the move were translated. Michael Newton has, however, argued that for most Gaelic-speaking settlers, migration continued to be viewed as an experience of dispossession well into the nineteenth century and that they compared their experience to that of the Natives, even while they were settling Native land. See Peter Womack, *Improvement and Romance: Constructing the Myth of the Highlands.* (London: MacMillan Press, 1989), 118–25; Michael Kennedy, " 'Lochaber No More': A Critical Examination of Highland Emigration Mythology," in *Myth, Migration and the Making of Memory: Scotia and Nova Scotia c.1700–1990* (Halifax: Fernwood Publishing, 1999), 267–97, and Michael Newton, *We're Indians Sure Enough: The Legacy of the Scottish Highlanders in the United States* (Auburn: Saorsa Media, 2001), 163–75 and 216–43.

19. The likely source for Smith's story is the Methodist minister, Reverend Robert Robinson, who emigrated from Ulster in 1844. He had worked as a preacher near Belfast and was received into the Methodist Church in Canada the year after he arrived in the colony. He served first at the Ashphodel Mission in the Cobourg District before obtaining his first congregation in Madoc Township in 1849. See *Case and His Contemporaries*, Vol. 4, 46–47, 108, 202. Similar complaints about the

lack of deference and the familiarity of servants are common in early Upper Canadian travel literature. For an example see the travelogue of the Edinburgh Physician John Howison, *Sketches of Upper Canada ... for the Information of Emigrants of Every Class.* (Edinburgh: Oliver and Boyd, 1822), 61–62.

20.　Adam Fergusson (1783–1862), a native of Perthshire, was the co-founder of the Town of Fergus and an influential writer and agriculturalist in Scotland and Canada. He founded the Agricultural Association of Upper Canada, served on the Board of Agriculture, and was a member of the Legislative Council from 1839 to 1862. As his statement on the Tories suggests, Fergusson was an ardent supporter of the Reformers and served as chair at the party's conventions in 1857 and 1859. Britton's comment, of course, was a double slur against both Fergusson's politics and his ethnicity. The speech was likely delivered at one of the Durham Meetings held in the summer and fall of 1839 in support of the reform proposals made by Lord Durham in his *Report* produced in the aftermath of the 1837 Rebellion. See Adam Fergusson, *Practical Notes Made During a Tour in Canada* (Edinburgh: 1839); Gilbert A. Stelter, "Combining Town and Country Planning in Upper Canada: William Gilkison and the Founding of Elora," in *Historic Guelph: The Royal City*, Vol. 24 (1985), 23–27; Elwood H. Jones, "Adam Fergusson," in *DCB*, Vol. 9 (1861–1870), 251–52; and Carol Wilton, *Popular Politics and Political Culture in Upper Canada 1800–1850* (Montreal: McGill-Queen's University Press, 2000), 194–220.

21.　Adam Johnstone Fergusson Blair (1815–67), the son of the Honourable Adam Fergusson, was a prominent political figure in Upper Canada. He was educated in Edinburgh before emigrating to Upper Canada with his parents in 1833. He was called to the Canadian Bar in 1839 and practiced law at Guelph. In 1842, he was named the first judge of the Wellington District Court, and in 1847 ran as a Reform candidate for Waterloo. He would remain active in politics until his death. He added Blair to his last name in 1862 after inheriting the Blair Estate in Perthshire, Scotland. See Bruce W. Hodgins, "Adam Johnstone Fergusson Blair," in *DCB*, Vol. 9 (Toronto: University of Toronto Press, 1976), 252–53.

22.　During the eighteenth century, a large number of educated single men, many of them from Scotland, travelled to the Caribbean sugar plantations to serve as managers, bookkeepers, physicians, or lawyers. They migrated on a temporary basis hoping to amass fortunes to bring back to Britain. Most were disappointed in this ambition, and by the end of the century many of the largest firms were experiencing difficulties that encouraged many individuals, such as Richard Stitt, to leave colonies like Jamaica. See Alan L. Karras, *Sojourners in the Sun: Scottish Migrants in Jamaica and the Chesapeake, 1740–1800* (Ithaca: Cornell University Press, 1992); and Douglas Hamilton, "Scottish Trading in the Caribbean: The Rise and Fall of Houston and Co.," in Ned C. Landsman, *Nation and Province in the First British Empire: Scotland and the Americas, 1600–1800.* (Lewisburg: Bucknell University Press, 2001).

23.   This is an obvious reference to the protagonist of the famous work written by Saavedra Cervantes (1547–1616) between 1597 and 1615. The first English translation of *Don Quixote* from the original Spanish was completed in 1620. See *Chambers Biographical Dictionary.* (Edinburgh: W & R Chambers, 1984), 262.

24.   Purvis Douglas Lawrason (1814–80) was born in Flamboro Township and was the eldest son of John Lawrason who moved his family to Dumfries Township in 1823. Purvis Lawrason became one of the leading farmers in South Dumfries, having accumulated nearly seven hundred acres, and, in 1858, he became the joint owner of the St. George Agricultural Works. He served briefly as a township councillor and was a prominent member of the St. George Methodist Church. See *The History of the County of Brant*, 668–69.

25.   Smith's recounting of Morrison's decline was typical of the cautionary tales employed by temperance advocates during the nineteenth century. At the time, "Gentleman" immigrants were viewed as being particularly prone to alcoholism. See Graeme Decarie, "Something Old Something New ... Aspects of Prohibitionism in Ontario in the 1890s," in Donald Swainson, ed., *Oliver Mowat's Ontario.* (Toronto: Macmillan, 1972), 154–173; James M. Clemens, "Taste Not; Touch Not; Handle Not: A Study of the Social Assumptions of the Temperance Literature and Temperance Supporters in Canada West Between 1839 and 1859," in *OH*, Vol. 64 (1972), 142–60; and Dunae, *Gentleman Immigrants*, 139–42.

26.   Susannah Strickland Moodie (1803–85) emigrated to Upper Canada in 1832, settling first on a purchased farm in Cobourg and then, in the spring of 1834, on uncleared land on the shore of Kutchawanook (Katchiwanooka) Lake in Douro Township, Peterborough County. Her *Roughing it in the Bush; or, Life in Canada* (London: R. Bentley, 1852) is one of the most discussed texts in early Canadian literature.

It has been viewed as a reflection of the nation's struggle with the landscape, a romantic novel, or a text reflecting the psychological conflict of a creative writer. More recently, scholars have focused on the manner in which the text was produced and have demonstrated that the book lacks coherence largely because it was assembled from previously published material, including contributions from Moodie's brother and husband, and was shaped by her London publisher and editor. Indeed, John Thurston has pointed out that the title was, in fact, a creation of the publisher and that despite reference to the bush experience nearly half of the text deals with the Moodie's first home on the cleared farm in Cobourg. Rather than reflecting a Canadian preoccupation with battling the land, Thurston argues that *Roughing it in the Bush* reflects the concerns of Moodie's gentry class and her attempt to continue a literary career first established in England. See John Thurston, *The Work of Words: The Writing of Susanna Strickland Moodie* (Montreal: McGill-Queen's University Press, 1996), 4–9 and 133–66; Michael Peterman, "Reconstructing the *Palladium of British America:* How the Rebellion of 1837 and Charles Fothergill helped Establish Susannah Moodie as a Writer in Canada," in *Papers of the Biographical Society of Canada*, 40 (1) (2002), 7–35; and Carl P.A. Ballstadt, "Susanna Strickland (Moodie)," in *DCB*, Vol. 11 (1881–1890), 857–61.

27.   John Wedderburn Dunbar Moodie (1797–1869), a native of Orkney, had served as an army officer during the Napoleonic War and, along with his brothers, had briefly settled in the Cape Colony at the end of the conflict. He shared with Susannah Strickland an interest in literary pursuits and would publish accounts of his exploits in the army and in South Africa. The couple met at the London home of Thomas Pringle, the Scots poet and former settler of South Africa, before they married and emigrated to Upper Canada. After spending several years in Cobourg and then Douro Township, "Dunbar" Moodie was appointed to the position of sheriff of the Victoria District, much to the chagrin of the local elite. The governor, Sir George Arthur, had been impressed with the loyalty of the Moodies during the 1837 Rebellion and the sheriff appointment was their reward. Her husband's new position allowed Susanna to leave Douro Township for Belleville in 1840 and his connections with publishers helped to provide her with the opportunity to continue publishing in Britain. See Carl P.A. Ballstadt, "John Wedderburn Dunbar Moodie," in *DCB*, Vol. 9 (1861–1870), 566–67; Peterman, "Reconstructing the *Palladium*,"

24–27; and John Thurston, *The Work of Words: The Writing of Susanna Strickland Moodie* (Montreal: McGill-Queen's University Press, 1996), 73–74 and 134.

28. Five Strickland sisters, (Agnes, Elizabeth, Catharine, Jane, and Susannah) turned to publishing their writing to maintain their Suffolk gentry home when their father died in 1818. Agnes and Elizabeth were particularly successful, the former producing many volumes including the *Lives of the Queens of England* (London: Henry Colburn, 1840), and the latter serving as editor of *The Lady's Magazine* that published some of Susannah's poetry. Catharine Parr Strickland (1802–99) was the first sister to publish her writing, starting with stories and then moving on to natural history. In 1832, she married Lieutenant Thomas Traill, a fellow Scot and friend of Dunbar Moodie, and emigrated with the Moodies to Canada. The sisters and their families would join their brother Samuel Strickland, the first member of the family to arrive in the colony, in attempting to settle Douro Township. Like her sister, Catherine Parr Traill continued to write and publish in Canada — some of her most notable works being her settler narrative, *The Backwoods of Canada* (London: C. Knight, 1836); her children's tale, *Canadian Crusoes* (London: A Hall, Virtue, 1852); and her natural history, *Studies of Plant Life in Canada* (Ottawa: A.S. Woodburn, 1885). Intriguingly, in their Canadian writing, Susannah Moodie and Catharine Parr Traill followed Anna Jameson in using a discussion of Native women to express their concerns regarding the position of women in their own society. See Thurston, 11–40; C. Ballstadt, E. Hopkins, and M. Peterman, eds., *Susanna Moodie: Letters of a Lifetime* (Toronto: University of Toronto Press, 1985); Michael Peterman, "Catharine Parr Strickland (Traill)," in *DCB*, Vol. 12 (1891–1900), 995–99; Michael Peterman, "In Search of Agnes Strickland's Sisters," in *Canadian Literature*, No. 121 (1989), 115–24; and Carole Gerson, "Nobler Savages: Representations of Native Women in the Writings of Susannah Moodie and Catharine Parr Traill," in *JCS*, Vol. 32, No. 2 (1997), 5–21.

29. The description of this potential journey is reminiscent of Susanna Moodie's recollection of the journey to her lot in Douro Township. Madoc Township is one of the northernmost townships in Hastings County. The township did not receive a railway link to Belleville until 1880, and even then the land above the northern terminus at Eldorado, the site of the first gold mine in Ontario, was sparsely settled. Many of the unoccupied lots in the most northern part

of the township, above Bannockburn, were owned by the Canada Company. It may have been one of these Canada Company blocks of land that Smith's brother-in-law was sent to investigate. See Moodie, *Roughing It in the Bush*, 1–17; *Illustrated Historical Atlas of the Counties of Hastings and Prince Edward, Ontario* (Toronto: H. Belden & Co., 1878); and N. & H. Mika, *Belleville: Friendly City* (Belleville: Mika Publishing, 1973).

Chapter 6: English and Scotch Immigrants

1. At the time Smith was writing, the Algoma District was defined as the area in northern Ontario stretching from Murillo in the north, North Bay in the East, Sault St. Marie in the west, and Bracebridge in the south. This region corresponded to the area surrendered by the Ojibwa in 1850 in the Robinson-Huron Treaty, which created the Native reserves where several Anglican missions were also later established. In return for the land surrender, the treaty provided an annual payment of £600 to be divided among various reserves. By the turn of the century, the Ontario Government was aggressively promoting settlement in the region with free land grants, but the soil was marginal and few farms survived. As a consequence, the lumber and mining industries came to dominate the region. See Olive Dickason, *Canada's First Nations: A History of Founding Peoples from Earliest* Times. (Toronto: Oxford University Press, 1997), 226–29; Frances Awdry and Eda Green, *By Lake and Forest: The Story of Algoma* (London: Eda Green, 1909); and Joseph Schull, *Ontario Since 1867* (Toronto: McClelland & Stewart, 1978), 47 and 57.

    A great deal of immigration to Manitoba occurred between 1876 and 1881, particularly to the Pembina Hills region in the southwest of the province. Indeed, in 1876 the rush of Ontario settlers into the region was described as "Pembina fever" by contemporaries. By the 1890s, however, migration from Ontario had declined despite the vigorous efforts of Manitoba's Premier Thomas Greenway to entice new settlers from his native province. See W.L. Morton, *Manitoba: A History* (Toronto: University of Toronto Press, 1957), 178–79, 187, 252. For a case study of secondary migration in nineteenth-century Ontario, see David Gagan, *Hopeful Travelers: Families, Land, and Social Change in Mid-Victorian Peel County, Canada West* (Toronto: University of Toronto Press, 1981).

2. The development of public transport systems, such as railways and trams, during the second half of the nineteenth century does appear to have developed a greater number of socially acceptable opportunities for single men and women to meet strangers. Indeed, Peter Ward's analysis of marriage practice in nineteenth-century Canada reveals a tendency of all ethnic groups to marry outside their communities as the century progressed. For example, between 1858 and 1860 Scots marrying within their ethnic group represented 40.4 per cent of total Scots who married, but between 1891 and 1895 that figure dropped to 13.3 per cent. See Peter Ward, *Courtship, Love, and Marriage in Nineteenth-Century English Canada* (Montreal: McGill-Queen's University Press, 1990), 77–79, 182.

3. Catholics often faced considerable discrimination in nineteenth-century Ontario, and the Orange Order, which perpetuated tensions between Protestant and Catholic, flourished. Initially the order was established as more of a local social club, but by the 1830s it was becoming increasingly political and anti-Catholic in outlook. In 1833, there were ninety-one Orange Lodges in Upper Canada with a claimed membership of ten thousand. By 1861, Orange Lodges could be found in most communities and membership had risen to over 100,000. Sectarian strife between Protestant and Catholic Irish immigrants was particularly intense in Toronto, which for a time was known as the "Belfast" of Canada, but anti-Catholicism was not restricted to Ontario. J.R. Miller has argued that anti-Catholicism assumed an almost "official posture" in nineteenth-century Canada, and Richard Lougheed has shown that by the end of the century it was even found among Québècois Protestants. The later varieties of anti-Catholicism were based largely on theological and nationalistic concerns, but in mid-nineteenth-century Ontario anti-Catholicism was very much associated with the anti-Irish sentiment that had grown in intensity with the arrival of the "Famine Irish." According to Alan Brunger, the Irish did tend to settle in separate areas, with the Protestant Irish occupying land in the western parts of the province and the Catholic Irish settling in the Eastern district where Scottish Catholics were also concentrated. See Donald Harmen Akenson, *The Irish In Ontario: A Study in Rural History*, second edition (Montreal & Kingston: McGill-Queen's University Press, 1999) 170–71; Hereward Senior, *Orangeism: The Canadian Phase* (Toronto: Ryerson, 1972); Brian P. Clarke, *Piety and Nationalism: Lay Voluntary Associations and the Creation of an Irish-Catholic Community*

in Toronto, 1850–1895 (Montreal: McGill-Queen's University Press, 1993); J.R. Miller, "Anti-Catholicism in Canada: From the British Conquest to the Great War," in T. Murphy and G. Stortz, eds., *Creed and Culture: The Place of English Speaking Catholics in Canadian Society, 1750–1930* (Montreal: McGill-Queen's University Press, 1993); R. Lougheed, "Anti-Catholicism among French-Canadian Protestants," in *Historical Papers 1995: Canadian Society of Church History*, 161–80; and A. Brunger, "The Distribution of the Scots and Irish in Upper Canada, 1851–71," in *The Canadian Geographer/Le Geographe canadien*, Vol. 34, No. 3 (1990), 250–58.

4. For an explanation of the term "Pennsylvania Dutch," see Chapter 3, Note 15 above. The German-speaking "Dutch" immigrants originally settled in the Niagara Peninsula, but by the time the Smith family arrived in Dumfries Township neighbouring Waterloo County had become the major centre of German settlement in Ontario. Lehmann, *The German Canadians*, 61–95; John Clarke and John Buffone, "Social Regions in Mid-Nineteenth Century Ontario," in *Histoire Sociale/ Social History*, Vol. 28, No. 55 (1995), 204–05.

5. The earliest Gaelic-speaking townships were found in eastern Ontario, most notably in Glengarry County. In the second half of the century they were joined by settlements in western Ontario and along the shores of Lake Huron. Among them were Aldborough Township, Elgin County, settled by Gaelic speakers from Argyllshire; Zorra Township, Oxford County, settled by Highlanders from Sutherland; and Huron Township, Bruce County, which saw a great deal of immigration from the Isle of Lewis. See Marianne McLean, *The People of Glengarry: Highlanders in Transition 1745–1820* (Montreal: McGill-Queen's University Press, 1991); Wilfred Campbell, *The Scotsman in Canada*. Vol. 1 (Toronto: Musson Book Company, 1911); Norman Robertson, *The History of the County of Bruce*, 415–26; Alexander M. Ross, "Loch Laxford to the Zorras: A Sutherland Emigration to Upper Canada," in *Scottish Tradition*, Vol. 18, (1993), 28–40; Stephen J. Hornsby, "Patterns of Scottish Emigration to Canada 1750–1870," in JHG, Vol. 18, No. 4, (1992), 397–416; and Lucille H. Campey, *The Scottish Pioneers of Upper Canada, 1784–1855: Glengarry and Beyond* (Toronto: Natural Heritage Books) 2005.

6. There is no question that the Scots had a profound impact on the character of Presbyterianism in Canada. American, German, Dutch, Irish, and Swiss Presbyterians did settle in Canada, but the Scots and their descendants dominated the church. This was aided by

the Church of Scotland, which, under the auspices of the Glasgow Colonial Society, sent out missionaries to the Scottish emigrant communities in the early nineteenth century. The Scottish influence was so profound that when the evangelical Free Church split from the Church of Scotland in 1843, the Canadian church followed suit. See W. Stanford Reid, "The Scottish Protestant Tradition," in W.S. Reid, ed., *The Scottish Tradition in Canada* (Toronto: McClelland & Stewart, 1976); J.S. Moir, *Enduring Witness: A History of the Presbyterian Church in Canada* (Toronto: Presbyterian Publications, 1974); J.S. Moir and E.A.K. McDougall, eds., *Selected Correspondence of the Glasgow Colonial Society 1825–1840* (Toronto: Champlain Society, 1994); and Richard W. Vaudry, *The Free Church in Victorian Canada, 1844–1861* (Waterloo: Wilfred Laurier Press, 1989).

7.   Smith may be referring to the activities of the American Home Missionary Society. This evangelical group, formed in 1826 with support from both the Congregationalists and Presbyterians, began sending missionaries to new settlements in Upper Canada in 1830. The Home Missionary movement was, however, also taken up later in the century by the Anglicans in northern Ontario and by Presbyterians and Methodists in the west of the province. In the early twentieth century the movement was carried on by the United Church. See C.B.G. Koontz, *Home Missions on the American Frontier, with Particular Reference to the American Home Missionary Society* (New York: Octagon Books, 1971); John Webster Grant, *A Profusion of Spires: Religion in Nineteenth Century Ontario* (Toronto: University of Toronto Press, 1988), 72–73, 188; and George C. Pidgeon, *Nation Building: A Review of the Work of the Home Missions* (Toronto: Board of Home Missions and Social Service, 1917).

8.   The Township of Bury, northeast of Cookshire in Quebec's Eastern Townships, was formerly established March 15, 1803. It was originally granted to a Mr. Calvin May and Associates, but within a short time was in the hands of the British American Land Company, which intended to settle impoverished English emigrants in the township. By the 1840s, the construction of roads by the company, as well as assisted passage support from England had facilitated the colonization of the township. As a consequence, 989 people, including a number of Scots, were settled in Bury by 1861. See Day, *History of the Eastern Townships*, 383–7; J.I. Little, *Nationalism, Capitalism, and Colonization in Nineteenth-Century Quebec: The Upper St. Francis District* (Montreal: McGill-Queen's University Press, 1989), especially 52–3; and J.I.

Little, *Crofters and Habitants: Settler Society, Economy, and Culture in a Quebec Township, 1848–1881* (Montreal: McGill-Queen's University Press, 1991), 17 and 54–55. See also, Campey, *Les Écossais: The Pioneers Scots of Lower Canada, 1763–1855*, 95, 96, 100–2, 104, and 107.

9. Lake Megantic is famous for being part of the route taken by Benedict Arnold in 1775, when he was to assist Montgomery's revolutionary forces in an attack on Quebec. The lake is approximately ten miles (sixteen kilometres) in length and the chief source of the Chaudiere River. It was therefore an important waterway and significant to the settlement of the Eastern Townships. Day, *History of the Eastern Townships*, 234.

10. Smith is probably referring to the Lake Megantic Presbyterian Church that in the nineteenth century was also connected to the Marsboro Presbyterian Church, both of which were in Frontenac County. See, "Marsboro Presbyterian Church Fonds," Eastern Townships Research Centre, Bishops University, Lennoxville, Quebec. Megantic was a stop for the Quebec Central Railway well into the twentieth century. See Omer Lavallee, "The Quebec Central," in *National Railway Historical Society Bulletin*, Vol. 13, No. 3, 1948. The Highland migration to the Eastern Townships is examined by J.I. Little in *Crofters and Habitants* and the Gaelic folklore of the region has been catalogued by Margaret Bennett in *Oatmeal and the Catechism: Scottish Gaelic Settlers in Quebec* (Montreal: McGill-Queen's University Press, 1998). See also Chapter 1, Note 6.

11. A type of projector arranged to combine two images of the same object or scene on a screen, giving an effect of solidity as in a stereoscope. Lesley Brown, ed., *The New Shorter Oxford English Dictionary*, Vol. 2 (Oxford: Clarendon Press, 1993), 3,052.

12. Benedict Arnold's invasion of Quebec began in Cambridge, Massachusetts, and followed a route that took his party to the eastern shore of Lake Megantic. James Kirby Martin, *Benedict Arnold: Revolutionary Hero* (New York: New York University Press, 1997), 118.

13. "Annual Presents" had been employed by the British to cement military alliances with First Nations since the eighteenth century. By the early nineteenth century they had also become the means of persuading Native Peoples to sign treaties that dispossessed them of their lands, in order to facilitate the allocation of lots to settlers. The full consequence of these treaties was unknown to the First Nations and is the subject of continuing resentment and dispute to this day. See Dickason, *Canada's First Nations*, 162–65; Schmalz, *The Ojibwa*

of Southern Ontario, 120–46. For a contemporary description of the gift-giving ceremony, see Scott A. McLean, ed., *From Lochnaw to Manitoulin,: A Highland Soldiers Tour Through Upper Canada* (Toronto: Natural Heritage Books, 1999). The steamer *Banshee* was a 400-ton (362.9 tonne) vessel owned by the Canadian Inland Navigation Company, which ran it on the Royal Mail Line that operated a daily service from Montreal to Kingston from 1855. The *Banshee* was removed from service in 1883 when its engines were transferred to another vessel. Captain McCoy skippered the *Banshee* in the early 1870s and may be the individual referred to by Smith. A detailed discussion of the steamship business is provided by Walter Lewis in "Steamboat Promotion and Changing Technology: The Careers of James Sutherland and the *Magnet*," in *OH*, Vol. 77, No. 3 (September 1985), 207–30. For more on the *Banshee*, see Robert Thomas, *Register of Ships of the Lakes and River St. Lawrence* (Buffalo: Wheeler, Matthews & Warren, 1864), 12; and the *Daily News* (Kingston) December 2, 1854; Ibid., February 22, 1855; Ibid., May 21, 1872; and Ibid., January 25, 1883.

14. Although a commonplace term for a Native female, "squaw" was a derogatory term in Smith's day as it remains in the present. Smith was aware of this fact. In his chapter on dialects, not included in this edition, Smith states "An Indian told me that ... their women do not like "squaw"; it was (to them) a displeasing corruption of their word for woman.

15. Archibald McKillop (1824–1905), born in Loch Ranza, Isle of Arran, Scotland, published a good deal of poetry in his lifetime. While he was alive, some were collected in his *Temperance Odes and Miscellaneous Poems* (Quebec: Thompson & Co., 1860). Others were published in the posthumous edition *Collected Verse, The Blind Bard of Megantic*, (Canada: n.p., 1913?). See Appendix B for a sample of Archibald McKillop's poetry "Megantic More Than Forty Years Ago."

16. This type of relationship between Gaelic and the Native language is also commented upon in a book published in Glasgow in 1841. See Robert MacDougall, Elizabeth Thompson, ed., *The Emigrant's Guide to North America* (Toronto: Natural Heritage Books, 1998), 39–40.

17. Professor John Stuart Blackie was chair of Greek at Edinburgh University (1852–82). It was largely through his enthusiastic efforts that a Celtic Chair was established in 1882. See A. Logan Turner, *History of the University of Edinburgh, 1883–1933* (Edinburgh: Oliver and Boyd, 1933), 229, 232.

18. The suggested link between Celtic and indigenous languages could allow the Gaels to claim a special, even ancient, affinity with the Natives of North America. This, in turn, could reinforce their claim as legitimate occupiers of the land as settlers. Of course, such a position also masked the role that Gaelic-speaking peoples played in dispossessing the indigenous peoples. Professor Blackie's derogatory comment, however, also suggests that the elite did not discriminate between Native and Highlander in their negative stereotyping. See Michael Newton, *We're Indians Sure Enough*; Krisztina Fenyo, *Contempt, Sympathy and Romance: Lowland Perceptions of the Highlands and the Clearances during the Famine Years* (East Linton: Tuckwell Press, 2000); and Robert F. Berkhofer, Jr., *The White Man's Indian: Images of the American Indian from Columbus to the Present* (New York: Knopf, 1978).

19. Despite Smith's claim, the strength of Reform politics among the settlers in Upper Canada suggests that a good many settlers retained their radical politics even after acquiring land of their own. Nevertheless, the desire to acquire a piece of land was a goal common to a great many English and Scottish immigrants of artisan and working-class backgrounds. English immigrants, however, tended to migrate to the areas already settled along the northwestern shore of Lake Ontario and Lake Erie, while Irish and Scottish immigrants tended to move inland to the new townships in the bush. This may suggest that on average English immigrants may have brought more capital with them, which allowed them to rent or buy farms in the more settled communities. Nevertheless, while some particular groups have been examined, there have been relatively few published studies of English immigration to Upper Canada. See Vance & Stephens, "Grits, Rebels and Radicals" in G. Martin and D. Pollard, eds. *Canada 1849* (Edinburgh: University of Edinburgh, Centre for Canadian Studies, 2002); A. Brunger, "The Distribution of the Scots and Irish" and "The Distribution of the English in Upper Canada, 1851–71," in *The Canadian Geographer/Le Geographe Canadien*, Vol. 30, No. 4 (1986), 337–43; Wendy Cameron and Mary McDougall Maude, *Assisting Emigration to Upper Canada: The Petworth Project 1832–1837* (Montreal: McGill-Queen's University Press, 2000); Terry MacDonald, " 'Come to Canada While You Have a Chance': *A* Cautionary Tale of English Immigrant Letters in Upper Canada," in *OH*, Vol. 91, No. 2 (1999), 111–30; and Bruce Elliot, "The English" in *An Encyclopedia of Canada's People.* (Toronto: University of Toronto Press, 1999).

20. Smith is referring to the Saugeen Peninsula in Bruce County. Under the terms of the treaty concluded at Manitowaning in 1836, the peninsula was to remain the possession of the Ojibwa in perpetuity. Nevertheless, in 1854, a further treaty with the Saugeen First Nations resulted in the surrender of most of the Saugeen Peninsula, leaving only a number of small reserves. The surrendered lands were auctioned off at Owen Sound on September 2, 1856. The proceeds of the sales were to be used to set up a fund, administered by the Indian Department, intended to provide annual payments to individuals on the reserves. Subsequent treaties reduced the size of Saugeen territory even further, ultimately leaving the Saugeen Reserve at the mouth of the Saugeen River, a smaller reserve above that at Chief's Point, another on the north side of Colpoy's Bay at Cape Crocker, and a small hunting ground at the northern tip of the peninsula. See N. Robertson, *The History of the County of Bruce*, 193–97, 193–97, and 525–28; and especially Peter S. Schmalz, *The History of the Saugeen Indians* (Ottawa: Ontario Historical Society, 1977), 232–35. See also, Mel Atkey, *When We Both Get to Heaven: James Atkey Among the Anishnabek at Colpoy's Bay* (Toronto: Natural Heritage Books, 2002).

21. Smith's humorous tone in this story hides the fact that both the 1836 and 1855 treaties, which surrendered 1.5 million acres of Saugeen land, were opposed by many Ojibwa at the time and, in the case of the 1855 treaty, agreement was achieved only through the use of threats. The dispossession meant an end to the traditional means of subsistence for the Saugeen people and, as occurred elsewhere in Ontario, relegated them to inadequate reserves. See Schmalz, *The Ojibwa of Southern Ontario*, 135–43; Smith and Rogers, eds., *Aboriginal Ontario*.

22. Reverend William Burgess (1802–86) emigrated from England in 1855. He served as a Congregational minister at Frome in Southwold Township, Elgin County, from 1855 to 1860 and at Edgeworth in east Tilbury, Kent County, from 1861 until his retirement in 1877. See Walkington, *Congregational Churches of Canada*.

23. Smith is referring to the eighteenth-century English novelist, Lawrence Sterne (1713–68). The quotation is from the chapter entitled *Maria* in Sterne's *Sentimental Journey Through France and Italy* (1768). The entire passage reads, "She had since that, she told me, strayed as far as Rome, and walk'd round St. Peters once — and return'd back — that she found her way alone across the Appennines — had travell'd over all Lombardy without money — and through flinty roads of savoy without shoes — how she had borne it, and how

she had got supported, she could not tell — but *God tempers the wind,* said Maria, *to the shorn lamb.*"

24. The stripping of lots for their timber, by both settlers and squatters, was a regular occurrence in mid-nineteenth-century Ontario. Some "settlers" merely occupied their lots until the valuable timber was taken off and then abandoned them. See J. David Wood, *Making Ontario: Agricultural Colonization and Landscape Re-creation Before the Railway* (Montreal: McGill-Queen's University Press, 2000), 101–09; Neil S. Folkey, *Shaping the Upper Canadian Frontier: Environment, Society, and Culture in the Trent Valley* (Calgary: University of Calgary Press, 2003), 75–96.

25. French Canadians had been settling in Essex and Kent counties since 1749. In Tilbury, most of the French-Canadian settlers were located in West Tilbury, Essex County, while the English and Scottish settlers were concentrated in East Tilbury, Kent County. The Tilbury station for the Canadian Southern Railway was close to Edgeworth where William Burgess was minister. After retiring, Burgess moved to Etobicoke where he was listed as a "market gardener" in 1877. None of his sons appears to have stayed in Tilbury. See Ernest J. Lajeunesse, *The Windsor Border Region: Canada's Southernmost Frontier* (Toronto: Champlain Society, 1960); Clarke and Buffone, "Social Regions in Mid-Nineteenth-Century Ontario," in *Illustrated Historical Atlas of the County of York* (Toronto: Miles & Co., 1878); and *Illustrated Atlas of the Dominion of Canada (*Toronto: H. Belden, 1881).

26. The Woman's Christian Temperance Union (WCTU) was founded in Cleveland, Ohio, in 1874. The organization was pledged to fight against the damaging effects of alcohol, but would later expand its activities to include abstinence from tobacco and drugs. By 1879, the organization was becoming more political in outlook and would be a driving force for women's suffrage in many states across the United States. See "Woman's Christian Temperance Union" at *http://www. wctu.org/earlyhistory.html*, accessed December 21, 2007.

27. Lady Henry Somerset was a leading English philanthropist and temperance advocate. She was president of the British Woman's Temperance Association (1890-1903) and founded the first British treatment centre for "inebriate" women at Duxhurst near Reigate on the coast of Kent. She visited America in 1891 when she attended meetings of the World's Woman's Christian Temperance Union in Boston, and was later, in 1898, elected president of that organization. The Ontario WCTU differed sharply with some of Lady Somerset's

views, particularly on the regulation of prostitution, but shared the view that alcohol was at the root of women's poverty and the source of domestic violence. The WCTU's provided a means for middle-class women to take on a broader public role in Victorian society that was not always as welcome as Smith's comments imply. See *DNB*, (1912–1921), 501–502; Sharon A. Cook, *"Through Sunshine and Shadow": The Women's Christian Temperance Union, Evangelicalism, and Reform in Ontario 1874–1930* (Montreal: McGill-Queen's University Press, 1995), especially 72–73; and "'Sowing the Seed for the Master': The Ontario WCTU and Evangelical Feminism 1874–1930," in *JCS*, Vol. 30, No. 3 (Fall 1995).

28. The use of "hair" as a verb comes from the Scots. To "hair" the butter, as Smith's tale suggests, is to remove impurities, such as hairs, by passing a knife through it in all directions. *CSD*, 260.

29. In 1881, there were several individuals with the surname Thomas located in Oro Township. Samuel Thomas (b. 1833) and Charles Thomas (b. 1836) shared lot 8, while T.M. Thomas (b. 1847) occupied lot 10 on Concession Line 3. See *Simcoe Supplement in the Illustrated Atlas of the Dominion of Canada* (1881).

30. Smith is referring to the Reverend Thomas Ford Caldicott (1803–69) of Northamptonshire England, who immigrated to Canada in 1827. Upon arrival at York, Caldicott opened a book and stationary store and soon after opened the York Commercial and Classical Academy, a private school, with his brother Samuel. In 1834, he was ordained as a Baptist minister, and soon after left for the United States, where he served the Baptist communities of New York State and Massachusetts for twenty-five years. He returned to Toronto in 1860, but not before being honoured with a doctorate from Madison University. During his career he was actively involved in the York Mechanic's Institute, the Religious Tract and Book Society, and the York Auxiliary Bible Society, as well as acting as editor of the *Canadian Baptist*. Marget H.C. Meikleham, "Thomas Ford Caldicott," in *DCB*, Vol. 9 (Toronto: University of Toronto Press, 1976), 112–13.

31. This is possibly Alfred Booker, Sr., a Baptist minister born in Nottingham, England, March 14, 1800. Alfred Booker decided to emigrate, arriving in Hamilton, Upper Canada, in 1842 with his wife and eight children. Thomas Melville Bailey, *DNB*, Vol. 1. (Hamilton: W.L. Griffin, 1981), 21.

32. For more on Levi French, see Chapter 2, above.

33. "Teague" and "Pat" are caricature names. They were commonly employed in the nineteenth-century music hall to denote dim-witted, comic Irishmen.

34. Smith is likely referring to the Reverend William Millard, an English Baptist minister who is listed as being sixty years of age and residing in St. James Ward, Toronto East, in the 1871 Census. See Library and Archives Canada [henceforth LAC], Record Group [henceforth RG] 31, microfilm Reel C9972. A Reverend W. Millard of Brampton is listed as one of the references for a ladies school called the Eclectic Female Institute. This may also be the individual to whom Smith is referring. See *Eclectic Female Institute* (Toronto: W.C. Chewett & Co., 1863), 4.

35. "Cutter" was a term used to refer to a horse-drawn sleigh equipped with iron runners for gliding over the snow.

36. Scholars have long noted the importance of family and friends in encouraging subsequent migration from the homeland. This type of "chain migration" from the Scottish Borders to Upper Canada was frequently directed through New York in the early nineteenth century. See Marjory Harper, *Adventurers and Exiles: The Great Scottish Exodus* (London: Profile Books, 2003); M. Vance, "Breaking the Power of a Metaphor: Toward a Social Interpretation of Emigration History," in C. Kerrigan, ed., *The Immigrant Experience* (Guelph: University of Guelph, 1992), 57–74; Vance, "Impressions of a Berlin Pioneer," 26–28; and E.J. Cowan "From the Southern Uplands to Southern Ontario," 72–73. See also, Campey, *The Scottish Pioneers, of Upper Canada*, (2005).

37. James Young writes that Telfer went to Scotland to induce intending emigrants to settle in Dumfries about the year 1820. It was in large part through the efforts of John Telfer that the northern part of Dumfries took on such a "Scottish character." James Young, *Reminiscences of the Early History of Galt and the Settlement of Dumfries.* (Toronto: Hunter, Rose and Co., 1880), 41–2.

38. James Hogg is best known as the author *Confessions of a Justified Sinner.* Like Burns before him, Hogg was both a well-known author and tenant farmer. For more on Hogg's life and works, see Nelson C. Smith, *James Hogg* (Boston: Twayne Publishers, 1980) 15–31. See also, Edith Batho, *The Ettrick Shepherd* (New York: Greenwood Press, 1969). According to James Young, it was William Dickson, Jr., not Telfer, who visited Hogg and offered him a farm in Dumfries. In Young's version, the poet is reported to have exclaimed "The

Yarrow couldna' want me!" For more on James Hogg, see Note 7 in Chapter 4.

39. "Reist" or "reest" is the Scots word meaning "to bring to a halt." *Scots Concise Dictionary*, 551.

40. In 1879, John Alexander, and A.G. Campbell were located beside each other on lots 65 to 68, Concession Line 2 in Wallace Township. This may be the family in Smith's tale. It is likely that he would have met them while he was minister at Listowel, which is also in the township. Wallace was the last township in Perth County to be settled since it was not surveyed until 1852. See *Illustrated Historical Atlas of the County of Perth, Ontario* (Toronto: H. Belden & Co., 1879); and William Johnston, *History of Perth County 1825–1902* (Stratford, ON: W.M. O'Beirne, 1903), 389–405.

41. According to James Young, Robert McLean was the teacher at the Galt Public School from 1846 to 1855. He was also an early member of the Galt Mechanics Institute. See Young, *Reminiscences of the Early History of Galt*, 205, 239.

42. As Catharine Wilson has shown, nineteenth-century "Bees" had elaborate codes of social obligation and hospitality associated with them and in the 1820s a barn could not be raised in Upper Canada without whisky. Indeed, one contemporary suggested that five gallons should be on hand for the sixteen men usually required to do the task. By the mid-century the drinking had brought about a contest between temperance and whisky advocates, which on occasion could degenerate into violence. From the 1870s, however, elaborate meals and entertainments had come to replace the generous quantities of strong drink offered earlier in the century. See C. A. Wilson, "Reciprocal Work Bees," in "Reciprocal Work Bees and the Meaning of Neighbourhood," in *CHR*, Vol. 82, No. 3 (September 2001), 443–44.

43. In a published version of this story, Smith claimed to have met James Easton in 1838, but did not see him again until after 1842. According to that article, Easton was well-known in the area around Agincourt in Scarboro Township. See W.W. Smith, "The Scot in Canada. II," in *The Scottish Canadian* (May 7, 1891), 10.

44. Smith may be referring to a biographical article on Reverend John Climie (1807–68) in the *Canadian Independent*. While he was editor of the paper, Smith wrote many articles on notable Congregational clergymen including Ludwick Kribs and Solomon Snider who also appear in these *Reminiscences*. See *Canadian Independent*, March

1888, 67; May 1892, 135. Reverend Climie was a stonemason who served as a lay preacher before being ordained in Bowmanville in 1855. He served as Congregational minister in that community from 1855 to 1857. Climie was subsequently the church's minister in Belleville from 1858 to 1867. See Walkington, *Congregational Churches of Canada.*

45. A "piece" is the Scots word for a snack, usually a piece of bread or scone spread with butter, jam, and the like. *Scots Concise Dictionary.* 492.

46. See the note relating to Dr. Stowe in Chapter 2, above.

47. Dr. Lachlan Taylor was a preacher, originally from Argyllshire, who joined the Methodists in 1839 at the age of twenty-two. At first he was an itinerant missionary in the Ottawa district, where his mother and father had a farm, but in 1853 he moved to Toronto to become agent of the Upper Canadian Bible Society. Taylor would travel extensively in Upper Canada to give lectures promoting the society. In a published article on the clergyman, Smith wrote that he had first met Dr. Taylor at the Smith home in St. George, but had also heard him lecture in Owen Sound in 1859, which corresponds to the date of this story. See Carroll, *Case and his Contemporaries*, Vol. 4, 263–64 and Vol. 5, 120; W.W. Smith, "The Scot in Canada III," in *The Scottish Canadian*, August 20, 1891.

48. The references to "mandrakes" are found in Genesis 30: 13–17.

49. After a short time as pastor of the Congregational Church in Listowel, Smith moved to Pine Grove, near Toronto, where he acted as Congregational minister for that community. See Caledonian Society of Toronto, "Rev. William Wye Smith" in *Selections From Canadian Poets*, (Toronto: Imrie, Graham and Company, 1900), 135.

50. The lecture must have occurred between 1870 and 1877 when Smith was minister at Pine Grove. William A. Wallis was a justice of the peace and one of the earliest settlers in Etobicoke Township. From 1824 he occupied lot 40 on Concession 1 above Smithfield. Weston, which is now part of greater Toronto, is located in the Township of North York on the border with Etobicoke Township. See *Illustrated Historical Atlas of the County of York* (1878).

51. In 1881, an Andrew Kyle was listed as a resident of Ayr, Waterloo County. This may have been a relative of Smith's friend Thomas Kyle. See *Illustrated Atlas of the Dominion of Canada* (1881).

52. In 1875, R. Graham, John Graham and Thomas Graham held lots on Concession Line 1 between St. George and Paris. It is possible

that Andrew Graham was related to these individuals. See *Illustrated Historical Atlas of the County of Brant* (1875).

53.   Smith is likely referring to Archibald Anderson who occupied lot 11 on Concession 3E in Caledon Township. The Toronto, Grey and Bruce Railway ran through his property. William Anderson was a mason from Renton, Dumbartonshire, who emigrated to Canada in 1834. See *Illustrated Historical Atlas of Peel County* (Toronto: Walker & Miles, 1877); and Maurice Lindsay, *The Burns Encyclopedia* (London: Hutchison, 1970), 28.

54.   Mary Campbell, "Highland Mary" (1763–86), was born near Dunoon, Argyllshire. In her early teens she moved to Ayrshire to work as a housemaid where she developed a relationship with Robert Burns. The nature of the relationship has been a matter of debate, but what is known is that she died of "fever" at Greenock apparently waiting for Burns. The poet wrote several songs and poems that were inspired by Mary Campbell and this led several nineteenth-century commentators, including Burns's first posthumous editor, James Currie, to suggest that she was the tragic "ideal maiden" who inspired Burns's art. This sentimental Victorian view persisted into the early twentieth century. See Maurice Lindsay, *Robert Burns: The Man; His Work; The Legend* (London: McGibbon & Kee, 1968); David Daiches, *Robert Burns* (London: Longman's, 1975); and F.B. Snyder, *Robert Burns, His Personality, His Reputation and His Art* (Toronto: University of Toronto Press, 1936).

55.   The Bible that Mary Campbell is supposed to have given Burns has not been found. See, M. Lindsay, *The Burns Encyclopedia*, London: Hutchison, 1970), 27–28.

56.   George MacDonald (1824–1905), born at Huntly in west Aberdeenshire, was a prolific writer of novels. His "Scottish Novels" were set mainly in the northeast where he was raised and educated before he moved to London to pursue his literary career. A recurring theme in MacDonald's work, that art provides a route to God, would have been particularly appealing to Smith. See David S. Robb, "Realism and Fantasy in the Fiction of George MacDonald," in *The History of Scottish Literature*, *Vol.* 3, (Nineteenth Century), 275–290; *DNB Supplement* (1901–1911), 513–15. The quotation is from MacDonald's *Robert Falconer* (London: Hurst & Blackett, 1868), Part 1, Chapter 12, "Robert's Plan of Salvation." The actual line reads "She cud hae wiled a maukin frae its lair wi'her bonnie heilan' speech." "Maukin" is the Scots word for a hare. *CSD*, 404.

57. John C. Becket (1810–79) was born in Kilwinning, Scotland. In 1831, he immigrated to New York, where he worked in the printing trade. In 1832, he arrived in Montreal where he set up a book and stationary store. Becket was deeply involved in the religious community of Montreal, was a teetotaller, and longtime member and president of the Montreal St. Andrew's Society. He had a connection with John Dougall, the founder of the *Montreal Witness*, and himself printed the *French Canadian Missionary Record*, the *Canada Miscellany*, and the *Canada Temperance Advocate*. John Irwin Cooper, "John C. Becket," in *DCB*, Vol. 10 (1972), 40–41.

58. Robert Weir was editor of the *Montreal Herald*, a "conservative, pro-British, anti-patriot" paper, from 1838 until his death in 1843. See Elizabeth Waterston, "David Kinnear," in *DCB*, Vol. 11 (1976), 429.

59. Rollo Campbell (1803–71) was born in Dunning-Mason, Perthshire. He emigrated to Montreal in 1822 from Greenock where he had apprenticed as a printer. Campbell was employed by the *Montreal Gazette* before he established his own printing business, which soon became one of Canada's largest. Campbell published several newspapers during his career, including the Reform paper, *The Pilot* (1849–62). He was also active in Reform politics and served on the city council. Campbell maintained his links with his homeland, and, in 1857, gave two lectures in Scotland that were subsequently published, encouraging his countrymen to emigrate to Canada. See Elizabeth Nish, "Rollo Campbell," in *DCB*, Vol. 10 (1871–1880), 129–30.

60. Smith published the results of his research on "Highland Mary" in John D. Ross's volume, *Highland Mary: Interesting Papers on an Interesting Subject* (Paisley: A. Gardner, 1894). A sketch taken from a photograph of Ms. Robertson, in Smith's possession, was also published in *The Scottish Canadian*, January 29, 1891, 3. "Highland Mary" appears to have also been a favourite topic of late nineteenth-century Burns enthusiasts in Canada. See *The Scottish Canadian* (July 23, 1891), 1.

61. "Creesh" is the Scots word for fat, grease, or tallow. *CSD*, 122.

62. Willie Kyle was a native of Dumfriesshire who settled in St. George in 1840 when he was in his sixties. He had been involved in the timber trade on the St. Lawrence earlier in the century, but the War of 1812 had ruined his business. Kyle rented his store, which served as a major social centre for the village, from Dr. Elam Stimson. See the Note in Chapter 3 above, and W.W. Smith, "The Scot in Canada. I," in *The Scottish Canadian* (April 23, 1891), 10.

63.   Penielheugh is a few miles outside of the Royal Town of Jedburgh, south of Edinburgh. Britain had been at war with Napoleon's France since May 1803, but the French invasion fleet was not assembled at Boulogne until July of 1804. Nelson's victory over the French fleet at Trafalgar the following year helped redirect Napoleon's attentions towards central Europe, and any idea of an invasion of the British Isles was abandoned. To commemorate the British victory over Napoleon at Waterloo the sixth Marquis of Lothian had a 150-foot-high monument erected in 1825. See Ian R. Christie, *Wars and Revolutions: Britain, 1760–1815* (Cambridge, MA: Harvard University Press, 1982), 257–80; and Michael Broers, *Europe Under Napoleon 1799–1815* (New York: St. Martin's Press, 1996).

64.   "Laverock," the Scots word for skylark, is derived from the Middle English "laverok." *CSD*, 360.

65.   James Goldie was born in Ayrshire, Scotland, on November 6, 1824. The Goldie family operated an important mill in Guelph, on the Speed River, and became influential members of the fast growing community. Apart from being an important business figure, James Goldie was also a director of the town's Mechanics Institute and on the Board of Management of the town library. See Leo A. Johnson, *History of Guelph.* (Guelph: Guelph Historical Society, 1977), 144–45 and 209–10.

66.   John Burroughs (1837–1921), the popular American nature writer, published extensively in the late nineteenth century. His article "Skylark on the Hudson" was published in *Scribner's Monthly*, Vol. 26 (February 1881), 518–19, not in *Harpers Monthly Magazine*. In the article Burroughs wrote: "The bird had, most likely, escaped from a cage, or, maybe, it was a survivor of a number liberated some time ago on Long Island." The story told to Smith is corroborated by a letter that Burroughs wrote to his brother, Evan, from Alloway, Scotland, in 1882. In the letter, Burroughs describes the encounter "about the ruins of an old castle," and identifies the young man as having the surname Scoular. Apparently, Scoular also had a brother and an uncle living in the United States near Burrough's home. See Clara Barrus, *Life and Letters of John Burroughs.* (New York: Russell & Russell, 1968), 239–42.

67.   The lack of songbirds in North America was a common complaint among nineteenth-century British travel writers and several attempts were made to "Europeanize" the continent by importing species from the Old World. The *Cincinnati Acclimatization Society* was formed in

1874 to introduce " foreign birds as are worthy of note for their song or their services to the farmer and the horticulturalist." As president of the Cincinnati, Hamilton and Dayton Railroad, Julius Dexter was a prominent Cincinnati citizen. See "More Birds for America," in *Manufacturer and Builder* (April 1874), 81; *Cincinnati Business Directory* (1890); and *Harper's New Monthly Magazine* (March 1874), 530.

Chapter 7: Irish and German Settlers

1. Although Smith is claiming personal knowledge, his characterization of the Irish settlers in based upon prevailing contemporary stereotypes. The image of the hard-drinking, illiterate, crafty, and occasionally violent Irishman, which was reproduced throughout the nineteenth century, was directed primarily at Irish Catholics immigrants. In Ontario, however, most of the Irish immigrants were Protestants who had literacy rates similar to the English and Scots settlers of the province. The majority of Irish immigrants arrived in Upper Canada between 1845 and 1860 when most of the best agricultural land had already been allocated. As a consequence, they either took up land in the more marginal areas, such as the region around Owen Sound, or joined the wage-labour market. Irish-Catholic settlement concentrated in the east of the province, but by 1871 a number of Irish Catholics had settled in Sydenham Township near Owen Sound. Most Irish-born settlers in the region were, however, Irish Protestants. For Irish stereotyping, see Donald Power, "The Paddy Image: The Stereotype of the Irishman in Cartoon and Comic," in Robert O'Driscoll and Lorna Reynold, ed., *The Untold Story: The Irish in Canada*. Vol. 1 (Toronto: Celtic Arts of Canada, 1988); L. Perry Curtis Jr., *Apes and Angles: The Irishman in Victorian Caricature* (Washington: Smithsonian Press, 1997) revised edition; R.F. Foster, *Paddy and Mr. Punch: Connections in Irish and English History* (London: Allan Lane, 1993), 171–94; and Richard Strivers, *A Hair of the Dog: Irish Drinking and American Stereotype* (University Park: Pennsylvania State University Press, 1977). For Irish settlement, see A. Brunger, "The Distribution of the Scots and Irish in Upper Canada," in *The Canadian Geographer/Le Geographe canadien*, Vol. 34, No.3 (1990), 254–57; Cecil J, Houston and William J. Smyth, *Irish Emigration and Canadian Settlement: Patterns, Links and Letters* (Toronto: University of Toronto Press, 1990); Donald H. Akenson, *The Irish Diaspora: A Primer*

(Toronto: P.D. Meany Company, 1993); and *The Irish in Ontario: A Study in Rural History*, 2nd ed. (Montreal, Kingston: McGill-Queen's University Press, 1999); Bruce S. Elliot, *Irish Migrants in the Canadas: A New Approach* (Montreal: McGill-Queen's University Press, 1988); and Catharine Anne Wilson, *A New Lease on Life: Landlords, Tenants and Immigrants in Ireland and Canada* (Montreal: McGill-Queen's University Press, 1994).

2. Arran Township in Bruce County was named after Arran, Scotland, and several Scots were among its first settlers. The Irish settlers, who were fewer in number, began settling in the township in 1853. See Robertson, *The History of the County of Bruce*, 262–77.

3. Nathaniel E. Wallace was the son of Thomas and Martha Wallace of Carney, County Sligo. He purchased lot 10, Concession 8 in Vaughan Township in 1833, and, in 1842, sold it to George Frazier Wallace, the brother of his wife Ann. It is not certain when Nathaniel Wallace moved to Woodbridge, but he was definitely there between 1851–53 when he served as a church warden for Christ Church, Anglican Church. Woodbridge was originally named Burwick after the original settler of the area, Rowland Burr. The name was changed in 1855 when the village applied for a post office. The Wallace family was prominent in the business community of the town during the second half of the nineteenth century. From 1865 to 1886, Alfred L. Gooderham was the postmaster at the Pine Grove post office in Vaughan Township. He was also one of the partners in Gooderham & Worts, the firm that operated the village's gristmill as well as a sawmill, general store, cooper shop, and distillery. The company also opened an operation in Toronto and became one of the largest distillers in Ontario; today the site is a popular tourist destination known as the Distillery District.

   The Toronto, Grey and Bruce narrow gauge railway was completed to Mount Forest in 1871, but in 1873 it was extended to Owen Sound. The CPR took control of the railroad in 1884. See Reaman, *A History of Vaughan Township*, 81, 115, 125–26, 224, and 285.

4. In this story and the ones that follow, Smith relies on two particular stereotypes found in nineteenth-century humour, the Irishman as a dim-witted oaf and the Irishman as an impish trickster. Both images were prevalent in popular literature and in popular theatre. Although they were intended to provoke laughter, at various times during the century such characterizations were employed to encourage anti-Irish prejudice. See Jennifer K. Harding, "The Caricature of the Irish

in British and U.S. Comic Art," in *Historian*, 1992, 54 (2), 283–88; Patrick O'Sullivan, "The Irish Joke"; Kathleen Donovan, "Good Old Pat: An Irish-American Stereotype in Decline," in *Eire-Ireland*, Vol. 15, No. 3 (1980), 6–14; D.G. Paz, "Anti-Catholicism, Anti-Irish Stereotyping, and Anti-Celtic Racism in Mid-Victorian Working Class Periodicals," in *Albion*, Vol.18, No.4 (1986), 601–16; and Dale T. Knobel, *Paddy and the Republic: Ethnicity and Nationality in Antebellum America* (Middletown, CN: Wesleyan University Press, 1986).

5. Reverend John Wood (1828–1905) was born in London, England. He was the Congregational minister in Brantford from 1852 to 1874, and served as minister in Ottawa and Canso, Nova Scotia, before retiring in 1897. Reverend Wood published several devotional works and a study of Canadian Congregational church history. See Reverend John Wood, *Memoir of Henry Wilkes, D.D., L.L.D., his Life and Times* (Montreal: F.E. Grafton, 1887); *Something From Our Hands: Historical Canadian Biography Based Upon Memoirs Recorded in 1899 by Rev. John Wood* (Hudson Heights, QC: Wood Family Archives, 1988); and Walkington, *The Congregational Churches of Canada.*

6. In the second half of the nineteenth century, Irish navies, who had earlier been employed in canal digging, became a key component of the labour force in railway construction throughout North America. The Irish railway-worker tale related by Smith unintentionally highlights the social tensions that characterized these workplaces. The unskilled, mainly Catholic, Irish workers were subjected to discrimination and to considerable social violence. See Ruth Bleasdale, "Conflict on the Canals of Upper Canada in the 1840s," in *Labour/Le Travail*, No. 7 (1981), 9–39; Daniel E. Bender, "An Uneasy Peace: Irish Labour on the Farmington Canal," in *Connecticut History*, Vol. 35, No. 2 (1994), 235–62; Peter Way, *Common Labour : Workers and the Digging of North American Canals, 1780–1860* (Cambridge: Cambridge University Press, 1993); Matthew E. Mason, "The Hands Here are Disposed to be Turbulent": Unrest among the Irish Trackmen of the Baltimore and Ohio Railroad, 1829–1851," in *Labor History*, Vol. 39, No. 3 (1998), 253–72; Jean-Pierre Kesteman, "Les travailleurs à la construction du chemin de fer dans la region de Sherbrooke (1851–1853) [The Railway Construction Workers in the Sherbrooke Region (1851–1853)] in *Revue d'Histoire de l'Amerique Francais*, Vol. 31, No. 4 (1978), 525–45; and David J. Hall, "The Construction Worker's Strike on the Canadian Pacific Railway, 1879" in *Labour/Le Travail*, Vol. 36 (1995), 11–35.

7. Reverend William W. Shepherd was a Methodist clergyman in Ontario. In 1865, he was listed as a Wesleyan Methodist student at Cobourg. See J.L. Mitchell and James Sutherland, eds., *Mitchell & Co.'s Canada Classified Directory for 1865–66* (Toronto: Mitchell & Co., 1865), 771.

8. This story appears to be an inaccurate gloss on Paul's 2nd Corinthians 8: 2–15 and Philippians 4: 10–20.

9. Jean Froissart (1333–1410) was a poet and medieval chronicler from Hainhault in the Low Countries. (The area today is in southern Belgium near the French border.) He moved in royal circles in England and France and is most famous for his *Chronicles* of the Hundred Years' War that recount the feats of arms by knights on all sides. See Cynthia Neville, "Jean Froissart," in D.R. Woolf, ed., *A Global Encyclopedia of Historical Writing* Vol. 1 (New York: Garland Pub., 1998), 337–38.

10. N. Reid & Company were listed as "marble dealers" in Newmarket in *Mitchell & Co.'s Canada Classified Directory for 1865–66*, 338.

11. Smith's tale is making light of the serious problem of infant mortality. Reformers were concerned with the high rate of infant death during the nineteenth and early twentieth century. See Larry A. Sawchuk and Stacie D.A. Burke, "Mortality in an Early Ontario Community: Belleville 1876–1885," in *Urban History Review*, Vol. 29, No. 1 (2000), 33–47; Cynthia Comacchio, "'The Mothers of the Land Must Suffer': Child and Maternal Welfare in Rural and Outpost Ontario, 1918–1940," in *OH*, Vol. 80, No.3 (1988), 183–205; and *"Nations are Built of Babies": Saving Ontario's Mothers and Children, 1900–1940* (Montreal: McGill-Queen's University Press, 1993).

12. David Willson (1778–1866) was born in Duchess County, New York, not in Ireland as Smith claims. His parents, John and Catharine Willson, had emigrated from County Down, Ireland, between 1768 and 1775. David Willson's wife, Phebe was a Quaker and the couple moved to Upper Canada to join the Quaker community there in 1801. David Willson split with the Quakers in 1812 and formed the millenarian movement, the Children of Peace. Inspired by Willson's theology, the sect sought to establish a church where God spoke directly to all and where both Jews and Christians could find a home while they awaited the coming of the Messiah. See James Reaney, "David Willson," *DCB*, Vol. 9 (1861–1870), 841–43; Albert Schrauwers, *Awaiting the Millennium: The Children of Peace and the Village of Hope, 1812–1889* (Toronto: University of Toronto Press,

1993), 226–7; W. John McIntyre, *Children of Peace* (Montreal: McGill-Queen's University Press, 1994); Gladys M. Rolling, *East Gwillimbury In the Nineteenth Century.* (Toronto: The Ryerson Press, 1967), 43; and Thomas Gerry, "The Religious Beliefs of David Willson and the Children of Peace," in *The York Pioneer,* Vol. 80, (1985), 32–44.

13. Like the Shakers, the Children of Peace attempted to live as a separate community, although they ran individual households rather than live communally. While Willson played a key role in the lives of the adherents, the movement did survive his death in 1866. In the later decades of the nineteenth century, however, the Children of Peace lost adherents and had ceased functioning by 1890. The Sharon Temple, however, still stands and is a spectacular building of unique proportions. Its square plan symbolized unity and justice; its three storeys represented the Trinity; the door in the centre of each side, at the cardinal points of the compass, allowed people to enter from all directions as equals; and the 2,952 panes of glass allowed the sun to illuminate the interior. Willson may have designed the temple, but the master builder was Ebenezer Doan, who had arrived from Pennsylvania in 1808, and helped with its construction between 1825 and 1832. See Rolling, *East Gwillimbury in the Nineteenth Century*, 43–5; Mathew Cooper, "Living Together: How Communal were the Children of Peace?" in *OH*, Vol. 79, No. 1 (1987), 3–17; Schrauwers, *Awaiting the Millennium*, 216–51; and McIntyre, *Children of Peace*, 47–81.

14. As Smith indicates, music was an integral part of the community at Sharon. See Anne Schau, "Sharon's Musical Past," in *The York Pioneer,* Vol. 80 (1985).

15. John David Willson (1797–1887) was born in New York State. He played a prominent role in the Children of Peace Band and acted as the sect's minister after his father's death. The Children of Peace's use of music, that combined both voice and instrument, may have been inspired by practices found in rural English parishes. The first choir performed in 1818 or 1819 and the band was formed shortly thereafter. The first Sharon feast, which may have been inspired by Methodist meals, was held in 1818. See Schrauwers, *Awaiting the Millennium*, 229; and McIntyre, *Children of Peace*, 82–107.

16. While he is mistaken on the origins of the term "Dutch," Smith's outline of the settlement of German speakers is largely correct. See Chapter 3 above; and Heinz Lehmann, *The German Canadians 1750–1937: Immigration, Settlement and Culture* (St. John's, NL:

Jesperson Press, 1986). The complexity of the various episodes of German migration to Upper Canada is illustrated by the Irish Palatines. This group left Germany in the early eighteenth century and first settled in Ireland. Some emigrated to New York later in the century and others went directly to Ontario in the early nineteenth century. Although these Palatine settlers had lost much of their German culture by the time they arrived in Canada, they did not consider themselves Irish, thus confounding the Irish and German ethnic categories established by Smith in this chapter. See Carolyn A. Heald, "The Irish Palatines in Ontario: Religion, Ethnicity and Rural Migration," in *Canadian Papers in Rural History*, Vol. 9 (1994), 17–185.

17.   Reverend Jeremiah Fishburn was pastor of the Zion Evangelical Lutheran Church in Sherwood, Vaughan Township, from 1854 to 1880. He was also the first president of the Canada Synod of the Lutheran Church. The Zion church had been established by settlers from Pennsylvania in 1808 and the first pastors came from the German settlement in Markham. Services in the church were conducted in German until 1850. See Reaman, *A History of Vaughan Township*, 156–58.

18.   German-speaking settlers from Waterloo County were among the first settlers to move into Bruce County. In Carrick Township they formed the majority of the population, but significant concentrations were also found in the adjacent Culross, Greenock, and Brant townships. The land had been surrendered in 1836 and a small number of squatters had made their way into Brant Township by the early 1840s. While nicknamed the "Banner Township" of Bruce County, extensive settlement did not occur until after the development of the Durham Road in 1848. The settlement of the county originally began with a double line of fifty-acre farm lots laid out on either side of the road, and since the government advertised free lots for settlers who were subjects of the Queen and at least eighteen years of age, the county was settled at a rapid pace. See Lehmann, *The German Canadians*, 83–85; Laura M. Gateman, *The History of the Township of Brant: 1854–1979* (Elmwood, ON: Brant Township Historical Society, 1979), 6–9; and Norman Robertson, *The History of the County of Bruce* (Toronto: William Briggs, 1906), 10–16 and 31–36. For the social role of blacksmiths in early Ontario, see William N.T. Wylie, *The Blacksmith in Upper Canada: A Study of Technology, Culture and Power* (Gananoque, ON: Langdale Press, 1990).

19. John McCallum was justice of the peace in Klienburg (Kleinberg, today, in the City of Vaughan) in 1870. Klienburg was named after John N. Klien (or Kline) who built a flour mill on lots 24 and 25, Concession Line 9, Vaughan Township in 1847. By 1870, the population of the village had grown to 350 and included Scots, English, and Irish settlers as well as the original German speakers. By employing the generic "Hans" to identify the German in this story, Smith is clearly employing conventional stereotypes. The "Dumb Dutchman" image, reflected in Smith's tale, appears to have first developed in Pennsylvania during the eighteenth century. See Reaman, *A History of Vaughan Township*, 56, 107–10; Achim Kopp, "'Of the Most Ignorant Stupid Sort of their Own Nation': Perceptions of the Pennsylvania Germans in the Eighteenth and Twentieth Centuries," in *Yearbook of German-American Studies*, Vol. 35 (2000), 41–55.

20. At the time Smith was writing, national characteristics, largely developed from prevailing ethnic stereotypes found in cartoons, Vaudeville shows, and popular literature, had come to be viewed as natural traits. Although these caricatures were often employed for humorous effect, they could also be utilized in virulently racist ways, as Smith's chapters below indicate. For examples of nineteenth-century ethnic caricature, see Arthur B. Maurice and Frederic T. Cooper, *The History of the Nineteenth Century in Caricature* (New York: Cooper Square Publishers, 1904); Perry L. Curtis Jr., *Apes and Angles: The Irishman in Victorian Caricature* (Washington: Smithsonian Press, 1997); and J.W. Bengough, *Bengough's Chalk-Talks: A Series of Platform Addresses on Various Topics* (Toronto: Musson Book Company, 1922), especially 51–53. For a more particular examination of stereotyping in the United States during the time Smith was writing, see James H. Dormon, "Ethnic Stereotyping in American Popular Culture: The Depiction of American Ethnics in the Cartoon Periodicals of the Guilded Age," in *Amerikastudien/American Studies [West Germany]*, Vol. 30, No. 4 (1985), 489–507; James H. Dormon, "American Popular Culture and the New Immigration Ethnics: The Vaudeville Stage and the Process of Ethnic Ascription," in *Amerikastudien/American Studies*, Vol. 36, No. 2 (1991), 179–93; and Henry B. Wonham, "An Art to be Cultivated": Ethnic Caricature and American Literary realism," in *American Literary Realism*, Vol. 32, No. 3 (2000), 185–219. For Reverend Solomon Snider, see Chapter 4 above; and Walkington, *The Congregational Churches of Canada*.

21. The German settlers of Norwich Township, Oxford County, were German Americans who had arrived in Upper Canada at the same time the Quakers and others had migrated from the United States. Reverend Snider was the Congregational minister in the township from 1861 to 1866. Lehmann, *The German Canadians 1750–1937*, 87; and Walkington, *The Congregational Churches of Canada*.

22. The persistence of the belief in witchcraft has also been noted among German immigrant groups in Waterloo County, Ontario, and in Lunenburg County, Nova Scotia. Helen Creighton's examination of witch folklore in Nova Scotia revealed similar beliefs regarding the bewitchment of butter, animals, and humans as well as the belief that witches could be defeated by a silver bullet. Such beliefs were not, however, restricted to the German communities. Researchers have also recorded tales regarding witches and fairies among French Canadian, Gypsy, and Scottish groups. Smith may have been surprised to learn that in 1817 adherents to the Church of Scotland in Pictou, Nova Scotia, complained that the local ministers refused to deal with "witches who were bothering the settlers" and successfully appealed to the Glasgow Colonial Society to have a minister sent out to tackle the problem. See W.J. Wintemberg, *Folk-Lore of Waterloo County* (Ottawa: King's Printer, 1950); Helen Creighton, *Folklore of Lunenburg County, Nova Scotia* (Toronto: McGraw-Hill Ryerson, 1976), 46–57; Jack Verney, "LaFollevill's Place: Low Life in the Cabarets of Old Montreal," in *The Beaver*, Vol. 76, No. 5 (1996), 24–27; Jan Perkowski, *Vampires, Dwarves and Witches among the Ontario Kashubs* (Ottawa: National Museum, 1972); and John S. Moir, *The Church in the British Era: From the British Conquest to Confederation* (Toronto: McGraw-Hill Ryerson, 1972), 134–35.

23. The townships of Durham, Victoria, and Ontario counties that border Lake Scugog were settled primarily in the 1850s. There does not appear to have been a concentration of German settlers in any of these areas. See Watson Kirkconnell, *County of Victoria Centennial History* (Lindsay, ON: Victoria County Council, 1967); J.E. Farewell, *Ontario County* (Whitby, ON: Gazette-Chronicle Press, 1907); *Illustrated Historical Atlas of the County of Ontario* (Toronto: J.H. Beers & Co., 1877); and *Illustrated Atlas of the Dominion of Canada* (Toronto: H. Belden & Co., 1881).

Chapter 8: The Indians

1. As with previous "ethnic" chapters, Smith is generalizing from his contact with a few particular groups. It is clear that in his discussion of the "Indians" he draws almost exclusively on his contact with the inhabitants of the Saugeen Reserves in the Owen Sound region, in particular, the Newash Reserve adjacent to Owen Sound, the Colpoy Bay Reserve beside Wiarton, and the Cape Crocker Reserve on the northern shore of Colpoy's Bay. While Smith resided in Owen Sound, both the Newash and Colpoy Bay reserves were surrendered to the Crown in 1857 and 1861, respectively, and their inhabitants relocated to the Cape Crocker Reserve. It is also clear that Smith had some contact with the Ojibwa of Manitoulin Island and the Spanish River Reserve in northern Ontario, as well as the Mohawk of the Six Nations Reserve centred around Brantford, but his account of the "Indians" is essentially based upon his experiences in Owen Sound. For the Saugeen First Nation, see Peter S. Schmalz, *The History of the Saugeen Indians* and *The Ojibwa of Southern Ontario;* for the Six Nations Reserve, see Charles M. Johnston, "The Six Nations in the Grand River Valley," in Smith and Rogers, eds., *Aboriginal Ontario,* 167–81.

2. In this paragraph, Smith slides from his previous chapters' identification of national characteristics into an overtly racist discussion, that is, a position that views other peoples as not only being different, but that sees a gap between "us" and "them" as permanent and unbridgeable because of the "other's" innate inferiority. See George M. Frederickson, *Racism: A Short History* (Princeton: New Jersey: Princeton University Press, 2002), 9. Here Smith demonstrates such ideas by repeating the ubiquitous late nineteenth-century myth that the indigenous populations would inevitably disappear because of their inability to adapt to "civilized" ways as well as the stereotypical caricature of the indolent, happy-go-lucky Black, which had originated in American minstrel shows of the 1840s and was repeated throughout the century. See Daniel Francis, *The Imaginary Indian: The Image of the Indian in Canadian Culture* (Vancouver: Arsenal Pulp Press, 1992), 16–43; and J. Stanley Lemons, "Black Stereotypes as Reflected in Popular Culture, 1880–1920," in *Journal of Popular Culture,* Vol.10, No. 1 (1976), 70–79.

3.   Charles Keeshick was a Potawatomi member of the Newash Reserve. In the 1840s, members of the Potawatomi, Ojibwa, and Odawa First Nations loyal to the British Crown moved from the United States and settled in Saugeen territory. They were joined by a number of other Ojibwa, including some Mississauga and a small number of Mohawks who were relocated from elsewhere in Canada. This resulted in considerable tension on the Newash Reserve with newcomers, such as Keeshick, challenging the authority of the hereditary chief, John Thomas Wahbahdick (Wahbatick). There were several points of conflict, but the role of the newcomers in negotiating the surrender of the Newash Reserve in 1857 was especially resented by the Saugeen members since most of them opposed any surrender. Charles Keeshick acted as translator during the 1857 negotiations. Smith met Charles Keeshick in 1855, and described him as "an intelligent and educated member of the band." See William Wye Smith, *Gazetteer and Directory of the County of Grey, 1865–66* (Toronto: The Globe Steam Press, 1865), 327; and Schmalz, *The History of the Saugeen Indians*, 36–43, 81–84, and 107–08.

4.   Smith is probably referring to William Waukay. In the early twentieth century, the Waukay family were the beneficiaries of Band Council patronage and held several appointments on the Cape Crocker Reserve. William's speech at Brantford may well have been an early attempt to ingratiate the family with potential benefactors. See Schmaltz, *History of the Saugeen Indians*, 208.

5.   Here Smith appears to be echoing the racism prevalent in late nineteenth-century popular American magazines. Articles in periodicals such as, *Harpers* and *Scribner's Monthly*, while claiming the inferiority of both indigenous peoples and Blacks, suggested that Blacks, properly trained and directed, could be more useful, since they were "a stronger race" and, while "lazy," were ambitious and suited to hard work. It was suggested, however, that Native North Americans were "too proud" to submit to White instruction and that they lacked the desire to "improve" themselves. See Charles R. Wilson, "Racial Reservations: Indians and Blacks in American Magazines, 1865–1890," in *Journal of Popular Culture*, Vol. 10, No.1 (1976), 70–79.

6.   Smith's reference to the physical characteristics of the early English suggests the influence of evolutionary biology on his thought. Rather than supporting notions of equality, such ideas were in fact employed by Smith's contemporaries in order to argue for a "scientific" basis for racial inequality and inferiority. For example, see Nancy Stephan,

The Idea of Race in Science: Great Britain, 1800–1960 (Hamden, CN: Archon Books, 1982).

7. Indigenous Peoples were navigating the Great Lakes for thousands of years prior to the arrival of Europeans and understood the hazards of travelling in open water. As in many other instances, Smith discounts traditional Native knowledge and practice to imply that First Nations were unwilling to adopt "superior" methods. See Dickason, *Canada's First Nations*, 56–58.

8. Smith is making a Biblical allusion. Jonah 1 recounts that after a casting of lots, Jonah was thrown overboard to lighten the load during a violent storm. He was subsequently swallowed by the whale.

9. Reverend Ludwick Kribs was the minister for the Congregational Mission at the Colpoy's Bay Reserve from 1853 to 1869. See Walkington, *The Congregational Churches of Canada*, and the note relating to Kribs in Chapter 4.

10. Sir William Johnson (1715–74), was a merchant and colonial administrator of considerable influence in the Mohawk Valley of New York. He was active in the fur trade, and during the Anglo-French wars often joined the Iroquois in attacks against the French, including the capture of Fort Niagara in 1759. See Julian Gwyn, "Sir William Johnson," *DCB*, Vol. 4 (1771–1800), 394–98. For the complex nature of Johnson's relations with the Native Peoples, see Richard White, *The Middle Ground: Indians, Empires, and Republics in the Great Lakes Region 1650–1815* (Cambridge: Cambridge University Press, 1991). Also see Howard Swiggett, *War Out of Niagara* (Port Washington, NY: Ira J. Friedman, Inc., 1963), 8–23.

11. This tale also reflects prevalent nineteenth-century racial stereotypes. It suggests not only a limited Native mental capacity, but also an essentially violent "savage" nature that could be revealed at a moments notice. See Francis, *The Imaginary Indian*, 65–66; Wilson, "Racial Reservations," 73; and Berkhofer Jr., *The White Man's Indian*, 90–97. The journey described by Smith was a well-travelled fur-trade route, which had been controlled by the Huron, Iroquois, and Ojibwa at various times. See Dickason, *Canada's First Nations*, 112–14; and White, *The Middle Ground*, 94–141.

12. Reverend Robert Robinson was minister of the Congregational Church in Owen Sound from 1863 to 1873. Robinson took over as minister at the Colpoy's Bay Indian Mission in 1874, the same year that Smith accompanied him on his journey to Algoma. Many Christian denominations sent missionaries into Northern Ontario,

but by the end of the century, the Anglican Church Missionary Society was the most active in the area visited by Smith and Robinson. By that time the Anglicans had established a church, as part of the Blind River Diocese, at Spanish beside the Spanish River Reserve, which is located on the North Channel south of the Town of Algoma and across from Manitoulin Island. See Walkington, *The Congregational Churches of Canada; The Canadian Independent*, May 1873; Croft, *Fourth Entrance to Huronia*, 59, 98, and 23. For Anglican missionary activity, see Edward F. Wilson, *Missionary Work Among the Ojebway Indians* (London: Society for Promoting Christian Knowledge, 1886); Awdry and Green, *By Lake and Forest: The Story of Algoma*; and Schmalz, *The Ojibwa of Southern Ontario*, xvi.

13. The missionary desire to "educate" and "civilize" the Natives resulted in the creation of the residential school system. In the late nineteenth century, separate boys' and girls' Native "industrial" schools were built in Spanish, Ontario, by the Roman Catholics to replace a school that had burned down on Manitoulin Island. As late as 1940 half of the Native pupil population of Ontario were being taught in such schools with devastating cultural, physical, and psychological consequences. See Schmalz, *The Ojibwa of Southern Ontario*, 181–89; and J.R. Miller, *Shingwauk's Vision: A History of Native Residential Schools* (Toronto: University of Toronto Press, 1996).

14. Smith's tale illustrates how the evangelical Christian emphasis on individual salvation was often in conflict with the communal nature of Native society. Individual conversions had created rifts in Native communities throughout Ontario, not only between those who held traditional beliefs and those who accepted Christian beliefs, but also between adherents of various Christian denominations. See Smith, *Sacred Feathers*, 98–111; and Schmalz, *History of the Saugeen Indians*, 22–55.

15. The Serpent River originates at Quirke Lake and drains into Lake Huron beside the Spanish Reserve. The Nahwegezhic (Nawageeshick) is a family name found in the Manitoulin Island region. See Schmalz, *The Ojibwa of Southern Ontario*, 234.

16. The tremendous range of Ojibwa beliefs are recorded in a wide variety of accounts, from collections of tales drawn from oral tradition written by contemporary Ojibwa authors to ethnographic accounts from outside scholars observing the communities. All agree that the water serpent was a powerful figure, a Manitou, with the power to both heal and injure people. According to some accounts of South

Eastern Ojibwa belief, the serpent was able to travel at great speed and was a shape shifter who often took the form of a man, revealing himself to individuals on vision quests. For an early ethnographic account, see Diamond Jenness, *The Ojibwa Indians of Parry Island, Their Social and Religious Life* (Ottawa: National Museum of Canada, 1935), 39–40. An Ojibwa discussion of Native belief can be found in Basil Johnston, *Ojibwa Heritage* (Lincoln, Nebraska: University of Nebraska Press, 1976) and Basil Johnston, *The Manitous: The Spiritual World of the Ojibwa* (New York: HarperCollins, 1995). For a discussion of the serpent motif in Ojibwa rock art see, Grace Rajinovich, *Reading Rock Art* (Toronto: Natural Heritage Books, 1994, 2nd printing 2002), 107–08.

17. Susannah Moodie recounts such an entrance by a Native. Published tales like hers may have been the source of Smith's account rather than his personal experience. See Susannah Moodie, *Roughing It in the Bush* (Toronto: McClelland & Stewart, 1989; originally published 1852), 291.

18. Smith has misunderstood the greeting "Boozhoo," which is an Ojibwa word and not a derivation of *bon jour.* "Usequebea" is the Scots word for whisky, derived from the Irish and Scottish Gaelic that was in use from the late seventeenth to the early twentieth century. Robinson, *CSD*, 756. As Smith suggests, the word would have been introduced by the Scots who dominated the fur-trade business in Canada. See Elaine Allan Mitchell, "The Scot in the Fur Trade," in W. Stanford Reid, ed., *The Scottish Tradition in Canada* (Toronto: McClelland & Stewart, 1976), 27–48.

19. In the 1840s, John Thomas Wahbahdick, the hereditary chief of the Saugeen people of the Newash Reserve, was involved in a bitter controversy with Reverend David Sawyer, a Mississauga Methodist minister who had come to the Reserve in the 1830s. Sawyer was unhappy with Wahbahdick's "secret council" with a Roman Catholic priest who wished to build a church on the reserve and on his refusal to allow the resettlement of six hundred members of his own Credit River Band on the reserve. Accusations of financial mismanagement and drunkenness followed and Wahbahdick was temporarily removed as chief. His dispute with the Indian Department was longstanding and began with his opposition to the surveying of Saugeen land in 1851 and 1855. See Schmalz, *History of the Saugeen Indians,* 22–41 and 89–90. See also Rhonda Telford, "The Anishinabe Presentation of the Fishing Rights to the Duke

of Newcastle and the Prince of Wales," in *Papers of the Algonquin Conference*, (30) (1999), 374–96.

20. The moralizing reflected in this passage is consistent with the temperance advocacy of Smith and his contemporaries. See, for example, F. Laurie Barron, "Alcoholism, Indians and the Anti-Drink Cause in the Protestant Indian Missions of Upper Canada, 1822–1850," in Ian A.L. Getty & Antoine S. Lussier, *As Long as the Sun Shines and the Water Flows: A Reader in Canadian Native Studies* (Vancouver: University of British Columbia Press, 1983), 191–202.

21. Smith's concern with language reflects the form of the nineteenth-century Ojibwa accounts of Native life. See Reverend George Copway [Kah-Ge-Ga-Gah-Bowh], *The Traditional History and Characteristic Sketches of the Ojibwa Nation* (London: C. Gilpin, 1850), 123–39; Reverend Peter Jones (Kahkewaquonaby), *History of the Ojebway Indians: With Special Reference to their Conversion to Christianity* (London: A.W. Bennett, 1861), 178–90. Smith devoted an entire chapter of this manuscript, not included in this edition, to words and their meanings. In this regard, Smith can be seen as seeking to be identified with his contemporary Victorian men and women of leisure and letters who volunteered their time to locate quotations for the *Oxford English Dictionary*. See Simon Winchester, *The Meaning of Everything: The Story of the Oxford English Dictionary* (Oxford: Oxford University Press, 2003).

22. It would appear that Smith failed to consider his contemporary, the famous Pauline Johnson (1861–1913), whose father was Mohawk and whose mother was English, an "Indian" poet. See Veronica Strong-Boag and Carole Gerson, *Paddling Her Own Canoe: The Times and Texts of E. Pauline Johnson (Tekahionwake)* (Toronto: University of Toronto Press, 2000). See also Sheila Johnston, *Buckskin and Broadcloth: A Celebration of E. Pauline Johnson — Tekahionwake* (Toronto: Natural Heritage Books, 1997).

23. In transcribing the Ojibwa translations of well-known hymns, Smith was following the example of the Mississauga Methodist minister, Reverend Peter Jones. See, for example, Jones, *A Collection of Ojebway and English Hymns: For the use of the Native Indians* (Toronto: Methodist Missionary Society, c.1877). Of course, in his own poetry, Smith was a slave to rhyme. See *The Selected Poems of William Wye Smith* (1908).

24. Smith clearly did not appreciate that drumming had numerous functions in Native society. Rather than drums being used exclusively for "war" dances, they were considered sacred instruments that could

be used at a variety of ceremonial occasions, a point that was made by Reverend Peter Jones in his account. See Jones, *History of the Ojebway Indians*, 134. See also Johnston, *Ojibway Heritage*, 134–48.

25. George Copway also noted the absence of the sounds "1," "f," and "r" as well as the absence of "v" and "x." Rather than viewing this as sounding "unusual," Copway noted that the softness of the vowels without the harshness of consonants, produced "a musical flow of words." See Copway, *Sketches of the Ojibway Nation*, 126.

26. The Mohawk on the Saugeen Reserve were Caughnawa (Kahnawake) Iroquois from the Sault Saint Louise Reserve south of Montreal. As compensation for their dispossession in Quebec, some of the Caughnawa had been promised land in Saugeen territory. The offer, to their traditional enemies, was deeply resented by the Saugeen and their opposition resulted in only a limited relocation of forty-four individuals from Quebec in 1852. An Ojibwa-Mohawk couple would likely have been treated with suspicion, perhaps accounting for a desire to identify with non-Native society. See Schmalz, *History of the Saugeen Indians*, 19, 45–54.

27. A "Cockit" hat was a boat-shaped, brimless, three-cornered hat made of thick cloth. Robinson, *CSD*, 106.

28. "Equa" was the spelling that Copway and Jones used for the Ojibwa word for woman. Copway, *Sketches of the Ojibwa Nation*, 158; Jones, *History of the Ojebway Indians*, 164. For a discussion of the White stereotypes for Native women, see Pauleena M. MacDougall, "Grandmother, Daughter, Princess, Squaw: Native American Female Stereotypes in Historical Perspective," in *Maine History*, Vol. 34, No.1 (1994), 22–39.

29. As he does throughout this chapter, Smith fails to understand the significance of the traditional Native economy based on hunting and fishing that he and other non-Native settlers were undermining. Leisured aristocratic gentlemen were responsible for the classification of fishing and hunting as "sport," and clearly Smith wished to be identified with such "sportsmen." As a consequence of these preoccupations, he neglects to include many Ojibwa games, which ranged from athletic competitions to ball games such as lacrosse, in his definition of sport. See Copway, *Sketches of the Ojibway Nation*, 42–54; Jones, *History of the Ojebway Indians*, 134–40.

30. Smith is referring to the Boat Lake in Bruce County rather than Huron County. Boat Lake is located west of Wiarton in Amabel Township, which was settled in 1857 after the land sale in Owen Sound. The

lake is approximately halfway between Colpoy Bay and the Saugeen
Reserve at Chief's Point on Lake Huron. See Robertson, *History of the
County of Bruce*, 206–10.

31. Access to the Georgian Bay and Lake Huron fishery would become a
source of conflict between Native and settler societies. In 1895, Joseph
Wahbezie, perhaps a relation of Frederick Wahbazee, opposed the
surrender of the last of the Georgian Bay islands still under Native
control. These islands had traditionally been used for exploiting
the fishery by the First Nations. See Schmalz, *History of the Saugeen
Indians*, 132–40 and 185–90; Peggy Blair, "Taken for 'Granted'":
Aboriginal Title and Public Fishing Rights in Upper Canada," in *OH*,
Vol. 92, No. 2 (2000), 31–55.

32. Magnesia is not necessarily harmless. It is used as a purgative, but in
sufficient doses can prove to be toxic. This story reveals that Smith
and Cameron did not understand the role of healers in Ojibwa
society. While somewhat hostile, Jones provides a useful account
of Native practice, *History of the Ojebway Indians*, 143–45. See also,
Jenness, *Ojibwa Indians*, 60–65; and Christopher Vecsey, *Traditional
Ojibwa Religion and its Historical Changes*, (Philadelphia: American
Philosophical Society, 1983), 144–59. Dr. Alan Cameron (1830–1912)
was educated at Glasgow University and settled in Owen Sound when
he came to Canada in 1854. He helped to found the Owen Sound
Hospital, served as medical officer of health, and was later chief
surgeon for the CPR. With his sons, D.A. and James, he also ran a
drugstore in Owen Sound. See Croft, *Fourth Entrance to Huronia*, 80.

33. Dr. William Francis was practising medicine at Manitowaning by
the 1870s. He gave medical testimony at a notorious murder trial in
1877 and was reported treating an attempted suicide victim in 1884.
See George Skippen, "Murder on the Manitoulin Island, 1877," in
Through the Years: Manitoulin District History and Genealogy, Vol. 10,
No. 4, February 1993; and *Manitoulin Expositor*, November 15, 1884.

34. The village of Manitowaning was established under the treaty of
1836 and was intended as the centre of government for the island. In
1838, a party consisting of thirty-eight people, including an Anglican
clergyman, a doctor, teacher, and several tradesmen, arrived and the
new village was begun. By 1842 the village contained "three workshops,
a store, barn, schoolhouse, sawmill, eleven houses for employees, and
thirty-seven Native houses." Despite what seemed to be early success
the settlement grew slowly, most Natives preferring to settle at the Jesuit
settlement at Wikwemikong. Shelley J. Pearen, *Exploring Manitoulin*

(Toronto: University of Toronto Press, 1992), 7, 131. Manitowaning was the site of the annual gift-giving ceremony held each year to maintain good relations between the British Colonial Government and the Natives of the region. For a good description of the gift-giving festivities at Manitowaning, see Scott A. McLean, ed., *From Lochnaw to Manitoulin: A Highland Soldier's Tour Through Upper Canada* (Toronto: Natural Heritage/Natural History, Inc., 1999), 27–37.

35. A carboy is a large glass bottle, usually encased in wicker.

36. The reserves on Manitoulin Island originated with the early nineteenth-century gift-giving ceremony held each year at Manitowaning by the British Colonial Government to maintain the loyalty of the Ojibwa in the region. In the 1830s, Sir Francis Bond Head initiated a scheme that sought to relocate the First Nations of southern Ontario onto the island. In 1836, Ojibwa leaders agreed to set aside Manitoulin as a reserve for Native settlement in perpetuity, but, by 1860, only 1,000 people had moved to the island. Those who did come had a difficult time adjusting to the poor agricultural conditions and had to increasingly rely on the fishery. A subsequent treaty, negotiated using dubious methods and signed in 1862, surrendered 600,000 acres on the island for European settlement and divided up the reserve lands. From 1838 Manitowaning served as the centre of government administration on the island and became a centre for settler society as well. See McLean, *From Lochnaw to Manitoulin*, 27–37; Schmalz, *The Ojibwa of Southern Ontario*, 162–65; David Nazar, "Nineteenth-Century Wikwemikong: The Foundation of a Community and an Exploration of its People," in *OH*, Vol. 86, No.1 (1994), 9–12; and Ruth Bleasdale, "Manitowaning: An Experiment in Indian Settlement," in *OH*, Vol. 66, No. 3 (1974), 147–57.

37. Smith's condescending attitude towards Ojibwa was not based on an intimate knowledge of the language, but stemmed from a desire to assert "White" superiority over the "primitive" Native. This is evident elsewhere in this chapter when he puts stock stereotypical phrases like "um" and "how" in his Native informants mouths, making them appear intellectually inferior. In contrast, Peter Jones argued that because of its literal imagery, Ojibwa "makes a deeper impression on the mind of both speaker and hearer than a language [such as English] composed of arbitrary or unmeaning sounds. Jones, *History of the Ojebway Indians*, 179.

38. Although Smith is likely referring to the Congregational Mission Church at Colpoy's Bay, there was also a Methodist Mission on the

reserve. The inhabitants of the Saugeen Reserves had proved capable of not only producing their own petitions on numerous occasions, but also detailed minutes of their council proceedings, but this anecdote allows Smith to suggest otherwise. See Schmaltz, *History of the Saugeen Indians*, 36, 37, 72, 76–77, and 122–28.

39. Smith's informant was confusing the name of the settlement, Manitowaning, with the name of the adjacent reserve, Wikwenmikong, which means the Bay of Beavers.

40. The beaver was considered a sacred animal by the Ojibway and other Native Peoples. It was not only admired for its intelligence, but for its meat and fur. The first beaver of the year that was caught was always eaten in a manner that reflected the respect given to this sacred animal. Norval Morriseau, *Legends of My People The Great Ojibway*, Selwyn Dewdney, ed., (Toronto: The Ryerson Press, 1967), 21. Lieutenant Andrew Agnew, when visiting Manitowahning in 1839, found a Native woman who had a beaver as a pet. He relates that "The lady of the wigwam, who lost her child last autumn and having found this little beaver this spring, has adopted it as a child and does look upon it as such." McLean, *From Lochnaw to Manitoulin: A Highland Soldier's Tour Through Upper Canada*, 32. See also, *The Adventures of Nanabush: Ojibway Indian Stories*, told by Sam Snake, Chief Elijah Yellowhead, Alder York, David Simcoe, Annie King; compiled by Emerson Coatsworth and David Coatsworth (Toronto: Doubleday Canada, Ltd., 1979), 17–22.

41. Birchton was a district in Westboro, Nepean Township, Carleton County, named after Thomas Birch, the original settler of the farm that was subdivided in the 1870s. W.E. Haughton & Charles A. Port, eds., *History of Westboro, Ontario: The Town of Possibilities, Ottawa's Westmount* (Westboro: n.p., 1927) and Bruce S. Elliott, *The City Beyond: A History of Nepean, Birthplace of Canada's Capital, 1792–1990* (Nepean: City of Nepean, 1991).

42. Smith failed to recognize that supplying the tourist market with woven hats and baskets was one of the few economic opportunities open to the Iroquois in the face of the systematic discrimination accompanied by an inadequate and oppressive educational system. According to F.W. Waugh, black ash was the "favorite Iroquois basketry material. The tree is cut into logs some six or eight feet (two to three metres) in length, the bark is removed and the outside pounded with the back of an axe or with a mallet, until the layers can be separated into strips." See F.W. Waugh, *Iroquois Foods and Food Preparation* (Ottawa: Government Printing Bureau, 1916), 61.

43. *Infra dig* is an abbreviation of the Latin phrase *infra dignatatem* meaning to be beneath one's dignity. *OED*, Vol. 5 (1933), 277.

44. Smith is clearly using the supposed treatment of dogs as an indictment of Native culture in general. He does not, however, appear to have been aware that according to Ojibwa custom, dogs, because of their relationship to wolves, needed to be kept from human ceremonies and away from sacred objects.

45. These kinds of conversion tales were commonplace among evangelical groups like the Baptists, Methodists, and Congregationalists, but Smith is clearly indicating that Joseph's well-being was also aided by "Indian money." What he neglects to mention is that the money was derived from a trust fund established by the proceeds of land sales of ceded Saugeen territory. The lack of access to suitable land for agriculture, let alone the traditional economy of hunting and fishing, had made the Saugeen dependent on the fund that was mismanaged by the Indian Department. See *History of the Saugeen Indians*, 166–190; and *The Ojibwa of Southern Ontario*, 170–74.

46. A "handsel" in this context means to use something for the first time. The word originated from the Old Norse *handsel*, "giving of the hand." Robinson, *CSD*, 266.

47. In ancient Greek mythology, Orpheus, the son of Apollo and Calliope, could play his lyre so beautifully that he entranced all of nature. See Simon Price and Emily Kearns, eds., *The Oxford Dictionary of Classical Myth and Religion* (Oxford: Oxford University Press, 2003), 394–95.

48. The quotation is from the romantic Irish poet, Tom Moore (1779–1852). The entire passage from *Ballad Stanzas* reads, "I knew by the smoke so gracefully curled, above the green elms, that a cottage was near, and I said, "If there's peace to be found in the world; A heart that is humble might hope for it here." *Thomas Moore's Complete Poetical Works* (New York: T.Y. Crowell & Co., 1895).

49. This striking passage clearly reveals Smith's belief in the superiority of "White" ways. His spelling and interpretation of Ojibwa words, however, cannot always be relied upon.

50. Smith appears to be referring to *The American Cyclopedia: A Popular Dictionary of General Knowledge*, Vol. 15 (New York: D. Appleton and Company, 1876), 448. The entry for sugar states that maple sugaring started in New England in 1752, and that it was practised by both Natives and settlers.

51. Francis Parkman (1823–93), one of the most popular and influential historians of his day, is considered by some to be the finest narrative

historian the United States has ever produced. Although virtually blind, Parkman produced an enormous body of work that was renowned for its literary quality, including: *The California and Oregon Trail* (1849); *The Jesuits in North America* (1867); and his best known nine volume series, *France and England in North America*. See Richard C. Vitzthum, "Francis Parkman," *American Historians, 1607–1865*. (Clyde N. Wilson ed.), *Dictionary of Literary Biography*, Vol. 30 (Ann Arbor, Michigan: Gale Research Company, 1984), 202–14.

52.   George Bancroft (1800–91) was an American statesman and historian. He wrote extensively, including: *History of the American* Revolution (1852); *History of the Formation of the Constitution of the United States* (1882); and is best known for his ten-volume *History of the United States From the Discovery of the American Continent to the Present Time*, (1834–1875). Kirk Wood, "George Bancroft," *American Historians, 1607–1865*, (Clyde N. Wilson, ed.), *Dictionary of Literary Biography*, Vol. 30, 6–21; and John W. Storey, "George Bancroft," in *A Global Encyclopedia of Historical Writing*, Vol. 1, 70.

53.   Although there is still some dispute over the origin of maple sugaring, archaeological evidence has made it clear that First Nations were engaged in the practice in the Great Lakes basin long before the arrival of European settlers in the region. See Margaret Holman & Kathryn C. Egan, "Maple Sugaring," in *Michigan History*, Vol. 74, No.2 (1990), 30–35; Robert H. Keller, "America's Native Sweet: Chippewa Treaties and the Right to Harvest Maple Sugar," in *American Indian Quarterly*, Vol. 13, No. 2 (1989), 117–35; and James F. Pendergast, *The Origin of Maple Sugar* (Ottawa: National Museums of Canada, 1982), 20–27.

54.   Smith clearly has difficulty grasping the communal approach to re-sources. His use of the word "pre-emption" illustrates that he is trying to explain the distribution in terms of non-Native society's land alloca-tion practices rather than attempt to understand Native attitudes.

55.   The romantic Scottish poet Thomas Campbell (1777–1844) published "The Beech Tree's Petition" in 1800. The stanza actually reads:

> And on my trunk's surviving frame
> Carved many a long forgotten name,
> Oh! By the sighs of gentle sound,
> First breathed upon this sacred ground;
> By all that have whispered here,
> Or beauty heard with ravished ear;

And love's own altar honor me;
Spare, woodman, spare the beechen tree!

The Complete Works of Thomas Campbell (Boston: Phillips, Sampson and Company, 1851), 220–21.

56. Again, Smith misunderstands the nature of Ojibwa communal society and the role of the totems. Marriage was forbidden between totem clan members and the qualities ascribed to the totem animals also appear to have influenced the division of labour. See Edward Benton-Banai, *The Mishomis Book: The Voice of the Ojibway* (Saint Paul, Minnesota: Indian Country Press Inc., 1981); and Johnston, *Ojibway Heritage*, 53.

57. Charles Rankin (1797–1886) who was born in Upper Canada, was appointed deputy provincial surveyor in 1820. Before 1840, Rankin lived in the Township of Malden, Essex County, southernmost tip of Ontario. In 1840, after marrying his wife Elizabeth Leech, he moved to Toronto and subsequently relocated to Owen Sound in 1850. Rankin conducted most of his professional survey work between 1833 and 1870 in the area surrounding Owen Sound where he resided until 1872. Rankin was intimately involved in pushing for the Newash land surrender in the 1850s, since he had a great deal to gain by lands being made available for survey and settlement near Owen Sound. See AO, F1018, Charles Rankin Fonds;" and Schmalz, *History of the Saugeen Indians*, 81, 89.

58. For an account of the early history of Penetanguishene, see A.C. Osborne, "Old Penetanguishene" in *Pioneer Papers*. No. 5–6. (Barrie: Simcoe County Pioneer and Historical Society, 1908; reprint, Belleville: Mika Publishing, 1974), 5–163. See also, Elsie McLeod Jury, *The Establishment at Penetanguishene*. Bulletin No. 12. (London: University of Western Ontario, 1959).

59. Rankin was referring to the 1818 Lake Simcoe-Nottawasaga Purchase in which 1.5 million acres was ceded by Chief Musquakie (Yellowhead) of the Lake Simcoe Ojibway in return for £1,200 worth in goods. See Robert J. Surtees, *Indian Land Surrenders in Ontario, 1763–1867* (Ottawa: Department of Indian and Northern Affairs, 1984); Schmalz, *The Ojibway of Southern Ontario*, 114, 128 and 144–45; and Smith, *Gazetteer and Directory of Grey County*, 56.

60. Sir John Colborne, 1st Baron Seaton, (1778–1863) was born at Lyndhurst, Hampshire, England. After an impressive military career that saw service in Egypt, Malta, Sicily, and in the Iberian Peninsula under the Duke of Wellington, Colborne was made lieutenant-

governor of Upper Canada. He arrived at York in November of 1828 amid a growing struggle between the Family Compact and radicals such as William Lyon Mackenzie. Colborne was cautious in his approach, avoiding being too closely associated with the Compact's leaders, and spent much of his time developing the young province's infrastructure. In particular, Colborne focused upon the development of new roads, bridges, and market facilities, facets of the colony he believed were essential if new immigrants were going to be attracted and settled effectively. In following this program, Colborne aimed to attract greater numbers of the masses of emigrants that were leaving Great Britain each year, and thus reducing American immigration and influence in Upper Canada. Alan Wilson, "John Colborne," *DCB*, Vol. 9 (1976), 137–43.

61. Although Smith is making light of his protest, Chief Wahbadick (Wahbatick) was one of several hereditary chiefs who a few years later would not sign the 1836 treaty and resisted surrender of Saugeen land. By that time, many Saugeen feared that they would be forced to move to Manitoulin Island as a consequence of Governor Head's policies. As late as 1849, Wahbadick was ordering another party surveying a road from Owen Sound to Southampton to cease work and threatening them when they refused. At several points during both the 1836 and 1854 surrenders there was deep concern that Native resentment could erupt in violence. Nevertheless, by 1865, Chief Wahbadick had also resettled in the Cape Croker Reserve. See Smith, *Gazetteer and Directory of the County of Grey*, 56, 326; Robertson, *History of the County of Bruce*, 6–7; and Schmalz, *History of the Saugeen Indians*, especially 66–75.

62. Smith is referring to the "influence" exerted by Captain John Moberly, a retired naval officer with land in the newly forming township. Captain Moberly was born in St. Petersburg (Russia) in 1789, entering the Navy in 1801 at the tender age of twelve. Moberly saw a great deal of action, rose quickly through the ranks, and in 1834 was appointed to the post of commander at Penetanguishene. His naval background no doubt influenced his prevailing upon Sir John Colborne to change the name of the settlement to Collingwood, to honour the great naval hero, Admiral Cuthbert Collingwood. For more on Captain Moberly, see A.C. Osborne, "Old Penetanguishene" in *Pioneer Papers*, Simcoe County Pioneer and Historical Society, No. 6. (Barrie: 1917; reprinted Belleville, ON: Mika Publishing, 1974), 106–10.

63. When W.R. Gibbard was instructed to lay out a town plan at the site of Meaford in 1845, he continued the association of the area with British naval heroes, naming the newly laid out streets Nelson, Collingwood, Sykes, and Bayfield, after the heroes possessing those names. Smith, *Gazetteer and Directory*, 151–56.

64. The Ojibwa word for swan is *Waabizii*. Smith is invoking another common stereotype in this passage, the Native as "noble savage." See Francis, *The Imaginary Indian*, 7–8, 16–17, and 46–47; and Berkhofer, Jr., *The White Man's Indian*, 72–79.

65. Smith is confused about the nature of Kitchi (Keeshi) Manitou (Great Mystery), which is better viewed as a force beyond the ability of human nature to comprehend. It would have appeared ridiculous to an Ojibwa to try to "speak" to Kitchi Manitou in the way Christians spoke or prayed to God. See Johnston, *The Manitous*, 1–7; and Vecsey, *Traditional Ojibwa Religion*, 80–82.

66. Smith is repeating European rather than Ojibwa perceptions of the wolf. According to Basil Johnston, the wolf was regarded as having the character traits of perseverance and guardianship (*Ojibwa Heritage*, 53), while the Ojibwa tales collected on Parry Island suggest Nanabush, the original man, and the wolf were brothers. When the wolf drowned after falling through the ice, Nanabush turned him away and sent him to preside over the dead in the west. From that point on wolves would remain separate from men. This may be why Smith's informant was so surprised to see wolf being used as a surname. See Jenness, *Ojibwa Indians of Parry Island*, 69.

67. Some Ojibwa customs insisted that the groom live with the bride and her parents to demonstrate that he could provide for them before a couple was allowed to marry. See Johnston, *Ojibwa Heritage*, 142–43; and Jenness, *Ojibwa Indians of Parry Island*, 98–99.

68. Smith chose to ignore or was unaware of the scale of the transformation in the Native economy as a consequence of the Saugeen land surrender. Over 1.5 million acres of traditional hunting ground had been surrendered severely reducing the Saugeen's ability to accumulate sufficient winter stores. In addition, attempts to introduce agriculture on the Newash Reserve by Natives who had migrated to the area, were thwarted when the land was surrendered in 1857 to allow for the expansion of Owen Sound. See Schmalz, *History of the Saugeen Indians*, 97–121. See also, Celia Haig-Brown, "Seeking Honest Justice in a Land of Strangers: Nahnebahauqua's Struggle for Land," in *JCS*, Vol. 36, No. 4 (2001–2002), 143–70.

69. The sun and moon feature prominently in Ojibwa belief. See Johnston, *Ojibwa Heritage*, 22, 149; and Jenness, 32–34.

70. Smith is following the common European practice of trying to explain Native beliefs by making parallels with ancient Roman or Greek gods and therefore imply, as Smith does, that Natives were at a lower stage of development. See Berkhofer Jr, *The White Man's Indian*, 45–46. Like Prometheus, Nanabush (Nanaboosh, Nanabohozho) purportedly stole fire for man, but Smith's parallel does not capture the complexity of belief regarding Nanabush. At times he is represented as a Manitou, an animal, a hero, a trickster or the archetypical human. Some Nanabush tales deal with his creation of the world after the flood from a piece of earth, while others deal with his skill as a hunter. Nevertheless, scholars have noted that some Nanabush tales were developed to explain the appearance of "White" men making Smith's story plausible. Unlike Nanabush, the Hiawatha tales were based on a traceable historical figure. See Johnston, *The Manitous*, 51–96, 243–44; *The Adventures of Nanbush*, told by Sam Snake et al; Vecsey, *Traditional Ojibwa Religion*, 84–100; and Nancy Bonvillain, *Hiawatha: Founder of the Iroquois Confederacy* (New York: Chelsea House Publishers, 1992).

71. The Mississauga name for the Credit River was Missinnihe, "trusting creek," where White traders did indeed give credit for the following year. The river had been a meeting place for the Mississauga at the western end of Lake Ontario for generations and as a consequence all the groups in the region became known collectively as the Credit River Indians. Their eventual dispossession led a few to resettle in the Saugeen reserves, but most Credit River Mississauga went to the Six Nations Mohawk territory. See Smith, *Sacred Feathers*, 21, 205–12.

72. Despite his own experience with Native sobriety, in this passage Smith employs the "drunken Indian" stereotype that was prevalent in late nineteenth-century popular literature. Drunkenness was viewed as another illustration of the Native's inability to adapt to "civilized life." See Wilson, "Racial Reservations," 74. It is intriguing, that despite Smith's condemnation of the whisky trader, he declines to name him. The Ojibwa clergyman George Copway suggests that such behaviour was part of a wider hypocritical attitude towards drink in White society. Copway, *Sketches of the Ojibwa Nation*, 264–65.

73. Smith clearly did not understand the social significance and the consensus building role of the Native Councils. As a consequence, he ridicules both their deliberations as well as their costume. For a

more empathetic account, see Copway, *Sketches of the Ojibway Nation*, 140–50; and Jones, 105–10.

74. Here Smith turns an act of hospitality into a demonstration of Native ignorance. He does not appear to be aware that Native societies from the Cree to the Inuit relied on unleavened "bannock" bread first introduced by Scots working for the Hudson's Bay Company. See Sarah Efron, "Bannock-making Recalls Native History," in *The Georgia Straight* (February 28, 2002).

75. The sentiments expressed by Smith's informant were clearly designed to ingratiate the speaker with his audience and he had sound reasons for doing so. The Potawatomi had settled in the Saugeen region only after 1841, when the Colonial government had issued notices that "presents" for visiting Natives from the United States would no longer be offered and that loyal allies should move to Canada if they wished continued support. This proved to be an appealing inducement for resettlement. By 1869, Potawatomi from Wisconsin, Illinois, and Michigan outnumbered the Saugeen on the reserves. Schmalz, *History of the Saugeen Indians*, 12–15; James A. Clifton, *A Place of Refuge for all Time: Migration of the American Potawatomi into Upper Canada, 1830 to 1850* (Ottawa: National Museums of Canada, 1975); and Copway, *Sketches of the Ojibway Nation*, 202.

76. It does not seem to have occurred to Smith that his host was too polite to complain about the defacement of a prized possession. The tale clearly reveals Smith's belief in his own superiority.

77. Although Smith acknowledges his society's colonization of the indigenous peoples, his blending of common stereotypes with pseudo-evolutionary theory attempts to justify it.

78. Listowel, Perth County, is located in the Huron Tract, an area comprising over two million acres that was purchased from the Chenail Ecarte, Ausabel River, and St. Clair River Ojibwa in 1827 for £1,375. Listowel was not settled until the 1850s. See Surtees, *Indian Land Surrenders in Ontario; and* Johnston, *History of Perth County*, 432–37.

Chapter 9: The Negroes

1. Here Smith is employing the conventional nineteenth-century term to describe Black people, but as with his earlier chapter on the First Nations, his stories are primarily concerned with the individuals he encountered near Owen Sound. The Black community in Owen

Sound consisted of former slaves, veterans of the War of 1812, and free Blacks from both British North America and the United States. Many found their way to Owen Sound and Collingwood when they were denied deeds to the land they had occupied in the Queen's Bush and in Artemisia and Holland townships. In recent years there have been several well-publicized attempts to preserve the memory of the early rural settlement of Black pioneers and their subsequent dispossession in Grey County, particularly at Negro Creek, south of Owen Sound in Holland Township, and Priceville in Artemisia Township. See Michael Wayne, "The Black Population in Canada West on the Eve of the American Civil War: A Reassessment Based on the Manuscript Census of 1861," in *Histoire Sociale/Social History*, Vol. 28, No. 56 (November 1995), 465–99; Linda Brown-Kubisch, *The Queen's Bush Settlement: Black Pioneers 1839–1865* (Toronto: Natural Heritage Books, 2004); Kate Russell, "Discrimination Charged Over Negro Creek Name Change," *The Enterprise*, July 5, 1997; Peter Meyler, ed., *Broken Shackles: Old Man Henson from Slavery to Freedom* (Toronto: Natural Heritage Books, 2001), new edition of the 1889 original publication, 201–04; and the documentary film, *Speakers of the Dead*, directed by Jennifer Holness and David Sutherland (Montreal: National Film Board of Canada, 2000).

2.   Although a significant proportion of the Black population in Upper Canada were former slaves who had been assisted in their escape by the "Underground Railroad," recent analysis of the census data suggests that by 1861 between 30 and 40 per cent of the Black population in the province were former slaves and their descendants. The remainder were primarily either descendants of the original Black population of Upper Canada or drawn from the free Black communities of the northern United States. Like other settlers, American free Blacks had come to Canada in search of land and established immigrant communities in the towns and rural settlements throughout southern Ontario. By emphasizing the flight from slavery and, after 1850, the Fugitive Slave Law in the United States, Smith and his contemporaries were, however, able to ignore Upper Canada's own slave-holding past. Indeed, in 1805, some slaves had fled Upper Canada to Detroit when the Michigan territory abolished slavery. Smith, however, was not alone in ignoring the fact that the original Black population in Upper Canada had arrived in slavery. See, Wayne, "The Black Population," 476; Peter Meyler & David Meyler, *A Stolen Life: Searching for Richard Pierpoint* (Toronto: Natural Heritage Books, 1999); Robin

Winks, ed., *Four Fugitive Slaves Narratives* (Don Mills, Ontario: Addison-Wesley Publishing Company, 1969); Thomas Smallwood, *A Narrative of Thomas Smallwood*, Richard Almonte, ed., (Toronto: The Mercury Press, 2000); Adrienne Shadd, "The Lord Seemed to Say 'Go': Women and the Underground Railroad Movement," in Peggy Bristow, et al, eds., "*We're Rooted Here and They Can't Pull us Up*": *Essays in African Canadian Women* (Toronto: University of Toronto Press, 1994), 41–68; Afua Cooper, "The Fluid Frontier: Blacks and the Detroit River Region, A Focus on Henry Bibb," in *Canadian Review of American Studies*, Vol. 30, No. 2 (2000), 133; Michael Power and Nancy Butler, *Slavery and Freedom in Niagara* (Niagara-on-the-Lake, ON: The Niagara Historical Society, 1993); and Adrienne Shadd, Afua Cooper, and Karolyn Smardz Frost, *The Underground Railroad: Next Stop, Toronto!* (Toronto: Natural Heritage Books, 2002, 2nd ed. 2005). See also Daniel G. Hill, *The Freedom Seekers; Blacks in Early Canada* (Toronto: The Book Society of Canada, 1981; reprinted by Stoddard Publishing Co. Ltd in 1992).

3.   The Black population in Owen Sound was located on the east hill, on the east side of Second Avenue between Twelfth and Thirteenth streets, and on both sides of the river at Jubilee Bridge. They were primarily employed in menial service work in town and on the ships that docked at the port. In this passage, Smith fails to recognize the economic disadvantages faced by this group nor that many of them had been forced out of their rural settlements by Irish and Scottish settlers. Despite these disadvantages, many Blacks owned and operated successful local businesses. Nevertheless, the racist stereotype of the lazy, shiftless Black was particularly prevalent in late nineteenth-century literature. The quotation from Barnes, if accurate, may be another example of an attempt to ingratiate the speaker by providing the listener with what he wishes to hear. Since Barnes was married to an Irish woman he may have been particularly keen on establishing cordial relations with his White neighbours. See Croft, *Fourth Entrance to Huronia*, 37, 66, 104, and 212; Brown-Kubisch, *The Queen's Bush*, 89 and 153–54; Gary E. French, *Men of Colour: An Historical Account of the Black Settlement on Wilberforce Street and in Oro Township, Simcoe County, Ontario, 1819–1949* (Stroud, ON: Kaste Books, 1978), 45–46, 90, and 119; Allan P. Stouffer, "'A Restless Child of Change and Accident': The Black Image in Nineteenth Century Ontario," in *OH*, Vol. 76, No. 2 (June 1984), 130; and Stanley J. Lemons, "Black Stereotypes" LAC, 1861 Census, C 1027, f. 44; 1871 Census, C 9954, Division 3, 38.

4.	The source of the poem is unclear, but the stereotype of the musical Black was common from the earliest days of slavery and was reinforced by the development of the minstrel show during the nineteenth century. See Pieterse, *White on Black*, 132–41. For the increasingly derogatory nature of the stereotype from the 1880s on, see James H. Dorman, "Shaping the Popular Image of Post-Reconstruction American Blacks: The 'Coon Song' Phenomenon of the Gilded Age," in *American Quarterly*, Vol. 40, No. 4 (1988), 450–71.

5.	The paternalistic attitude expressed here by Smith was particularly prevalent among dissenting White clergymen like himself. The sentiment was mobilized in support of refugee Blacks in 1851 with the creation of the Anti-Slavery Society of Canada. Nevertheless, paternalistic attitudes created resentment among the Black population and demonstrated a continuing sense of superiority among the Whites. Smith reflects this with his exclusion of Blacks from his "nation," even though by the time he was writing, unlike Smith himself, most of the Black population in Canada had been born in the country. Such exclusionary attitudes reinforced segregationist tendencies in Canada as well as the United States. See Allen P. Stouffer, *The Light of Nature and the Law of God: Anti-Slavery in Ontario 1833–1877* (Montreal: McGill-Queen's University Press, 1992); George M. Fredrickson, *Racism: A Short History.* (Princeton: Princeton University Press, 2002), 79–82; Wayne Edward Kelly, "Race and Segregation in the Upper Canada Militia," in *Journal of Army Historical Research*, Vol. 78 (2000), 264–77; Winks, *The Blacks in Canada*, 337–45 and 362–80.

6.	A major motive of both free and enslaved American Blacks to emigrate to Canada was the opportunity to legally hold property and to pass land on to family members, a right that could be defended in court. See Brown-Kubisch, *The Queen's Bush*, 6–7, 25–33; Mary Ann Shadd, *A Plea for Emigration, or, Notes of Canada West*, Richard Almonte, ed., (Toronto: The Mercury Press, 1998); Sharon A. Roger Hepburn, "Crossing the Border from Slavery to Freedom: The Building of a Community at Buxton, Upper Canada," in *American Nineteenth-Century History*, No. 2 (2000–03), 26–68.

7.	The tale reported here follows closely the form of published nineteenth-century slave narratives. See Winks, ed., *Four Fugitive Slave Narratives*; Smallwood, *A Narrative*.

8.	Elsewhere Smith considers such actions as humorous, but the widespread belief of his contemporaries that Blacks were particularly prone to criminal behaviour results in Smith turning this episode into part of a moral tale that is completed below. For White attitudes towards Blacks and crime, see George M. Fredrickson, *The Black Image in the White Mind: The Debate on Afro-American Character and Destiny 1817–1914* (New York: Harper & Row, 1971), 251–52, 273–75.

9.   Henry Clay (1775–1852) was a United States statesman and speaker of the House of Representatives. From 1831–42 he served in the Senate and unsuccessfully ran for president on three separate occasions. He was one of the leading proponents of the war with Britain in 1812, which led to the failed invasion of Canada. David Crystal, *The Cambridge Biographical Encyclopedia.* (Cambridge: Cambridge University Press, 1995), 214. For more on Henry Clay, see Kimberley C. Shankman, *Compromise and the Constitution: The Political Thought of Henry Clay* (Lanham, MD: Lexington Books, 1999); and *DAB*, Vol. 4, 173–79.

10. There does not appear to be any record of a Black man with Levi as either a given or a surname residing in Vaughan Township. The 1871 census does, however, record a Black farmer by the name of John Thomas as residing in Vaughan, indicating that Blacks did settle in the township. Levi was a common slave name and may have been used by Smith and his neighbours as a stereotypical nickname for this particular individual. The idea that Blacks had a diminished mental capacity was a prevalent nineteenth-century stereotype embodied in the "Sambo" character that was particularly applied to plantation slaves. See Joseph Boskin, *Sambo: The Rise & Demise of an American Jester* (New York: Oxford University Press, 1986).

11. Smith may have been witnessing a personal celebration of Emancipation Day, which was much more significant than he indicates. On August 1, throughout the nineteenth century, Black communities across Ontario commemorated the abolition of slavery in the British Empire in 1834. By the second half of the nineteenth century, Emancipation Day was an occasion for parades, dances and sporting events in which both Blacks and Whites participated. These days were, however, also used by the Black communities to protest their continued experience of segregation and discrimination and to remind Ontario's White population of the promise of equality created by the British in 1834. Smith would have been aware of this since Emancipation Day had been celebrated in Owen Sound since the 1860s and still is observed on August 2 as a major celebration in Owen Sound. (The year 2008 marks the 146th anniversary of this event, currently chaired by Dennis Scott, a descendant of the early Black population

of Owen Sound.) See Collin McFarquhar, "A Difference of Perspective: Blacks, Whites, and Emancipation Day Celebrations in Ontario, 1865–1919," in *OH*, Vol. 92, No. 2 (2000); Brown-Kubisch,
The Queen's Bush, 153 and 171.

12. Smith is referring to early types of light vehicles propelled by the
rider. These took many forms including four- and three-wheeled
varieties, but by the latter decades of the nineteenth century, the
two-wheeled "bicycle" became dominant. Velocipedes were one
variation propelled by pedals attached to the front wheel. Their
introduction sparked a sport that was enthusiastically embraced
by the menmen and women who could afford to purchase the new
machines. For more on velocipedes and the development of the
bicycle in Canada, see Glen Norcliffe, *The Ride to Modernity: The
Bicycle in Canada, 1869–1900* (Toronto: University of Toronto Press,
2001); and Sharon Anne Babaian, *The Most Benevolent Machine: A
Historical Assessment of Cycles in Canada* (Ottawa: National Museum
of Science and Technology, 1998).

13. The advertisement from the fictitious Professor Laurens of
Cincinnati, not Buffalo, appeared in the April 1, 1869, edition of the
Daily Spectator. Smith appears to have confused this story with a later
story in the April 6 edition of the same paper reporting on the prizes
awarded by S.J. Sherman & Co. in an amateur velocipede-riding
contest. That company did offer instruction in riding.

14. The details given, and the relish taken, in reporting the incident
strongly suggests that the *Spectator* reporter was behind the stunt.
The Black men involved are harder to identify, although the report
does name Solomon "Rainbow" as the rider of the wheelbarrow. This
may be a reference to Solomon Curtis who, in the 1871 Census, is
listed as a seventeen-year-old resident of St. Mary's Ward, working
as a tobacconist. The stunt was clearly plugging into the happy-
go-lucky Black Sambo stereotype. Nevertheless, by having Black
men as riders, the stunt was also using racial stereotypes as a means
to ridicule the pretensions of the gentlemen amateur athletes of
the type that competed for S.J. Sherman's cup. See *Daily Spectator*,
April 1, April 2, April 5, April 9, April 10, 1869; LAC, 1871 Census,
C 9926, Division 1, 66. For the marginalized condition of the
Black community in Hamilton, see Michael B. Katz, *The People
of Hamilton, Canada West: Family and Class in a Mid-Nineteenth-
Century City* (Cambridge: Harvard University Press, 1975), 61–68;
Winks, *The Blacks in Canada*, and the accounts in Benjamin Drew's

The Refugee; or, The Narratives of Fugitive Slaves in Canada Related by Themselves (Toronto: Coles Publishing Company, 1972, reprint of the 1856 edition).

15. Reverend George Willet (?–1921) was ordained in the Congregational Church in 1878. He served as minister at Vankleek Hill from 1878 to 1879. See Walkington, *The Congregational Churches of Canada*.

16. Reverend John McKillican (1824–1911) was born at Vankleek Hill. His father Reverend William McKillican, who was a minister in Aberdeen before emigrating to Canada in 1816, ran Congregational missions to settlers in Eastern Ontario from Vankleek Hill between 1816 and 1829. John McKillican was ordained in 1851, and from 1860 to 1890 served as secretary of the Sunday School Union while living in Danville and Montreal, Quebec. See Walkington, *The Congregational Churches of Canada*; and Reverend John Wood, *Something From Our Hands*, 27–29, 32, and 39.

17. Smith is referring to Emily Wells, the widow of James P. Wells. Emily and her husband were both Congregationalists, and, like Smith, were born in Scotland. According to the census, Emily Wells was sixty-nine in 1881 and had a live-in Irish domestic servant, Lizzie McMillan. There is no mention of any permanent Black residents in Hawkesbury West, where Vankleek Hill is located, in either the 1871 or 1881 census reports. See LAC, 1871 Census, C 10,010, Division 2, 65; and LAC, 1881 Census, C 13228, Division 6.

18. The Black community of St. Catharines was one of the largest in Ontario. It was an early terminus for the Underground Railroad and the location for several anti-slavery groups, mutual aid societies and a number of Black congregations. The tendency to separate Black and White congregations in Ontario, as reflected in Smith's story, was also replicated in the school system, which also served to reinforce segregation and discrimination in the province. See Drew, *The Refugee*; Brown-Kubisch, *The Queen's Bush Settlement*; and Winks, *The Blacks in Canada*.

19. The conversation between Nicodemus and Christ is recounted in John 3:1–21. In this exchange, Christ emphasized the need to be "born again," one of the key theological components of nineteenth-century evangelical Christianity. The commitment to evangelism among slaves and their descendants has been examined closely by scholars, with many viewing it as a crucial element in Black resistance to slavery and discrimination. According to the 1861 census, Samuel Barnes, aged fifty, was employed in Owen Sound as a teamster and

he and his Irish wife, Elizabeth, aged twenty-eight, were both listed as Wesleyan Methodists. See Eugene Genovese, *Roll Jordan Roll: The World the Slaves Made* (New York: Vintage Books, 1976), 232–55; LAC, 1861 Census, C 1027, f. 44.

20.   Smith edited the *Sunday School Dial*, the first illustrated Sunday School paper published in Canada, while he was in Owen Sound. See Caledonian Society of Toronto, "Rev. William Wye Smith," *Selections from Scottish Canadian Poets*, (Toronto: Imrie, Graham and Company, 1900), 135.

21.   Reverend William King (1812–95) was the Presbyterian minister at Buxton near Chatham, Ontario, from 1851 to 1883. King was born in Ireland but emigrated to America in the 1830s and settled in Louisiana in 1835. He married Mary Phares, the daughter of a local planter and in the process became a slave holder despite being a confirmed abolitionist. After the death of his wife and child in 1843, King attended divinity school in Edinburgh and determined to free his slaves by relocating them to Upper Canada. William King had a considerable influence in the segregated Black community he helped to create at Buxton, but he was far from alone in advocating rural settlement in Upper Canada as a means for Blacks to obtain economic self-sufficiency. Several Black writers, notably Mary Ann Shadd, advocated the same goal through their journalism. Recent scholarship has also demonstrated that the Buxton, or Elgin, Settlement was indeed successful, but that this was largely the consequence of the efforts of the settlers themselves rather than the paternalistic direction of Reverend King. See Donald Walkington, *Presbyterian Ministers in Upper and Lower Canada* (Toronto: United Church Archives, 1984); Walkington, *Ministers of the Presbyterian Church in Canada 1875–1925;* Howard Law, "'Self-Reliance is the True Road to Independence': Ideology and the Ex-Slaves in Buxton and Chatham," in *OH*, Vol. 77, No. 2 (June 1985), 105–21; Heather Murray, *Come, Bright Improvement!: The Literary Societies of Nineteenth Century Ontario.* (Toronto: University of Toronto Press, 2002), 62–74; Peggy Bristow, "'Whatever You Raise in the Ground You Can Sell It in Chatham' " in *We're Rooted Here and They Can't Pull Us Up;* and Hepburn, "Crossing the Border from Slavery to Freedom." See also Victor Ullman, *Look to the North Star: A Life of William King* (Toronto: Umbrella Press, 1994) originally published by Beacon Press of Boston, Massachusetts in 1969.

22.   Smith is likely referring to the 13,000 ton (11,800 tonne) tug *Rescue* that was built in Buffalo and owned by Cook and Brothers of Montreal.

See Robert Thomas, *Register of the Ships of the Lakes and River St. Lawrence* (Buffalo, NY: Wheeler, Matthews & Warren, 1864), 89.

23. The reference is to John Wesley (1703–91), the famous English evangelical minister and founder of Methodism. Despite much persecution during the early days of the Methodist movement, Wesley persevered and late in life was a well-respected and influential minister and writer. Crystal, *Cambridge Biographical Encyclopedia*, 993. For an account of Wesley's career, see Vivian H. Green, *John Wesley* (London: Nelson, 1964).

24. The Penetanguishene Reformatory for Boys was established in 1859. Before that time male juvenile offenders in Upper Canada were imprisoned in adult institutions. The reformatory was intended to educate as well as punish, but in the 1860s reformers complained that the boys, like adults, were housed in cells and that the major emphasis was on work, such as quarrying, road building, and brick making, rather than on education. Such criticisms resulted in the closure of the reformatory in 1904 and the boys were transferred to the industrial school system. It is unclear how many of the reformatory's inmates were from Ontario's Black communities. See Andrew Jones and Leonard Rutman, *In the Children's Aid: J.J. Kelso and Child Welfare in Ontario* (Toronto: University of Toronto Press, 1981), 104–07.

25. Reverend Samuel Ringgold Ward (1817–66) was born into slavery in Maryland. The Ward family later fled to New Jersey allowing Samuel the opportunity to study law and medicine, but he found his calling as a Congregational minister. Ward emigrated to Upper Canada to avoid arrest for aiding a fugitive slave and became intimately involved in the Anti-Slavery Society of Canada. In 1852, he embarked on a province-wide speaking tour on behalf of the society and this is the likely date of the sermon in what is now the town of Kleinburg. As the verbal attack on Ward indicates, education and social class did not isolate Black immigrants from White racism in Upper Canada. See Robin Winks, "Samuel Ringgold Ward," *DCB*, Vol. 9, 820–21; Brown-Kubisch, *The Queen's Bush Settlement*, 146–47, 226–31, 246; Samuel Ringgold Ward, *Autobiography of a Fugitive Negro; His Anti-Slavery Labours in the United States, Canada & England* (Chicago: Johnson Publishing Co., 1970; reprint of the 1855 edition).

26. James Addams Beaver (1837–1914) was promoted from the field to become a Brigadier-General of the Union Army during the Civil War and he later served as Governor of Pennsylvania from 1886 to 1891. See *DAB*, Vol. 2, 112–13.

27. This appears to be a reference to Bishop Benjamin Arnett (1838–1906) who was a minister in the African Methodist Episcopal Church. Smith appears, however, to be mistaken since Arnett was born a free man in Brownsville, Pennsylvania, although he was prominent in fighting Ohio's segregation laws. In the late nineteenth century Arnett was a leading speaker on African American issues and served as the Republican representative for Greene County, Ohio, in the state legislature. As a Methodist Episcopal clergyman, Arnett served parishes in the Ohio cities of Toledo, Cincinnati, and Columbus, before being elected Bishop of South Carolina and Georgia in 1888. The International Sunday School Convention met in Pittsburgh in 1890. See Richard R. Wright, *The Bishops of the African Methodist Episcopal Church* (Nashville: A.M.E. Sunday School Union, 1963).

28. In the 1861 census, Mary Taylor was listed as a forty-eight-year-old mulatto woman and her husband John was listed as a fifty-four-year-old mulatto blacksmith. Both were identified as being from the United States as was a third member of the household, Rogena Taylor, a nineteen-year-old mulatto woman. LAC, 1861 Census, C 1027, f. 43.

29. While Smith raises the issue of economic discrimination in this passage, he underrates its significance for restricting Black employment opportunities in Upper Canada. By the second half of the nineteenth century, as a consequence of such discrimination, most Blacks in Canada were occupied in menial, unskilled labouring jobs. This economic segregation was also accompanied by strict social segregation. Throughout the nineteenth century sexual liaisons between Black men and White women were particularly frowned upon and their occurrence often provoked White violence. The mulatto children produced by these relationships were viewed as a particular challenge to the social order and were, as a consequence, viewed with considerable suspicion by White society. In these circumstances it is remarkable that a couple such as the Taylors were able to pursue any public business at all. Linda Brown-Kubisch, "The Black Experience in the Queen's Bush Settlement," 108–16; Susanna Moodie, *Roughing it in the Bush*, 210–11; Barrington Walker, "The Tale of Ida Jane and George: Murder, Miscegenation, and Bastardy in 1893 Raleigh, Ontario," in *Canadian Review of American Studies*, Vol. 30, No. 2 (2000), 211–27; and Patricia Morton, *Disfigured Images: The Historical Assault on Afro-American Women* (New York: Greenwood Press, 1991), 21–22.

30. John Mills was a prominent figure in the early history of Owen Sound. Apart from acting as bailiff, he is listed as one of the executive members of the Owen Sound Boating Club (his boat was called the *Heather Bell)*. He is also mentioned as being one of a number of people offering free land for the site of the proposed County building in 1853. Croft, *Fourth Entrance to Huronia*, 52, 125.

31. Since pie-making could be considered a "natural" extension of a women's domestic role, Mary Taylor was able to be accepted as an independent business woman by Smith and his contemporaries. Nevertheless, such public roles could also result in stereotyping as the later development of the Aunt Jemima character, which represented the female equivalent of the happy-go-lucky Sambo, reflects. Mary Taylor's public role obviously came with taunts from the local youths and criticisms of her domestic life, all of which served to minimize and denigrate her accomplishment. For a discussion of nineteenth-century Black female stereotypes, see Shirley J. Lee, "Gender Ideology and Black Women as Community-Builders in Ontario, 1850–70," in *CHR*, Vol. 75, No. 1, (March 1994), 53–73; and Pieterse, *White on Black*, 154–56.

32. Sir Samuel White Baker (1821–93), the English explorer, was born in London. He was the son of a West Indian merchant, but was himself disinclined to a career in business. He began his career in African exploration in 1861 and in 1864 was the first European to see Albert N'yanza (Lake Albert) in the Upper Nile region. He was honoured by the Royal Geographical Society and knighted in 1866. Baker published two best-selling accounts of his journeys. See Samuel Baker, *The Albert N'yanza, Great Basin of the Nile, and Explorations of the Nile Sources* (London: Macmillan, 1866) and *The Nile Tributaries of Abyssinia* (London: Macmillan, 1867); James S. Olson and Robert Shadle, eds., *Historical Dictionary of the British Empire*, Vol. 1 (Westport, CT: Greenwood Press, 1996), 99–100.

33. According to the 1861 census, John Edwards was a twenty-eight-year-old Black labourer who emigrated from the United States. His household was comprised of his wife Charlotte, aged twenty-eight, also born in the United Sates, and their two children, Mary and Sanford, aged eight and five respectively, who were both born in Upper Canada. The census also listed Martha Jones, aged sixty-seven, as another Black member of the household. She may have been Charlotte's mother. See LAC, 1861 Census, C 1027, f. 30.

34. George M. Butchart, who had been born in Scotland, was a tinsmith. After arriving in Owen Sound, he and his brother R.P. Butchart opened a hardware store on Main Street in 1842. By the 1870s, he had become one of the town's leading businessmen and prominent citizens, serving as city councillor from 1869 to 1872. See LAC, 1861 Census, C 1027, f. 28; and Croft, *Fourth Entrance to Huronia*, 106, 125, 127, 144, and 199.

35. According to the 1861 census, Bailiff Paul Dunn, aged fifty-one, had been born in England and was an Episcopalian. Croft reports that he was an original settler on St. Vincent Line and was still bailiff in 1863 when Smith resided in the town. See LAC, 1861 Census, C 1027, f. 3; and Croft, *Fourth Entrance to Huronia*, 29, 103.

36. Smith's tale reflects both the suspicion many Blacks had of authority and their intense concern with maintaining possession of their land. Given the Black experience of dispossession in rural Grey County, this was a natural preoccupation.

37. As early as the 1850s Owen Sound was involved in the Temperance debate, and perhaps with good cause: In 1851 the village had five taverns but only two churches completed. William Wye Smith was actively involved in the campaign for Temperance, as were many of the friends he mentions in his reminiscences, including John Frost, Thomas Lunn, and the Reverend Ludwig Kribs. See Ken Barker, "Owen Sound in the Early 1850s," *Owen Sound Sun Times*, September 10, 1999 and September 24, 1999; and Jan Noel, *Canada Dry: Temperance Crusades before Confederation*. (Buffalo, NY: University of Toronto Press, 1995).

38. Reverend Walter Inglis, who was born sixteen miles (twenty-five kilometres) from Edinburgh in Brothersheils, arrived in Canada in 1855. He was the first minister of the Presbyterian Church at Riversdale, Bruce County, which was established in 1857. He then served as minister at Kincardine from 1859 to 1868, and at Ayr from 1869 to 1884. See William Cochrane and Walter Inglis, *Memoirs and Remains of the Reverend Walter Inglis, African Missionary and Canadian Pastor* (Toronto: Robinson, 1887), 9, 94–110; Walkington, *Presbyterian Ministers in Upper and Lower Canada*; Walkington, *Ministers of the Presbyterian Church in Canada 1875–1925* and Norman Robertson, *History of the County of Bruce*, 408.

39. This reference is to the famous missionary/explorer David Livingstone (1813–73) born in Blantyre, Scotland. He first went to Africa in 1841 under the auspices of the London Missionary Society, partly

due to the encouragement of fellow Scottish missionary, Dr. Robert Moffat (1795–1883). When Livingstone joined Moffat in southern Africa, he met and married Moffat's daughter Mary. In Scotland, the Moffats had been a farming family at Ormiston, East Lothian, and Dr. Moffat's mission station at Kuruman, Bechuanaland, replicated this settled life. After their marriage, the Livingstones were stationed several hundred miles northward at Mobosta. Walter Inglis was sent out by the London Missionary Society to provide Livingstone support at his station, much to Livingstone's chagrin. The two men had previously been students together for a year and a half. Inglis ended up establishing a separate missionary station, but had to abandon it and return to Britain in 1853 when conflict broke out between the Boers and the native Africans. By 1849, Livingstone had become dissatisfied with mission station life and began his series of explorations into the interior of the African continent for which he would become famous. After getting lost on one expedition he was located by Henry Morton Stanley, who had been sent to find him, a meeting that led to the famous quote, "Dr. Livingstone I presume?" See "David Livingstone," *DNB*, Vol. 11, 1263–76; "Robert Moffat," *DNB*, Vol. 13, 544–48; Tim Jeal, *Livingstone* (New York: G.P. Putnam's Sons, 1973), 20 and 63; and Cochrane and Inglis, *Memoirs and Remains of the Reverend Walter Inglis*, 60–93 and 206–23.

40. By placing this tale at the end of the chapter, Smith not only links the Blacks of Ontario with "exotic" Africa, but he also suggests that Black deference to authority was a natural trait. This sits well with the paternalistic attitudes expressed throughout the chapter. See Pieterse, *White on Black*; and Frederickson, *The Black Image in the White Mind*.

Chapter 10: Literature in the Bush

1. There was a failed attempt to produce a daily newspaper, the Toronto *Daily Standard*, in 1836, but Smith is referring to the Toronto *Globe*, which became a daily not in 1851, but in 1853. See Paul Rutherford, *A Victorian Authority: The Daily Press in Late Nineteenth-Century Canada* (Toronto: University of Toronto Press, 1982), 36–41. For further details on early Canadian publishing, see H. Pearson Gundy's standard account "Literary Publishing" in *Literary History of Canada: Canadian Literature in English*, Vol. 1, Carl F. Klinck, ed. (Toronto: University of

Toronto Press, 1976); and Mary Lu MacDonald, *Literature and Society in the Canadas, 1817–1850* (Lewiston: Edwin Mellon, 1992), 39–65.

2. Smith is referring to the nine muses of classical antiquity. One of Smith's earliest poems, "The Voice of the Nine," (*Alazon, and Other Poems*, 92), adopted the same theme, when a cold winter blast prompts a visit from the muses who inspire the young poet to pick up the pen.

3. William A. Stephens (1809–91) contributed verse in the "Old Country idiom" to various newspapers from Niagara to Owen Sound. Born in Belfast, Northern Ireland, Stephens originally worked on the family farm at Norval near Hamilton, but in 1850 he was appointed collector of Customs at Owen Sound where he would have met with Smith. See Henry Morgan, *Bibliotheca Canadensis, or A Manual of Canadian Literature.* (Ottawa: 1867); Carl F. Klinck, "Literary Activity in Canada East and West, 1841–1880," in *Literary History of Canada*, 166; and MacDonald, *Literature and Society*, 321, 19, 21, 53, and 81. There are several volumes older than Stephen's published in Upper Canada. Some of these are: James Lynne Alexander's *Wonders of the West, or A Day at the Falls of Niagara in 1825* (York: Charles Fothergill, 1825); James Martin Cadwell, *The Wandering Rhymer, A Fragment, with other Poetical Trifles* (York: Upper Canada Gazette Office, 1826); A.J. Williamson's *Original Poems on Various Subjects* (Toronto: W.J. Coates, 1836); and Daniel Haydn Mayne's *Poems and Fragments* (Toronto: W.J. Coates, 1838). See also, MacDonald, *Literature and Society*, 269–70.

4. Hugh Scobie (1811–53) was a prominent publisher and political figure in mid-nineteenth-century Upper Canada. Born in Fort George, Scotland, Scobie emigrated with his family in 1833, settling in West Gwillimbury Township near Bradford. Scobie was an energetic defender of Scottish interests in Upper Canada and was active in the Church of Scotland. Apart from a successful career in publishing, Scobie was a Freemason, a founding member of the Toronto Literary and Historical Society, a magistrate and an advocate for educational reform, his efforts seeing him appointed to the province's first board of education. See David Ouellette, "Hugh Scobie," *DCB*, Vol. 8 (1985), 789–91. Smith's first volume of poetry was entitled *Alazon and Other Poems: Including Many of the Fugitive Pieces of Rusticus*. He had previously published many of the poems under the pseudonym "Rusticus" in New York's *Saturday Emporium* and in local papers in Upper Canada. See also Appendix A.

5. Alexander McLachlan, (1817–96) was one of the most celebrated of the Scottish immigrant poets in Canada. McLachlan was born in Johnstone, near Paisley, and would later apprentice as a tailor in Glasgow where he became active in Chartist reform politics in the 1830s. He emigrated to Upper Canada in 1840 to take up the farm in Caledon Township he inherited from his father. He made a living as a part-time tailor, lecturer, and writer, publishing his first collection of poems *The Spirit of Love, and Other Poems* in 1846. In this passage Smith is referring to his second volume, *Poems: Hamely Rustic Jingle* (Toronto: John C. Geikie, 1856), and his third volume, *Lyrics* (Toronto: A.H. Armour, 1858). McLachlan would subsequently publish a volume that included his most famous poem, *The Emigrant and Other Poems* (Toronto: Rollo & Adam, 1861) as well as *Poems and Songs* (Toronto: Rose Pub. Co., 1874). In addition, William Briggs, the Methodist publisher that Smith had hoped would publish his own "Reminiscences," later issued a posthumous collection, *The Poetical Works of Alexander MacLachlan* (Toronto: W. Briggs, 1900). See Elizabeth Waterston, "Alexander McLachlan" in *Canadian Writers Before 1890*, W.H. New, ed., *Dictionary of Literary Biography*, Vol. 99 (Detroit: Gale Research Inc., 1990), 242–43; Mary Jane Edwards, "Alexander MacLachlan," *DCB*, Vol. 12, 660–64; and Norman Murray, *The Scottish Hand-Loom Weavers 1790–1850: A Social History* (Edinburgh: John Donald, 1978), 168–71.

6. John Cunningham Geikie (1824–1906) was born in Edinburgh and educated at Queen's College in Kingston, later being ordained in the Presbyterian Church in 1848. He opened a bookstore in Toronto that specialized in religious works, but also carried a large supply of medical and scholarly publications. During the 1850s he was involved in the fierce struggle over the supply of educational books to schools, which was, in the opinion of many booksellers, monopolized by the government through Egerton Ryerson. In 1860, Geikie sold out to one of his employees and retired to England, where he pursued a successful career writing children's literature. George L. Parker, *The Beginnings of the Book Trade in Canada* (Toronto: University of Toronto Press, 1985), 124–26.

7. There may be an element of jealousy in Smith's criticism. Although both men produced poetry in Scots dialect, it was McLachlan who was dubbed the "Canadian Burns" and praised by leading American poets like Emerson, Thoreau, Longfellow, and others. McLachlan was also more prominently featured in the first anthology of Canadian poetry

edited by Edward Hartley Dewart, which included ten poems by McLachlan to Smith's five. See E.H. Dewart, *Selections from Canadian Poets* (Montreal: J. Lovell, 1864). For a discussion of the impact of Robert Burns on Canadian poetry, see Elizabeth Waterston, *Rapt in Plaid: Canadian Literature and Scottish Tradition* (Toronto: University of Toronto Press, 2001), 12–42.

8.   Smith is referring to a lack of financial recognition, since Charles Sangster (1822–93) was well-received by his contemporaries and was, along with McLachlan, the most prominently featured poet in Dewart's first Canadian anthology. Sangster's work, in particular the romantic poem *The St. Lawrence and the Saguenay* (1856), continues to be regularly reproduced in published anthologies. Nevertheless, his literary career was adversely affected by personal tragedy and his struggle to obtain employment. Sangster worked as a clerk and as a journalist in his native Kingston, Ontario, and as a civil servant in the Post Office Department in Ottawa. These onerous, ill-paid jobs, as well as the untimely death of several family members, affected his mental health, ultimately resulting in several breakdowns. Despite the encouragement from many contemporary literary figures, Sangster proved unable to produce a great deal more original poetry after the volumes Smith mentions. Two later collections, *Norland Echoes and Other Strains and Lyrics* and *The Angle Guest and Other Poems and Lyrics* were not published until the 1970s. See Frank M. Tierney, "Charles Sangster," *DCB*, Vol. 12, 944–48.

9.   Evan MacColl (1808–98) born in Kenmore, Lochfyne, was the son of a Highland tenant farmer reputed to have a vast knowledge of Gaelic songs. When the family emigrated in 1831, MacColl remained behind, pursuing a career as a customs officer in Liverpool. He gained a reputation as a poet through the publication of *The Mountain Minstrel* (1836), while living in Scotland. In 1850, he joined his family in Upper Canada, settling in Kingston where he became an important fixture of the Scottish community. He continued to write poetry in Canada, though mostly on Scottish themes, and later in life brought out a collection, *The English Poetical Works of Evan MacColl* (Toronto: Hunter, Rose, 1883). Several of MacColl's English poems were included in Dewart's first Canadian anthology, and, like Smith's and McLachlan's, were featured in *Selections from Scottish Canadian Poets, Being a Collection of the Best Poetry Written by Scotsmen and Their Descendants in the Dominion of Canada* (Toronto: Caledonian Society of Toronto, 1900). See John Ferns, "Evan MacColl," *DCB*, Vol. 12, 588–89.

10. Charles Heavysege was a popular and highly celebrated poet during the 1860s and 1870s. He was born in Yorkshire, England, in 1816, and worked as a woodcarver before emigrating to Montreal in 1853. He continued in his trade, but also began a career in journalism, reporting first for the *Montreal Transcript*, and then the *Daily Witness*, where he eventually became city editor. Heavysege published his volumes of poetry, which tended to focus on Biblical themes, between 1852 and 1865, but the ill-paid daily grind of newspaper work affected his ability to produce literature during the last decade of his life. His major works include: *The Revolt of Tartarus: A Poem* (1852); *Saul: A Drama in Three Parts* (1857); *Count Filippo, or The Unequal Marriage: A Drama in Five Acts* (1860), and *The Advocate: A Novel* (1865). See Sandra Djwa, "Charles Heavysege" in *Canadian Writers Before 1890*, W.H. New, ed., *Dictionary of Literary Biography*, Vol. 99 (Detroit: Gale Research Inc., 1990), 158–60; and J.C. Stockdale, "Charles Heavysege," *DCB*, Vol. 10, 346–48.

11. Thomas D'Arcy McGee (1825–68), born in Carlingford, County Louth, Ireland, was a prominent politician representing the Montreal Irish-Canadian community in the mid-nineteenth century. Besides holding public office, McGee made a living from journalism and was a prolific writer, producing many histories and biographies as well as poetry. In his youth, McGee was heavily influenced by the Young Ireland Movement and became an Irish nationalist. Nevertheless, he later rejected the revolutionary republican Fenian movement, which in the eyes of many Irish nationalists made him a turncoat. By the time McGee settled in Montreal, he had come to believe that a federation of the colonies of British North America offered the best protection to minorities, including Irish Catholics in North America, and worked towards the creation of such a state. He believed that the production of a Canadian literature was also essential to this goal and promoted the Montreal Literary Club as a means to encourage the creation of a national literature. Apart from the volume of poetry mentioned by Smith, a collection, *The Poems of Thomas D'Arcy McGee* (Montreal: Sadlier, 1869), was published after McGee's death. The "tragic end" cited by Smith was a reference to McGee's assassination in Ottawa in 1868. The Fenians were held responsible and James Patrick Whelan, an Irish immigrant, was hanged for the crime. Seemingly, no connection was established between Whelan and the Irish revolutionary movement and doubts remain concerning Whelan's guilty verdict. See Thomas D'Arcy McGee, *The Mental Outfit of the*

New Dominion (Montreal: n.p., 1867) and Robin B. Burns, "Thomas D'Arcy McGee," *DCB*, Vol. 9, 489–94.

12. Carroll Ryan (1839–1910), born in Toronto, served as a volunteer in the Crimean War. When he returned to Canada he embarked upon a career in journalism. In addition to the volume mentioned by Smith, Ryan also published *Songs of a Wanderer* (Ottawa: G.E. Desbarats, 1867) and *Poems, Songs, Ballads* (Montreal: J. Lovell, 1903), as well as biographies of George Airey Kirkpatrick (1890), Sir Richard J. Cartwright (1892) and Wm. Cornelius Van Horne (1892). See T.H. Rand, *A Treasury of Canadian Verse* (Toronto: W. Briggs, 1900), 401.

13. According to Theodore Rand, J.R. [Andrew] Ramsay (1839?–1907) was born near West Flamboro, Ontario, and pursued a career as a house decorator, winning recognition for his landscape designs. By 1900 he was residing in Westover, Ontario, near Hamilton. In addition to *The Canadian Lyre* (Hamilton: Donnelly, 1859), which contains the poem, "Spinning Wheel," Ramsay published at least three other volumes of poetry: *Win-on-ah, or, The Forest Light: and Other Poems* (Toronto: Adam, Stevenson, 1869); *One Quiet Day: A Book of Prose and Poetry* (Hamilton: Lancefield, 1873); and *Muriel, the Foundling, and Other Original Poems* (Toronto: A.H. Hovey & Co., 1886). See Rand, *A Treasury of Canadian Verse*, 399–400.

14. It is noteworthy that Smith emphasizes Ascher's Jewish faith rather than his Scottish birth. Isidore Gordon Ascher (1835–1914) was born in Glasgow and emigrated to Canada with his family in 1844. He studied law at McGill College and was called to the bar in 1862. Besides publishing *Voices from the Hearth: A Collection of Verses* (Montreal: John Lovell, 1863), Ascher contributed regularly to British and American magazines. Later in his career, Ascher was drawn to novel writing and published *An Odd Man's Story* (Montreal: W.F. Brown, 1889); *The Doom of Destiny* (London: Diprose & Bateman, 1895); and *A Social Upheaval* (London: Greening & Co., 1898). His *Collected Poems* (London: Elliot Stock, 1929) was published posthumously. Jean Ingelow (1820–97), who was born in Boston, Lincolnshire, was a prominent nineteenth-century poet and novelist who was also well-known for her children's stories set in her native county. She spent most of her life in London where she likely met Ascher. See Morgan, *Bibliotheca Canadensis*, 12–13; and Maureen Peters, *Jean Ingelow, Victorian Poetess* (Ipswich: Boydell Press, 1972).

15. John Fraser (Cousin Sandy) (1810–72) was born in Portsoy, Banffshire, Scotland. His father and mother emigrated to the Eastern Townships

of Quebec in 1831, but Fraser went to London to run a merchant-tailor business. The failure of Fraser's business as well as his known involvement with the English Chartists may have encouraged him to join his family in Stanstead, Quebec, where he continued to work as a tailor. He later moved his family to Montreal where he published several poems and stories as "Cousin Sandy," particularly in the *Herald*. Fraser also published an account of his Chartist days in the *Northern Journal*, but the volume that Smith is alluding to was *A Tale of the Sea, and Other Poems* (Montreal: Dawson, 1870). Although a tub is featured in the book's title poem, Smith appears to have confused the work with the more famous satirical poem by Jonathan Swift. An inquest found that Fraser had died by accidental drowning in Ottawa on the seventh of June 1872, at the age of sixty-one. See *Canadian Illustrated News*, Vol. 5, No. 24 (June 15, 1872), 374; and No. 25 (June 22, 1872), 390.

16. Augusta Baldwyn (1821?–84) was the daughter of the Anglican rector at St. John's on the Richelieu River south of Montreal. From the late 1830s she regularly contributed poetry to both Canadian and American publications, including the *Literary Garland* (Montreal) and the *Christian Mirror* (Boston). After the publication of her collection, *Poems*, she continued to publish poetry in periodicals such as the *Ladies Repository* (Cincinnati, Ohio), the *Cultivator* (Boston) and the *Family Herald* (Montreal). Despite Smith's dismissal of her work, two of Baldwyn's poems were also included in Edward H. Dewart's *Selections from Canadian Poets* (1864). See Morgan, *Bibliotheca Canadensis*, 17–18.

17. Harriett Annie Wilkins (1829–88) born in Bath, England, was the daughter of a Congregational minister, Reverend John Wilkins, who had come to Hamilton in 1846. After the death of her father a year later, Wilkins supported her family by teaching music and conducting a seminary for young ladies in the family home. She supplemented her income by writing poetry for the Hamilton *Spectator* and contributed regularly to the paper's "Poet's Corner." She published five books of poems, four of which *The Holly Branch* (1851); *The Acacia* (1860); *Autumn Leaves* (1869); and *Victor Roy, a Masonic Poem* (1882) were published by the *Spectator*. Her collection, *Wayside Flowers* (1876) was published by Hunter, Rose & Company in Toronto. While Smith is condescending towards the women included in his summary of published poets, Wilkins had four poems in the Dewart collection, almost as many as Smith himself. In addition, Smith makes no

mention of Susannah Moodie's poetry. While Moodie had not published a collection of poems in Canada, she was well-known as a poet and also had four selections in the Dewart volume. The lack of appreciation for female authors, however, appears to have been widespread in nineteenth-century Canada. Women born before 1899 accounted for only 13.5 per cent of Canadian authors worthy of inclusion in Canadian reference books. See Katherine Greenfield, "Harriet Wilkins," *DCB*, Vol. 11, 925; Susannah Strickland [Moodie] *Enthusiasm: and other Poems* (London: Smith, Elder, 1831); Thurston, *The Work of Words*, 29–35 and 85–91; and Carole Gerson, *A Purer Taste: The Writing and Reading of Fiction in English in Nineteenth-Century Canada* (Toronto: University of Toronto Press, 1989), 8.

18. The *Dumfries Courier* was published in Galt as a weekly from 1844–47. Only three copies of the paper survive, none of which contain Smith's poem. See Gilchrist, *Inventory of Ontario Newspapers*, 23.

19. The *Brantford Courier* began publishing as a weekly in 1840. From 1870 to 1918 it ran as a daily paper. Very few copies of the paper survive before the 1870s. See Gilchrist, *Inventory of Ontario Newspapers*, 17.

20. This story of Smith's young friend's early attempt at publishing appeared in Smith's tale "Leafing Out," part of a series entitled "John Kanack's Experiences" published in the *New Dominion Monthly*, May, 1873.

21. Newspapers and literary magazines provided one of the few opportunities for writers to get into print in early nineteenth-century Canada and they continued to be an important vehicle for the publication of fiction throughout the century. Protestant men, like Smith, of Scottish or English descent predominated among both writers and editors. Of these, the majority were drawn from the educated middle class with a little than half of the writers being either lawyers or clergymen. See Gerson, *A Purer Taste*, 8–11; and MacDonald, *Literature and Society in the Canadas*, 13–65.

22. The poem rhymes when it is pronounced with a Scots accent. For example, "Vaugh*on*" would rhyme with "m*on*." For Robert King, see Chapter 3, Note 18, above.

23. A "Hornbook" was a paper containing the alphabet, often with the Lord's Prayer, mounted on a thin piece of flat wood with a handle at the bottom. The paper was often covered with a thin, transparent sheet made from animal horn to preserve it. See Andrew W. Tuer, *History of the Horn-Book* (London: Leadenhall Press, 1897, reprinted 1968).

24. According to James Young, the establishment of schoolhouses in Dumfries Township was a slow process. In these circumstances, it is understandable that temporary classes were established by various settlers. By calling such impromptu arrangements "hedge schools," Smith is alluding to the illegal outdoor schools established during the eighteenth century in Ireland after Catholic schools were abolished by the "Penal Laws" of the Protestant Ascendancy. See Young, *Reminiscences of the Early History of Galt*, 89; and S.J. Connolly, ed., *Companion to Irish History* (Oxford: Oxford University Press, 1998), 237–38.

25. Alexander Davidson (1794–1856) published several versions of his textbook with its daunting title, *The Canada Spelling Book: Intended as an Introduction to the English Language, Consisting of a Variety of Lessons, Progressively Arranged in Three Parts: With an Appendix, Containing Several Useful Tables, the Outlines of Geography, a Comprehensive Sketch of Grammar, and Morning and Evening Prayers for Every Day in the Week*. Smith is likely referring to the 1845 edition published by Davidson himself in Niagara, Upper Canada.

26. With the *British Colonist*, Hugh Scobie aimed to provide a moderate alternative to the existing Reform and Tory newspapers in Toronto. The paper was published, first as a weekly, then as a tri-weekly, from 1838 to 1859. Smith's poems entitled, "The Carrier Boy's New Year's Address," were published earlier than he indicates in 1850 and 1851. See Ouellette, "Hugh Scobie," 789–91; and the *British Colonist*, No. 956 (January 1, 1850) and No. 1059 (January 3, 1851).

27. William Walter Copp (1826–94) is best known as one of the founders of the publishing firm, Copp, Clark and Company. William Copp had emigrated to Toronto from Great Torrington, England, in 1842 and worked for Hugh Scobie. When Scobie died in 1853, Copp, in partnership with Thomas MacLean and William Chewitt, bought parts of Scobie's business. Elizabeth Hulse, "William Walter Copp," *DCB*, Vol. 12 (1990), 212–13.

28. John MacDonald (1824–90), who was born in Perth, Scotland, was appointed to the Senate in 1887. MacDonald, a devote Methodist and initial opponent of Confederation, had been elected in 1864 as a Reformer and in 1875 as Independent Liberal MP for Toronto Centre, where his influential dry goods business was located. Sir John A. MacDonald nominated him for the Senate partly as a reward for the support that he had occasionally given the Tory government in the 1870s. See Michael Bliss, "John MacDonald," *DCB*, Vol. 11,

551–52. For a discussion of the early Toronto literary societies, see Murray, *Come Bright Improvement*, 23–52 and 245–59.

29. Mackenzie published his *Colonial Advocate* from 1824 to 1834. The paper was extremely critical of the Tory elite, a position that sparked a famous incident in 1826 when a group of young Tories ransacked his office and threw his press into Lake Ontario. Mackenzie ceased publishing the *Advocate* when he entered municipal politics and became Toronto's first mayor, but started a new paper, the *Constitution*, when the Reformers were defeated in the violent 1836 election. It was the *Constitution* that provided Mackenzie a public platform in the immediate lead up to the 1837 Rebellion. The *Message* (later the *Toronto Weekly Message*), in which Mackenzie continued to attack government corruption and patronage, was founded in 1852, three years after he had received amnesty for his role in the rebellion. The paper began its decline in 1858 when Mackenzie resigned from the legislature and ceased publication at his death in 1861. See Armstrong & Stagg, "William Lyon Mackenzie," *DCB*, Vol. 9 (1861–70), 497–507; Paul Romney, "From the Types Riot to the Rebellion: Elite Ideology, Anti-legal Sentiment, Political Violence, and the Rule of Law in Upper Canada," in *OH*, Vol. 79, No. 2 (June 1987), 115–44; and Cecilia Morgan, "'When Bad Men Conspire, Good Men Must Unite!': Gender and the Political Discourses in Upper Canada, 1820s-1830s," in Kathryn McPherson et al, eds., *Gendered Pasts: Historical Essays in Femininity and Masculinity in Canada* (Don Mills, Ontario: Oxford University Press Canada, 1999), 12–28.

30. James Lesslie (1802–85), was one of the leading merchants and prominent citizens of Toronto during the nineteenth century. Lesslie was, like Mackenzie, a Reformer, but he had adamantly opposed the use of violence in 1837. Lesslie's negative assessment of Mackenzie's leadership qualities may have been a consequence of the fact that he had been harassed and imprisoned in the aftermath of the rebellion as a consequence of his association with Mackenzie. Smith, however, uses the tale to once again personalize and thus trivialize the rebellion. The Mackenzie and Lesslie families had been closely connected in their native Dundee. Besides employing Mackenzie, who had apprenticed as an apothecary and an accountant, as his bookkeeper, Edward Lesslie had financed the general store and circulating library that Mackenzie and his mother ran in Alyth, twenty miles (thirty-two kilometres) north of Dundee. When the business collapsed in 1820 and Mackenzie emigrated to Canada, he was accompanied by James

Lesslie. In 1822, Mackenzie and the Lesslies were briefly partners in a general store in Dundas, Upper Canada, but the partnership was dissolved in 1823. Intriguingly, both William Lyon Mackenzie and James Lesslie went into journalism as a means of forwarding their shared goal of political reform in Upper Canada — Mackenzie in 1824 with the *Colonial Advocate* and Lesslie in 1838 with the *Examiner.* J.M.S. Careless, "James Lesslie," *DCB*, Vol. 11, 516–19, Armstrong and Stagg, "William Lyon Mackenzie," 497; and Vance and Stephen, "Grits, Rebels and Radicals," 188–89, 197–98.

31.   Peter Jaffray (1800–64) was born in Stirling, Scotland, and had been involved in the printing trade in Edinburgh and Shrewsbury before he emigrated to Upper Canada in 1844. Jaffray and his sons had initially helped produce the *Dumfries Courier,* which was edited by Ben Herle, but Jaffray began printing his own *Galt Reporter* in 1847–48, after the failure of the *Dumfries Courier.* The *Reporter* was published first as a weekly and then, after 1896, as a daily until 1922. See James Young, *Reminiscences of the Early History of Galt and the Settlement of Dumfries,* 196–98 and 219; and Gilchrist, *Inventory of Ontario Newspapers,* 23.

32.   J.A. Smith's stories appeared in his *Humourous Sketches.* In the published version of the tale, Ike Sickle fails to win the hand of his intended because of an embarrassing incident at a quilting bee. In 1886, Prof. W.S. Vallance was identified as the professor of elocution at Glasgow University in the promotional flyer for a series of his recitals held in Toronto. See Smith, *Humourous Sketches,* 45–49; and *Shaftsbury Hall Tuesday and Wednesday Evg's, Feb. 9 & 10, Recitals by the Eminent Scotch Elocutionist, Prof. Vallance, F.S.Sc.* (S.1.: n.p., 1886) held by the Metropolitan Toronto Library, Canadian History Department.

33.   John Dougall (1808–86), born in Paisley, Scotland, emigrated to Canada in 1826 to establish a branch of the family's textile distribution business. As part of his operation in Montreal, Dougall also ran a book and stationary shop, which ultimately led him into publishing, first as editor of the *Canada Temperance Advocate* and then, in 1846, with his own weekly Montreal *Witness.* Part of the financial backing for Dougall's publishing activities came through his business partnership with the sugar-refining Redpath family as a consequence of his marriage, in 1840, to Elizabeth Redpath. For Dougall, who was an evangelical Protestant who had converted to Congregationalism at the time of his marriage, newspaper publishing was not merely a business but a means to forward the evangelical cause. Like many of his readers, Dougall advocated temperance, sabbatarianism, and free

trade, and was intensely anti-Catholic, so much so that the English-speaking Catholics of Montreal felt compelled to respond in 1850 with the rival *True Witness and Catholic Chronicle*. Despite such hostility, the *Witness* flourished, becoming a daily in 1860, and survived under the editorship of Dougall's son, John Redpath Dougall, until 1913. See J.G. Snell, "John Dougall," *DCB*, Vol. 11, 270–71; and Lorraine Vander Hoef, "John Dougall (1808–1886): Portrait of an Early Social Reformer and Evangelical Witness in Canada," in *Journal of the Canadian Church Historical Society*, Vol. 43 (2001), 115–45.

34. The *Daily Witness* reported on the Congregational Union Confer-ence, which ran from June 11 to June 15, 1869. Smith made several presentations, including an essay on "Revivals" and was present on Monday June 14 when Dougall addressed the assembly. Smith took up his position at Pine Grove, Ontario, after the conference. In order to maintain the evangelical tenor of his paper, John Dougall had a strict advertising policy. He would not accept advertisements for patent medicines, liquor, or tobacco, or for "morally question-able" entertainments, such as races or the theatre. The *Witness* did not publish brand-name advertising until 1879, when John Red-path Dougall assumed management of the paper. See *Daily Witness*, June 11, 12, 14, and 15, 1869; and Vander Hoef, "John Dougall," 125–26.

35. John Dougall believed that the periodical industry had a duty to promote the evangelical cause and the *New York Daily Witness* (1871–77) was intended to further that goal in the United States. Despite absorbing much of Dougall's energy and family resources, the paper failed between 1877 and 1878. However, the *New York Weekly Witness*, also founded in 1871, was transformed by Dougall's son, James Duncan Dougall, into the weekly *Sabbath Reading and New York Witness, and* it continued to be published until 1920. See Vander Hoef, "John Dougall," 129–32 and 138.

36. John Lovell (1810–93) was a prominent Montreal printer and publisher. Born in Ireland, Lovell emigrated with his family to Lower Canada in 1820, where the family took up a farm near Montreal. In 1823, he began an apprenticeship to a printer and from there would become one of the eras prominent publishers. His companies would publish a variety of works, including: magazines; music books and sheet music; newspapers, directories, and government publications; and school textbooks. He published the work of several Canadian poets including Charles Sangster, Alexander McLachlan and Susannah

Moodie, as well as E.H. Dewart's first anthology of Canadian poetry. As Smith rightly notes, Lovell made a significant contribution to Canadian literature. In 1847, Lovell published the *Snow Drop* or, *Juvenile Magazine*, the first children's magazine in the colony. In 1864, Lovell offered to the public the first anthology of Canadian poetry with *Selections from Canadian Poets*. Lovell also actively supported the development of French-Canadian literature with the printing of such works as Michel Bibaud's *L'encyclopedie Canadienne*, James Huston's, *Le Repertoire National*, and the second edition of Francois-Xavier Garneau's, *Histoire du Canada*. Perhaps his greatest impact on Canadian publishing came, however, with his continued agitation for changes to Canadian and British copyright legislation that would enable Canadian publishers to better compete with their American counterparts. By 1866, Lovell's Canadian printing operations were employing 150 people and running twelve steam presses, and by the time of his death, John Lovell and Son had grown into an international publishing company with printing operations in New York State and Montreal. George L. Parker, "John Lovell," *DCB*, Vol. 12 (1990), 569–73. See also, H. Pearson Gundy, *Book Publishing and Publishers in Canada Before 1900* (Toronto: The Bibliographical Society of Canada, 1965), 15–17.

37. In 1877, James McClelland was listed as being located at the southern edge of Alton, Caledon Township, on Concession Line 4 West, lots 22 and 23. See *Illustrated Historical Atlas of the County of Peel, Ont.* (Toronto: Walker & Miles, 1877), 211.

38. The *New Dominion Monthly* (1867–79) was published by John Dougall to coincide with Confederation. As with his other publications, it was designed to be morally uplifting and was directed at a family audience. The *New Dominion Monthly* did offer the opportunity for Canadian authors, like Smith, to contribute original articles and stories. See Vander Hoef, "John Dougall," 127–28 and 138; Gerson, *A Purer Taste*, 7; and Fraser Sutherland, *The Monthly Epic: A History of Canadian Magazines 1789–1989* (Markham, ON.: Fitzhenry & Whiteside, 1989) 38–45. For a list of Smith's "John Kanack" articles, see Appendix A.

39. Reverend James A.R. Dickson (?–1915), was ordained as a Congregational minister in 1865. He served in London, Ontario, until 1870 and then in Toronto until 1878. In 1879, Dickson joined the Presbyterian Church of Canada and moved to Galt where he served until 1914. See Walkington, *The Congregational Churches of Canada*.

40. William McDougall, (1822–1905), a radical lawyer of Scots parentage, published the *North American* on a semi-weekly basis from 1850–54. He had previously been involved in journalism with his weekly papers: the *Canada Farmer,* the *Agriculturalist & Canadian Journal* and then the *Canadian Agriculturalist,* all of which were related to his interest in agricultural improvement. The *North American* was founded in response to McDougall's dissatisfaction with the pace of reform under the Baldwin-LaFontaine coalition government. See Suzanne Zeller, "William McDougall," *DCB*, 632–36.

41. The "Clear Grits" had a much more radical platform than Smith suggests. The group, which had a remarkably high proportion of Scots in its membership, was demanding wholesale democratic reform of the newly united governments of Upper and Lower Canada, including the adoption of universal suffrage and vote by ballot. Although historians have tended to argue that the Clear Grit platform was derived from American Republicanism, it contained striking parallels with the contemporary British Chartist manifesto. George Brown (1818–80), the well-known Lowland Scottish reformer and founder of the *Globe,* adopted the label to describe the group when one of its members informed Brown that he would not be welcome since the group only wanted those Reformers who were "clear grit." As Smith indicates, by the mid-1850s Brown had come to dominate the Reform Party and the term "Grits" came to describe all reform members. The term was ultimately applied to the members of the Reform Party's successor organization, the Liberal Party of Canada. See Vance and Stephen, "Grits, Rebels and Radicals," 181, 193, and 203; Michael E. Vance, "Scottish Chartism in Canada West: An Examination of the 'Clear Grit' Reformers," in *Scottish Tradition,* Vol. 22 (1997), 56–102; and J.M.S. Careless, "George Brown," *DCB*, Vol. X, 91–103. Smith's allusion to the Cave of Adullam is another Biblical reference. Samuel 1:22 describes how David gathered all those who were "distressed," "discontented," or "in debt" at the cave.

42. *The Church* was published in Cobourg, from May 1837 to July 1846, and then in Toronto from July 1846 to July 1855. The *Examiner* was a weekly newspaper published in Toronto from 1838 to 1855, when it was absorbed by the *Globe.* Samuel Lount (1791–1838) and his family came to Upper Canada from Pennsylvania after the War of 1812. Lount worked as a blacksmith and ran successfully for Simcoe County as a Reformer in the 1834 election. His defeat in the 1836 election encouraged him to join the rebellion. Peter Matthews (1789?–1838)

was the son of a United Empire Loyalist family born in the Bay of Quinte region. By 1837, Matthews was a popular farmer in Pickering Township who had served in the local militia during the War of 1812. During the rebellion he led a contingent of rebels from Pickering. Both men were tried for treason in Toronto and, despite numerous appeals for clemency, were hanged in the courtyard of the Toronto jail on April 12, 1838. See Gilchrist, *Inventory of Toronto Newspapers*, 164; Ronald J. Stagg, "Samuel Lount," *DCB*, Vol. 7, 518–19; "Peter Matthews," *DCB;* Paul Romney and Barry Wright, "The Toronto Treason Trials, March-May 1838," in Murray Greenwood and Barry White, eds., *Canadian State Trials, Vol. II: Rebellion and Invasion in the Canadas, 1837–1838* (Toronto: University of Toronto Press, 2002), 62–99.

43. Dudley and Burns were located at 11 Colborne Street in Toronto. Besides printing Smith's *Poems* (1888) and his brother's *Humourous Sketches* (1875), the firm specialized in producing Upper Canadian Baptist literature as well as publishing the rules and regulations of various Toronto societies, including the Toronto Gun Club, the Ontario Historical Society, the Victoria Club, and the Toronto University Medical Society. See Elizabeth Hulse, *A Dictionary of Toronto Printers, Publishers, Booksellers, and the Allied Trades, 1798–1900* (Toronto: Anson-Cartwright, 1982).

44. Smith is referring to William Hutton (1723–1815) and his volume, *The Court of Requests* (Edinburgh: W. & R. Chambers, 1840). Hutton also published *The History of Derby* (Birmingham: Thomas Pearson, 1791) and several editions of *The History of Birmingham* (Birmingham: James Guest, 1835). See *DNB*, Vol. 10, 361–63.

45. Judge Frederick T. Wilkes was born in England and emigrated to Canada in 1820, settling first in Brantford. He was the appointed county judge when Grey County was established in 1854, and he was also a member of the Owen Sound Congregational Church. Wilkes was no longer living when Smith published his *Gazetteer of Grey County* in 1865. See Smith, *Gazetteer,* 215; Croft, *Fourth Entrance to Huronia*, 58, 99; and *History of the County of Brant*, 213–14.

46. In his *Gazetteer* Smith lists several men with the last name Doherty in St. Vincent Township, but only one John Doherty, who shared lot 10 on Concession Line 10 with a Thomas Doherty. The 1857 edition of the *Canada Directory* lists Smith as clerk of the Division Court and John Lee as a watchmaker on Poulette Street, but by the time Smith compiled his *Gazetteer,* John Lee was listed as a shoemaker and Messrs.

Vick and Forham were listed as the watchmakers for Owen Sound. All of that tends to suggest that the case was probably heard in the late 1850s. See *Canada Directory for 1857–1858* (Montreal: John Lovell, 1857), 500; and Smith, *Gazetteer of Grey County*, 247, 268, 290.

47. Since the division court was essentially a small claims court, Wilkes did not have the authority to sentence individuals to Kingston Penitentiary. Only judges in criminal courts had that discretion. See Margaret A. Banks, "The Evolution of Ontario Courts, 1788–1981," in David H. Flaherty, ed., *Essays in the History of Canadian Law*, Vol. 2 (Toronto: University of Toronto Press, 1983), 492–772; and David Murray, *Colonial Justice: Justice, Morality, and Crime in the Niagara District, 1791–1849* (Toronto: University of Toronto Press, 2002), 25–8, 69, and 151–53. For Kingston Penitentiary, see Oliver, *Terror to Evil-Doers*, 86–97, 105–11, 119–25, and 501.

48. Smith's account of the division court's operation in nineteenth-century Ontario can be compared with W.S. Herrington's, *Pioneer Life on the Bay of Quinte, and the Court of Requests* (Napanee: Lennox and Addington Historical Society, 1915). Not only did disputes over property account for most of the cases in the lower courts in the 1850s, they also represented a great deal of the business of the higher courts. According to R.B.C. Risk, property cases were the second most common type of dispute to come to the higher courts, and requests for enforcement of claims against debtors were the fourth most common. See R.B.C. Risk, "The Law and the Economy in Mid-Nineteenth-Century Ontario," in David H. Flaherty, ed., *Essays in the History of Canadian Law*, Vol. 1 (Toronto: University of Toronto Press, 1981), 92.

49. The Maus Plains School was founded in 1830. Both the school and the plains were named after the pioneer family that donated the land for the building. The "Galt Subscription and Circulating Library" was formed in 1836 and was located on the corner of Main and Ainslie streets until it was incorporated into the library of the Galt Mechanics' Institute in 1854. "John Smith," listed as one of the original members of the Circulating Library, may have been Smith's father. Subscription libraries organized by groups of settlers, at times supported by a wealthy patron, were the most common form of library in the early years of the nineteenth century, but by mid-century the labouring men's mechanics' institutes held the largest collections of what were essentially public libraries. In 1851, the Toronto Mechanics' Institute held 1,300 volumes available for the members "self-improvement" and the collection would form the core of the Toronto Public Library

when it was founded in the 1880s. See *The History of the County of Brant*, 444–8 and 669–70; Young, *Reminiscences of the Early History of Galt*, 123–26 and 239; Gerson, *A Purer Taste*, 4–5; Murray, *Come Bright Improvement*, 26–31 and 40–44; and the *Canada Directory 1851* (Montreal: John Lovell, 1851), 555.

50. Here Smith is suggesting that Scottish readers were less apt to read fiction, instead opting for religious or educational works. While the figures for the Mitchell Library that Smith quotes may well be accurate, he masks the fact that there was a great struggle over readers in Scotland and that fiction, often of a sensational character, was rapidly superceding other forms of literature. Of the 45,000 books published in England between 1816 and 1851, over 10,000 were religious works, far outdistancing the next category — history and geography with 4,900. Yet the circulation of these works was often limited, and many of the religious works published were in fact produced to combat the spread of fictional works and the perceived negative effects they might have upon young readers, women, and the working class in general. For a more complete discussion of these and related issues, see R.K. Webb, "The Victorian Reading Public," *Universities Quarterly*, 12 (November 1957); Robert A. Colby, "Rational Amusement: Fiction vs. Useful Knowledge in the Nineteenth Century," in *Victorian Literature and Society*, James R. Kincaid and Albert J. Kuhn, ed. (Ohio: Ohio State University Press, 1984) and G.A. Cranfield, *The Press and Society*. (London: 1978), in particular see Chapter 5, "The Growth of a New Reading Public and the Struggle to Control It."

51. Such figures appear confirmed by the fact that in 1870 novels comprised two-thirds of the Montreal Mechanics' Institute's circulation, and in 1880 novels represented over three-quarters of the Toronto Mechanics' Institute's circulation. Gerson, *A Purer Taste*, 17–35.

52. In the nineteenth-century debate over the perils of novel reading, women were highlighted as being particularly prone to suffer from an excessive indulgence in "light" reading. In general, prose fiction was viewed as less serious reading with a particular appeal to women and young readers. Nevertheless, by the 1880s it was being argued that historical novels, of the variety produced by Walter Scott, had a valid educational function. By recounting this tale, however, Smith is clearly implying that the young woman in question did not have the ability to make informed judgements over her choice of reading material. See Gerson, *A Purer Taste*, 17, 22, and 93–94; and Robert A. Colby, "Rational Amusement vs. Useful Knowledge in the Nineteenth

Century," in James R. Kincaid and Albert J. Kuhn, eds., *Victorian Literature and Society* (Ohio: Ohio State University Press, 1984). For a re-examination of the female reader stereotype in an early period in an American context, see Cathy N. Davidson, "The Novel as Subversive Activity: Women Reading, Women Writing" in Alfred F. Young, ed., *Beyond the American Revolution* (DeKalb: Northern Illinois University Press, 1993), 283–316.

53.   A reference to the English poet, Alexander Pope (1688–1744).

54.   Captain Charles Cunningham Boycott (1832–97) was land agent for Lord Erne's estate at Lough Mask, County Mayo. In 1873, while acting as land agent, Captain Boycott opposed the Land League, under the leadership of Charles Stewart Parnell, and its demands for rent reductions. Catholic labourers refused to harvest crops on the estate, which meant they would spoil, until fifty Orangemen, escorted by over 1,000 troops, were called in. "Boycotting" became an effective weapon of the Land League against the unfair rents, evictions, and other abuses rife within the antiquated landholding system in Ireland. See D.J. Hickey, J.E. Doherty, ed., "Captain Charles Cunningham Boycott," *A Dictionary of Irish History Since 1800* (Dublin: Gill and Macmillan, 1980), 42.

55.   The passage is found in Luke 14:21.

56.   William Cullen Bryant (1794–1878), was a well-known American poet and editor. After making a name for himself as a poet of considerable merit, Bryant was offered the co-editorship of the *New York Review* and *Athenaeum Magazine*, a post that brought him into contact with New York's literary elite. In 1826, he was offered the position of assistant editor of the *New York Evening Post*, one of the countries leading papers. In 1829, he assumed the editorial chair, a position he would hold until his death in 1878. Allen Johnson and Dumas Malone, eds., "William Cullen Bryant," *DAB*, Vol. 2 (New York: Charles Scribner's Sons, 1958), 200–5.

57.   According to the *Oxford English Dictionary*, the first use of "inimical," meaning harmful or hostile, was in 1643. See *OED* (second edition, 1989), Vol. 7, 974.

Chapter 11: Backwoods Experiences

1.   Since the *Reporter* was not founded until 1847, the story must have been published after that date.

2. Charles Durand (1811–1905) was the son of Captain James Durand who emigrated from England around 1800. Charles Durand was born in Barton Township, Upper Canada, and studied law in Hamilton. The Durand family were involved in Reform politics and Charles became entangled with the leadership of the 1837 Rebellion. He was tried for treason and spent several years in exile in the United States before being pardoned in 1844 when he returned to practise law in Toronto. In the 1830s, Durand had contributed several poems and works of prose to the *Canadian Casket* and *Canadian Garland*, and then later in the 1840s to the *Canadian Gem* and *Family Visitor*. A Methodist and militant Temperance advocate, Durand owned and edited the *Canadian Son of Temperance* from 1851–54. See Charles Durand, *Reminiscences Of Charles Durand of Toronto, Barrister* (Toronto: Hunter, Rose, 1897); Read and Stagg, eds., *The Rebellion of 1837 in Upper Canada*, iii–iii, and 95; MacDonald, *Literature and Society in the Canadas*, 305; and Greenwood & Wright, eds., *Canadian State Trials*, Vol. 2, 70, 72, 77–79, and 297.

3. Pedro II (1825–91) was the second emperor of Brazil. Like Smith, Pedro II was an ardent abolitionist, even though this weakened his support from the powerful slave-owning class in Brazil. Their opposition, along with a rising militarism in the country, resulted in the declaration of a Brazilian Republic in 1889 and the exile of the royal family. Pedro II died in Paris in 1891. See R.J. Barman, *Citizen Emperor: Pedro II and the Making of Brazil, 1825–1891* (Stanford: Stanford University Press, 1999); E.V. Da Costa, *The Brazilian Empire: Myths and Histories* (Chapel Hill: The University of North Carolina Press, 2000); and Michael M. Smith, "Pedro II," in *The McGraw-Hill Encyclopedia of World Biography*. (New York: McGraw-Hill, Inc., 1973), 343–44. The Emperor's journey was also described in *The Daily News* (Kingston) June 9, 1876, 1.

4. The *Spartan* was a Royal Mail steamer that plied the St. Lawrence and Lake Ontario. In August of 1865, the steamer sank near Caughnawaga when the captain became confused by smoke from a bush fire that was sweeping across the river. By October the ship had been successfully refloated and towed to Montreal for repairs, afterwards being operated as a passenger carrier between Hamilton and Montreal. See, "Hamilton Harbour 1826–1901, 1865" at *http://www.hhpl.on.ca/GreatLakes/Documents/Brookes/*; and The Department of Marine and Fisheries [Canada], *Annual Report … for the Year Ending 30th June 1871*, 57, accessed April 20, 2006.

5.   Here Smith is referring to the "Battle of the Windmill," which took place in November of 1838. After the failure of William Lyon Mackenzie's rebellion in 1837, there was widespread skirmishing along the American border. On November 11 a force of about four hundred men set out from New York State for Prescott, Upper Canada, where they intended to capture Fort Wellington and sever communications between Upper and Lower Canada. Upon landing they fortified themselves in a windmill and some surrounding buildings, however, the reinforcements they believed would be arriving never materialized, and they were soundly defeated by a combined force of British regulars and local militia. For an account of the battle see, Scott A. McLean, "The Battle of the Windmill Revisited," in *Canadian Military History*, Vol. 9, No. 4 (Autumn 2000), 65–72.

6.   In this discussion, Smith is following the lead of Catharine Parr Traill (1802–99) who published a great deal on the natural history of Upper Canada and, in particular, on the utility of local plant life for settlers in her volume *The Canadian Emigrant Housekeeper's Guide* (Montreal: J. Lovell, 1861).

7.   Lobelia is named after the botanist Mathias de Lobel, who died in London in 1616. It is an erect annual or biennial herb that stands one to two feet (thirty to sixty centimetres) high, with a pale violet-blue flower. The plant was well-known to native North Americans long before Europeans "rediscovered" its medicinal qualities. It was often used as an expectorant and was believed by many to be an excellent treatment for bronchitis. See "Lobelia Inflata" at *http://www.Botanical. com*, accessed December 24, 2007.

8.   Sassafras is a small tree that stands between twenty and forty feet [six and twelve metres] high, with slender branches and broadly oval leaves. Its roots are believed to have medicinal qualities and have long been used as a treatment for rheumatism, syphilis, and skin diseases. In Louisiana the leaves are used as a condiment in sauces and for thickening soups. It is also commonly used to make tea and as a flavouring in soft drinks. See, "Sassafras Officinale" at *http://www. Botanical.com*, accessed on December 24, 2007.

9.   According to Catharine Parr Traill, settlers first learned about the medicinal qualities of sassafras from the First Nations, and many drank it as a substitute for tea. See Traill, *Canadian Emigrant Housekeeper's Guide*, 78–79.

10. Smith's source for Sir Walter Raleigh's (1552–1618) idiosyncratic spelling is not clear. The *Oxford English Dictionary*, however, identifies

the origin of the word "sassafras" with the Spanish explorers of the early sixteenth century. On his voyages to the Americas, Raleigh is certain to have come in contact with both Spanish and the indigenous inhabitants who were the first to introduce the plant to Europeans. See *OED*, 2nd ed., Vol. 16, 493; and Raleigh Trevelyan, *Sir Walter Raleigh* (London: Allen Lane, 2002).

11. Sarsaparilla is a widely used alternative medicine. A climbing vine native to tropical America and the West Indies, it is most commonly used as a treatment for rheumatism and psoriasis. See, "Sarsaparilla" at *http://www.healthy.net*, accessed on December 24, 2007.

12. A temperance society had been established in Beverly Township as early as 1829. See C.M. Johnston, *The Head of the Lake: A History of Wentworth County* (Hamilton: Wentworth County Council, 1967), 88.

13. The 1871 Census lists an Albert Huson as a forty-seven-year-old resident native of the United States and resident of Paris, Ontario. His occupation was listed as "Bailiff," which would be consistent with Smith's story. See LAC, C-9916, Division 2, 1.

14. A John McRoberts is recorded in the 1871 Census as a fifty-one-year-old native of Scotland, an Independent, and a law clerk. Although he was residing in Guelph, this could be the McRobert's in Smith's account. See LAC, C-9945–6, Division 2, 66.

15. This story of the Beverly choir appeared in Smith's story "Leafing Out," part of his series entitled "John Kanack's Experiences" published in the *New Dominion Monthly* (May, 1873).

16. The presence of Beverly Swamp in the early days of settlement helped create the poor reputation of the township, but by the 1870s, much of the land had been drained and had proved to be extremely fertile. As a consequence, many of the settlers, most of whom were Scots, became quite prosperous. Indeed, in the 1870s, Beverly Township was described as "by far the largest and wealthiest" in Wentworth County. See *Illustrated Historical Atlas of the County of Wentworth, Ont.* (Toronto: Page & Smith, 1875), vii and x. The "Old Hundred" is a reference to Psalm 100 set to music in 1551. "Ortonville," or "All Things Work Out For Good," was written in 1837 by Thomas Hastings (1784–1872). See D. Dewitt Wasson, *Hymntune Index and Related Hymn Materials* (Lanham, Maryland: The Scarecrow Press, 1998), 1437 and 2002.

17. Salt was discovered in 1866 by Sam Platt nearly 1,000 feet (300 metres) below Goderich harbour. Platt was not particularly surprised by the discovery since First Nations people in the area had told

him of rock salt deposits in the region. Mass production of the salt deposits began in 1880, and since 1955, Goderich salt has been sold worldwide under the brand name "Sifto." See *The Canadian Encyclopedia* (Edmonton: Hurtig Publishers, 1988), 613, 1927.

18. Tales of being lost in the woods were common in the early accounts of pioneer life and many settlers would have been familiar with the "Indian captivity narratives" that emerged in literature of the Seven Years' War in North America. This may account for the idea that the children were taken by members of the First Nations when there was no evidence that this ever occurred in Grey County. See Linda Colley, *Captives: Britain, Empire, and the World, 1600–1850* (New York: Anchor Books, 2002), 168–202 and 382–83; Kathryn Zabelle Derounian-Stodola and James Arthur Levernier, *The Indian Captivity Narrative, 1550–1900* (Toronto: Maxwell Macmillan Canada, 1993); and Samuel Gardner Drake, *Indian Captivities, or, Life in the Wigwam: Being True Narratives of Captives Who Have Been Carried Away by the Indians* (Auburn, New York: Derby and Miller, 1851).

19. Smith, *Gazetteer and Directory of Grey County*, 186. Melancthon Township would later become part of the County of Dufferin when that county was formed in 1888.

20. The shortage of currency in Upper Canada made the credit system attractive to those wishing to establish themselves as commercial farmers. Indeed, it was essential to farmer and storekeeper alike. While debt levels remained high, few farmers failed as a consequence of the credit system. See McCalla, *Planting the Province*, 142–47.

21. For the treatment of debtors in Upper Canada, see Chapter 4, Note 21, above.

22. The earliest Agricultural Society in Upper Canada was started in Niagara in 1793, but it was in the 1830s that most district agricultural societies were founded, due in large part to support from the government. As early as the 1820s, prizes were offered at Agricultural Fairs for the best plowing. Smith appears to be referring to the Dumfries Agricultural Society, which rotated its fair across Galt, Paris, and St. George, but was not founded until 1839. The development of plow technology over the course of the century also helped to improve practice. See J.J. Talman, "Agricultural Societies of Upper Canada," *Ontario Historical Society Papers and Records*, 27 (1931), 545–52; *History of the County of Brant*, 461; and Alan E. Skeoch, "Developments in Plowing Technology in Nineteenth-Century Canada," in *Canadian Papers in Rural History*, Vol. 3 (1982), 156–77.

23. Smith may be referring to one of the many editions of *Punch and Judy, With Twenty-Four Illustrations, Designed and Engraved by George Cruikshank, and Other Plates, Accompanied by the Dialogue of the Puppet-Show, An Account of its Origin, and of Puppet Plays in England*. The fourth edition, published in London in 1859 by T.C. Lacy, was ninety-four pages in length. The surname "Starnaman" is of German origin and not frequently found in Upper Canada. The 1871 Census records three Starnamans, all in the Haldimand District. They may have been related to the Starnaman in Smith's tale. See LAC, C-9916 Division 1, 30, C-9918, 24; C-9917, Division 1, 40.

24. While the Ottawa Valley would produce lumber longer, in the first half of the nineteenth century the industry, comprised of small-scale sawmills, employed more hands in areas of the colony closer to the Great Lakes. The trade supplied a voracious demand for timber in New York State, particularly from the high-quality pine forest of southwestern Ontario. The activity produced a tremendous rate of deforestation. For example, in 1850 Vaughan Township, 47.2 per cent of the land was wooded, but by 1900 only 5.6 per cent of the land remained in forest. See Wood, *Making Ontario*, 105–9.

25. In the first phase of settlement, the local sawmill was as important as the local gristmill. The gristmill converted grain crops into a marketable commodity, and the sawmill did the same for the logs produced through clearing. The erection of a sawmill was often a major local event that represented the transition from an economy based upon subsistence pioneering to one engaged in agricultural production, but most mills were of a temporary nature and became obsolete once the majority of land in an area had been cleared. Although lumbering and pioneer agriculture enjoyed a symbiotic relationship, by 1860 the two could come into conflict as lands were taken up merely to clear logs rather than contribute to settlement. See Wood, *Making Ontario*, 109; Neil S. Forkey, *Shaping the Upper Canadian Frontier: Environment, Society, and Culyure in the Trent Valle* (Calgary: University of Calgary Press, 2003), 42–43, 55, 88–89; and Guillet, *Early Life in Upper Canada*, 246–48. Nathaniel E. Mainwaring (?–1852) arrived in South Dumfries from Connecticut in 1820 and became one of the township's most successful farmers. See *History of the County of Brant*, 188.

26. Going "off in a pet" means going away in a fit of bad temper.

27. Smith is referring to the verse novelette *Enoch Arden* by Lord Alfred Tennyson (1809–92). In Tennyson's tale, Arden leaves his wife and

children to venture to China and to seek a fortune but returns to find that she has married again. See Alfred Tennyson, *Enoch Arden* (London: E. Moxon, 1864). For the California Gold Rush, see H.W. Brands' general account, *The Age of Gold: the California Gold Rush and the Birth of Modern America* (New York: Double Day, 2002); Kenneth N. Owens, ed., *Riches for All: The California Gold Rush and the World* (Lincoln: University of Nebraska Press, 2002), especially Chapter 2; and Malcolm J. Rohrbough, "'We Will Make Our Fortunes — No Doubt of It': The Worldwide Rush to California," in Kenneth N. Owens, ed., *Riches for All: The California Gold Rush and the World* (Lincoln: University of Nebraska Press, 2002), 55–70.

28. Reverend Joseph Unsworth (18?–1914) was ordained as a Congregational minister in 1853. He served at Georgetown (1855–81), at Stouffville (1883–91), and then at Toronto (1892–1913). See Walkington, *The Congregational Churches of Canada*.

29. In the first half of the nineteenth century, Upper Canada was essentially a rural community but in the second half of the century, urbanization, fuelled by both migration from the countryside and immigration, increased dramatically. As early as 1851, some rural communities reached their population peak, and by 1911 the urban population of Ontario became greater than the rural population. See Wood, *Making Ontario*, 137–44.

30. The decline in sugar-making was directly related to the pace of deforestation. Later in the century, the commercialization of sugar production also resulted in fewer individuals participating in the activity. See Guillett, *Early Life in Upper Canada*, 255–58, and Wood, *Making Ontario*, 91, 163–64.

31. Reverend R.J. Williams was ordained as a Congregational minister in 1849. He served in Alton, Caledon Township (1855–56) and in Newmarket (1877). See Walkington, *The Congregational Churches of Canada*.

32. For the early nineteenth-century history of the Royal Dockyard at Woolwich, which closed in 1869, see Philip MacDougall, "Hazardous Waters: Naval Dockyard Harbours During the Age of Fighting Sail," in *Mariner's Mirror*, Vol. 87, No.1 (2001), 15–29; and "The Woolwich Steam Yard," in *Mariner's Mirror*, Vol. 85, No. 2 (1999), 172–81.

33. The connection between romance and sugar-making was also noted in Upper Canada. Bulwer is located in Eaton, one of the Eastern Townships, where Smith was briefly minister. See Guillett, *Early*

Life in Upper Canada, 259; and Day, *History of the Eastern Townships,* 388–89.

34. John Watson was born at the Shotts near Glasgow, on June 12, 1820. At the age of eight he was apprenticed as a moulder, a trade which would serve him well during his lifetime. He emigrated to North America in 1842, landing at Boston and making his way to the Niagara region in search of work. He plied in his trade in Hamilton and Galt, and in 1846 decided to open his own foundry in the village of Ayr. Initially, he manufactured cast iron cooking pots, stoves, and by 1871 the foundry was manufacturing "nearly every thing a farmer needed from a plow to a threshing machine ..." In 1876, the company won the only gold medal given to a Canadian at the Centennial Exhibition in Philadelphia for agricultural implements. *Archival Records on John Watson.* Ayr, Ontario, Ayr Public Library.

35. Hugh Miller, (1802–56) the popular geologist and author was born in Cromarty, Scotland. At sixteen he was apprenticed as a stonemason, work that exposed him to the world of geology and fossils. He began writing at an early age, writing on a tremendous range of subjects and contributing to popular publications such as *Wilson's Tales of the Borders* and *Chambers's Edinburgh Journal.* He became well-known for the story of his early years in *My Schools and School Masters* (1854), but is best known for his geological works, *The Old Red Sandstone* (1841), *Footprints of the Creator* (1850), and *The Testimony of the Rocks* (1857), works designed to combat the evolutionary theories of Robert Chambers and Charles Darwin and reconcile his biblical knowledge with his scientific observations. See Rosemary Goring, ed., "Hugh Miller," *Chambers Scottish Biographical Dictionary.* (Edinburgh: Chambers Publishing, 1992), 314; and Lester Borley, ed., *Celebrating the Life and Times of Hugh Miller: Scotland in the Early Nineteenth Century: Ethnography & Folklore, Geology & Natural History, Church & Society* (Cromarty: Cromarty Arts Trust & Elphinstone Institute of the University of Aberdeen, 2003).

36. For folklore in southern Ontario see, Chapter 7, Note 22.

37. The commissioner was likely a representative of the Colonial Land and Emigration Commission that had been established by the Colonial Office in 1840. The commission was later replaced, in 1866, by the Emigrant's Information Office, which operated until 1918. See Marjory Harper, *Emigration from the Northeast of Scotland* (Aberdeen: Aberdeen University Press, 1988), Vol. 1, 14–17; Vol. 2, 4–5.

38. The "professional" pioneer, usually North American-born, was a

noted figure in nineteenth-century Ontario, although not all were successful as Smith implies. The link between the lumber and agricultural economies in Upper Canada is particularly apparent with this group of settlers. See Wood, *Making Ontario*, 106–9; and Forkey, *Shaping the Upper Canadian Frontier*, 75–95.

39. In 1870, John Underhill (1847–?), an Upper Canadian-born farmer, resided on Concession 5, lot 1 in Burford Township. In the *1875 Atlas*, the lot is listed as belonging to the Underhill estate, suggesting that he may have left for Manitoba in the intervening years. See *County of Brant Gazetteer and Directory for 1869–70: Containing Brief Historical and Descriptive Sketches of the Townships, Towns and Villages, with the Names of Residents in Each Locality* (Toronto: James Sutherland, 1870) and *Illustrated Historical Atlas of the County of Brant, Ont.* (Toronto: Page & Smith, 1875); and LAC, 1871 Census, C-9914, Division 1, 47.

40. As road construction expanded during the early nineteenth century, so too did the system of stagecoaches. The system reached the height of its development in the 1840s when both Hamilton and Toronto had become major coaching centres. Complaints about the riding experience were, however, universal. See Wood, *Making Ontario*, 126 and 145; Guillet, *Early Life in Upper Canada*, 548–72; and J.J. Talman, "Travel in Ontario Before the Coming of the Railway," in *Ontario Historical Society Papers and Records*, Vol. 29, (1933), 85–102.

41. Robert Spence (1811–68) was born in Dublin, Ireland, and emigrated to Upper Canada in 1836. He taught school in Dundas before founding the *Dundas Warder*, which was published as a weekly from 1846 to 1859. Spence was elected as a moderate Reformer in the 1854 election and ended up supporting the Tory-Reform coalition of Sir Alan McNab and Augustin-Norbert Morin. As a consequence, he was awarded the postmaster general position. He was defeated in the 1857 election by the less compromising "Clear Grit" reformer, William Notman. See P.G. Cornell, "Robert Spence," *DCB*, Vol. 9, 735–6; and Gilchrist, *Inventory of Ontario Newspapers*, 39.

42. The reference is to the poem "Lord Ullin's daughter" by Thomas Campbell (1777–1844). See *The Complete Poetical Works of Thomas Campbell*, 154–56.

43. Reverend Thomas Stevenson was the Presbyterian minister in Owen Sound from 1860 to 1869. Before that he briefly served in Stratford (1857–58). See Walkington, *Presbyterian Ministers in Upper & Lower Canada*, 56.

44. Smith is using the title "old" to distinguish the elder Nathaniel E.

Mainwaring from his son Dr. Nathaniel Mainwaring. Dr. Mainwaring (1816–?) went to the United States to study medicine and then opened a practice in St. George. He married Rebecca Stimson, the daughter of Dr. Elam Stimson. See *History of the County of Brant*, 188, 669.

45.   The businesses in rural centres tended to be associated with agricultural production or were of the general merchant variety. These stores thrived while transportation remained difficult, but when the railway system developed in the mid-nineteenth century many small village businesses found they could not compete with the suppliers in larger urban centres. See Wood, *Making Ontario*, 141–56; and Thomas F. McIlwraith, *Looking for Old Ontario: Two Centuries of Landscape Change* (Toronto: University of Toronto Press, 1997), 262–70.

46.   In the first phase of settlement, there was little concern with the amount of field space occupied by fencing. The fence described by Smith was, however, unusual as most early settlers employed the "snake rail fence" that was both stable and movable. As settlement intensified, fences that were more permanent and occupied less land, like the post and rail fence, became far more common. See McIlwraith, *Looking for Old Ontario*, 194–202 and 338.

47.   Smith's recounting of the overly familiar reference to Queen Victoria was in direct contrast to how the royal visit was portrayed in the Canadian press at the time which sought to present the nation as cosmopolitan and progressive rather than backward and provincial. Ian Radforth has pointed out, however, that this did not apply to members of First Nations, who were pressured to appear at the tour's major events in "traditional" costume rather than the dress that reflected their adaptation to current colonial realities. See Ian Radforth, "'Called to the Attention of the Whole Civilized World': The Visit of the Prince of Wales to British North America, 1860," in *Zeitschrift fur Kanada-Studien*, 20 (1) (2000), 185–204; and "Performance, Politics, and Representation: Aboriginal People and the 1860 Royal Tour of Canada," in *CHR*, Vol. 84, No. 1 (March 2003), 1–32.

48.   For a recent general account of the Red River settlement, see Lucille H. Campey, *The Silver Chief: Lord Selkirk and the Scottish Pioneers of Belfast, Baldoon and Red River* (Toronto: Natural Heritage Books, 2003). See also J.M. Bumsted, *The People's Clearance: Highland Emigration to British North America, 1770–1815* (Edinburgh: Edinburgh University Press, 1982); and *The Collected Writings of Lord Selkirk*, Vols. 1 and 2 (Winnipeg: Manitoba Record Society, 1984, 1987).

49.   Smith is making a derogatory reference to a Métis guide. The Mé-

tis people originated with the intermarriage between First Nations' women and both French-speaking coureurs de bois and the Scottish fur-trade company men, particularly those recruited in Orkney and Lewis. Tensions between settlers and Métis would ultimately contribute to the outbreak of the North West Rebellion in 1885. See Sylvia Van Kirk, *Many Tender Lies: Women in Fur-Trade Society* (Winnipeg: Watson & Dwyer, 1980, 1999); and Dickason, *Canada's First Nation's*, 280–88.

50. The group, which included James, Angus, and Donald Sutherland, James Wallace, John Armstrong, George Bannerman, Donald MacKay, and Arthur Campbell, formed a "Scottish Settlement" on the Third Concession, West Gwillimbury, County Simcoe, in 1819. The community established an "Auld Kirk" Presbyterian Church on Concession 6, lot 8 in 1823. See Campey, *The Silver Chief*, 82–85, 90–95, 152–53, and 204; *Illustrated Atlas of the County of Simcoe* (Toronto: H. Belden and Co., 1881), 12–3; and Andrew F. Hunter, *A History of Simcoe County* (Barrie, ON: The County Council, 1909), 21–22 and 311–12.

51. Concern over illegal whisky-making was also apparent in the Highlands of Scotland in the early nineteenth century. Although there was a moral aspect to the attack on the production of illicit spirits, the main concern was the loss of tax revenue that such stills represented. See T.M. Devine, "The Rise and Fall of Illicit Whisky-Making in Northern Scotland, 1780–1840," in *Scottish Historical Review*, Vol. 54, No. 58 (October 1975), 155–77.

52. Reverend John Black (1818–82), who was born in Eskdalemuir, Dumfriesshire, did not arrive in Red River until 1851. Black emigrated as a young boy with his family to New York and later moved to Toronto where he attended Knox College. He was working in Montreal as a Presbyterian minister when he agreed to serve the Scottish colonists in Red River. Black reversed a trend in nineteenth-century Scottish emigration that saw congregations, particularly of evangelical denominations, follow their ministers to new settlements in British North America. See, Campey, *The Silver Chief*, 137–40; Hartwell Bowsfield, "John Black," *DCB*, Vol. 11, 79–80; Walkington, *Presbyterian Ministers in Upper & Lower Canada*; and Donald Meek, "Evangelicalism and Emigration: Aspects of the Role of Dissenting Evangelicalism in Highland Emigration to Canada," in Gordon MacLennan, ed., *Proceedings of the First North American Congress of Celtic Studies: Held at Ottawa from 26th–30th March, 1986* (Ottawa: Chair of Celtic Studies, University of Ottawa, 1988), 15–37.

53.   William Gregg (1817–1909) had been a Presbyterian minister in Belle-
      ville (1848–58) and Toronto (1858–72) before becoming a professor
      at Knox College (1873–95). Although Gregg does not mention Smith
      by name, he does refer in his *History* to Angus Sutherland, one of the
      West Gwillimbury Red River settlers who died in March 1885. See
      Walkington, *Presbyterian Ministers in Upper & Lower Canada*, 24; Walk-
      ington, *Ministers of the Presbyteriuan Church in Canada, 1875–1925*, 109;
      and William Gregg, *History of the Presbyterian Church in the Dominion
      of Canada, from Earliest Times to 1834* (Toronto: Presbyterian Print and
      Pub. Co., 1885), 218. Sir Roderick William Cameron (1825–1900), the
      son of the North West Company's Duncan Cameron (c.1764–1848),
      was born in Glengarry County, Upper Canada. Cameron moved to
      New York in 1852 and established a successful company, R.W. Cam-
      eron & Company, that specialized in shipping to Australia. He was a
      member of the Geographical Society of New York and vice-president
      of the Canadian Club of New York City. See Jennifer S.H. Brown,
      "Duncan Cameron," *DCB*, Vol. 7, 137–39; and R.C. MacGillivary, "Sir
      Roderick William Cameron," *DCB*, Vol. 12, 149–50.

54.   The abandoned anchor is still on display at Anchor Park, Holland
      Landing, East Gwillimbury, York County. It is not clear what vessel
      the anchor was intended for, but a view of Penetanguishene drawn in
      1817 still shows a hull on the stocks. Two vessels, the *Tecumseth* and
      the *Newash* were sent to the Lake Huron naval station in 1815, but
      by 1817 they had been reduced to floating hulks. See Hugh Francis
      Pullen, "The March of the Seamen," and John R. Stevens, "The Story
      of the Armed Schooner *Tecumseth*," *Occasional Paper No. 8–9* (Halifax:
      Maritime Museum of Canada, 1961), 20, 25.

55.   Smith's obituary refers to a Mrs. Gowan as his daughter living in
      Buffalo, but a later article refers to his daughter as Mrs. James A.
      Adie living in Florida. This may be the same individual. See *Canadian
      Congregationalist*, Vol. 24, No. 3 (January 18, 1917), 3; and W.F.R.,
      "Rev. William Wye Smith: He Translated the New Testament," *The
      Express* (St. Catharines), October 4, 1967.

56.   Smith published the same version of this tale in his *Gazatteer.* See
      Smith, *Gazatteer and Directory of Grey County*, 96–97.

57.   Thomas Chalmers (1780–1847) was a theologian and preacher born
      in Anstruther, Fife. He published a variety of theological works, but
      is best known for his social experiment in the Tron Parish of Glasgow
      and his role in the Disruption of the Church of Scotland in 1843. In
      that year Chalmers and 470 ministers seceded from the Church of

Scotland to form the Free Church of Scotland. The sermon to which Smith refers was on John 2:15, in which Chalmers argued that to avoid the folly of "loving the world," affections had to be diverted to the "love of God." See Stewart J. Brown, *Thomas Chalmers and the Godly Commonwealth in Scotland*, (Oxford: Oxford University Press, 1982); Rosemary Goring, ed., "Thomas Chalmers," in *Chambers Scottish Biographical Dictionary*. (Edinburgh: Chambers Publishing, 1992), 81; William Hanna, ed., *Selected Works of Thomas Chalmers, D.D, LL.D.* (Edinburgh: Thomas Constable & Co., 1859), Vol. 3 Sermons; John F. Mccaffrey, "Thomas Chalmers and Social Change," in *The Scottish Historical Review*, Vol. 9. No. 169, (April 1981); and Stewart Mechie, *The Church and Scottish Social Development*. (London: Oxford University Press, 1960).

58. St. Catharine's jail, also known as the Lincoln County jail, was opened in 1866 and closed in 1973. Thomas P. Blain, who was born in Niagara in 1838, ran a dry goods and clothing business on Regent Street. See *Illustrated Historical Atlas of the Counties of Lincoln and Welland, Ontario* (Toronto: H.R. Page & Co., 1876), 86.

59. *Illustrated Tid-Bits* [later *Illustrated Bits*] was published in London, England, from 1884 to 1917.

60. For Smith's research on "Highland Mary" see his chapter in Ross, *Highland Mary* (1894) and Chapter 6, above.

61. As conditions became more settled in southern Ontario, there were fewer complaints about Sabbath-breaking, but in the middle of the century, a petition with over twenty thousand signatures requesting that all public works and offices be shut on Sundays was sent to the government. The request had almost universal support but some, like the Anglican Bishop John Strachan, saw it as a violation of the separation of church and state and saw such enforced Sabbatarianism as a "Scottish" imposition. There is no doubt that the sabbath was strictly observed in Victorian Scotland, and it is perhaps not surprising that Daniel Defoe's *Robinson Crusoe* (1719) was based on the story of the marooned Scotsman, Alexander Selkirk (1676–1721). See Moir, *The Church in the British Era*, 188–89; Grant, *A Profusion of Spires*, 164–65, 189–90; T.C. Smout, *A Century of the Scottish People, 1830–1950* (New Haven: Yale University Press, 1986), 182–84; and Diana Souhami, *Selkirk's Island: The True and Strange Adventures of the Real Robinson Crusoe* (New York: Harcourt, 2002).

62. This may be a reference to Stephen Piper (1820–?) an Englishman

who held a hundred acres on Concession 8, lot 6, in Garafraxa West. A James McKee (1841–?) is listed in the 1871 Census as a Canadian-born miller of Irish descent living in Guelph. This could be the individual identified by Smith. The Census also lists several McKees in Garafraxa, including Robert McKee (1826–?), an Irish-born farmer who could have been James's brother. See *Topographical and Historical Atlas of the County of Wellington, Ontario* (Toronto: Walker & Miles, 1877); and LAC, 1871 Census, C-9947, Division 1, 61; *Ibid.*, C-9945 Division 1, 1; Ibid., C-9947–8, Division 2, 7.

63. William "Tiger" Dunlop (1792–1848) was an army officer, surgeon, politician, and Canada Company official, born in Greenock Scotland. The well-travelled William Dunlop is best remembered for his role in the Canada Company where he worked alongside John Galt to develop two-and-a-half million acres of land in western Upper Canada along the shore of Lake Huron. Dunlop was present at the founding of Guelph, and soon after himself founded the Town of Goderich. In 1832, he published a guide for emigrants entitled, *Statistical Sketches of Upper Canada, For the Use of Emigrants*, a work aimed at attracting young emigrants, and one that had considerable influence. Dunlop would part ways with the Canada Company in 1838, but continue to remain a force in local politics. See, Gary Draper and Roger Hall, "William Dunlop," *DCB*, Vol. 7 (Toronto: University of Toronto Press, 1988), 260–63. For more information on Dunlop's involvement with John Galt and the Huron Tract, see Robert C. Lee, *The Canada Company and the Huron Tract*, 1826–1853.

64. Bishop John Strachan (1778–1867), the well-known teacher, clergyman, and officeholder born at Aberdeen, Scotland. Strachan was educated at the Aberdeen Grammar School, King's College, Aberdeen, and would later, while teaching near St. Andrews, be befriended by Thomas Chalmers. In 1799, he took up an offer to teach in Kingston, Upper Canada, and, in 1804, was ordained a priest in the Church of England. Strachan moved to Cornwall in 1803 and began teaching in earnest. He quickly established himself as one of the leading educators of the province, offering his own unique brand of education which drew heavily upon the Scottish model, but also well-suited to circumstances in Canada. G.M. Craig, "John Strachan," *DCB*, Vol. 9 (1976), 751–55.

Afterword

Reverend William Smith and Identity

1. *Globe*, January 8, 1917; Theodore H. Rand, *A Treasury of Canadian Verse: With Brief Biographical Notes* (Toronto: W. Briggs, 1900), 344, 402. E.H. Dewart in his introduction to *The Poetical Works of Alexander McLachlan* (Toronto: W. Briggs, 1900) referred to W.W. Smith as being "in the vanguard of our poetic writers," 15.

2. Lionel Stevenson, *Appraisals of Canadian Literature* (Toronto: Macmillan Company, 1926) 212–13; and J.D. Logan & Donald G. French, *Highways of Canadian Literature: A Synoptic Introduction to the Literary History of Canada (English) from 1760 to 1924* (Toronto: McClelland & Stewart, 1924), 50

3. Norah Story, *The Oxford Companion to Canadian History and Literature* (Toronto: Oxford University Press, 1967), 644.

4. *Canadian Congregationalist*, Vol. 24, No. 3 (January 18, 1917).

5. Susan Thorne, *Congregational Missions and the Making of an Imperial Culture in Nineteenth-Century England* (Stanford: Stanford University Press, 1999), 53–88.

6. John Wood, *Memoir of Henry Wilkes* (Montreal: F.E. Grafton, 1887); John Wood, *Something From Our Hands* (Hudson Heights, Quebec: Wood Family Archives, 1988); Cecilia Morgan, *Public Men Virtuous Women: The Gendered Languages of Religion and Politics in Upper Canada* (Toronto: University of Toronto Press, 1996), 118–21.

7. See John Tosh, *A Man's Place: Masculinity and the Middle-Class Home in Victorian England* (New Haven: Yale University Press, 1999).

8. William Wye Smith, *The New Testament in Braid Scots* (Paisley: A. Gardner, 1901); and William Wye Smith, *The Gospel of Matthew in Broad Scotch* (Toronto: Imrie, Graham, 1898).

9. John A. Smith's wife, Elizabeth, was born in Upper Canada but could have been Kyle's sister. [See LAC, 1871 Census, RG 31 reel C-9940, Division 4, 45; 1901 Census, District 102, Oxford South, Subdistrict A-2, Burford (Village), 3]. Smith's marriage took place on October 5, 1851, in Wellington County and Margaret Chisolm was recorded as being from Grey County. The witness, John Chisholm, is likely the same man listed in 1871 census as a forty-six-year-old "Scotch" resident of Owen Sound. See Dan Walker and Fawne Stratford-Devai,

"Part 1, Wellington District 1840–1852," in *The Marriage Registers of Upper Canada/Canada West*, Vol. 9 (Delhi: Nor Sim Research & Publication, 1997); and LAC. 1871 Census, RG 31, reel C-9954, Owen Sound Town, Division 3, 1.

10. In this passage Smith overlooks the trip he made to Scotland in 1862, an account of which he latter published in the *Scottish Canadian*, Vol. 1, No. 6 (December 18, 1890); Vol. 1, No. 8 (January 1, 1891); Vol. 1, No. 13 (February 5, 1891); Vol. 1, No. 15 (February 19, 1891); Vol. 1, No. 19 (March 19, 1891); and Vol. 1, No. 20 (March 26, 1891).

11. William Wye Smith, *The Poems of William Wye Smith* (Toronto: 1888), 26.

12. William Wye Smith; Angelo McCallum Read, *The Canadian Flag Song: Two Part Song for Use in Schools* (Toronto: Anglo-Canadian Music Publishers Association, 1913).

13. Carl A. Berger, *A Sense of Power: Studies in the Ideas of Canadian Imperialism 1867–1914* (Toronto: University of Toronto Press, 1970).

14. See T.M. Devine, *Scotland's Empire 1600–1815* (London: Allen Lane, 2003), 290–319; and Diana M. Henderson, *Highland Soldier: A Social Study of the Highland Regiments, 1820–1920* (Edinburgh: John Donald, 1989).

15. Thorne, *Congregational Missions and the Making of an Imperial Culture*, 124–170; Edward Said, *Culture and Imperialism* (New York: Knopf, 1993).

16. Jane Samson, *Race and Empire* (London: Longman, 2005) 124–70.

17. Matthew Frye Jacobson, *Whiteness of a Different Color: European Immigrants an the Alchemy of Race* (Cambridge, MA.: Harvard University Press, 1998).

18. J. Murray Gibbon moved to Scotland as a child to be educated and, after graduating from the University of Oxford, worked as a journalist in London before accepting a job as publicity agent for the CPR, which brought him to Montreal in 1913. See Stuart Henderson, " 'While There is Still Time …': J. Murray Gibbon and the Spectacle of Difference in Three CPR Folk Festivals, 1928–1931," in *Journal of Canadian Studies*, Vol. 39, No. 1 (Winter 2005), 139–74; and John Murray Gibbon, *Canadian Mosaic: The Making of a Northern Nation* (Toronto: McClelland & Stewart, 1938).

Bibliography

Achenson, Donald Harman. *The Irish in Ontario: A Study in Rural History*. Montreal, Kingston: Gill-Queen's University Press, 1984, 2nd ed., 1999.

Ascher, Isidore Gordon. *Voices from the Hearth: A Collection of Verses*. Montreal: John Lovell, 1863.

____. *Collected Poems*. London: Elliot Stock, 1929.

Bailey, Thomas Melville, ed. *Dictionary of Hamilton Biography*. Vol. 1. Hamilton, ON: W.L. Griffin Limited, 1981.

Ballstadt, Carl P.A., and Michael Peterman, eds. *Susanna Moodie: Letters of a Lifetime*. Toronto: University of Toronto Press, 1985.

Bell, William. *Hints to Immigrants; in a Series of Letters from Upper Canada*. Edinburgh: Waugh and Innes, 1824.

Bennett, Margaret. *Oatmeal and the Catechism*. Montreal: McGill-Queen's University Press, 1998.

Berchem, F.R. *The Yonge Street Story, 1793–1860*. Toronto: Natural Heritage/Natural History Inc., 1996.

Berkhofer, Robert F. Jr. *The White Man's Indian: Images of the American Indian from Columbus to the Present*. New York: Knopf, 1978.

Birkwood, Susan. "True or False: Anna Jameson and the Position of Women in Anishinaubae Society." *Nineteenth-Century Feminisms*. No. 2 (Spring/Summer 2000).

Blair, Peggy. "'Taken For Granted': Aboriginal Title and Public Fishing Rights in Upper Canada." *Ontario History*. Vol. XCII, No. 2 (2000).

Bleasdale, Ruth. "Conflict on the Canals of Upper Canada in the 1840s." *Labour/Le Travailleur*. No. 7 (1981).

____. "Manitowaning: An Experiment in Indian Settlement." *Ontario History*. Vol. 66, No. 3 (1974).

Bonnycastle, Sir Richard. *The Canadas in 1841*. London: H. Colburn, 1841.

Borley, Lester, ed. *Celebrating the Life and Times of Hugh Miller*. Cromarty: Cromarty Arts Trust & Elphistone Institute of the University of Aberdeen, 2003.

Bristow, Peggy, D. Brand, L.Carty, A.P. Cooper, S. Hamilton, and A. Shadd. *We're Rooted Here and They Can't Pull Us Up: Essays in African Canadian Women*. Toronto: University of Toronto Press, 1994.

Brown, John. *Rab and His Friends*. 1859.

Brown, Stewart J. *Thomas Chalmers and the Godly Commonwealth in Scotland*. Oxford: Oxford University Press, 1982.

Brown-Kubisch, Linda. *The Queen's Bush Settlement: Black Pioneers 1839–1865*. Toronto: Natural Heritage Books, 2004.

Brunger, A. "The Distribution of the Scots and Irish in Upper Canada, 1851–71." *The Canadian Geographer/Le Geographe Canadien*. Vol. 34, No.3 (1990).

____."The Distribution of the English in Upper Canada, 1851–71." *The Canadian Geographer/Le Geographe Canadien*. Vol. 30, No.4 (1986).

Bumsted, J.M. *The People's Clearance: Highland Emigration to British North America, 1770–1815*. Edinburgh: Edinburgh University Press, 1982.

____. *The Collected Writings of Lord Selkirk*. Vols. 1 & 2. Winnipeg: Manitoba Record Society, 1984, 1987.

Byerly, A.E. *Fergus*. Elora, ON: 1934.

Byers, Mary, and Margaret McBurney. *The Governor's Road*. Toronto: University of Toronto Press, 1982.

Caledonian Society of Toronto. *Selections from Scottish Canadian Poets*. Toronto: Imrie, Graham & Company, 1900.

Caldwell, James Martin. *The Wandering Rhymer: A Fragment, with Other Poetical Trifles*. York [Toronto]: Upper Canada Gazette Office, 1826.

Cameron, Wendy, and Mary McDougall Maude. *Assisting Emigration to Upper Canada: The Petworth Project 1832–1837*. Montreal: McGill-Queen's University Press, 2000.

Campbell, Thomas. *The Complete Poetical Works of Thomas Campbell*. Boston: Phillips, Sampson and Company, 1851.

Campbell, Wilfred. *The Scotsman in Canada*. Vol. 1. Toronto: Musson Book Company, 1911.

Canadian Biographical Dictionary and Portrait Gallery of Eminent and Self-made Men: Ontario Volume. Toronto: American Biographical Publishing Co., 1880.

Canadian Illustrated News.

Caniff, William. *The Medical Profession in Upper Canada*. Toronto: W. Briggs, 1894.

Careless, J.M.S. *Brown of the Globe*. Toronto: Dundurn Press, 1989.

Carroll, Francis M. *A Good and Wise Measure: The Search for the Canadian American Boundary, 1783–1842*. Toronto: University of Toronto Press, 2001.

Carroll, John. *Case and His Contemporaries, or, The Canadian Itinerant's Memorial: Constituting a Biographical History of Methodism in Canada from its Introduction into the Province to the Death of Rev. Wm. Case in 1855*. Vols. 3 & 4. Toronto: Wesleyan Conference, 1871–1877.

Christmas, Rev. Henry. *The Emigrant Churchman in Canada*. Vol. 1. London: Richard Bentley, 1849.

Clarke, John, and John Buffone. "Social Regions in Mid-Nineteenth Century Ontario." *Histoire Sociale/Social History*. Vol. 28, No. 55 (1995).

Clarkson, Betty. *At the Mouth of the Credit*. Cheltenham, ON: The Boston Mills Press, 1977.

Clemens, James M. "Taste Not; Touch Not; Handle Not: A Study of the Social Assumptions of the Temperance Literature and Temperance Supporters in Canada West between 1839 and 1859." *Ontario History*. Vol. 64 (1972).

Coatsworth, Emerson, and David Coatsworth (comp). *The Adventures of Nanabush: Ojibway Indian Stories*. Toronto: Doubleday Canada Ltd., 1979.

Cochrane, William, and Walter Inglis. *Memoirs and Remains of the Reverend Walter Inglis, African Missionary and Canadian Pastor*. Toronto: Robinson, 1887.

Colby, Robert A. "Rational Amusement: Fiction vs. Useful Knowledge in the Nineteenth Century." *Victorian Literature and Society*. Eds. James R. Kincaid and Albert J. Kuhn. Ohio: Ohio State University Press, 1984.

Cook, Sharon A. *'Through Sunshine and Shadow': The Women's Christian Temperance*

Union, Evangelicalism, and Reform in Ontario 1874–1930. Montreal: McGill-Queen's University Press, 1995.

Cooper, Afua. "The Fluid Frontier: Blacks and the Detroit River Region, a Focus on Henry Bibb." *Canadian Review of American Studies.* Vol. 30, No. 2 (2000).

Copway, Rev. George. *The Traditional History and Characteristic Sketches of the Ojibwa Nation.* London, ON: C. Gilpin, 1850.

Cornell, John A. *The Pioneers of Beverly.* Dundas: Roy V. Somerville, 1889.

County of Brant Gazetteer and Directory for 1869–79: Containing Brief Historical and Descriptive Sketches of the Townships, Towns and Villages, with the Names of Residents in Each Locality. Toronto: James Sutherland, 1870.

Cowan, E.J. "From the Southern Uplands to Southern Ontario: Nineteenth-Century Emigration from the Scottish Borders." *Scottish Emigration and Scottish Society.* Edited by T.M. Devine. Edinburgh: John Donald Ltd., 1992.

Croft, Melba Morris. *Fourth Entrance to Huronia: The History of Owen Sound.* Owen Sound: Stan Brown Printers Ltd., 1980.

Curtis, L. Perry Jr. *Apes and Angles: The Irishman in Victorian Caricature.* Washington: Smithsonian Press, 1997. (Revised Edition).

Daily News (Kingston)

Daily Spectator (Hamilton)

Day, C.M. *History of the Eastern Townships.* Montreal: John Lovell, 1869. (Reprint, Belleville, ON: Mika Publishing Company, 1989.)

Dewart, Edward Hartley. *Selections From Canadian Poets.* Montreal: 1864.

Dickason, Olive. *Canada's First Nations: A History of Founding Peoples from Earliest Times.* Toronto: Oxford University Press, 1997.

Dictionary of Canadian Biography.

Dorland, Arthur Garratt. *A History of the Society of Friends in Canada.* Toronto: MacMillan and Co., 1927.

Drew, Benjamin. *The Refugee; or, The Narratives of Fugitive Slaves in Canada Related by Themselves.* Toronto: Coles Publishing Company, 1972 — reprint of the 1856 edition.

Durand, Charles. *Reminiscences of Charles Durand of Toronto, Barrister.* Toronto: Hunter, Rose, 1897.

Durham Historical Committee. *A History of the Town of Durham, 1842–1994.* Owen Sound, ON: Stan Brown Printers, Ltd., 1994.

Elliot, Bruce. *The City Beyond: A History of Nepean, Birthplace of Canada's Capital 1792–1990.* Nepean, ON: City of Nepean, 1991.

Irish Migrants in the Canadas: A New Approach. Montreal: McGill-Queen's University Press, 1988.

English, John, and Kenneth McLaughlin. *Kitchener, an Illustrated History.* Waterloo, ON: Wilfred Laurier University Press, 1983.

Ennals, Peter, and Deryeck W. Holdsworth. *Homeplace: The Making of Canadian Dwelling Over Three Centuries.* Toronto: University of Toronto Press, 1998.

Farewell, J.E. *Ontario County.* Whitby, ON: Gazette-Chronicle Press, 1907.

Fenyo, Krisztina. *Contempt, Sympathy and Romance: Lowland Perceptions of the Highlands and the Clearances during the Famine Years.* East Linton, UK: Tuckwell Press, 2000.

Fergusson, Adam. *Practical Notes Made During a Tour in Upper Canada.* Edinburgh: 1839.

Folkey, Neil S. *Shaping the Upper Canadian Frontier: Environment, Society, and Culture in the Trent Valley.* Calgary: University of Calgary Press, 2003.

Foster, C.H. *The Rungless Ladder: Harriet Beecher Stowe and New England Puritanism.* New York: Cooper Square Publishing, 1970.

Francis, Daniel. *The Imaginary Indian: The Image of the Indian in Canadian Culture.* Vancouver: Arsenal Pulp Press, 1992.

Fraser, John. *A Tale of the Sea, and Other Poems.* Montreal: Dawson, 1870.

French, Gary E. *Men of Colour: An Historical Account of the Black Settlement on Wilberforce Street in Oro Township Simcoe County, Ontario, 1819–1949.* Stroud, Ontario: Kaste Books, 1978.

Friedland, Martin L. *The University of Toronto: A History.* Toronto: University of Toronto Press, 2002.

Gagan, David. *Hopeful Travellers: Families, Land, and Social Change in Mid-Victorian Peel County, Canada West.* Toronto: University of Toronto Press, 1981.

Gateman, Laura M. *The History of the Township of Brant: 1854–1979*. Elmwood, ON: Brant Township Historical Society, 1979.

____. *Echoes of Bruce County*. St. Jacobs, ON: St. Jacobs Printery, 1982.

Gerson, Carole. *A Purer Taste: The Writing and Reading of Fiction in English in Nineteenth-Century Canada*. Toronto: University of Toronto Press, 1989.

Gifford, Douglas, ed. *The History of Scottish Literature: Volume 3 Nineteenth Century*. Aberdeen: Aberdeen University Press, 1988.

Gilchrist, J. Brian. *Inventory of Ontario Newspapers 1793–1986*. Toronto: Micromedia, 1987.

Gow, James. "Charles Rankin's Survey of the Owen Sound Road." *Wellington County History*. Vol. 2 (1989).

Grant, George Monro. *Picturesque Canada*. Toronto: Beldon Bros, 1882.

Grant, John Webster. *A Profusion of Spires: Religion in Nineteenth Century Ontario*. Toronto: University of Toronto Press, 1988.

Greer, Allan. *The Patriots and the People: The Rebellion of 1837 in Rural Lower Canada*. Toronto: University of Toronto Press, 1993.

____. "1837–38: Rebellion Reconsidered." *Canadian Historical Review*. Vol. LXXVI, No. 1 (1995).

____. "From Folklore to Revolution: Charivaris and the Lower Canadian Rebellion of 1837." *Social History*. Vol. 15, No. 1 (1990).

Gregg, William. *History of the Presbyterian Church in the Dominion of Canada, From Earliest Times to 1834*. Toronto: Presbyterian Print and Publishing Co., 1885.

Guillet, Edwin C. *Early Life in Upper Canada*. Toronto: University of Toronto Press, 1969.

____. *Pioneer Inns and Taverns*. Vol. 4. Toronto: Ontario Publishing, 1958.

____. *The Pioneer Farmer and Backwoodsman*. Toronto: Ontario Publishing Co., 1963.

____. *The Lives and the Times of the Patriots*. Toronto: University of Toronto Press, 1968.

Haig-Brown, Celia. "Seeking Honest Justice in a Land of Strangers: Nahnebahauqua's Struggle for Land." *Journal of Canadian Studies*. Vol. 36, No.4 (2001–02).

Hawkins, J.J. "Early Days in Brantford." *Brant Historical Society Papers, 1908–1911.* Brantford, ON: Brant Historical Society.

Harper, Marjory. *Adventurers and Exiles: The Great Scottish Exodus.* London: Profile Books, 2003.

_____. *Emigration from Northeast Scotland.* Vols. 1 & 2. Aberdeen: Aberdeen University Press, 1988.

Haughton, W.E., and Charles A. Port (eds.). *History of Westboro, Ontario: The Town of Possibilities, Ottawa's Westmount.* Westboro: s.n., 1927.

Head, Sir Francis Bond. *Narrative of Recent Events in Canada.* London: J. Murray, 1839.

_____. *The Emigrant.* London: J. Murray, 1846.

Heald, Carolyn, A. "The Irish Palatines in Ontario: Religion, Ethnicity and Rural Migration." *Canadian Papers in Rural History.* Vol. IX (1994).

Heavysege, Charles. *The Revolt of the Tartarus.* London: 1852, Montreal: 1855.
_____. *Jephthah's Daughter.* Montreal: 1865.

Hornsby, Stephen J. "Patterns of Scottish Emigration to Canada 1750–1870." *Journal of Historical Geography.* Vol. 18, No. 4 (1992).

Houston, Cecil J. and William J. Smyth. *Irish Emigration and Canadian Settlement: Patterns, Links and Letters.* Toronto: Toronto University Press, 1990.

Houston, Susan E., and Alison Prentice. *Schooling and Scholars in Nineteenth-Century Ontario.* Toronto: University of Toronto Press, 1988.

Howison, John. *Sketches of Upper Canada ... For the Information of Emigrants of Every Class.* Edinburgh: Oliver and Boyd, 1822.

Hulse, Elizabeth. *A Dictionary of Toronto Printers, Publishers, Booksellers, and the Allied Trades, 1798–1900.* Toronto: Anson-Cartwright, 1982.

Hunter, Andrew F. *A History of Simcoe County.* Barrie, ON: The County Council, 1909.

Hutton, William. *The Court of Requests.* Edinburgh: W & R. Chambers, 1840.

Illustrated Atlas of the County of Peel, Ontario. Toronto: Walker & Milles, 1877.

Illustrated Atlas of the Dominion of Canada. Toronto: H. Belden, 1881.

Illustrated Historical Atlas of the County of Brant. Toronto: Page & Smith, 1875.

Illustrated Historical Atlas of the Counties of Lincoln and Welland, Ontario. Toronto: H.R. Page & Co., 1876.

Illustrated Historical Atlas of the County of Ontario. Toronto: J.R. Beers & Co., 1877.

Illustrated Atlas of the County of Simcoe. Toronto: H. Belden and Co., 1881.

Illustrated Atlas of the County of Wellington. Toronto: Walker & Miles, 1877.

Illustrated Historical Atlas of the County of Wentworth. Toronto: Page & Smith, 1875.

Illustrated Historical Atlas of the Counties of Hastings and Prince Edward, Ontario. Toronto: H. Belden & Co., 1878.

Illustrated History of the County of York, and the Township of West Gwillimbury and Town of Bradford, in the County of Simcoe, Ontario. Toronto: Miles & Co., 1878.

Jameson, Anna. *Sketches* in *Canada: and Rambles Among the Red Men.* London: Longman, Brown, Green and Longmans, 1852.

____. *Winter Studies and Summer Rambles* in *Canada.* London: Saunders and Otley, 1838.

Johnson, Leo A. *History of Guelph.* Guelph, ON: Guelph Historical Society, 1977.

Johnston, C.M. *Brant County: A History 1784–1945.* Toronto: Oxford University Press, 1967.

____. *The Head of the Lake: A History of Wentworth County.* Hamilton, ON: Wentworth County Council, 1967.

Johnston, Judith. *Anna Jameson: Victorian, Feminist, Woman of Letters.* Aldershot, UK: Scolar Press, 1997.

Johnston, William. *History of Perth County 1825–1902.* Stratford, ON: W.M. O'Beirne, 1903.

Jones, Rev. Peter. *History of the Ojebway Indians: With Special Reference to Their Conversion to Christianity.* London: A.W. Bennett, 1861.

Karras, Alan L. *Sojourners in the Sun: Scottish Migrants in Jamaica and the Chesapeake, 1740–1800.* Ithaca, NY: Cornell University Press, 1992.

Katz, Michael B. *The People of Hamilton, Canada West: Family and Class in a Mid-Nineteenth Century City.* Cambridge, MA: Harvard University Press, 1975.

Kirkconnell, Watson. *County of Victoria Centennial History*. Lindsay, ON: Victoria County Council, 1967.

Klinck, Carl F. (ed.) *Literary History of Canada: Canadian Literature in English*. Vol. 1. Toronto: University of Toronto Press, 1976.

Kopp, Achim. "'Of the Most Ignorant Stupid Sort of their own Nation': Perceptions of the Pennsylvania Germans in the Eighteenth and Twentieth Centuries." *Yearbook of German American Studies*. 2000.

Lehmann, Heinz. *The German Canadians 1750–1937: Immigration, Settlement and Culture*. Saint John's: Jesperson Press, 1986.

Lemons, J. Stanley. "Black Stereotypes as Reflected in Popular Culture, 1880–1920." *Journal of Popular Culture*. Vol. 10, No. 1 (1976).

Little, J.I. "The Mental World of Ralph Merry: A Case Study of Popular Religion in the Lower Canadian-New England Borderland, 1798–1863." *CHR*. Vol. 83, No. 3 (September 2002).

_____. "From the Isle of Arran to Inverness Township: A Case Study of Highland Emigration and North American Settlement, 1829–34." *Scottish Economic and Social History*. Vol. 20, Part 2 (2000).

_____. "Agricultural Improvement and Highland Clearance: The Isle of Arran 1766–1829." *Scottish Economic and Social History*. Vol. 19, Part 1 (1999).

_____. "The Bard in a Community in Transition and Decline: Oscar Dhu and the Hebridean Scots of the Upper St Francis District, Quebec." *Canadian Papers in Rural History*. Vol. 10 (1996).

_____. *Crofters and Habitants: Settler Society, Economy, and Culture in a Quebec Township, 1848–1881*. Montreal: McGill-Queen's University Press, 1991.

MacColl, Evan. *The English Poetical Works of Evan MacColl*. Toronto: Hunter, Rose, 1883.

MacDonald, Mary Lu. *Literature and Society in the Canadas 1817–1850*. Lewiston, NY: Edwin Mellen Press, 1992.

MacDougall, Pauleena, M. "Grandmother, Daughter, Princess, Squaw: Native American Female Stereotypes in Historical Perspective." *Maine History*. Vol. 34, No. 1 (1994).

Macrea, Marion, and Anthony Adamson. *Cornerstones of Order: Courthouses and Town Halls of Ontario, 1784–1914*. Toronto: C. Irwin, 1983.

Mannen, Douglas A. *From Bauslaugh's Mill to the Present*. Paris, ON: J.R. Hastings Printing, 1987.

Mayne, Daniel Haydn, *Poems and Fragments*. Toronto: W.J. Coates, 1838.

McCabe, J.D. *Illustrated History of the Centennial Exhibition*. Philadelphia: The National Publishing Co., 1876.

McFarquhar, Collin. "A Difference of Perspective: Blacks, Whites, and Emancipation Day Celebrations in Ontario, 1865–1919." *Ontario History*. Vol. XCII, No. 2 (2000).

McGee, Thomas D'Arcy. *The Poems of Thomas D'Arcy McGee*. Montreal: Sadlier, 1869.

McIntyre, James. *Poems of James McIntyre*. Ingersoll, ON: Office of the Chronicle, 1889.

McIntyre, W. John. *Children of Peace*. Montreal: McGill-Queen's University Press, 1994.

McKillop, Dugald McKenzie. *Annals of Megantic County, Quebec*. Lynn, MA: D. McKillop, 1902.

McLachlan, Alexander. *The Poetical Works of Alexander McLachlan*. Toronto: W. Briggs, 1900.

McLean, Mariane. *The People of Glengarry: Highlanders in Transition 1745–1820*. Montreal: McGill-Queen's University Press, 1991.

McLean, Scott A. *From Lochnaw to Manitoulin: A Highland Soldier's Tour Through Upper Canada*. Toronto: Natural Heritage Books, 1999.

____."The Battle of the Windmill Revisited." *Canadian Military History*. Vol. 9, No. 4 (Autumn 2000).

Meek, Donald. "'The Fellowship of Kindred Minds': Some Religious Aspects of Kinship and Emigration from the Scottish Highlands in the Nineteenth Century." *Hands Across the Water: Emigration from Northern Scotland to North America*. Aberdeen: Aberdeen & Northeast Scotland Family History Society, 1995.

Meyler, Peter (ed.). *Broken Shackles*. Toronto: Natural Heritage/Natural History Inc., 2001.

Mika, N. & H. *Belleville: Friendly City*. Belleville, ON: Mika Publishing, 1973.

Miller, J.R. *Shingwauk's Vision: A History of Native Residential Schools*. Toronto: University of Toronto Press, 1996.

Mitchell and Co's Canada Classified Directory for 1865–66.

Moir, J.S. *Enduring Witness: A History of the Presbyterian Church in Canada*. Toronto: Presbyterian Publications, 1974.

Moodie, Susanna. *Life in the Clearings*. Toronto: The MacMillan Company, 1959.

_____. *Roughing it in the Bush, or, Life in Canada*. Toronto: McClelland and Stewart, 1991.

_____. *Enthusiasm: and Other Poems*. London: Smith, Elder, 1831.

Moore, Christopher. *The Loyalists: Revolution, Exile, Settlement*. Toronto: McClelland and Stewart, 1984.

Moore, Thomas. *Thomas Moore's Complete Poetical Works*. New York: T.Y. Crowell & Co., 1895.

Moran, James E. *Committed to the Asylum: Insanity and Society in Nineteenth Century Quebec and Ontario*. Montreal: McGill-Queen's University Press, 2000.

Morgan, Cecilia. "History, Nation and Empire: Gender and Southern Ontario Historical Societies." *Canadian Historical Review*. September 2001.

Morgan, Henry James. *Bibliotheca Canadensis, or, A Manual of Canadian Literature*. Ottawa: 1867.

_____. *Canadian Men and Women of the Time; a Handbook of Canadian Biography*. Toronto: W. Briggs, 1898.

Morriseau, Norval. *Legends of My People, the Great Ojibway*. Ed. Selwyn Dewdney. Toronto: The Ryerson Press, 1967.

Mulvany, Charles Pelham, et al. *History of Toronto and County of York*. Toronto: C.B. Robinson, 1885.

Murray, David. *Colonial Justice: Justice, Morality, and Crime in the Niagara District, 1791–1849*. Toronto: University of Toronto Press, 2002.

Murray, Heather. *Come, Bright Improvement! The Literary Societies of Nineteenth-Century Ontario*. Toronto: University of Toronto Press, 2002.

Murray, Norman. *The Scottish Hand Loom Weavers 1790–1850: A Social History*. Edinburgh: John Donald, 1978.

Mutrie, R. Robert. *The Long Point Settlers*. Ridgeway, ON: Log Cabin Publishing, 1992.

National Archives of Canada. *1881, 1871, 1861 Census*.

Oliver, Peter. *'Terror to Evil-Doers': Prisons and Punishments in Nineteenth Century Ontario*. Toronto: University of Toronto Press, 1998.

Parr Trail, Catharine. *The Canadian Settler's Guide*. London: E. Stanford, 1860.

____. *The Canadian Emigrant Housekeeper's Guide*. Montreal: J. Lovell, 1861.

Palmer, Brian D. "Discordant Music: Charivaris and Whitecapping in Nineteenth Century North America." *Labour-La Travail*, Vol. 3 (1978).

Parker, George L. *The Beginnings of the Book Trade in Canada*. Toronto: University of Toronto Press, 1985.

Peters, Maureen. *Jean Ingelow, Victorian Poetess*. Ipswich, UK: Boydell Press, 1972.

Pieterse, Jan Nederveen. *White on Black: Images of Africa and Blacks in Western Popular Culture*. New Haven, CT: Yale University Press, 1992.

Power, Donald. "The Paddy Image: The Stereotype of the Irishman in Cartoon and Comic." in The *Untold Story: The Irish in Canada*, edited by Robert O'Driscoll and Lorna Reynolds. Vol. 1. Toronto: Celtic Arts of Canada, 1988.

Power, Michael, and Nancy Butler. *Slavery and Freedom in Niagara*. Niagara-on-the-Lake, ON: The Niagara Historical Society, 1993.

Radforth, Ian. "Performance, Politics, and Representation: Aboriginal People and the 1860 Royal Tour of Canada." *Canadian Historical Review*. Vol. 84, No. 1 (March 2003).

Ramsay, J.R. *The Canadian Lyre*. Hamilton, ON: Donnelly, 1859.

Ramsay, Philip A. *The Works of Robert Tannahill, With a Life of the Author, and Memoir of R.S Smith, the Musical Composer*. London: A. Fullerton & Co., 1838.

Rand, T.H. *A Treasury of Canadian Verse*. Toronto: W. Briggs, 1900.

Reaman, G. Elmore. *A History of Vaughan Township*. Toronto: University of Toronto Press, 1971.

Reid, C., and R. Stagg. *The Rebellion of 1837 in Upper Canada*. Ottawa: 1988

Reville, F. Douglas. *History of the County of Brant*. Brantford, ON: Hurley Printing Co., 1920.

Reynolds, John C. (ed.) *Kincardine: 1848–1984*. Owen Sound, ON: Stan Brown Ltd., 1982.

Robertson, John. *History of the Brantford Congregational Church, 1820–1920*. Renfrew, ON: Renfrew Mercury Print, 1920.

Robertson, Norman. *History of the County of Bruce*. Toronto: William Briggs, 1906.

Roger-Hepburn, Sharon A. "Crossing the Border from Slavery to Freedom: the Building of a Community at Buxton, Upper Canada." *American Nineteenth Century History*. Vol. 3, No. 2 (2002–03).

Rogers, Edward S., and Donald B. Smith. *Aboriginal Ontario: Historical Perspectives on the First Nations*. Toronto: Dundurn Press, 1994.

Rolling, Gladys M. *East Gwillimbury in the Nineteenth Century*. 1967.

Romney, Paul. "From the Types Riot to the Rebellion: Elite Ideology, Anti-legal Sentiment, Political Violence, and the Rule of Law in Upper Canada." *Ontario History*. Vol. LXXIX, No. 2 (June 1987).

Romney, Paul, with Barry Wright. "The Toronto Treason Trials, March–May 1838." *Canadian State Trials, Vol. II: Rebellion and Invasion in the Canadas, 1837–1838*. Edited by Murray Greenwood & Barry Wright. Toronto: University of Toronto Press, 2002.

Rooklidge, J.W. *Directory of the County of Bruce, Canada West*. Montreal: John Lovell, 1867.

Ross, Alexander M. "Loch Laxford to the Zorras: A Sutherland Emigration to Upper Canada." *Scottish Tradition*. Vol. XVIII (1993).

Rutherford, Paul. *A Victorian Authority: The Daily Press in Late Nineteenth-Century Canada*. Toronto: University of Toronto Press, 1982.

Ryan, Carroll. *Poems, Songs, Ballads*. Montreal: J. Lovell, 1903.

Sawchuck, Larry A., and Stacie D.A. Burke. "Mortality in an Early Ontario Community: Belleville 1876–1885." *Urban History Review*. Vol. 29, No. 1 (2000).

Schmalz, Peter S. *The Ojibwa of Southern Ontario*. Toronto: University of Toronto Press, 1991.

Schrauwers, Albert. *Awaiting the Millenium: The Children of Peace and the Village of Hope, 1812–1889.* Toronto: University of Toronto Press, 1993.

Senior, Hereward. *Orangeism: The Canadian Phase.* Toronto: Ryerson, 1972.

Shadd, Mary Ann. *A Plea for Emigration, or, Notes of Canada West.* Edited by Richard Almonte. Toronto: The Mercury Press, 1998.

Sharpe, Roger, *The Village of Brantford in 1830.* Brantford, ON: Brant Historical Society, 2001.

Silverman, Jason H. *Unwelcome Guests: Canada West's Response to American Fugitive Slaves, 1800–1865.* New York: Associated Faculty Press, 1985.

Smaller, Harry. "Teachers and Schools in Early Ontario." *Ontario History.* Vol. LXXXV, No.4 (December 1993).

Smallwood, Thomas. *A Narrative of Thomas Smallwood.* Edited by Richard Almonte. Toronto: The Mercury Press, 2000.

Smith, Donald B. *Sacred Feathers: The Reverend Peter Jones (Kahkewaquonaby) and the Mississauga Indians.* Toronto: University of Toronto Press, 1987.

Stein, Stephen J. "The 'Not-so-faithful' Believers: Conversion, Deconversion and Reconversion among the Shakers." *American Studies.* Vol. 38, No.3 (1997).

Stelter, Gilbert A. "Combining Town and Country Planning in Upper Canada: William Gilkison and the Founding of Elora." *Historic Guelph: The Royal City.* Vol. XXIV (1985).

Stephan, Nancy. *The Idea of Race in Science: Great Britain, 1800–1960.* Harnden, CN: Archon Books, 1982.

Sterne, Lawrence. *Sentimental Journey through France and Italy.* 1768.

Stouffer, Allan P. "'A Restless Child of Change and Accident': The Black Image in Nineteenth Century Ontario." *Ontario History.* Vol. LXXVI, No. 2 (June 1984).

_____. *The Light of Nature and the Law of God: Anti-Slavery in Ontario 1833–1877.* Montreal: McGill-Queen's Press, 1992.

Sullivan Historical Society. *A History of Sullivan Township, 1850 to 1975.* Desboro, ON: Richardson, Bond and Wright Ltd., 1975.

Surtees, Robert J. *Indian Land Surrenders in Ontario, 1763–1867.* Ottawa: Department of Indian and Northern Affairs, 1984.

Sutherland, Fraser. *The Monthly Epic: A History of Canadian Magazines 1789–1989.* Markham, ON: Fitzhenry & Whiteside, 1989.

Talman, J.J. "Agricultural Societies of Upper Canada." *Ontario Historical Society Papers and Records,* 27. 1931.

____. "Travel in Ontario before the Coming of the Railway." *Ontario Historical Society Papers and Records.* Vol. 29 (1933).

Telford, Rhonda. "The Anishinabe Presentation of the Fishing Rights to the Duke of Newcastle and the Prince of Wales." *Papers of the Algonquin Conference.* Vol. 30 (1999).

Templin, Hugh. *Fergus, the Story of a Little Town.* Fergus, ON: 1933.

Thomson, William. *A Tradesman's Travels in the United States and Canada in the Years 1840, 1841, 1842.* Edinburgh: Oliver & Boyd, 1842.

Thurston, John. *The Work of Words: The Writing of Susanna Strickland Moodie.* Montreal: McGill-Queen's University Press, 1996.

Topographical and Historical Atlas of the County of Wellington, Ontario. Toronto: Walker & Miles, 1877.

Vance, Michael E. "Advancement, Moral Worth, and Freedom: The Meaning of Independence for Early Nineteenth-Century Lowland Emigrants to Upper Canada." *Nation and Province in the First British Empire: Scotland and the Americas, 1600–1800.* Edited by Ned C. Landsman. Lewisburg, NY: Bucknell University Press, 2001.

____. "Scottish Chartism in Canada West: an Examination of the 'Clear Grit' Reformers." *Scottish Tradition.* Vol. 22 (1997).

____."Breaking the Power of a Metaphor: Toward a Social Interpretation of Emigration History." *The Immigrant Experience.* Edited by C. Kerrigan. Guelph, ON: University of Guelph, 1992.

____."Impressions of a Berlin Pioneer — The Emigrant Letters of Dr. John Scott." *Waterloo Historical Society Journal.* Vol. 77 (1989).

Vander Hoef, Lorraine. "John Dougall (1808–1886): Portrait of an Early Social Reformer and Evangelical Witness in Canada." *Journal of the Canadian Church Historical Society.* Vol. XLIII (2001).

Vaughan, Edgar. "Scottish Settlers for Canada from Venezuela: A Bureaucratic Problem in 1827." *Historic Guelph: The Royal City.* Vol. XVIII (April 1979).

____. "The Guayrians at Guelph in Upper Canada: Some Additional Notes." *Historic Guelph: The Royal City*. Vol. XIX. April 1980.

Vaundry, Richard W. *The Free Church in Victorian Canada, 1844–1861*. Waterloo, ON: Wilfred Laurier Press, 1989.

Waldie, Jean. *Brant County: The Story of Its People*. Paris, ON: Brant Historical Society, 1984.

Walkington, Donald. *The Congregational Churches of Canada: A Statistical and Historical Summary*. Toronto: United Church Archives, 1979.

____. *Presbyterian Ministers in Upper and Lower Canada*. Toronto: United Church Archives, 1984.

____. *Ministers of the Presbyterian Church in Canada 1875–1925*. Toronto: United Church Archives.

Ward, Peter. *Courtship, Love, and Marriage in Nineteenth-Century English Canada*. Montreal: McGill-Queen's University Press, 1990.

Ward, Samuel Ringgold. *Autobiography of a Fugitive Negro: His Anti-Slavery Labours in the United States, Canada, and England*. Chicago: Johnson Publishing Co., 1970 — Reprint of the 1855 edition.

Waterston, Elizabeth. *Rapt in Plaid: Canadian Literature and Scottish Tradition*. Toronto: University of Toronto Press, 2001.

Wayne, Michael. "The Black Population of Canada West on the Eve of the American Civil War: A Reassessment Based on the Manuscript Census of 1861." *Histoire Sociale/Social History*. Vol. 28, No. 56 (1995).

Weaver, John C. *Crimes, Constables, and Courts: Order and Transgression in a Canadian City, 1816–1970*. Montreal: McGill-Queen's University Press, 1995.

Webster, J.C. *Rural Schools of South Dumfries Township*. Ayr, ON: Brant Historical Society, 1992.

White, Paul. *Owen Sound: The Port City*. Toronto: Natural Heritage/Natural History Inc., 2000.

Whiteside, Margaret., *Belfountain and the Tubtown Pioneers*. Cheltenham, ON: Boston Mills Press, 1975.

Williamson, A.J. *Original Poems on Various Subjects*. Toronto: W.J. Coates, 1836.

Willis, N.P., and W.H. Bartlet. *Canadian Scenery Illustrated*. London: G. Virtue, 1842.

Wilson, Catharine Anne. "Reciprocal Work Bees and the Meaning of Neighbourhood." *Canadian Historical Review*. Vol. 82, No. 3 (September 2001).

Wilson, Charles R. "Racial Reservations: Indians and Blacks in American Magazines, 1865–1890." *Journal of Popular Culture*. Vol. 10, No. 1 (1976).

Winks, Robin W. *The Blacks in Canada: A History*. 2nd ed. Montreal: McGill-Queen's University Press, 1997.

Wintemberg, W.J. *Folklore of Waterloo County*. Ottawa: King's Printer, 1950.

Womack, Peter. *Improvement and Romance: Constructing the Myth of the Highlands*. London: MacMillan Press, 1989.

Wood, Rev. John. *Memoir of Henry Wilkes, D.D. LL.D.; His Life and Times*. Montreal: F.E. Grafton, 1887.

_____. *Something From Our Hands: Historical Canadian Biography Based Upon Memoirs Recorded in 1899 by Rev. John Wood*. Hudson Heights, QC: Wood family Archives, 1988.

Wood, John David. *Making Ontario: Agricultural Colonization and Landscape Recreation before the Railway*. Montreal: McGill-Queen's University Press, 2000.

Index